HAWKER
HURRICANE

HAWKER HURRICANE
THE MULTIROLE FIGHTER

PHILIP BIRTLES

FONTHILL

Fonthill Media Language Policy

Fonthill Media publishes in the international English language market. One language edition is published worldwide. As there are minor differences in spelling and presentation, especially with regard to American English and British English, a policy is necessary to define which form of English to use. The Fonthill Policy is to use the form of English native to the author. Philip Birtles was born and educated in Croydon; therefore British English has been adopted in this publication.

Fonthill Media Limited
Fonthill Media LLC
www.fonthillmedia.com
office@fonthillmedia.com

First published in the United Kingdom and the United States of America 2017

British Library Cataloguing in Publication Data:
A catalogue record for this book is available from the British Library

Typeset in Minion Pro 10pt on 13.5pt
Printed and bound in England

Contents

Introduction

The Hawker Hurricane propaganda was largely overshadowed by the Spitfire during the Second World War. The main reason was that the Hurricane was a monoplane developed from a long line of Hawker biplane combat aircraft and at the end of its development, while the Spitfire was at the start of its creation. The Spitfire was undoubtedly faster than the Hurricane, but it was more challenging to produce initially, while the rugged construction of the Hurricane resulted in it being more resistant to battle damage. Its wide-track undercarriage was more suitable for operations from basic airfields and was easier to maintain. Without the Hurricane, there would not have been a Battle of Britain as there would not have been enough suitable fighters for the defence against the Nazi invasion. Without the Spitfire, we would probably not have won the Battle of Britain. The role of the Hurricanes was to destroy the Luftwaffe bombers attacking British airfields, later London and other major cities, while Spitfires attacked the escorting Luftwaffe fighters.

The Luftwaffe were at a disadvantage as the range of their fighters limited them to only a short time over Britain, and the crew of any enemy aircraft shot down were either killed or taken prisoner, reducing the hordes of Luftwaffe combat aircraft available to attack Britain. When RAF pilots were shot down, if they were lucky to survive the onslaught, they could at least parachute to safety on home soil. Hurricane pilots were responsible for more victories than all other forms of defence during the Battle.

With the Battle of Britain won and RAF fighter pilots tasked with hazardous offensive operations across occupied Europe, Hurricanes became very vulnerable to enemy defences; losses increased alarmingly. More pilots were killed or taken prisoner than during the Battle of Britain, many of them very experienced.

In other theatres of operation, Hurricane pilots continued to excel despite flying—by then—out-dated aircraft, particularly in the battles for Malta, 6 Squadron's anti-armour

Hurricanes in the North African campaigns, and against the Japanese over the impenetrable Burmese jungle.

This book is in memory of all those brave young men who paid the ultimate price, allowing us to have the freedom we enjoy now, which they were unable to experience.

1

Sopwith: Pioneer Test Pilot, Aircraft Designer and Manufacturer

THE HAWKER HURRICANE came from a long line of fighter aircraft that commenced during the First World War. The Sopwith Aircraft Company was founded as Sopwith Aviation by Tom Sopwith, who was one of Britain's aviation pioneers.

Thomas Octave Murdock Sopwith, better known as Tom Sopwith, was attracted to flying when John Moisant landed near Dover on 18 September 1910 as the first to fly across the English Channel carrying a passenger in a rather frail Bleriot. The intention had been to make a flight from Paris to London, but a series of mishaps and difficulties with rough English summer weather resulted in the pair not arriving in London until 6 October.

Tom Sopwith was fortunate to have a private income from his father, an education in engineering, and an interest in motorcycles that progressed to motorcars and motorboats in his late teens, with a brief attempt at ballooning. However, it was the cross-Channel flight that infused him with an enthusiasm for aeroplanes, and it was not long before he visited Brooklands, the centre of British aviation, where he paid for two circuits in a Henry Farman aircraft. He was so impressed by the aerial experience that he decided to acquire an aeroplane of his own, and after discussions with the pioneer designer Howard T. Wright, Sopwith bought a Howard Wright monoplane for £630.

Although he had not received flying lessons, Sopwith felt he was capable of flying this machine. The machine took off on his first attempt on 22 October after a run of 300 yards; however, in pulling the control stick back too hard, the aeroplane climbed to some 40 feet, stalled, and crashed, breaking the propeller and undercarriage with damage to the wing. Following repairs on 4 November, Sopwith made more cautious progress with taxiing, hops, straight flights, and finally circuits of Brooklands, rapidly gaining experience and confidence. He then bought the latest Howard Wright biplane with a more powerful 60-hp E. N. V. engine.

9

Tom Sopwith standing in his Howard Wright monoplane watching the designer, Howard T. Wright, inspect the engine ready for flight. (*BAE Systems*)

Tom Sopwith in the two-seat Howard Wright biplane. (*BAE Systems*)

By 21 November, he felt confident enough to apply for his pilot's certificate, which required three flights, each of 3 miles, around a circular course without landing. The three flights need not be completed on the same day, but on completion of each flight, the pilot had to land within 150 yards of a spot defined by the examiners. Tom Sopwith was awarded Certificate No. 31, making him one of Britain's aviation pioneer pilots.

Having proved his capabilities as a pilot, Sopwith planned an attempt on the British Empire Michelin Cup together with a prize of £500 for the longest flight made before 31 December 1910. The conditions stipulated that the pilot must be a British national and the aeroplane must be entirely of British manufacture. Sopwith notified the Royal Aero Club of his intention to compete for the record on 10 November by flying around a fixed circuit of just over 1 mile. The person to beat was Cody, who qualified for the prize having already flown 94.5 miles in two hours and twenty-four minutes.

Although tedious, the circuit was deemed fairer as a point-to-point flight may have given rise to suspicions of an intermediate landing en route. As he built up the circuits around the course, his supporters on the ground maintained a count of his progress that was displayed on a board for him to see. The aircraft flew smoothly as the hours ticked by with Sopwith experiencing the extreme cold from exposure in an open cockpit. When he had completed ninety-five circuits, Sopwith knew he had beaten Cody and continued his progress to cover 100 miles. Having taken off at 10.05 a.m., he finally landed at 13.16 p.m., having recorded 107.75 miles in three hours, twelve minutes, and forty seconds in qualification for the trophy.

With very little official interest in aviation expressed by the Government at the time, the only way to make progress in the air was by a combination of sponsors, the press, and pioneers. Baron de Forest offered a prize of £4,000 for the longest flight from England to the Continent. As with the previous record, the conditions were that the pilot must be a British national, flying an all-British aeroplane, with the deadline for completion being 31 December 1910.

There were a number of other competitors for the prize waiting to leave from Dover. After waiting at Eastchurch from 5 December for suitable weather, Sopwith was able to depart at 8.16 a.m. on Sunday 18 December in his Howard Wright biplane with 20 gallons of fuel. He flew over Canterbury and was logged over Dover at 9 a.m. with a speed of 50 mph at 1,200 feet. Visibility was poor and the compass unreliable; the plan was to make for Chalons near Paris, covering a distance of 240 miles. The French coast could just be seen from mid-Channel, while dense cloud blotted out the sun and made navigation very difficult. As he flew on over unknown towns and villages the weather became gusty, which resulted in the aircraft becoming too difficult to control. Sopwith made a forced landing near a village with 11 gallons of fuel still remaining in the tank. Making enquiries about his whereabouts from two ladies in a cottage, he established that he had arrived at Beaumont in Belgium, about 9 miles from the French frontier. Despite the post offices being closed on a Sunday, Sopwith was able to send a cable from a local railway station confirming his location, and asked his friend and engineer Fred Sigrist to travel to Belgium and make the aircraft safe for a possible further attempt at the record if someone else flew further before the deadline. However, bad weather at Dover wrecked some of the aircraft when a hangar collapsed. Sopwith had achieved a distance of 177 miles in three hours and forty minutes with no serious challenger due to the bad weather, and finally claimed the £4,000 prize.

Sopwith in the Howard Wright Biplane in which he won the Baron de Forest £4,000 prize. (*BAE Systems*)

He was not as fortunate with the Michelin Cup. He was beaten by Alex Ogilvie, who flew 130 miles at Rye on 28 December. After a number of attempts, Sopwith managed to fly 150 miles in four hours and seven minutes to improve his own best time and better Ogilvie's, although the cup was not to be his as Cody achieved 195 miles in four hours and fifty minutes over Laffan's Plain on the last day of the year to claim the prize.

As a result of his exploits, King George V expressed an interest in Tom Sopwith flying to Windsor Great Park. On 1 February 1911, Sopwith arrived in the morning at Brooklands in cold fog that lasted until at least mid-day. On telephoning Windsor, he was told that there was bright sunlight, so he decided to take-off in the mist. He departed at 1 p.m. and, climbing to 1,000 feet on a compass heading, he emerged into sunlight. After twenty minutes, he saw Datchet church and he landed on the golf course where he was met by his sister and brother-in-law who took him to lunch. After lunch, Sopwith drove to Windsor to select a suitable place to land in the park, choosing the East Lawn as the best option for landing and take-off. By the time Sopwith had returned to Datchet for the aircraft, a large crowd had formed to welcome him to the Park. On landing he was presented to his Majesty, who inspected the machine together with Princes Henry, George, and John, where it was noted that the radiator was leaking due to damage caused by the frost.

Sopwith took off again for Datchet, where he landed in rising mist, before returning the next day to Brooklands.

The Howard Wright Biplane flown on to the East Terrace of Windsor Castle by Sopwith to be viewed by HRH King George V, Prince Henry, Prince George, and Prince John. (*BAE Systems*)

Following a highly successful aviation tour of the USA from May to October 1911, in which Sopwith took part in a number of aircraft events and also flew premium passengers, he returned to Brooklands and started The Sopwith School of Flying, offering lessons on four different types of aircraft for £75 from 1 February 1912. Tom Sopwith was the chief instructor with Fred Sigrist in charge of maintenance and repairs. To allow a greater freedom of operation when other flying duties came up, Fred Raynham was hired as chief pilot and instructor of the school to undertake routine instruction, while Sopwith gave air experience flights, which encouraged further custom for the school. On Sunday 5 May, Sopwith was responsible for the maiden flight of the first Coventry Ordnance Biplane, built by Howard Wright and designed by W. O. Manning, which was the beginning of his career as a test pilot.

Sponsored by the Daily Mail, Britain's first Aerial Derby was held on 8 June 1912 over an 81-mile circuit starting and finishing at Hendon. There were fifteen entrants in total, and Tom Sopwith achieved the best time of one-hour, twenty-three minutes and eight seconds to confirm himself the winner after some debate.

The flying school continued to be busy. Among those who learned to fly was Major Trenchard, later to become the 'Father of the Royal Air Force'; Captain Ellington, later to become Marshal of the RAF; Sir Edward Ellington; the aircraft designer Howard Wright; and the Australian Harry Hawker, who was to have a profound effect within the Sopwith organisation and British aviation.

The 1912 Three-seater was the first true Sopwith-designed aircraft. Although it had a tailskid, it normally operated on the main and nose wheels. (*BAE Systems*)

The 1913 Sopwith Floatplane was flown in *The Daily Mail* Circuit of Britain race. (*BAE Systems*)

Harry Hawker with the first true Sopwith design, the three-seat biplane at Brooklands. (*BAE Systems*)

Despite Tom Sopwith being busy with test, instruction, competition, and passenger flying, he still found time to enter the entirely new challenge of aeronautical design. A tractor biplane powered by a 70-hp Gnome engine was built by the school staff and successfully flown on 4 July 1912, later carrying two of the mechanics as passengers.

Sopwith's enthusiasm for nautical and aeronautical modes of transport soon resulted in an attempt to combine his interests. He commissioned S. E. Saunders of Cowes to build a hull while wings were constructed at Brooklands under the direction of Fred Sigrist.

Australian Harry G. Hawker joined Tom Sopwith as a mechanic on 12 July 1912 and having learned to fly became a test pilot. Meanwhile, Sopwith entered his improved Burgess Wright biplane for the Michelin Duration prize of £500, flown Hawker, who had completed his first test flights on 15 October 1912.

On the fourth attempt, Harry Hawker flew for eight hours and twenty-three minutes over Brooklands on 24 October 1912 to achieve a new British Duration Record.

By this time, there was an abundance of flying schools at both Brooklands and Hendon. Sopwith decided to run down the flying instruction and concentrate on the production of aircraft with Sigrist in charge of the construction and Hawker as test and demonstration pilot. The first draughtsman was hired on 21 October, marking the beginning of the Sopwith Aviation Company.

The company's first sale was of a Sopwith tractor biplane to the Admiralty, with its delivery by Hawker on 23 November 1912 to Eastchurch after a precautionary landing en route the

The Australian Harry Hawker was the chief test and demonstrator pilot for Sopwith at Brooklands.

The Sopwith hangars at Brooklands, with other early aviation company hangars in the background. (*BAE Systems*)

The Batboat featured a Saunders-built hull and was powered by a 100-hp Green engine. (*BAE Systems*)

previous day. The proceeds of this sale allowed for the purchase of a disused skating rink in Canbury Park Road at Kingston-upon-Thames for the manufacture of aircraft, with flight testing continuing at Brooklands. The first Bat Boat flying boat was constructed in the newly acquired premises utilising the hull built by Saunders and the wings and airframe built by Sopwith.

With the challenge of Mr A. Mortimer Singer offering a prize of £500 for an aircraft capable of operating from both land and water, plans were made to adapt the Bat Boat, resulting in the employment of more workers. After being exhibited at the Olympia Aero Exhibition on 14 February, where it created much interest, the Bat Boat was taken to Cowes for trials, but neither Sopwith nor Hawker could coax it off the water. After beaching the aircraft, the pair retired to a hotel for the night, only to find it wrecked the next morning due to high winds. An improved replacement was planned with ailerons in place of wing-warping. Meanwhile, the production of an improved tractor biplane for the Admiralty continued—one example successfully passed War Office tests at Farnborough on 8 May 1913. On 31 May, Hawker took the aircraft up to 11,450 feet, which was confirmed as a new British height record.

Work continued on an improved Bat Boat. Wheels were fitted to allow operations from land, but it was found to be unstable in flight when flown again by Harry Hawker on 25 May. With adjustments and repairs made, it was prepared for the Mortimer Singer Prize. The conditions of the prize were that both entrant and pilot must be British subjects and the aircraft had to be of British manufacture. The aircraft was required to fly a series of land and sea and vice versa flights with a passenger over a distance of no less than 5 miles. A minimum altitude was specified of 750 feet with at least 1,500 feet on one flight. After some practice attempts at Cowes, Hawker won the Mortimer Singer prize of £500 for Sopwith Aviation on 8 July 1913 flying from the Hamble River. The Bat Boat therefore became the first practical British amphibian, adding to the widening range of aircraft being produced by the company. The Admiralty took advantage of the new type, as well as three floatplane versions of the tractor biplane, the first of which was delivered in June 1913. With additional orders coming in, Sopwith Aviation continued to expand its workforce, and records continued to be broken, particularly those related to carrying passengers to altitude.

The Daily Mail announced sponsorship of a Circuit of Britain Race in May, offering a £5,000 prize for the first completion of a prescribed course around Britain within a seventy-two-hour period from 16 August 1913. The entrants and pilots had to British subjects and the aircraft had to be of British manufacture. Although four entrants paid their £100 entry fee, only Sopwith qualified. Cody was one entrant, but was killed in his seaplane over the August Bank Holiday weekend.

Although it was expected that the Bat Boat would be entered, Sopwith competed with a new floatplane powered by a 100-hp Green engine of British manufacture. Hawker made an initial unsuccessful attempt on 16 August, but his place was taken by Sydney Pickles due to illness. Hawker was fit again for another start on 25 August, but 15 miles north of Dublin decided to land to make engine adjustments, and as he was making the landing his foot slipped from the rudder bar and the aircraft crashed into the water, injuring the passenger. Despite failure, Sopwith was the only entrant for the race and the Daily Mail rewarded Hawker with £1,000 for covering 1,043 miles.

In the autumn of 1913, work started on a new compact, single-seat racing tractor biplane known as the Tabloid, the first of the line of Sopwith scouts. This new type was ready for demonstration at Farnborough on 29 November, where its good performance was met with approval. The aircraft went into production in early 1914. Meanwhile, a variety of types were in production for the Admiralty. The Sopwith works were visited by Winston Churchill in his capacity as First Lord of the Admiralty in February. In March 1914, the company was formally reconstituted as The Sopwith Aviation Co. Ltd; a private company with the registered office in Canbury Park Road. At the end of March, the first seaplane for the Greek Naval Air Service was ready for testing, increasing the company's business into the export market as well as the UK Admiralty and War Office. The naval aircraft could be fitted with a unique folding wing arrangement to save space on board ships.

With no idea that the First World War was soon to start, Sopwith began to plan for the new season competitions—the primary event being the Schneider Trophy contest. There had been no British entry in the 1913 event, but Sopwith entered a float-equipped Tabloid for the 1914 race held in Monaco.

The day of the race was 20 April. Two Nieuport monoplane seaplanes were entered by the French; a Swiss flying boat; and the only other British contestant, Lord Carbery, entered a Deperdussin monoplane seaplane.

Howard Pixton, the Sopwith pilot, followed the French and Swiss entrants into the air in the Tabloid; Lord Carbery retired after one lap due to engine problems. Despite his later start

The Sopwith Schneider floatplane was the only entrant to complete the course at the 1914 Monaco Schneider Trophy contest, flying laps after the race to achieve a world record speed of 92 mph. (*BAE Systems*)

Pixton passed the French aircraft, who had to drop out after engine failures caused by the pilots increasing their speed. Pixton continued with one of the nine cylinders on his engine misfiring, but passed the Swiss entrant when he had to land to take on more fuel to cross the finishing line the winner after completing the twenty-eight laps, covering 280 km in two hours and thirteen seconds. Instead of landing, Pixton risked his overtaxed engine and flew two more laps to achieve the 300 km world record at 92 mph. The remaining entrants from France and America realised that there was no chance in them gaining victory and withdrew. It was also interesting that the French had believed that to achieve success in speed events the monoplane configuration would be much more suitable and that the biplane layout was considered inferior. As a result, the French lead in aeronautics was lost and taken over by Britain in the next four years.

Meanwhile, Harry Hawker had returned to Australia during the British winter season of 1913–1914, taking with him the prototype Tabloid and demonstrating it around the country where he had been born in January 1889.

Hawker had left school at the age of twelve and, giving his age as fourteen, went to work for a motor company. Having a natural mechanical aptitude, he soon became an expert with cars and earned enough money to travel to Britain where he arrived in May 1911 and managed to continue his career in the motor trade. He was fortunate to be able to start work with Sopwith as a mechanic on 12 July 1912. The money Hawker saved from his salary had been in case he needed the fare back home, but he instead offered it to Sopwith in exchange

Harry Hawker took the Sopwith Tabloid prototype two-seater on a demonstration tour of Australia in 1913–1914. (*BAE Systems*)

for flying lessons. His subsequent successes made him famous both in Britain and Australia, where he returned with the two-seat Tabloid on 13 January 1914. He made his first flight in Australia on 27 January. By offering flights at £20 a time and attending flying exhibitions, the tour of Australia was self-supporting. After a very successful stay in Australia, the Tabloid was dismantled and shipped back to Brooklands with Hawker in late April 1914. After six weeks at sea, Hawker arrived back at Tilbury on 7 June, from where he went straight to Brooklands and was flying a Tabloid that afternoon.

Sopwith entered at least one aircraft to all major aviation events; the 'First Race from London to Manchester and Back' sponsored by the Daily Mail was no exception. The 100-hp Tabloid from the Schneider Trophy success flown by Hawker was entered, but he had to retire and return due to ill health having only managed to reach Coventry. While preparations were made for entering further events, the competition was growing from other manufacturers, which all ceased when Britain declared war on Germany on 4 August 1914. The result was an increase in orders, and to avoid a conflict of interest between the Admiralty and War Office, Sopwith became a designated contractor to the Royal Navy (RN).

Work levels increased in the workshops at Kingston. Brooklands was taken over as a military camp under the command of the Army—No. 2 Reserve Flying Squadron RFC was formed there and the Bristol School's aircraft were taken over. Security was increased dramatically.

The British Expeditionary Force (BEF) commenced its move to France on 9 August, and news soon began to come through about Sopwith aircraft in action with both the Army and

RN, with Tabloids serving with 3 and 4 Squadrons. Meanwhile, the RN were using Sopwiths in action on the Western Front as defence against German Zeppelins in the bombing role, but with the advances of the enemy by the end of 1914 not a single serviceable Sopwith aircraft remained in the war zone, although the factory was still busy supplying flying boats to the Admiralty. Due to poor serviceability with the engines of the Sopwith floatplanes, by mid-1915 Short's aircraft had taken over the reconnaissance duties in France, and Sopwith Two-Seat Scouts and Tabloids were allocated to home defence both from East Coast bases and converted cross-Channel ferries, but with ineffective results.

Following Tom Sopwith's visit to the BEF in France in June 1915 when no Sopwith aircraft were in operation, he gained a better understanding of what type of aircraft was needed. This allowed future Sopwith designs to lead British aviation. The first of these was a two-seat biplane that became known as the 1½ Strutter, the drawings of which were released for manufacture on 12 December 1915, followed early in 1916 with a single-seat Scout and a Triplane, allowing the company to expand rapidly. By February, the first 1½ Strutters were being flight tested at Brooklands, and on 12 April, Hawker took one of the biplanes to a new British height record of 24,408 feet (7,200 metres).

The first Triplane made its maiden flight on 30 May 1916. Hawker was so pleased with its performance that he looped it three times during this first test.

While Sopwith was still a designated supplier to the Admiralty, the Army also needed the Sopwith 1½ Strutter armed with its fixed forward-firing Vickers gun (complete with its interrupter gear to allow it to fire through the propellers) to combat the scourge of the enemy Fokkers.

Sopwith 1½ Strutter A6901 with the half-struts at the wing centre-section. (*RAF Museum*)

The Sopwith Triplane was powered by a 110-hp Clerget rotary engine. (*BAE Systems*)

Sopwith 1½ Strutter N5220. (*BAE Systems*)

The 1916 Sopwith Baby floatplane 8124. (*BAE Systems*)

The expanding Sopwith factories were fully occupied with supplying the RNAS, and with the growing urgency for the new aircraft at the Battle of the Somme offensive, an agreement was achieved for the RFC aircraft to be built by a group of sub-contractors with a royalty paid to Sopwith. The first of these sub-contractors was Ruston Proctor of Lincoln, followed by Fairey Aviation, Hooper & Company, and Vickers. The Scout, later to be named the Pup, was also selected for both the RNAS and RFC, which rapidly increased the production volumes both for Sopwith and the sub-contractors, while the Standard Motor Company and Whitehead Aircraft were added to the sub-contractors. There were also plans for the Triplane to be adopted for service; from its humble beginnings as a small local business the company becoming a very large industrial complex. The Schneider version of the Tabloid was developed into the Sopwith Baby floatplane for the Admiralty, which were carried on board ships and lowered when required to operate, but they were only able to fly from the sea in relatively calm conditions.

When further Babies were required for home defence in late 1916, the production line was moved to the Blackburn Aeroplane and Motor Company at Brough near Hull.

Sopwith then concentrated on the design and construction of land-based aeroplanes, the company specialising in fighter aircraft. The first Sopwith 1½ Strutters were delivered to No. 5 Wing in France on 24 April with the first action on 21 May when three enemy aircraft were engaged and driven off. In addition to the synchronised forward-firing Vickers gun, the 1½ Strutter also had a Lewis gun mounted on a Scarff ring and operated by a gunner in the rear cockpit, which was separated by a fuel tank and hampered communications between the two crew members.

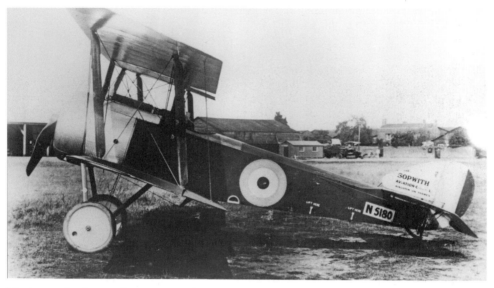

N5189 was the first production Sopwith Naval Pup for the Admiralty. (*BAE Systems*)

Next to enter service was the Pup, which went for service trials in France in May 1916 and into series production at W. Beardmore and Sons in Scotland. This was followed by the Triplane prototype, which was delivered to the RNAS in France in mid-June and went into action on 1 July with one enemy biplane damaged. The Pup finally went into combat on 24 September with the RFC.

Production Triplanes began to arrive at Dunkirk in early 1917 to equip No. 8 (Naval) Squadron, with the first victory on 1 February. Both the Pup and Triplane were armed with a single fixed Vickers gun synchronised to fire through the propeller blades. The major problems in these early stages were engine failures and gun stoppages—the latter caused by the oil becoming less viscous with the colder higher altitudes reached by the Sopwith types. Some of the 1½ Strutters were completed as single-seat bombers, with the bombs carried internally in place of the rear cockpit, which went into operation on 2 August.

Replacement of the 1½ Strutters commenced in the RNAS on the Western Front with Pups on 16 November 1916. Naval 8 became the first squadron to be fully equipped with the type under the control of the RFC, and they made good use of the improved performance benefits.

No. 54 Squadron was the first RFC squadron to be equipped with Pups on 24 December 1916, going into action in early 1917. In addition to air-to-air combat, the aircraft were also used very effectively for ground attack. When the Battle of Arras opened on 9 April 1917, 32 per cent of the fighter squadrons, consisting of three RNAS and five RFC units, were equipped with the three types of Sopwith fighters to maintain air superiority over the Western Front.

The Sopwith menagerie was about to gain a new member with the first Camel having made its maiden flight.

The Sopwith Dove at the Shuttleworth Trust has been preserved as the first production Naval Pup for the Admiralty. (*Author's photo*)

Sopwith Camel armed with a synchronised Vickers machine gun mounted on the engine top-decking. The major recognition feature was the straight top wing. (*Systems Museum*)

Meanwhile, No. 3 Wing RNAS were equipped with Sopwith 1½ Strutters to form the world's first strategic bomber force from 1 July 1916. Operations commenced on 30 July and achieved a high level of success against military and industrial targets. Despite the successes, No. 3 Wing RNAS was disbanded in June 1917 due to representations made by the Army regarding the costs involved and the perceived lack of achievements. By the end of hostilities, over 5,400 Sopwith 1½ Strutters had been built by Sopwith and sub-contractors both in Britain and Europe.

During 1916, the Sopwith Company had expanded beyond all recognition but was unable to undertake major aircraft assembly due to the limitations in factory space. With the assembly allocated to sub-contractors, Sopwith began to investigate an expansion into more suitable premises and a government factory at nearby Ham was leased, ensuring that the company was able to assemble aircraft in the quantity it was designing, and to manufacture the parts for them.

Although the Pup was very effective as a fighter, there was a need to replace it with a higher performance fighter to combat the enemy aircraft then entering service. The first Camel prototype was powered by a 110-hp Clerget engine and armed with twin Vickers guns firing through the propeller arc. The first F.1 prototype was passed by the Sopwith Experimental Department on 22 December 1916, and the first production order came from the RNAS in January 1917, followed by the RFC in May, with its service entry in June. The major recognition feature of the Camel was the straight top wing with a dihedral on the lower wing, and the main power plant in service aircraft was the 130-hp Clerget.

The Sopwith Camel with a fixed forward-firing Vickers machine gun firing through the propeller arc and a Lewis gun over the wing centre-section. (*BAE Systems*)

The Camel did have a reputation for being difficult to handle by inexperienced pilots, with a tendency to spin caused by propeller torque when making tight turns, which resulted in a number of deaths during training. By early August, the RNAS Pups and Nieuports had been replaced by Camels within a number of squadrons. The RFC replaced their 1½ Strutters with Camels and gained the first recorded victory against a German fighter on 27 July 1917. Like the Pups, in addition to its success as a fighter, Camels were also adapted for ground attack armed with four under-fuselage mounted 20-lb bomb racks. They first went into action in this capacity with 70 Squadron RFC on 19 September in preparation for the Third Battle of Ypres.

Meanwhile, Camel production was building up to equip the expanding squadrons in France, which would be involved in defending against the great German Spring offensive of 1918.

The next major type to be developed by Sopwith was the Dolphin, which had an armament of twin fixed Vickers guns firing through the propeller arc and a pair of elevated Lewis machine guns—the world's first multi-gun fighter.

Designed to fly faster than the Camel and be more manoeuvrable than the S.E.5, the Dolphin had backward staggered biplane wings, with the top wing attached to the fuselage top giving the pilot good visibility. The first prototype, powered by a 200-hp Hispano engine made its maiden flight by Harry Hawker from Brooklands on 23 May 1917, and was evaluated at Martlesham Heath for the RFC. The Expeditionary Force was so impressed with the potential of the Dolphin that Sopwith received their largest order to date for 500 aircraft on 29 June 1917. Deliveries commenced in November, although there were a number of teething troubles in early service that the Sopwith team worked hard to correct. One of

The Sopwith Dolphin featured backward stagger biplane wings to give the pilot a better view. Armament was two elevated Lewis machine guns for defence against airships and a pair of fixed synchronised Vickers machine guns above the engine. (*BAE Systems*)

the most serious problems was with the Hispano engine suffering connecting rod failures, which Hispano-Suiza blamed on Sopwith and refused to assist with any corrections. It was therefore recommended that the well-proven Bentley BR.2 rotary engine be fitted in place of the Hispano while Sopwith was urgently dealing with the other development problems.

By the end of 1917, nearly twenty Dolphins had been flown to France, and 19 Squadron RFC was selected to introduce the new type. The first aircraft were received in January 1918 and achieved their first victory on 8 March. No. 23 Squadron soon followed 19 Squadron's use of Dolphins in preparation for the launch of the German offensive. Both squadrons were used for ground-attack duties against the advancing enemy troops, which was hardly the role this high-altitude fighter was intended for. The high-altitude performance was particularly useful against high-flying enemy reconnaissance aircraft, and the type continued on strafing, interception, line patrols, observation balloon bursting, and bomber escorts until the final Dolphin major operation of the war on 30 October 1918, less than a month before the Armistice. No. 19 Squadron had accounted for sixty-four enemy aircraft destroyed; 87 Squadron flew Dolphins scoring a total of eighty-nine victories. Despite over 1,000 Dolphins being delivered to what by then had become the RAF, four squadrons—19, 23, 79, and 87—were the only units equipped with Dolphins in France. The type remained in service on training duties until the last was withdrawn in June 1919.

Despite the entry into service of the Dolphin, the Camels still continued to be active in combat both in ground attack and air-to-air fighting. Three Camel squadrons—28, 45, and 66—were allocated against the Austro-Hungarian Air Service, and on 30 March the sole Camel VC was awarded to Lt A. Jerrard of 66 Squadron for his gallantry in Italy following combat against superior numbers of Albatros D.IIIs on 30 March. He had shot down at least three enemy aircraft and destroyed more on the ground when he was finally shot down and taken prisoner, later escaping.

With the German advances commencing on 21 March, it was essential to bomb and strafe the enemy troops and supply convoys that were advancing on a massive scale. As the British troops fell back, airfields were abandoned, sometimes when the aircraft were already airborne, resulting in landings in whatever fields were available and were often without facilities. The Camels were used to damage the roads with bomb craters to slow down enemy traffic. They killed horses pulling wagons with machine gun fire to further block the roads as well as shooting at the scattering troops. There were a total of ten Camel Squadrons on the Western Front accounting for some 40 per cent of the total fighter strength.

With the superiority of the Camel on the Western Front, it became the mount of a number of aces; it was Camel B7270 of 209 Squadron, flown by Captain Roy Brown, which was credited with shooting down Baron Manfred von Richthofen on 21 April 1918, although there was some controversy over who really was responsible for the death of the Red Baron, the leading ace of the First World War. Other British aces included Captain R. A. Little, who was eighth in the list of British aces in 203 Squadron, and his colleague Raymond Collishaw—the highest scoring ace to survive the war. Captain H. W. Woollett of 43 Squadron had a number of successes against enemy observation balloons, achieving six victories in one day against these well-defended targets. D. R. MacLaren became the commanding officer of 46 Squadron who, by the end of the war, was sixth in the list of British high-scoring aces.

Despite these successes, the overall wastage to the Camels reached eighty aircraft in a period of five months in addition to the other types in service. In August 1918, there were signs of the battle turning to the advantage of the Allies and the Camels were used to strafe the retreating ground troops and attack enemy airfields. On 4 November, within a week of the Armistice, Camels of 65 and 204 Squadrons met some forty enemy scouts and in the ensuing combat claimed nine enemy aircraft destroyed, six driven down out of control, and two others driven down, making for a total of seventeen enemy aircraft lost, with one RAF pilot missing, and another taken prisoner. This engagement was described as 'the record combat of the war in the air'. By the time of the Armistice on 11 November 1918, 65 Squadron had claimed 219 victories, of which 136 enemy aircraft were destroyed; the squadron had moved to France on 24 October 1917. At the end of the First World War, there were twenty-two squadrons equipped with Sopwith aircraft—some 50 per cent of the total fighter strength on the Western Front.

Although the Camel was very manoeuvrable at low level when used for ground attack, a more heavily armed and armoured aircraft was required to fill this demanding role. Sopwith therefore developed the Salamander, which was first flown from Brooklands on 27 April 1918.

With the Americans joining the Allies from late 1917, it was realised that the Germans would attempt a massive offensive before the Americans could enter the war in force. Therefore, an armoured trench fighter was specified to help defend against the attempt to drive back the Allied forces. Originally, the aircraft were to be fitted with downward-firing machine guns, but it was more effective to have two synchronised Vickers guns firing at a small angle of depression rather than acutely depressed guns firing from underneath the aircraft.

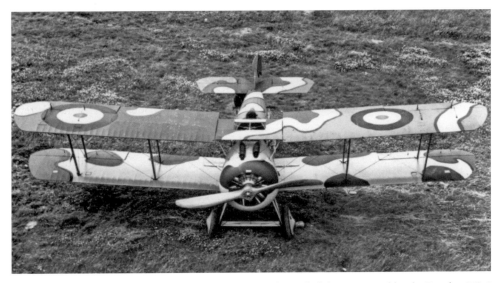

The Sopwith Salamander was produced as an armoured trench fighter powered by the Bentley B.R.2 rotary engine—but too late to see service during the First World War. (*BAE Systems*)

The German offensive commenced on 21 March 1918. With the Salamander desperately required, the first aircraft was sent to France on 9 May for service evaluation. The reports were favourable and the type was ordered into production in early June with a substantial contract to Sopwith. The armour plating increased the weight of the aircraft, increasing the speed in a dive, and the aircraft was heavy on lateral control, which made it tiring to fly. However, Sopwith was also busy with the Snipe and did not have the resources to further develop the Salamander. The Salamander, powered by a Bentley BR.2 rotary engine, could carry the same war load as the Camel, which was either four 20-lb bombs, or one 112-lb bomb. Unfortunately the Salamander was not ready for service before the Armistice, and although (like the Camel) it was not declared obsolete at the end of the First World War, the fifty or so stored for possible use until the early 1920s never saw squadron service.

Meanwhile, following a specification A. F. Type I Single-seat Fighter (High Altitude) issued by the Air Board in late 1917, one of two designs submitted by Sopwith was the 7F.1 Snipe, powered by the Bentley B.R.2 rotary engine.

There were eight contenders for this requirement, including a group powered by the radial Wasp engine with which Sopwith entered the monocoque fuselage structure Snail. By early March, most of the Bentley-powered contenders were under test at Martlesham Heath

The Sopwith Snipe was a single-seat fighter powered by the Bentley B.R.2 rotary engine to replace the Camels and Dolphins. (*BAE Systems*)

The Richard Road Works in Kingston was constructed for the mass production of combat aircraft during the First World War since the existing Sopwith manufacturing facilities were totally inadequate. This photograph, taken in December 1918, shows the factory full of Snipes, Dolphins, and Salamanders. The Richard Road Works was leased to Leyland Motors from 1928 until 1948, and later became the main Hunter and Harrier production line. (*BAE Systems*)

where the Snipe prototype was flown by Captain J. B. McCudden, who by then had destroyed fifty-seven enemy aircraft in aerial combat. After a fifteen-minute flight, he was full of praise for the new Sopwith fighter, while the other contenders lacked manoeuvrability, which was essential in combat. As a result, the Ministry of Munitions placed orders for 1,700 Snipes. The Snail, and its Wasp-powered competitors, did not progress due to the unreliability of the engine, although the monocoque structure of the fuselage was to be adopted in later designs.

The Sopwith organisation continued to expand at a rapid rate to cope with the high volume of combat aircraft for the war effort.

Early in 1918, the first Snipes were built for evaluation at Martlesham Heath, and the new Ham factory was being prepared for volume production of the new fighter planned to replace the Camel in service. The first Snipe was flown from Brooklands on 27 April 1918 with the first example sent to France on 9 May for evaluation—its armament a pair of synchronised Vickers guns firing downwards at a slight angle. Following favourable reports, the type was confirmed for production in June. Hawker continued to be busy test flying the new proto-types from Brooklands, including a number of types that never entered production, such as Rhinos and Hippos. All the prototypes were constructed in the experimental department within the old skating rink and disassembled for transport to Brooklands where they were reassembled for flight testing, but it soon became obvious that the RAF, newly formed on 1 April 1918, had found an air-superiority fighter with the Snipe. The origins of the Snipe are obscure. The first documentary evidence is a report to the Air Board, from August 1917, of an aircraft similar to the Camel but with the improved view of the Dolphin, making it a better fighting machine. The first Snipe probably flew in September 1917, but the initial performance was disappointing and changes were made to the fuselage, which made a great improvement. However, there was an accident on 16 November when the prototype crashed while landing in fog.

The Air Board ordered six prototypes for development trials, which were flown during the winter of 1917–1918. When compared with the Camel, the climb rate to 10,000 feet was the same for both types, but the Snipe was faster, had a greater range, and carried more than double the ammunition. After extensive trials that were concluded successfully, 43 Squadron introduced the Snipe into service on 23 September 1918, and the first combat was by 4 (Australian Flying Corps) Squadron on 22 October when five enemy aircraft were shot down. The Snipes were superior to the best of the enemy fighters, and in the closing weeks of the war the Snipe squadrons increased their scores with minimal losses, making the type the finest fighter from any country to operate in the First World War.

The concept of the Snipe was developed as the Salamander for ground attack. Sopwith fighters were also used as night fighters for home defence, anti-submarine coastal patrols; the Sopwith T.1, later to be named the Cuckoo, was a torpedo-carrying anti-shipping defence, as well as pioneering in operations made from the decks of ships.

Progress with the design and operation of aircraft had been rapid during the First World War due to the ever-pressing needs of combat. The performance and reliability of both aircraft and aero engines had advanced dramatically, but with the signing of the Armistice on 11 November 1918 the Great War machine rapidly began to wind down. However, there were still challenges, one of which was left over from 1914 when the Daily Mail had offered a prize of £10,000 for the first non-stop crossing of the Atlantic. Sopwith was keen to make an early attempt for this prize and planned as a basis the Sopwith B.1 bomber, powered by a 360-hp Rolls-Royce Eagle and with a deeper fuselage to accommodate the extra fuel, as well as an increased wing area to carry the extra load. Naturally, the pilot was to be Hawker, together with Lt Cdr K. K. Mackenzie-Grieve as navigator. The new aircraft was ready in six weeks and had a number of unique features, including a jettisonable undercarriage to reduce drag, reinforced wooden runners on the longerons, and an inverted boat built into the top fuselage decking. On 20 March 1919, the Sopwith Atlantic, as it had been named, sailed with its crew across the Atlantic to St John's, Newfoundland, where a suitable departure field had been prepared.

Poor weather delayed the departure, but reassembly of the aircraft commenced so that it would be ready to depart as soon as the snow and ice thawed.

The Sopwith Atlantic was produced very quickly by Sopwith after the end of the First World War for an attempt on being the first aeroplane to be flown across the North Atlantic. Flown by Harry Hawker, it departed from Newfoundland on 18 May 1919, but had to make a forced landing in the sea. The crew were rescued by a Danish ship. (*BAE Systems*)

There was plenty of competition for the prize and the Atlantic departed at 17.45 GMT on Sunday 18 May, dropping the undercarriage after crossing the coast. With poor weather encountered during the night, the engine began to overheat. After a number of unsuccessful attempts to correct the problem, Hawker headed south to the main shipping lanes and force-landed close to a Danish ship, whose crew rescued the two aviators. As the ship was not equipped with radio, the news of the rescue could not be sent home and it was assumed that both had been lost at sea until the Danish ship was able to signal by flags to the Butt of Lewis that the crew were aboard. They were collected by HMS Woolston and taken to Scapa Flow to catch a train to London. The wreckage was later salvaged and exhibited on the roof of Selfridges in London.

In peacetime, RAF Camels were replaced by Snipes, equipping squadrons overseas in a number of trouble spots. Some of the earlier types, which were obsolete to the RAF, were supplied to overseas air forces. Eleven squadrons were equipped with Snipes in Britain, including 80 Squadron in Egypt and 1 Squadron in Iraq. The Snipes were withdrawn from overseas service in 1926 and declared obsolete with the RAF in 1928, replaced by Hawker fighters.

At the end of the war, in addition to the subcontractors, the four Sopwith plants—the experimental department in the original skating rink, the works in Canbury Park Road, the assembly line at Ham, and the flight testing at Brooklands—employed some 3,500 people, of which over 1,000 were women. With the signing of the Armistice, the older workers and most of the women left, but there were still too many employees for the much reduced workload.   Despite efforts to diversify into the motor trade and furniture industries using the skills of the workforce, Sopwith was unsuccessful. Efforts were also made to produce aircraft for the civil market and participate in sporting events, including the 1919 Schneider Trophy contest, but with no success.

In spite of all the efforts to keep the factories busy, the economic slump of 1920 proved too much, resulting in the company being wound up on 10 September and going into voluntary liquidation. Sopwith were not the only company in aviation to be closed, with many others also going out of business.

In the place of Sopwith, the H. G. Hawker Engineering Co. Ltd was formed on 15 November 1920 with the aim of manufacturing motorcycles and as dealers in all kinds of steam and internal combustion engines, cars, and aircraft. Initial orders were received for spares for Camels and reconditioned Snipes for home defence with the RAF.

While practicing for the 1921 Aerial Derby, Harry Hawker was killed on 12 July in a Nieuport Goshawk for unknown reasons. His death was not only a great loss to the company and his colleagues but also to the country, with condolences coming from the King and Prime Minister.

The first aircraft produced by Hawker was the Sopwith-designed Duiker, a high wing monoplane first flown in 1923. W. G. Carter became chief designer, and a promising young draughtsman, Sydney Camm, joined the company from Martinsyde in 1923.

The Sopwith/Hawker Duiker was the final Sopwith design and produced by H. G. Hawker Engineering. It was not very successful and did not enter production. (*BAE Systems*)

The first Hawker aircraft to be ordered into production was the Woodcock. A total of sixty-four were built for the RAF, replacing the Snipes of 3 and 17 Squadrons. One Woodcock was retained by the company and entered in the King's Cup Race of 1925 flown by Flt Lt P. W. S. 'George' Bulman, later to become the company's chief test pilot. Bulman was later responsible for flight testing the Hurricane, in addition to the family of combat biplanes. He was known as 'George' as he had difficulty remembering names and therefore called everyone George.

With the trend moving from wood to metal construction, Sopwith asked Sigrist and Camm to work on metal structures, resulting in the Hawker-developed system of bolted duralumin tubes, which was a construction system continued through to the Hurricane.

The new company of Hawker Aircraft Ltd was formed in 1933 to cope with raising the additional capital to finance the production of the Hawker Hart series of fighters and light bombers. Since the Ham works had been leased to Leyland Motors, Hawker bought the Gloster Aircraft Company and the production of certain Hawker types of aircraft was transferred to the Gloster works at Hucclecote. In 1935, the shares of the Armstrong Siddeley Development Company were acquired to form the Hawker Siddeley Aircraft Company, which became Hawker Siddeley Aviation, with Armstrong Siddeley Motors, Armstrong Whitworth Aircraft, A. V. Roe (Avro), and Air Service Training.

With the RAF Expansion Scheme getting under way in the early to mid-1930s, more factory space was needed, which resulted in the construction of a new factory and airfield at Langley that soon became busy with Hurricane production. In 1963, Sir Thomas Sopwith, who had been knighted in 1953, resigned as chairman of the Hawker Siddeley Group to become president of what had become a multi-national aerospace and engineering organisation. He died in 1989 having reached his 100th year.

2

The Hawker Biplane Fighters

W HEN SYDNEY CAMM joined the Hawker team at Kingston in 1923, he became chief designer in 1925 and continued the unrivalled fighter family. Until 1966, he had overall responsibility for the classic biplane fighters including the Hart and Fury, to the first monoplane fighter–the Hurricane, and into the jet age with the Hunter and finally the early versions of the unique V/STOL Harrier.

Sydney Camm was born on 5 August 1893. As a schoolboy he had made model aeroplanes, which started his interest in aviation, and was proud of the fact that he was able to turn a boyhood hobby into a career. In 1914, Camm joined Martin & Handasyde at Brooklands initially as a woodworker, but he was later promoted to the drawing office. Like all the aircraft companies after the end of the First World War, it was increasingly difficult to create sufficient work to continue business, but he worked with the small design team of what had become the Handasyde Company. After working on a competition monoplane glider and a motor glider for the 1924 light aircraft competition, Handasyde went into liquidation in the autumn of 1923. In November 1923, Camm was taken on as the senior designer of H. G. Hawker, with W. G. Carter as chief designer. Camm's first task was to produce a modern version of the Tabloid with half the power and half the weight. This was to be the first professional design with Camm in charge and emerged as the Cygnet, gaining a winning place at the 1924 Lympne Light Aircraft Trials.

When Carter resigned from Hawker in 1925, Camm was appointed his successor as chief designer. He ruled the design office and was a hard taskmaster who would not allow any argument from his team, but he was a perfectionist in detail design, personally checking every drawing.

Having been involved in the development of metal tubular structures replacing wood, Camm started with the classic Hart biplane family in 1928, initially designed as a high speed, light day-bomber, but later adapted to become a two-seat fighter and trainer.

Sydney Camm joined the Hawker team in November 1923 as a senior designer under George Carter. He was appointed chief designer from 1925 when George Carter moved to Glosters. Not only was Sydney Camm responsible for the design of the Hawker biplane combat aircraft, but also the Hurricane and the advance into the jet age with the Hunter. (*BAE Systems*)

Camm's first design of his own was the Hawker Cygnet for the Lympne Light Aircraft Competition in 1924, which it won. (*BAE Systems*)

The old Canbury Park Road offices used by Sopwith and taken over by H. G. Hawker Engineering in 1920. They remained in use until 1959 when the new offices were built in Richmond Road. (*BAE Systems*)

The Hawker Hart bomber prototype J9052 at Brooklands in its original configuration was first flown by George Bulman in June 1928 and powered by a Rolls-Royce F.XIB engine, later to become the 525-hp Kestrel. This was the basis for a number of the Hawker biplane combat aircraft and, as a two-seat day bomber, had a fixed forward-firing synchronised Vickers gun operated by the pilot, while the observer had a Lewis gun in the rear cockpit. (*Author's collection*)

Power was generally produced by a single 525-hp Rolls-Royce Kestrel, but other engines were also installed and variants exported to Estonia and Sweden where they were built under licence.

The Hart was designed to specification 12/26 as a day-bomber with a top speed of 160 mph, and the tender was submitted in December 1926. The primary structure used the Hawker steel tube construction method with a fabric covering, single bay wings, and an undercarriage with pneumatic shock absorbers.

The Hawker tender was accepted and the construction of a mock-up commenced in early 1927, with the prototype flown for the first time by George Bulman in June 1928. A production contract was placed for fifteen development aircraft, with a successful introduction to RAF service with 33 Squadron in January 1930.

Among the early production aircraft was a company owned G-ABMR, which survived in airworthy condition for many years until presented to the RAF Museum, where it is now preserved. This Hart was used for engine test bed work and tested many of the features of later versions within the family. The Hart bomber was faster than the RAF fighters, and an experimental flight of Hart Fighters, later named Demons, served with 23 Squadron at Kenley in 1931. The size of Hart orders for RAF operations at home and overseas was so

The Hart Trainer prototype K1996 looping with the Brooklands motor racing track in the background. The Hawker sheds were located by the lower part of the race track loop, with the Vickers factory later built close to the start of home straight. (*BAE Systems*)

The single-seat Hawker Fury fighter, powered by a close-cowled Rolls-Royce Kestrel engine, was first flown by Gerry Sayer from Brooklands on 25 March 1931. Fury K1938 was part of the initial production batch and delivered to 43 Squadron at Tangmere in May 1931. (*RAF Museum*)

great that 665 were built under sub-contract by Vickers, Armstrong Whitworth, and Gloster, mostly going to the RAF flying training schools. By 1936, Harts on operational squadrons were being replaced by Hawker Hind day-bombers, many of the surplus being passed to the South African Air Force.

The next major fighter development was the Hawker Fury, similar in layout to the Hart, but designed as a single-seat interceptor and also powered by a close-cowled Kestrel engine.

The Fury was probably the ultimate in biplane fighter design produced as a private venture in 1929, following on from the one-off Hornet, which flew at over 200 mph during trials at Martlesham Heath. Not only was the Hornet-Fury fast, but it had excellent handling qualities and a high structural strength, resulting in the RAF placing production orders with Hawker in 1930. Construction was generally similar to the earlier Hart—the fabric-covered wing structure with metal spars and spruce ribs. Armament was provided by two fixed synchronised Vickers guns in the top decking of the nose. The initial order for twenty-one Fury Is was placed in August 1930, and a further six were ordered by Yugoslavia. The first production Fury K1926 was from Brooklands on 25 March 1931, and all the initial orders for the RAF and Yugoslavia had been completed and flown within three weeks. The first RAF unit to receive Furies was 43 (Fighter) Squadron based at Tangmere, with sixteen aircraft delivered in May 1931. With further production orders, 25 (Fighter) Squadron re-equipped with Furies at Hawkinge, followed by 1 (Fighter) Squadron at Tangmere in May 1932—all three squadrons performing outstanding formation aerobatics.

A formation of Fury Is with 1 Squadron. (*BAE Systems*)

One Fury, powered by an Armstrong-Siddeley Panther, engine was delivered to Norway but did not go into production, and sixteen Furies were ordered by the Persian Government.

Development of the Fury was carried out by Hawker at company expense initially with what was known as the Intermediate Fury, registered G-ABSE, followed by the High Speed Fury, which first flew on 3 May 1933, but was adopted by the Air Ministry as K3586 to Specification F.14/32.

These two prototypes were used to test a range of engines, including the Rolls-Royce P.V.12 later to become the Merlin.

There was no urgency to replace the Fury Is in RAF service as they remained the fastest fighter in the air defence of Britain. However, between 1936 and 1938, half a dozen squadrons needed more advanced fighters, to fill the gap before the arrival of the Hurricane, which was progressing as a project. Based on the High Speed Fury fitted with a Kestrel engine, the new aircraft reached 228 mph on trials, and the new specification F.6/35 issued in March 1935 called for additional fuel capacity, the provision for which reduced the top speed to 223 mph. This version became the Fury II, with twenty-three aircraft built by Hawker and a further seventy-five sub-contracted to General Aircraft at Hanworth. The first production aircraft from Hawker flew on 3 December 1936 and they were issued to RAF squadrons, starting

One Fury, powered by a 530-hp Armstrong Panther radial engine, was delivered to Norway as 401. (*RAF Museum*)

The High Speed Fury was the ultimate development of this classic fighter, and K3586 first flew on 3 May 1933 initially as a private venture powered by a Kestrel VI S engine. It was subsequently used as a test bed for a number of engines. (*RAF Museum*)

with 25 (Fighter) Squadron, in early 1937. Other squadrons to be equipped with the new variant were 41 Squadron at Catterick, 43 and 87 Squadrons at Tangmere, and 73 Squadron at Mildenhall. However, by 1939 all had been withdrawn from front-line service and been replaced by Gladiators, Hurricanes, and Spitfires.

The world's only surviving Fury I, K5674, was restored to its former glory over a period of eighteen years, carrying the 43 Squadron markings it wore at Tangmere and now based at Duxford.

Meanwhile, the Hart and Fury development continued for aircraft in a variety of roles. The Hawker Nimrod was a fleet fighter very similar to the Fury, although it had been developed entirely separately as it was conceived under a widely different requirement.

In 1930, Specification N.16/30 was raised around Hawker's Kestrel fleet-fighter proposals, and the Nimrod was similar structurally to the Fury. An order was placed for thirty-five aircraft with Hawker, and the first production aircraft was flown by Gerry Sayer on 14 October 1931. The first aircraft were delivered in 1932 to 408 Flight on HMS Glorious, followed by 402 and 409 Flights, all replacing Flycatchers. An improved version, the Nimrod II, was developed with production commencing in September 1933 and deliveries of the first of thirty-six from March 1934. Nimrods remained in service with the Fleet Air Arm (FAA) until May 1939, when the last were replaced by Sea Gladiators.

A pair of Nimrods—a Mk I and a Mk II—have been restored to flying condition and are generally operated from Duxford.

Hawker Nimrod I S1621 Fleet Fighter was operated by 800 NAS and powered by a Kestrel IIS. (*BAE Systems*)

The Hawker Demon was developed as the fighter version of the Hart, with a pair of fixed forward-firing Vickers machine guns and a Lewis gun for the observer in the rear cockpit. The first production Demon was flown on 10 February 1933. Demon K3776 was issued to 65 Squadron, and photographed on 29 April 1935. (*RAF Museum*)

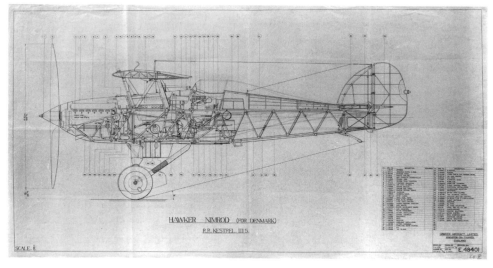

The Hawker Nimrod for Denmark, powered with a Rolls-Royce Kestrel IIS engine shows the classic Hawker tubular construction which continued into the Hurricane. (*BAE Systems*)

Specification F.9/32 was issued because of difficulties experienced by the rear-seat gunner in the Hart Fighter, and a contract placed with Hawker for seventeen Demons.

The first of these was flown on 10 February 1933. By April the initial batch was complete, allowing 23 Squadron to exchange its Bulldogs for the new Demons. Additional contracts were placed for sixty-two Demons powered by the 485-hp Kestrel IIS engine to equip a number of the Auxiliary Air Force squadrons. The eventual total for the RAF was increased by 108 aircraft, in addition to sixty-four Demons for the RAAF, with the engines being changed to Kestrel Vs.

In 1934, 41 (Fighter) Squadron replaced its Bulldogs with Demons and, later in the year, 64 (Fighter) Squadron in Egypt was equipped with Demons. To give the gunner additional protection from the elements, a Frazer-Nash hydraulically operated turret was fitted for trials and later adopted in production. By September 1939, the Demon was declared obsolete and had been replaced on all RAF operational squadrons. One has been restored to flying condition, operating regularly from Duxford.

An adaptation of the basic Hart design for fleet spotter and reconnaissance duties to Specification O.22/36 was the Hawker Osprey, with its rearward folding wings for stowage on Carriers.

Early Ospreys were flying from Brooklands in 1932, and in August of that year began to replace Flycatchers aboard the carriers HMS Eagle and Courageous—the early aircraft being of conventional aluminium construction and strengthened for catapult launching. Towards the end of 1932, a change was made to the primary structure by construction from stainless steel to protect against corrosion from the salt-laden sea air. In 1933, the Osprey became

The Hawker Osprey was a fleet spotter and reconnaissance aircraft that featured rearward folding wings for stowage aboard ships. (*Author's collection*)

the standard ship-board, two-seat reconnaissance aircraft serving on many ships and units with the RN. However, withdrawal from service began during 1938, with some remaining on target-towing duties until they were declared obsolete in 1940.

Similarly, adaptations were made to the basic Hart for the RAF as an Army co-operation aircraft to Specification 7/31 for service at home and the Middle East. An early production aircraft was evaluated in the Army co-operation role and an initial order placed for 40 of what became the Audax—the first being flown by Gerry Sayer on 29 December 1931. The standard Hart armament of a fixed forward-firing synchronised Vickers gun and an observer's Lewis gun in the rear cockpit was retained, and the first unit was 4 (AC) Squadron at Farnborough in 1932. Additional orders allowed a number of home and Middle East squadrons to replace their Wapitis, which were based on the First World War DH.9a. A number of overseas sales were made of the Audax, and with the RAF Expansion Scheme from 1935 to 1937, many of the flying training schools were equipped with the Audax. Production ended in 1937 and the type was used as glider tugs. Hawker construction total of the Audax was 265, with a further 453 built by subcontractors. The RAF also required a special adaptation for policing duties in Iraq, the Hardy, of which forty-seven were built by Gloster, and there was another SAAF adaptation named the Hartbees.

The final Hawker biplane combat aircraft was the Hind, built to Specification G.7/34 as an interim replacement for the Hart bomber for the RAF pending entry into service of the more modern Battles and Blenheims.

The Hawker Hind was the ultimate biplane day bomber, the prototype of which made its maiden flight on 12 September 1934. In addition to serving with the RAF in Britain, some were sent to the Middle East, and Hind K5552 was still operating in Egypt in 1941. (*RAF Museum*)

Hind I L7213 visited Panshanger and served with 611 Squadron. (*BAE Systems*)

The surviving Hinds were those that served in Afghanistan, with at least nine being recovered for restoration. One Hind was restored in time for the Royal Review of the RAF by HRH The Queen at Abingdon in June 1968 and is now preserved in the RAF Museum at Cosford. (*Author's photo*)

One of three Hinds for Latvia was 178, powered by a Bristol Mercury radial engine. and seen at Brooklands prior to delivery. (*BAE Systems*)

Although the layout of the Hind was similar to the two-seat Hart, its engine was the more powerful 640-hp Kestrel V, while improvements were also made to the rear cockpit, including a prone bomb-aiming position. The prototype Hind was first flown on 12 September 1934, with the aircraft being very close to production standards. After a development programme, the first production Hind flew on 4 September 1935. Following the initial development order, contracts were placed for 193 aircraft for the RAF, and a further order for 244 was placed in April 1937. A total of 338 Hinds were in service with the main Bomber Command squadrons, with 114 in service with seven squadrons in the Auxiliary Air Force.

With the delivery of Battles and Blenheims to the RAF from the autumn of 1937, many of the Hinds were converted for training duties and withdrawn from operational duties by the outbreak of the Second World War. Hinds were popular with overseas air forces including Afghanistan, where eight new aircraft were delivered in 1938 and an additional twelve transferred from the RAF.

Surprisingly, a large number of ex-Afghanistan Hinds have survived, including an airworthy aircraft with the Shuttleworth Trust and six recently recovered from Afghanistan, which are stored in the Hastings area.

An Audax replacement for the RAF was the Napier Dagger-powered Hector, which incorporated many of the Hind rear-cockpit improvements as well as a tailwheel replacing the skid.

The Hawker Hector prototype K3719 was an Army co-operation aircraft powered by a Napier Dagger III 'H' engine. (*BAE Systems*)

The prototype was first flown by George Bulman on 14 February 1936, and 178 were ordered from Westland with the first production aircraft flying in February 1937. First deliveries were made to Odiham to replace the Audax in February 1937, but replacement commenced with Lysanders in December 1938 and the Hectors were withdrawn from the regular RAF squadrons in 1939. Some Hectors saw action with the Auxiliary squadrons when six Hectors of 613 Squadron dive-bombed enemy troops in the Calais area on 26 May 1940 with the loss of two aircraft, after which the type was withdrawn.

This brought to an end Sydney Camm and Hawker's programme of high-performance combat single-engined biplanes, ready for the challenge of the new monoplane fighter that became the Hurricane.

3

Hurricane Design, Development and Production

WITH FULL ORDER books from the RAF and overseas customers, the Hart family of combat aircraft were helping the Hawker Company to make more money than any other British aircraft manufacturer. This welcome success resulted in the company staying with the tried and tested, but rapidly dating, tubular steel construction and biplane configuration, while other manufacturers, including Bristol and Supermarine, were developing the monoplane layout. Hawker had considered a monoplane fighter design powered by a Bristol Jupiter radial engine in 1925, but tendered a metal structure fabric-covered fuselage biplane for Specification F.7/30 in competition with the other monoplane designs.

Due to delays with some of the competing aircraft for F.7/30, the RAF trials were held up until late 1934 and early 1935, giving Camm the opportunity to study a monoplane fighter based on the Fury.

This became the Hawker Interceptor Monoplane to Specification F.3/34, leading to the Hurricane prototype K5083 to Specification F.36/34.

When Camm started this development, he must have had the approval of both Sopwith, who was spending much time on his many other interests, and Sigrist, who was in the powerful position of being responsible for the day-to-day running of the business and had already seen off two earlier designers. Camm was appointed to the Board of Directors in 1935, giving him a higher level of authority within the overall organisation.

When the Hurricane was ordered into production in 1936, it was already outdated with its fabric-covered rear fuselage and tubular metal structure.

Six months after the Hurricane's first flight, the Fairey Battle and Spitfire flew. Both featured all-metal monocoque structures, but it was not until 1937 and 1938 that Camm's design team began to use metal monocoque forms in the rear fuselage of the Tornado and Typhoon.

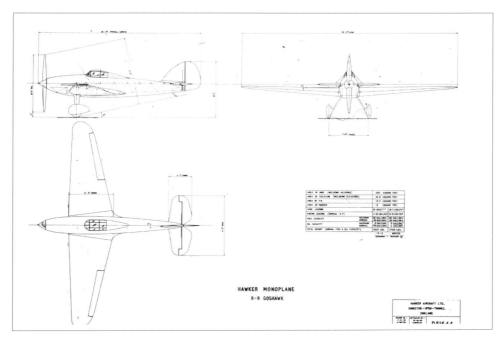

Sydney Camm made some early studies of a Hawker monoplane fighter powered by a single Rolls-Royce Goshawk engine. (*BAE Systems*)

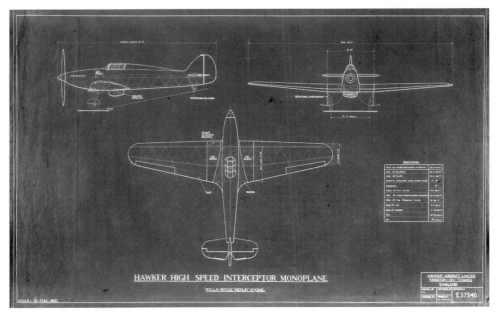

The layout of the Hawker High Speed Interceptor Monoplane powered by a Rolls-Royce Merlin engine was very similar to the Hurricane Mk I. (*BAE Systems*)

The prototype Hurricane K5083; official photo at Brooklands in late October 1935 with a 6-foot scale pole by the nose fitted with the original minimally framed canopy. (*Author's collection*)

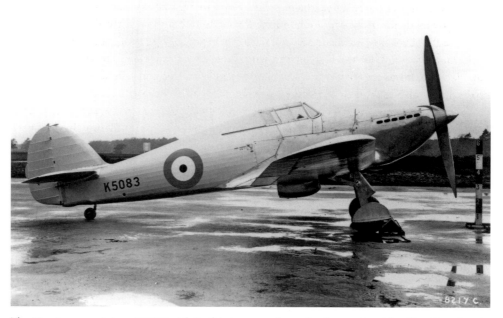

The Hurricane prototype K5083 with its fabric-covered rear fuselage and rudder. The hinged main undercarriage doors were fitted and the tailwheel was retractable. (*IWM photo*)

Even then, the centre fuselage and engine mounts were of steel-tube construction—a style continued until the end of the Tempest's production run. When the prototype Tornado flew in December 1939, the majority of British, American, and European production lines were producing all-metal stressed skin monocoque combat aircraft.

However, this is not a criticism of Hawker production methods, which were right for the time and for rapid production in the Hawker factories with their skilled workforce and appropriate tooling. With the growing fear of German production outstripping the UK's capability it was important to exploit the known technical skills to maximise production. In fact, the Hurricane experienced far fewer production difficulties than the all-metal monocoque Spitfire, ensuring that sufficient Hurricanes were available for the critical Battle of Britain. It has been said that the Battle of Britain would not have been won if it was not for the Spitfire, but there would not have been a Battle of Britain at all if the Hurricanes had not been available. Hurricane performance was generally inferior to that of the Spitfire, but it was of a rugged construction and could absorb battle damage. Its pilots were able to concentrate on trying to stop the Luftwaffe's bomber attacks, while the higher performing Spitfires countered their escorting Messerschmitt Bf 109s and protected the Hurricanes.

However, Camm was not averse to progress. When new ideas were suggested he challenged them, but if he found them acceptable he would defend them against criticism. Nothing in the design of the Hurricane was unique except for the provision of eight machine-guns in the wings as had been specified by the Air Ministry. The unbraced monoplane wing, flaps, enclosed cockpit with sliding canopy, hydraulic systems, and retractable undercarriage had all been used in the past. The Hurricane's wide-track, inward-retracting undercarriage also allowed operations from austere airfields, while the narrow-track undercarriages of the Spitfire and Bf 109 made for tricky ground handling throughout their service lives.

Above all things, the Hurricane benefitted from being in the right place at the right time. Its performance was not outstanding, but more than adequate. It was easy to fly and an excellent gun platform. It was easy to produce in quantity, and its rugged construction made it easy to repair. It was also capable of adaptation to different roles in the ever-changing demands of battle, later becoming an extremely effective ground attack and anti-armour aircraft. Camm lead a modestly sized team in the mid-1930s, in very basic accommodation, but with the Hurricane they changed the course of history and helped preserve the British way of life.

In the hands of the majority of 'the few', the Hurricanes were able to combat the enemy air armada and turn them from day to night attacks later in 1940, which reduced the accuracy of bombing and resulted in Adolf Hitler's plans for invasion being abandoned. In service sooner than the Spitfire and available in greater numbers, the Hurricanes shot down more enemy aircraft during the Battle of Britain than all other air and ground defences combined.

Camm continued his design leadership into the jet age with the classic Hunter and the unconventional P.1127/Harrier, which was a project he was not entirely happy with since it used entirely new technology and was outside his comfort zone. Camm died in 1966, but the Kingston project team survived until the end of 1988 when, after seventy-five years of continual technical and commercial success, responsibility for Harrier and Hawk support moved to Warton near Preston, Lancashire.

Well before development of the Hart and Fury series of aircraft ended, there were thoughts on the next step in combat aircraft development beyond the current technology. It was clear that the biplane layout was limited; studies commenced in 1933 on what was known as the Fury Monoplane. The Rolls-Royce Goshawk engine was the chosen power plant, but the project still featured a fixed undercarriage because Camm was not clear whether the drag saved would be cancelled out by the increased weight and complexity of retractable gear. During the twelve months of the study, the more powerful and less complex Rolls-Royce PV.12, later developed into the Merlin, became available. Its increased power and improved reliability, encouraged Camm to specify a retractable undercarriage, with a wide track for stable operations from unprepared fields. This proved to be a wise decision as during the Second World War, Hurricanes had operated from all types of surfaces, from the North African desert to the ice fields of the Arctic and clearings in the Burmese jungle.

In August 1934, Hawker's F.36/34 proposal had reached the design stage, and in spite of the change of configuration to a monoplane with a retractable undercarriage and eight guns in the wings, the prototype flew just eleven and a half months later. It was remarkable that the company could create a high-performance monoplane fighter using existing production capabilities. The construction methods used in the Hurricane differed very little from those of the earlier biplane fighters. Its fuselage retained Hawker's traditional Warren criss-cross girder square tubular structure, and the wing used the conventional dumbbell section spar. The wing was given the necessary torsional stiffness by using dumbbell-boomed rib section with Warren bracing in plain view. Initially, fabric covering was placed over the metal wing ribs, but it was later replaced by more robust metal skins. Although stressed skin would have been more desirable with lower structural weight, it would have required new tooling and skills, whereas the aircraft needed to be produced as quickly as possible using current manufacturing techniques and without major changes to the existing tooling.

Camm preferred to work closely with the end user of an aircraft—initially satisfying their basic requirements, trying it, and then gradually adjusting the design to meet the factors that were of major importance in the specification. The development of the Hurricane was a good example of the design team working closely with Major Buchanan, the Director of Technical Development, and Squadron Leader Ralph Sorley. Both were of the Air Ministry Operations Branch, and the resulting agreement was to fit eight Browning machine guns in the wings, which was the heaviest armament of any aeroplane at the time. The Hurricane Mk II was also to be armed with four of the more destructive 20-mm cannons.

In the mid-1920s, with the German war threat apparently removed by the Armistice, the perceived threat could only come from France, and with the official doctrine that the bomber would always get through, the air defence of Britain was in a very poor state. The majority of the inadequate defence budget was put into bomber development, with very little left over for air defence. It was Air Marshal Sir John Salmond, Air Officer Commander-in-Chief, Air Defence of Great Britain (ADGB), who in 1925 highlighted the deficiencies in Britain's air defences, and it was thanks to his efforts that both the RAF and aircraft industry began to prepare for a more effective air defence.

There was little point in having large RAF Expansion Scheme bomber stations if they could easily be put out of action by enemy bombers. RAF fighters had to have the performance and armament to be capable of intercepting enemy bombers before they destroyed British bomber bases. While the RAF Expansion Scheme concentrated on building bomber stations, the fighter squadrons were generally based at the First World War vintage stations with rudimentary facilities. With Sir John Salmond's departure from the ADGB, his place was taken by Air Marshal Sir Edward Ellington, who was more of a bomber man. Fortunately, a key command appointment in the Fighting role was Air Vice-Marshal Hugh Dowding, who was fully aware of the shortcomings of the RAF fighter force.

Dowding argued the fighter case so strongly that, in 1930, he was promoted as Air Member for Research and Development on the Air Council, where he could exercise his influence on new aircraft for the RAF. A further significant change happened in 1929 with the retirement of Sir Hugh Trenchard as Chief of the Air Staff, to be replaced by Sir John Salmond on 1 January 1930, confirming a strong support from the top for air defence. An initiative began to modernise the entire RAF from 1929 continuing for the next three years. Although there was broad agreement on the overall interceptor requirement, there were a number of areas of difference, particularly in power-plant configuration, the type of armament, and whether night operation should be in the basic requirements.

In terms of performance, it was decided that there should be a maximum speed of 250 mph at 10,000 feet—an arbitrary figure 75 mph faster than the maximum speed of the Bristol Bulldog then in service. While the technical discussions were continuing, there were also economic considerations regarding the overall costs of new designs and the development of engines. The in-line engine provided reduced drag and therefore higher speeds, but its cooling system and radiator created additional weight and vulnerability. Weight of armament was critical to achieving an acceptable hit expectancy; the aircrafts' higher engagement speeds allowed for only shorter bursts of fire with reduced destructive capability. Better armament performance could be achieved by mounting guns outside the propeller arc, dispensing with the traditional interrupter gear and therefore increasing the rate of fire. Finally, the main concern with night operations was whether the aircraft could take-off, be flown, and landed in the dark. These technical points were the responsibility of the aircraft designers to solve.

The Air Ministry was concerned with the overall costs not only of production, but also the overall cost of ownership. There would also be the more demanding training programmes for aircrew and engineering support. Larger production contracts would help bring down unit costs and, at this stage, the target date for service entry was to allow participation in the annual air exercises of 1934. Specification F.7/30 had been drawn up to satisfy this requirement but was premature, although it did result in the Hawker Fury biplane entering service, which could only achieve 207 mph at 14,000 feet.

When Germany abandoned the International Disarmament Conference in 1932 and subsequently withdrew from the League of Nations there was no longer any control over its armament programme, further underlining the need for Britain to modernise its air defences, especially with the knowledge of developments with German aircraft. It was soon realised that not only had Specification F.7/30 not been pitched highly enough, but that by the time prototypes were ready for evaluation they would be obsolete.

Camm was therefore encouraged to study the benefits of a monoplane fighter with a retractable undercarriage. Initial proposals used the Fury fuselage fitted with a low mono-plane wing, but with the Kestrel engine, top speed was going to be only in the region of 270 mph. As studies progressed, Camm proposed a rectangular wing centre-section with a fairly deep aerodynamic section, to which the two-spar outer wings would be bolted. The main undercarriage would be hinged at the outer edge of the centre section, retracting inwards, the wheels almost meeting on the centre-line of the aircraft. The length of the main under-carriage legs was dictated by the diameter of the propeller and in turn determined the span of the wing stub centre-section. The wide-track undercarriage was retracted hydraulically by a hand pump alongside the pilot's seat. Meanwhile, Rolls-Royce was developing the Kestrel into the PV.12, later to become the Merlin—this new engine being adopted for what had become the Hawker Interceptor Monoplane.

The cantilever wing, as described, brought increased structural weight that, when com-bined with the greater weight of the engine, cancelled out the benefits of the retractable undercarriage and increased engine power. Gun armament was again increased, from two machine-guns to four. Traditionally, guns had been mounted within reach of the pilot because of their unreliability, but firing through the propeller arc restricted the rate of fire and a more suitable location had to be found.

Among the reliability problems associated with the Vickers guns was the poor standard of the large stocks of First World War ammunition remaining, but also the weapons themselves were totally out of date by world standards. As a result, all the available guns were tested in 1933—the American Colt coming out as the best available in rate of fire, penetration, range, and reliability. It was designed to fire 0.303-inch rimless ammunition, and was therefore unable to fire British wide-tolerance 0.303-inch rounds without reducing the 1,200 rounds per minute rate of fire. In January 1934, it was confirmed that the Colt could be adapted for British ammunition and plans were made for licence manufacture in Britain.

Assuming these guns would be available, the Air Ministry discussed a draft Specification F.5/34, with a target maximum speed of 300 mph, with both Camm and Supermarine's Mitchell. Although the designers were not given details of each other's designs for commercial reasons, Camm was aware that the Supermarine design was to be of stressed skin construction. Armament was to be at least six guns—this requirement being specified by Sqn Ldr Ralph Sorley, director of Operational Requirements—who suggested that both designs should be capable of carrying eight guns.

By March 1934, detail design of a prototype F.5/34 Interceptor Monoplane was under way in the Hawker experimental design office, and no detailed information was available on the Colt guns, provision was being made for four, fixed, fuselage side-mounted Vickers guns. However, the project team was also studying the best method for accommodating eight guns in the outer wings, and tests confirmed that the aircraft would have satisfactory aerodynamic qualities up to 350 mph with an all-up weight (AUW) of 4,600 lb on the power of a 1,000-hp Merlin engine.

A detailed Specification F.36/34 written around the Hawker submission was sent to Camm during the last week in August 1934 and a formal design was tendered to the Air Ministry on 4 September. On 17 November, the first manufacturing drawings were issued to the experimental department, allowing for the manufacture of jigs and tools. In parallel, Supermarine was commencing work on what was to become the Spitfire to Specification F.37/34 with a top speed in level flight of 330 mph at 15,000 feet, while Camm's design was only required to fly at 320 mph at the same altitude. This difference was based on lower drag for the Supermarine design, but in fact both aircraft exceeded these speeds by 4 to 5 per cent when they entered service.

At the end of November, Rolls-Royce advised Hawker that engine weight had increased by 80 lb—increasing AUW to 4,800 lb—but on 18 December, Rolls-Royce increased take-off power rating to 1,025 hp at 2,900 rpm, with installed weight to be no more than 1,200 lb and giving a power-to-weight ratio of 0.85. Meanwhile, a wooden mock-up of the aircraft was constructed at Canbury Park Road for studies of cockpit layout, pilot field of view, undercarriage retraction, cooling ducting, radiator location, and gun mountings. In late December, an unserviceable PV.12 engine was delivered for installation in the mock-up.

The final design conference was held at Kingston on 10 January 1935. The RAF was represented to discuss the results of studies made with the mock-up, and there was an urgent need to confirm the wing gun installation before manufacture of the prototype wings became too far advanced. A design had already been prepared for eight guns, but they could only be fitted if a satisfactory licence agreement for the Colt guns was confirmed. Details of licence manufacture had already been provided to the Birmingham Small Arms (BSA) Company, the terms of which were being studied.

A contract was placed with Hawker on 18 February for the manufacture of a prototype with the serial number K5083, but there was still no confirmation on armament. Six weeks later, it was agreed not to fit guns to the prototype but to make ballast provision for two fuselage-side mounted Vickers guns and a Colt in each wing. This was a curious configuration—if the Colt guns did become available, why mix the armament? It would have been logical to confirm the eight Colt guns to avoid delays.

Detailed performance estimates were submitted by Hawker on 21 February, including a take-off weight of 4,900 lb for a wing loading of 19 lb per square foot, and a flying weight of 4,480 lb. Maximum speed was estimated to be 330 mph at 15,000 feet, the service ceiling 32,500 feet, and the absolute ceiling at 34,800 feet. Landing speed at a weight of 4,200 lb using flaps was to be around a modest 73 mph. It was expected that the time needed to reach a height of 20,000 feet would be in the region of twelve minutes, but since specific fuel consumption had not been finalised by Rolls-Royce, no range or endurance figures were available. All performance and weights assumed an armament of four guns.

Final agreement was reached between Colt and BSA for the gun licence in July, and the Air Ministry confirmed on 1 August that the prototype should be ballasted for eight wing-mounted Colt guns. The wings were still fabric covered, which was considered adequate for the aircraft's speed range, but there was concern that battle-damaged fabric might disintegrate. With the RAF in the middle of a major expansion programme, the Hawker board justified investment in tooling for metal stressed skin construction using relatively inexpensive plant, particularly for the wings. The first set of wings with stressed metal skins was completed in 1938. The new stressed skin techniques for wings and fuselage were later used on the Typhoon and Tempest, although the major production lines for those types were sub-contracted while the Hawker factories at Kingston, Langley, and Brooklands concentrated on Hurricane production. The PV.12, by now named Merlin, was ready for installation in the Hurricane prototype in the engine 'C' version. However, a fairly large radiator was required for cooling the engine. To smooth the airflow over the retracted main undercarriage, 'D' doors were hinged to the main legs to cover flush over the wheels. By this time, the AUW had grown to about 5,400 lb.

As the prototype neared completion, space at Canbury Park Road became increasingly limited. In addition to the prototype Hurricane in the 90-foot by 60-foot Experimental Department, there was also the Hurricane wooden mock-up and prototypes of the Hector, Fury II, and Henley under construction. Each aircraft was completed on the Canbury Park Road production line and the wings were removed for the road journey to Brooklands where the aircraft were reassembled for flight. Although Hawker owned a large factory off Richmond Road in Kingston, it had been leased to the Leyland Motor Company for a further twelve years and the lease could not be broken.

Hitler broke the military clauses in the Treaty of Versailles on 21 May 1935 and commenced a massive rearmament programme for Germany, increasing tension throughout Europe and creating an increased urgency for Britain to rearm. Seven weeks before Hitler's denunciation of the Peace Treaty, Hermann Göring revealed the new Luftwaffe, which already had 20,000 personnel and some 3,000 in flight training. Its first fighter squadrons were operating the Heinkel He 51, which was a match for the RAF's Furies, and specifications were being issued to German industry for modern types including the Bf 109 fighter, the Do 17 and Heinkel He 111 bombers. The prototype Bf 109 made its first flight in September 1935 powered by an imported Rolls-Royce Kestrel engine before the ultimate German engine was available, and production versions of the fighter were to go into action during the Spanish Civil War long before Hurricanes and Spitfires entered service with the RAF.

Following preliminary certification of the Merlin 'C' for an initial fifty hours flying time, engine No. 11 was delivered to Canbury Park Road for initial systems checks. On 23 October, the Hurricane prototype was loaded under wraps on a special lorry and taken to the assembly shed at Brooklands. On arrival, the fabric-covered wings were reassembled to the aircraft and flight preparations made, including undercarriage retraction functions and engine ground runs. The Hawker design team was dealing with the sometimes difficult combination of a new airframe combined with a new engine, but the combination turned out to be a winner. When the aircraft was weighed in its take-off configuration with full fuel, oil, ballast, and pilot, the total came to 5,416 lb and the centre of gravity (C of G) was within 0.5 inches of its design position.

On 3 November, P. W. S. 'George' Bulman began taxi trails on the grass at Brooklands to become familiar with the Hurricane's enclosed cockpit and bulky nose, remarking that without the top wing of a biplane, the cockpit was brighter, and the view was 'marvellous'.

George Bulman had always had difficulty in remembering people's names, and tended to refer to everyone as 'George', hence his nickname. He had been appointed to the Hawker Board in mid-1935 at the same time as Camm. As chief test pilot, he had been assisted by P. E. G. 'Gerry' Sayer from 1930, and P. G. 'Philip' Lucas from 1931—the three pilots were responsible for the enormous flying programme until they were joined by John Hindmarsh and Maurice Summers in 1935.

Maurice Summers was the younger brother of Mutt Summers, the chief test pilot at Vickers who flew the Spitfire prototype on its maiden sortie. Maurice soon joined his older brother who was based with Vickers, also at Brooklands. Gerry Sayers moved to Gloster in 1935, later making the maiden flight of the E.28/39, Britain's first jet aircraft, but lost his life in combat. As the Hurricane was readied for its first flight, the test flying team therefore consisted of Bulman, Lucas, and Hindmarsh.

A setback occurred on 4 November when Rolls-Royce advised the Hawker Board that the Merlin had failed its full fifty-hour certification test, although there was no obvious reason for a loss of power after forty hours. Bulman suggested that the first flight could go ahead without certification provided there was no magneto-pause and the engine oil filter was inspected after each flight to ensure there were no metal particles. This was agreed with Fred Sigrist and the Rolls-Royce engineers, who allowed Bulman to taxi out for the maiden flight from Brooklands on 6 November 1935.

The aircraft turned into wind. The Merlin opened up, driving the large, fixed-pitch wooden Watts propeller, the tail lifted as speed built up, and the aircraft was off the ground and flying low over the banking of the motor racing track. After about thirty minutes, Bulman returned in the shiny silver dope and polished metal monoplane, side-slipping over the boundary and, bringing the aircraft straight in with the engine ticking over, dropping gently to a perfect three-point landing. The eighty or so workers cheered as Sopwith and Camm drove out in the chairman's Rolls-Royce car to welcome George back. The flight had been kept secret from the media and, as far as is known, no photographs exist of this momentous occasion.

There was no formal, written flight-test report, but Bulman briefed Sopwith and Camm orally in the Brooklands watch office. He reported that the engine temperature built up quickly while taxiing and that directional control was effective on take-off. He was critical of the cockpit canopy, which flexed continually during flight. When the flaps were lowered for landing, the engine temperature again began to increase rapidly, probably due to the centre-section flaps blocking the exhaust from the radiator duct. The flight concentrated on investigating general handling characteristics without measuring performance, but Bulman had performed a slow roll and a gentle dive at around 300 mph. He was enthusiastic about the stalling capabilities, finding that with the undercarriage down with just over half the fuel remaining and flaps up, the aircraft stalled at about 80 mph. Stall recovery was immediate with only slight pressure forward required on the stick.

As a result of Bulman's complaints about the canopy, it was eventually redesigned with more robust framing throughout. There were concerns about possible tail flutter in a dive, and the tailplane was braced with a single strut, which was later found to be unnecessary. Overheating on the ground was a constant problem with the Merlin-powered Hurricanes and

The silver overall Hurricane prototype K5083 at Brooklands fitted with the two-blade Watts wooden fixed-pitch propeller and the original exhaust system, but featuring the stronger canopy. (*Author's collection*)

Spitfires, and to improve the situation on the Hurricane, the radiator fairing was redesigned. The folding 'D' doors on the main undercarriage legs were prone to damage from stones during take-off and landing, and they were therefore removed.

After five test flights, all by Bulman, a provisional airworthiness certificate was issued on 6 December for the Merlin 'C', but only three more flights were made with No. 11, all of which suffered engine problems before it was replaced by Merlin 'C' No. 15. The Merlin 'C' was relegated to test use, with engine development concentrating on the F version, later to become the Merlin I. Bulman made a further two flights before agreeing that the aircraft was ready for service assessment at Martlesham Heath for the compilation of a production specification allowing a production contract to be raised. The prototype was flown to the Aeroplane and Armament Experimental Establishment (A&AEE) at Martlesham Heath on 5 March 1936, the day the Spitfire made its maiden flight.

Initial service trials commenced with a thorough technical examination including ease of servicing, ground handling, systems, and cockpit layout. The technical officers were very enthusiastic about the undercarriage configuration and the ease of accessibility of the gun bays, refuelling points, and radio compartment. Following the successful engineering evaluation, the aircraft was handed over to the responsible RAF test pilot, Sergeant 'Sammy' Wroath. His task was to evaluate the Hurricane and report on handling and performance measurements for submission to the commanding officer for consolidation in a single A&AEE report.

The prototype Hurricane K5083 went to the A&AEE at Martlesham Heath in February 1936, but without armament or canopy strengthening. (*Author's collection*)

Prototype Hurricane K5083 fitted with the improved cockpit canopy, but without armament and retaining the struts under the tailplane. (*Flight photo*)

The early Merlin engines were still troublesome and three different units were used. The aircraft made a short visit to Hucknall, the Rolls-Royce test and development airfield, where most of the problems were corrected, allowing the evaluation to continue.

The A&AEE submitted its findings to the Air Ministry and apart from aileron and rudder control becoming rather heavy at high speeds, the overall result was that all departments were pleased with the Hurricane, and even though the original unstiffened canopy was still fitted, it did not produce any comments. The performance included a maximum speed of 315 mph at 16,200 feet, climb to 15,000 feet from take-off in 5.7 minutes, and to 20,000ft in 8.4 minutes. Service ceiling was estimated at 34,500 feet, which proved optimistic with the Merlin 'C' engine, and absolute ceiling at 35,400 feet. Take-off into a 5-mph headwind at an AUW of 5,672 lb gave a ground run of 265 yards and the landing ground run, using brakes, was 205 yards.

With the anticipated capability of the Hurricane to carry eight machine-guns in its wings, Camm submitted a proposal on 23 April 1936 for a more destructive version of the aircraft equipped with four 20-mm cannons, but there was no official interest in the configuration at the time. The four-cannon Hurricane Mk IICs finally entered RAF service in 1941.

This lack of interest was probably fortunate, since had it gone ahead in place of the Colt-armed aircraft, production might have been delayed so drastically that no Hurricanes would have been in service at the outbreak of war.

The four, 0.303-machine guns mounted in the starboard wing of a Hurricane Mk I with ammunition feeds. (*Author's collection*)

Production of the 20-mm cannon that armed Hurricane Mk IIs at Langley. (*Author's collection*)

With the prospect of a major production contract, in March 1936, Camm instructed the Hawker production drawing office to begin creating a full set of manufacturing drawings while preparations were also made for the new production line. To ease the problem of restricted space, production of seventy-eight Hector Army co-operation aircraft was sub-contracted to Westland Aircraft at Yeovil to follow on from the Audax. The majority of Fury II production was sub-contracted to General Aircraft at Hanworth, where Harts and Hinds were also being converted to trainers. This allowed 24,000 square feet of shop-floor space to be available by 1937, and a further 14,000 square feet of space was made available at Brooklands for final assembly and completion.

Despite the urgent need for a modern fighter aircraft, the Air Ministry delayed placing a contract, and Hawker decided to prepare for the production of 1,000 aircraft at its own expense, clearing the space and ordering aluminium sheets, steel tubing, and recruiting 280 skilled machinists and fitters. These preparations stimulated the Air Ministry to create a new Production Scheme 'F' on 1 June calling for 1,000 fighters, for delivery of the total, less 100 Hawker fighters, by 1 January 1939. On 3 June, the Hawker Board received a formal contract for 600 monoplane fighters. Five days later, all the manufacturing drawings were issued to the production departments in Canbury Park Road—the name 'Hurricane' was officially approved by the Air Ministry on 27 June when the prototype was first displayed publicly during the RAF Pageant at Hendon. On 20 July, Hawker at last received Specification 15/36 from the Air Ministry confirming the full production standard of the Hurricane.

The Hurricane wing centre-section was produced complete with main undercarriage and fuel tanks; a woman inspects it before it joins the final assembly line. (*RAF Museum photo*)

Female labour was vital to maintaining the high levels of wartime production and undertaking the work normally done by men, many of whom were serving in the military. Here, two women are fitting the fire wall on to a Hurricane Mk IIC. (*RAF Museum photo*)

Prototype flying continued with few snags since very little had been criticised at the A&AEE, and Rolls-Royce was busy improving the reliability of the Merlin. The first production-configuration Merlin 'F' improved reliability by reducing rated altitude and shortening the time at full power, although these restrictions caused concern for both the Hurricane and Spitfire design teams since they affected sustained combat performance.

In addition to the removal of the main undercarriage 'D' doors, the centre-section of the flaps was removed to improve airflow through the radiator, this latter configuration being flown for the first time on 16 July. K5083 was then dismantled for the return to Canbury Park Road and installation of the fabric-covered eight-gun wings, and a cockpit gun sight. The tailplane struts were removed and a ground adjustable rudder trim tab fitted.

The prototype returned to Brooklands on 17 August fitted with a Merlin 'C' engine ready for continued development flying in preparation for the aircraft to return to the A&AEE in September ahead of service acceptance trials the following spring. However, the RAF was not happy with the reliability of the Merlin 'F', and the prototype returned to Hucknall for fight trials during September and October for investigations into why its performance was not up to standard. The main result of the tests was that cooling had to be improved drastically.

By this time, the Merlin 'G' was being run on the bench—the entire camshaft mounting, rocker, and valve gear having been redesigned and a number of other improvements incorporated. These promised smoother running at full power, as well as reduced temperature limitations. However, the Rolls-Royce engineers were still keen for an improved radiator design. The Merlin I was therefore withdrawn from use in both the Hurricane and Spitfire, and the 180 or so built were allocated to Fairey Battle production, the light bomber being less demanding on full power operation. The 'G' version, known as the Merlin II, was adopted for both fighters, but work on Hurricane production was stopped in November while the cowlings around the newly shaped engine were redesigned, tooled, and manufactured.

Hawker and the Air Ministry were in agreement that little could be done to improve the prototype without a further delay to final service trials apart from fitting a new radiator fairing and a revised rudder with an inflight adjustable trim tab. With the new rudder installed, both Bulman and Lucas undertook initial spinning trials. Spin recovery was shown to be within the limits required by the RAF, but it was noticed that with the tailwheel in the down position, recovery was slightly improved.

At the end of March 1937, Bulman returned the prototype to Martlesham Heath, by which time the eight Colt guns had been fitted along with their ammunition feed, as had a radio, lengthened radiator fairing, a strengthened windscreen and canopy, and a fixed tailwheel. As K5083 was still fitted with a Merlin 'C', it was agreed that its performance and handling would not influence the ultimate report. The final stage of the service assessment was commenced by Sammy Wroath on 3 April.

With the RAF Expansion Scheme fully established, the Hawker Board needed to generate considerable additional production capacity in anticipation of major orders for Hurricanes. The other factories within the Hawker Siddeley Group were fully committed to their own designs, so a whole new facility was demanded. RAF Fighter Command had been created in mid-1936 under the command of Air Marshal Sir Hugh Dowding with a requirement for

The Hurricane production line at Langley, with the metal rear tubular fuselage structure surrounded by wooden skin ready for covering by fabric. This structure was very rugged and resistant to damage by enemy gunfire. (*Author's collection*)

fifty-two fighter squadrons, each with twenty aircraft, to defend Britain. With the retirement of the majority of the earlier biplane fighters, there were insufficient orders to fully equip these squadrons with Hurricanes and Spitfires and provide adequate reserves. The capital of the Hawker Siddeley Group was considerably increased with a substantial investment from the 'City' to build a new production factory. Following negotiations with Buckinghamshire County Council, a site was selected on farmland at Langley where a new factory with grass airfield was built for all Hurricane production from early 1939.

While the Hurricane programme was still in Camm's experimental design office, work was being undertaken on a light bomber to Specification P.27/32 to replace the Hart and Hind in RAF service. The aircraft selected for this specification was the three-seat Fairey Battle, powered by the early Merlins rejected for the Hurricane and Spitfire, but with an AUW almost twice that of the Hurricane. The Battle, with its load of eight 250-lb bombs, was only able to achieve a maximum speed of 174 mph at 8,000 feet, making it extremely vulnerable. Its requirement was therefore replaced by Specification P.4/34, which took into account the anticipated improved performance of the modern monoplane fighter and had a bombload of 1,000 lb and a top speed of at least 250 mph.

The Hawker design team proposed a two-seat, manoeuvrable dive-bomber powered by the Merlin and using the outer wings and tail of the Hurricane. With the requirement for an internal bomb carriage, a deeper fuselage was designed, with the main undercarriage track width increased in an enlarged wing centre-section. With the bomb-bay in the centre-section, the radiator fairing was moved forward directly below the engine. This design, which was to become the Henley, was submitted to the Air Ministry in 1935 and a prototype was ordered.

Although the armament specified was two machine-guns, one in the starboard wing and the other in the rear cockpit, Hawker pointed out that since the Hurricane wings were being used, up to eight wing-mounted guns could be fitted. With the Hurricane programme naturally taking priority during 1936, the Henley prototype suffered delays and did not fly until 10 March 1937.

A production order for 350 aircraft was sub-contracted to Gloster, but in the event only 200 were completed and relegated to target towing. The reason for this change of role was concern in the Air Ministry caused by public indignation against the German Junkers Ju 87 Stuka dive-bomber terror weapons, which if the Henley had continued in its intended role, would have suggested that the RAF condoned this form of aerial warfare.

The withdrawal of the Henley from the dive-bombing role left the Battles at the mercy of the Bf 109s during the Battle of France, resulting in its unfortunate crews being massacred, although there was no guarantee the Henley would have survived any better. The reduced Henley production allowed Gloster to produce more Hurricanes just when they were needed desperately for the Battles of France and Britain.

George Bulman flying the Hurricane prototype K5083 with the Henley prototype K5115, which first flew on 24 March 1937, in close formation. (*Author's collection*)

The Hawker Henley, using wings and other assemblies from the Hurricane, was originally designed as a two-seat, all-metal light dive bomber powered by a Merlin engine, but the small batch built were used for target-towing duties with the winch fitted on the port side of the fuselage by the canopy. (*BAE Systems*)

Only one Hawker Hotspur was built, the prototype K8309, using some Hurricane assemblies and powered by a Merlin II engine. It was built to the same specification as the Boulton Paul Defiant and was fitted with a Boulton Paul turret behind the pilot armed with four .303-inch Browning machine guns. (*BAE Systems*)

The Hawker Hotspur was also built in prototype form as a two-seat turret fighter to the same ill-conceived specification as the Boulton Paul Defiant.

Both types had a gun turret mounted behind the pilot's cockpit, and the Hotspur used many components similar to those of the Hurricane and Henley, but was too late to compete with the Defiant. The main weakness of the Defiant was that it did not have forward-firing machine guns, and with limited manoeuvrability was vulnerable to attack from below and behind, as well as head-on. At least the Hotspur with Hurricane outer wings might have had forward-firing machine guns fitted.

The Hurricane prototype, K5083, continued flying at the A&AEE during the spring of 1937, but could no longer contribute to the flight development programme and was taken on RAF charge at Martlesham Heath on 25 May. Being unrepresentative of the planned production version, K5083 was made available to MGM at Martlesham Heath and flown by Sammy Wroath on fourteen occasions for a film called Test Pilot, starring Clarke Gable and Myrna Loy, after which it faded into oblivion.

Meanwhile, the initial Hurricane production lines were gaining momentum at Kingston and Brooklands, and the first production example, L1547, was rolled out of the Brooklands flight shed to be flown for the first time by Philip Lucas on 12 October 1937.

By this time, more than seventy Bf 109s had been built, and twenty-four were in service with Franco's Nationalist forces in the Spanish Civil War flown by German pilots, who were gaining valuable experience in combat conditions. Although these early Bf 109s were

The first production Hurricane Mk I L1547 at Brooklands with the Vickers factory in the background. This aircraft made its maiden flight on 12 October 1937 and was issued to 312 Squadron, with whom it was lost on 10 October 1940 when it crashed into the River Mersey. (*Author's collection*)

under-powered and under-gunned, a month after the maiden flight of the first production Hurricane, a Bf 109 powered by a 1,650-hp Daimler Benz engine was flown to a new world air speed record of 378.39 mph.

Unlike the British Air Ministry, which generally ordered single combat prototypes, the Luftwaffe ordered up to six, followed by a dozen or so pre-production aircraft, which allowed a large range of trials before full production was authorised. The Air Ministry policy of ordering one prototype meant that if the hand-built aircraft was lost in an accident, there was no replacement immediately available, causing major delays or an abandonment of the programme. This resulted in considerable development work being done on the early production aircraft as they entered service with the RAF squadrons.

RAF plans were to establish four Hurricane and two Spitfire squadrons during 1937, but this was not achieved due to the problems with the Merlin Is. The first Merlin II was delivered to Kingston on 19 April to allow for preparation of manufacturing drawings for the cowlings around the new engine shape.

Once established, a model of the new design had to be tested in a wind tunnel to ensure that there was no serious change in drag or airflow that might affect the Hurricane's performance and handling. This work took until 8 September when L1547 was moved to Brooklands for final assembly and preparation for flight.

The Merlin installation in an early Hurricane Mk I in early 1938, with the two-blade Watson wooden fixed-pitch propeller fitted. (*Flight photo*)

The first production Hurricane Mk I L1547 at Brooklands, with 'kidney' exhaust stubs and the lower hinged main undercarriage doors removed. (*Author's collection*)

Once airborne, L1547 was flown at various centre of gravity positions up to the military AUW of 5,993 lb, which included full fuel and ammunition. By the end of the month, full production standard Merlin IIs were available and L1547's early example was replaced with a new engine—the aircraft flying again by 11 November. By now, three more production Hurricanes were in the flight development programme.

While L1547 was retained at Brooklands for six months before delivery to the A&AEE for two years of trials, each production Hurricane was given around six flights to check handling, performance, and systems, and to allow adjustments before delivery to the RAF. Flight testing was intensive; Hawker pilots made four or five sorties each per day, resulting in some 3,200 flights from Brooklands during 1938, not including delivery flights to the RAF. This was prior to the establishment of maintenance units (MUs), so manufacturers were responsible for the fully equipped aircraft up until it was accepted by the Service, when ownership passed to the Air Ministry.

Any loss of Hurricane prior to handover had to be rectified by the manufacturer and the aircraft replaced. John Hindmarsh was killed on 6 September 1937 while testing Hurricane L1652 and replaced by Dick Reynell, who was in turn killed on 8 September 1940 while flying Hurricanes on a temporary posting with 43 Squadron to evaluate the combat capabilities of the aircraft. With the establishment of MUs, the RAF became responsible for fitting service-supplied equipment, including radios, which reduced the manufacturer's production test-flying burden.

The early metal tubular structure of a Hurricane Mk I ready for equipping with the systems and equipment. (*Flight photo*)

In some cases, squadron commanders arranged for some of their pilots to visit the manufacturers to make a familiarisation flight in the Hurricanes before taking delivery themselves since there were no operational conversion units (OCUs) available at the time. Squadrons were responsible for their own conversion; pilots were faced with conversion from Gloster Gauntlet biplane fighters with a maximum speed of 230 mph, an open cockpit, and fixed undercarriage, to a modern 330-mph monoplane with an enclosed cockpit, landing flaps, and a hand-pumped retractable undercarriage.

By mid-December 1937, nine production Hurricanes had flown and four were ready for delivery to the type's first front-line RAF unit, 111 Squadron, at Northolt, which was conveniently close to Brooklands and Kingston and allowed round-the-clock support for the new type's introduction. Although re-equipping was to commence on 1 January 1938, arrangements were made for these four aircraft (L1548–L1551) to be delivered immediately. All arrived before Christmas, although they were not on official RAF charge until the allotted date. Four more aircraft were delivered during January, and a total of sixteen Hurricanes had arrived by the end of February, allowing for six aircraft per flight and four in reserve, usually on maintenance or repair.

Hurricane development work continued apace at Brooklands, where Bulman was not entirely happy with the aircraft's spin recovery characteristics. Additional wind tunnel tests were carried out to examine the airflow under the tailplane with the aircraft in the stalled condition. It was found that there was a complete breakdown of airflow along the lower half of the fuselage, resulting in the bottom half of the rudder being ineffective in spin recovery. To overcome this problem, a ventral spine was fitted under the rear fuselage with a cutaway to accommodate the fixed tailwheel, extended back to the rudder, which was increased at its base by about 7 inches.

The modification was flown on L1547 from 19 January 1938 until 9 March, during which time exhaustive spinning trials were carried out. This transformed the Hurricane's spin recovery and improved lateral control with wheels and flaps down for approach and landing. By this time the fiftieth Hurricane was almost complete, and it was decided to incorporate the ventral fairing from the sixty-first aircraft, resulting in none of the first three squadrons receiving Hurricanes with this modification made during the initial deliveries.

By mid-1938, Hurricane production was at a rate of five per week, but this reduced temporarily in July and August while a number of modifications were incorporated on the production line. In addition to the spin fairing, these modifications included the removal of the Venturi from the port side of the fuselage, the relocation of the radio, the strengthening of the oxygen bottle mounting, and a small alteration to the nose cowling to permit the introduction of ejector exhaust manifolds in place of the kidney type.

The propeller initially used on the Hurricane Mk Is was the wooden two-bladed fixed-pitch Watts type that had been in widespread use for more than a decade and was effective at speeds up to 360 mph. Above that, the aircraft drove the propeller at such a speed that its tips experienced compressibility as they approached the speed of sound, and overspeeding the propeller with its coarse pitch could seriously damage the engine. These problems were understood, however, and the first variable-pitch propeller that governed engine speed entered trials in the late 1920s. It was Hamilton Standard in the USA that devised the first successful pitch-changing design. This was licence produced by de Havilland Propellers from 1934 initially with a two-bladed propeller, but then on a three-blade version for the Hurricane and Spitfire, as well as many other types in development. In addition, a constant-speed propeller was developed by Rotol that allowed the pitch (angle to the airflow) of the propeller blades to be optimised by a hydraulically operated constant-speed unit (CSU); fine pitch was selected for take-off and coarse pitch for combat. When fitted with the three-blade Rotol airscrew, the Hurricane's rate of climb was improved and endurance improved dramatically, contributing to the aircraft's combat success in the Battle of Britain.

The first de Havilland licence-built Hamilton Standard two-pitch three-bladed propeller was fitted to Hurricane Mk I L1562 and first flown on 29 August. After adjustments it proved successful. Mechanically operated, it did not require the hydraulic power lines as with the Rotol propeller and could easily be fitted to the shaft of the Merlin II. Not only was the Rotol unit hydraulically operated, but it required a different shaft, and the CSU installed on the front of the engine behind the propeller. Rolls-Royce therefore introduced the Merlin III with a universal shaft to fit any propeller likely to be fitted in the foreseeable future.

The Air Ministry was reluctant to make changes to the initial production contract for 600 Hurricanes, but Hawker persuaded the RAF to release damaged Hurricane L1606 from

A later production standard Hurricane Mk I at Brooklands, with a three-blade propeller; metal covering replacing the fabric covering of the wings; the under-fin anti-spin fairing; a fixed tail wheel; and a bullet-resistant windscreen. (*Flight photo*)

After being damaged while with 56 Squadron, Hurricane Mk I L1606 was returned to Hawkers where it was repaired, registered G-AFKX, and used for Merlin engine development. It originally flew on 24 January 1939 with a Merlin III engine, which gave it a top speed in a dive of 460 mph. It was later fitted with a Merlin XX. (*Peter Green collection*)

56 Squadron, and in November 1938 a Merlin III was delivered with the CSU and Rotol constant-speed propeller and fitted to the fully repaired Hurricane. It was allocated the civil registration G-AFKX, and was first flown by Philip Lucas on 24 January 1939.

On 7 February, Bulman flew it for a performance assessment and recorded a maximum level speed of 344 mph at 15,100 feet—the fastest yet flown by a Hurricane. The aircraft had improved acceleration, and the Merlin ran smoothly over the entire speed range. In a dive from 21,000 feet, an indicated speed of 460 mph was noted at full power and 2,850 rpm, with no tendency to overspeed.

As RAF deliveries built up in 1939, the experimental design work on the Hurricane at Kingston had been passed to the Production Design Office and Camm was busy with two new, all-metal designs: the Tornado and Typhoon. These required new machinery in the factory, which would also make metal skinned wings for the Hurricane possible. Although the Air Ministry did not support this change in case it slowed the vital production rate, Camm was successful in having one of the trials aircraft, L1877, allocated for a preliminary assessment of the prototype stressed wings, and on 26 April 1939, Philip Lucas flew its first flight. A new set of wings, built in a production-type jig with full provision for eight guns, was then fitted to G-AFKX with a first flight in this configuration on 4 July by K. G. Seth-Smith—a recent addition to the flight test team at Brooklands. These new all-metal wings proved so successful that the Air Ministry asked Hawker to produce them with great urgency; a contract for 400 sets was placed to be used as replacements for damaged wings on aircraft returned for repair, and

The cockpit of a Hurricane Mk I with the side panel removed to give access to the tubular structure and systems. (*Author's collection*)

A Hurricane Mk IIA was retained by Hawkers for the defence of Langley factory and airfield, and although it was kept at permanent readiness, there is no record of any action. (*HSA photo*)

later to deliver stocks to maintenance units to modify aircraft before delivery to operational squadrons. Meanwhile, Hawker continued to build Hurricanes with fabric-covered wings—the Air Ministry sticking to its belief that any alteration in the basic terms of the original contract for 600 aircraft might delay the production deliveries to the RAF.

However, by 1938, Hawker had received new contracts for 800 aircraft, with another 1,700 to be built by Glosters—none of which had been started, so they could have been specified with metal wings without any disruption to deliveries. Not only was it a complete waste of materials and production capacity, but there were still many aircraft in operation during 1940 with fabric-covered wings while large stocks of metal wings remained with the manufacturers and at maintenance units that required no more than three hours per aircraft to change. When the full situation was explained to Dowding, steps were taken to fit metal wings during manufacture, although the Air Ministry still insisted that some Hurricanes be fitted with fabric-covered wings, only to be changed to metal wings when delivered to an MU before delivery to the operational squadrons.

4

RAF Service Entry

T HE HURRICANE OFFICIALLY entered RAF service with 111 Squadron at Northolt from 1 January 1938.

The commanding officer was Sqn Ldr John W. Gillan who, along with his flight commanders, was responsible for converting pilots to the Hurricane from the Gauntlet biplanes at the same time as learning to fly and fight with the new monoplane fighters themselves.

There were no advanced trainers to help, as the Miles Master and North American Harvard did not enter service with the RAF for another year.

Also, the Hurricane training system had not been set up; there were no OCUs, and there was no two-seat Hurricane.

As was to be expected, there were a number of accidents, one of which was fatal.

To build confidence in his pilots, Gillan planned a high-speed flight from Northolt to Turnhouse near Edinburgh, but on the northerly flight on 10 February he encountered strong headwinds delaying his arrival in Scotland. Landing at 4 p.m., he decided to take advantage of the strong tailwinds on the return leg and had the Hurricane quickly refuelled before departing for Northolt. He took off as dusk was gathering and climbed to 17,000 feet, flying above cloud and without oxygen. Spotting the lights of Bedford through a gap in the clouds, Gillan began his descent, breaking cloud over Northolt and landing soon after 6 p.m. He had covered the 327 miles from Turnhouse in forty-eight minutes at an average speed of 408.75 mph with the Merlin at full power without problems. Gillan had taken full advantage of the 80 mph tailwind to achieve this spectacular time and was known from then on as 'Downwind' Gillan. He was rewarded with an Air Force Cross (AFC) for his leadership and dedicated training, bringing the squadron up to full operational standard.

The next unit to receive Hurricanes was 3 (Fighter) Squadron based at Kenley and commanded by Sqn Ldr Hugh Lester, a forty-year-old RFC veteran of the First World War.

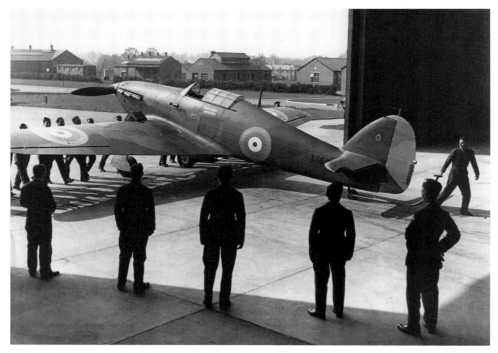

No. 111 Squadron was responsible for the introduction of the Hurricane to the RAF with the first aircraft arriving at Northolt in December 1937, in advance of the official acceptance date of 1 January 1938. The CO, S/Ldr John Gillan, flew L1555 in record time from Edinburgh to Northolt on 10 February 1938. (*Flight photo*)

Hurricane Mk Is of 111 Squadron lined up at Northolt in mid-1939 for a practice scramble. (*Peter Green collection*)

Ground crews also had to learn how to maintain the advanced Hurricane, although fortunately the structure was fairly traditional. An early 111 Squadron Hurricane Mk I was being serviced at Northolt in 1938. (*RAF Museum photo*)

Hurricane Mk I P2617, which was first delivered to the RAF in January 1940, with its fixed-pitch wooden Watts two-blade propeller being started by the ground crew winding up the inertia starter. This method was later replaced by ground-based trolley battery starters known as 'Trolley Acks'. (*Author's collection*)

A pilot climbing aboard a 111 Squadron Hurricane with his seat parachute behind him. (*RAF Museum photo*)

Sgt Brown of 111 Squadron showing what a best dressed pilot needs to wear when operating the Hurricane. There was no cockpit heating or pressure cabin to make high altitude flying more comfortable. (*Author's collection*)

No. 111 Squadron operated Hurricane Mk Is from December 1937 until April 1941, replacing the early aircraft with ones fitted with the anti-spin fairing and non-retractable tail-wheels. The squadron moved from Northolt to Acklington on 27 October 1939 and returned to Northolt on 13 May 1940. (*RAF Museum photo*)

Hurricane Mk I L1582 from the first production batch was delivered to 3 Squadron at Kenley. (*Author's collection*)

Hurricane Mk Is of 3 Squadron in the Warren Truss hangars at Kenley with Gladiators in the background. (*RAF Museum photo*)

The squadron had been flying Bulldogs for eight years when it began to re-equip with Gladiator biplane fighters in March 1937. Hurricanes began arriving with 3 Squadron in March 1938, but there were difficulties operating the new fighters from the then relatively small airfield, resulting in a number of accidents as pilots attempted to avoid the boundary fence.

When a pilot was killed and two Hurricanes written-off, it was decided to revert to Gladiators while the airfield at Kenley was enlarged, later to become a vital sector station within 11 Group during the Battle of Britain.

Number 3 Squadron then re-equipped with Hurricanes in July 1939, by which time it had moved to Biggin Hill.

The third unit to equip with Hurricanes was 56 Squadron based at North Weald; twenty aircraft were delivered during May and June 1938.

The complement of aircraft for each squadron had been increased on 1 April so that nine Hurricanes were allocated to each flight, three of which were assigned for conversion training. The squadron had been operating Bulldogs, Gauntlets, and Gladiators over the previous three years and was led by Sqn Ldr Charles Lea-Cox, who was also an RFC veteran. The transition to Hurricanes went smoothly, and by August, the squadron had been declared operational by day and night.

During September 1938, with the Munich crisis approaching, Fighter Command brought its squadrons to readiness, with the urgency to introduce the Hurricane and Spitfire paramount. Instead of the dozen or so RAF squadrons scheduled to be equipped with the new fighters,

No. 3 Squadron received their first Hurricane Mk Is at Kenley in March 1938. Here, the pilots are preparing for the Empire Air Day display. Due to inadequate landing distances for the Hurricanes, the squadron reverted to Gladiators at Biggin Hill while Kenley was improved. (*Author's collection*)

The third unit to equip with Hurricanes was 56 Squadron at North Weald, using the early versions with the original rudder and Watts propeller, which was delivered between May and June 1938. (*RAF Museum photo*)

Three flights of 111 Squadron flying early Hurricanes without the anti-spin strake under the rudder and with retractable tailwheels. (*Author's collection*)

only 56 and 111 Squadrons were operational with Hurricanes, and a small number of early Spitfires were with 19 Squadron at Duxford.

While Spitfire deliveries continued at a slow pace, the production of Hurricanes accelerated rapidly and, with work carried out around the clock, by October enough Hurricanes were being delivered to re-equip one squadron every month, replace losses, and with the introduction of the fully modified aircraft with anti-spin fairings, replace the earlier machines on the initial squadrons. By the end of 1938, Hawker was producing thirty aircraft per month.

In July and August, 85 and 87 Squadrons at Debden began replacing their Gladiators with Hurricanes—85 Squadron being declared operational in November with the arrival of Sqn Ldr David Atcherley as commander.

In August, 73 Squadron began re-equipping at Digby; followed by 32 Squadron at Biggin Hill in September; then the three units at Tangmere 1 Squadron in October; and 43 and 79 Squadrons in November.

The final squadron to receive Hurricanes in 1938 was 151 at North Weald commanded by Sqn Ldr Edward Donaldson.

Within a couple of months of the Munich Crisis, a further three Hurricane squadrons had been declared operational and five others were working up on the type. Meanwhile, only 19 and 66 Squadrons had received Spitfires and neither was operational.

Full-production Hurricane Mk I L1683 in 1938 with the anti-spin strake, the fixed tail-wheel, and the Merlin II engine driving a fixed-pitch wooden Watts two-blade propeller. (*RAF Museum photo*)

Hurricane Mk I L1648 from the first production batch showing the traditional wing planform. It was later operated by 85 Squadron in France. (*Author's collection*)

No. 87 Squadron took delivery of its first Hurricanes at Debden during July 1938, and Mk I PD-P is seen at readiness during exercises in August 1939, just before war was declared. (*Author's collection*)

The first Hurricane Mk I deliveries were made to 87 Squadron at Digby in July 1938, replacing Gladiator biplane fighters. Mk I L1831 PD-R was at readiness during the summer of 1939. (*P. H. T. Green collection*)

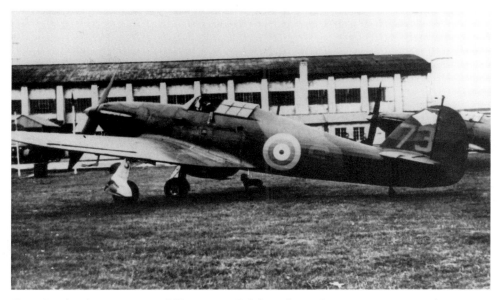

No. 73 Squadron began to equip with Hurricanes at Debden within 12 Group in August 1938. Early Hurricane Mk I L1568 was at an APC at Sutton Bridge soon after the new aircraft arrived. (*Peter Green collection*)

No. 73 Squadron began to take delivery of Hurricanes at Digby in August 1938, Mk I HV-W being an example in service during 1939. (*P. H. T. Green collection*)

No. 73 Squadron began to receive Hurricane Mk Is at Digby in 12 Group during July 1938. The squadron moved to France on 9 September 1939 and returned to Britain at Church Fenton on 18 June 1940. A move was made to Castle Camps on 5 September 1940 and the squadron was posted to the Middle East on 6 November 1940. Hurricane Mk I HV-Z:73 Squadron was at Manston in August 1939 before going to France. (*Peter Green collection*)

Hurricane Mk Is fitted with the wooden Watts fixed-pitch propeller were delivered to 32 Squadron at Biggin Hill from September 1938, and later replaced by the improved performance examples with three blade variable pitch propellers. (*P. H. T. Green collection*)

No. 1 Squadron was the first of the three units at Tangmere to receive Hurricanes in October 1938 to the early configuration. (*Peter Green collection*)

No. 79 Squadron was the third unit in the Tangmere Wing to receive Hurricane Mk Is from November 1938. Mk I L1719 AL-F:79 Squadron is being prepared for flight in 1939. (*P. H. T. Green collection*)

No. 151 Squadron began to receive Hurricanes in December 1938 when based at North Weald. The squadron continued to operate the Mk I Hurricanes until June 1941, but had moved to Martlesham Heath on 13 May 1940 for the Battle of Britain. (*Author's collection*)

No. 501 Squadron Auxiliary Air Force began to re-equip with Hurricane Mk Is in March 1939 at Filton for the protection of the aircraft and aero-engine factories at Bristol. Hurricane Mk I L1869 suffered a mishap at Filton. The squadron moved to Tangmere from 27 November 1939 until 10 May 1940. (*RAF Museum photo*)

No. 504 Squadron in the Auxiliary Air Force began to receive Hurricanes at Hucknall in February 1939 for the protection of the Rolls-Royce factories against enemy attack. (*RAF Museum photo*)

Hurricane Mk I P3774 TM-V:504 Squadron at readiness. The squadron re-equipped with Hurricane Mk Is at Hucknall in May 1939 to protect the Rolls-Royce aero engine factories, but was posted to Digby on 27 August, and Debden and Martlesham Heath on 9 October before going to France on 12 May 1940. On returning from France on 21 May, the squadron went to Debden and the next day moved to Wick before moving to Castletown on 21 June. A move was made to Catterick on 2 September and then to Hendon four days later. The squadron moved to Filton on 26 September and Exeter on 18 December 1940. (*Author's collection*)

No. 17 Squadron started re-equipping with Hurricane Mk Is at North Weald in June 1939, continuing to operate this mark until February 1941. The squadron moved to Croydon on 2 September 1939 and then operated from Debden and Martlesham Heath until May 1940. (*RAF Museum photo*)

The pace of Hurricane deliveries continued to increase in 1939, with 213 Squadron re-equipping at Wittering in January, 46 Squadron at Digby in February, as well as two Auxiliary Air Force (AAF) squadrons—501 at Filton in March 1939, and 504 at Hucknall in May.

The latter represented a new move by the Air Ministry, since up to that time the 'Weekend Warriors' as they were known, had been flying light bombing and Army co-operation duties, and when it was decided to supply some with fighters, it was assumed that they would receive biplanes. These two squadrons received Hurricanes ahead of regular squadrons, but they were part of the Special Reserve, which included more very experienced pilots, their duties being to protect the vital aero engine factories of Bristol and Rolls-Royce. However, the conversion of pilots was slow, although early in the Second World War, many of the part time AAF pilots were as effective as the pilots of the regular RAF squadrons, with equal skill and courage in combat.

More squadrons continued to be equipped with Hurricanes in the year leading up to the war, with Hawker's production rate outstripping the RAF's squadron capacity for new fighters by April. It was therefore possible to begin supplying aircraft to the training units, including No. 11 Advanced Training Pool at Andover, assisting the operational squadrons with pilot conversion. Station Flights, used to keep pilots serving temporary ground duties current, became station training flights with Hurricanes.

On 1 September 1939, the day Britain declared war on Germany, deliveries of Hurricanes to the RAF were considered entirely satisfactory by the Air Ministry, with sixteen Hurricane squadrons fully operational—605 AAF Squadron was in the process of working up on the new type. These squadrons had a total of 280 aircraft in operation, mostly still with fabric-covered wings and Merlin II engines, and an additional 133 were with maintenance units, training units or test establishments. With a total of 572 Hurricanes completed by the outbreak of the Second World War, the remaining 169 had either been sold to foreign air forces, written-off in accidents, were under repair, or awaiting collection from Brooklands, leaving only twenty-eight of the original order for 600 Hurricanes to be completed. At the same time, there were only seven fully operational Spitfire squadrons—five with Bristol Blenheim night fighters, three with Gladiators, and one with Gauntlets—for a total of thirty-two squadrons, twenty short of the fifty-two squadron target.

5

The Battle of France

O NE OF THE support units for the battle of France was 151 Squadron based at North Weald commanded by Sqn Ldr Edward 'Teddy' Donaldson, which began to receive Hurricane Mk Is in December 1938. Teddy collected L1794 (GG-M) from Hawker at Brooklands on 1 December as his first Hurricane flight, and the first of a complement of twelve aircraft with two on immediate reserve and another four on Command reserve. Teddy began putting his pilots through a rigorous training programme to prepare them for the anticipated war, which was declared on 3 September when Hitler's forces invaded Poland.

Prime Minister Neville Chamberlain made the announcement on BBC radio to the Nation:

> I am speaking to you from the Cabinet Room at No. 10 Downing Street. This morning the British Ambassador in Berlin handed the German government a final note stating that, unless we heard from them by eleven o'clock that they were prepared at once to withdraw their troops from Poland, a state of war would exist between us. I have to tell you now that no such undertaking has been received and that consequently this country is at war with Germany. Now may God bless you all. May He defend the right. It is the evil things that we shall be fighting against, brute force, bad faith, injustice, oppression and persecution and against them I am certain that the right will prevail.

Following the declaration of war by Britain and France against Germany, the British Expeditionary Force (BEF) was sent across the English Channel to take up positions along the Franco-Belgian border as part of an established agreement. The RAF contributed two elements: one was the Air Component of the BEF, and the other was the Advanced Air Striking Force (AASF). The former was tasked with the support and protection of the BEF and included 85 and 87 Squadrons equipped with Hurricanes.

When war was declared, No. 87 Squadron with Hurricane Mk Is was the first to move to France, arriving at Rouen on 4 September 1939. Their aircraft had the anti-spin fairing under the rudder, but were still powered by the Merlin II driving the two-blade Watts propeller. (*Author's collection*)

The AASF-operated vulnerable Battles and Blenheim bombers that the Hurricanes of 1 and 73 Squadrons were tasked with protecting both in the air and on the ground, as well as providing air defence over the British-occupied areas in Northern France.

No. 87 Squadron was the first to go to France on 4 September 1939 arriving at Rouen, followed by the other three Hurricane squadrons on 9 September, 85 also going to Rouen, while 1 Squadron was initially based at Octeville and 73 Squadron at Le Havre.

Among the pilots with 87 Squadron was Dennis David, based at Lille Seclin in the autumn of 1939, where the accommodation was built on wooden piles about eighteen inches off the ground.

As the most severe winter approached, the bitter cold assaulted the pilots from all sides, top and bottom, the only heating being from a small solid fuel stove in the middle of the hut. Despite piling everything available on top of the beds, including greatcoats, they could not get warm, and ice formed on the inside of the windows. A flight of three Hurricanes was always at thirty-minute readiness during daylight hours, and on special occasions such as VIP visits, the pilots would be at two-minute readiness, sitting in the cockpits for several hours in all weathers maintaining R/T contact with flying control. On 6 December 1939, a day more bitterly cold than usual, Dennis was section leader of three aircraft designated as the stand-by, when HRH King George VI visited on inspection of the station accompanied by the Dukes of Windsor and Gloucester with other high ranking officers.

No.1 Squadron moved to France on 9 September 1939 as part of the AASF equipped initially with the early standard Hurricane Mk Is with the Watts two-blade propeller and without the spin fairing under the extended rudder. This Hurricane Mk I L1681 was lost in France in May 1940. (*Author's collection*)

Ground crew arm a 73 Squadron Hurricane Mk I in the harsh winter conditions in France in 1939. (*P. H. T. Green collection*)

No. 73 Squadron flew to France as part of the AASF on 9 September 1939 based at Le Havre. This Hurricane Mk I was fitted with the Watts two-blade propeller and was usually flown by Sgt P. V. Ayerst, and is seen landing on one of the temporary grass airfields in May 1940. (*IWM photo*)

Hurricane Mk I L1628 of 87 Squadron, flown by the CO S/Ldr W. E. Cooper force-landed in Belgium on 4 November 1939 and was the first Hurricane to be interned. (*Author's collection*)

HRH King George IV visited Lille-Seclin Aerodrome on 6 September 1939, where both 85 and 87 Squadrons had just arrived. Hurricane Mk Is of 85 and 87 Squadrons were on display, together with three Gladiators and a Blenheim IV. (*IWM photo*)

The King stopped his car near Dennis's Hurricane, got out, and walked towards the aircraft, while Dennis unstrapped himself, climbed down to find the King waiting for him by the propeller with his hand outstretched for a handshake, surrounded by the royals. The King conversed with Dennis without any stutter and was well informed about the current situation.

Meanwhile, the Armée de l'Air (French Air Force) contribution was largely ineffective since the majority of its fighters were so antiquated that they were generally incapable of matching the modern Luftwaffe. Dowding resisted French demands to despatch an additional six RAF fighter squadrons, but did agree with some reluctance for 607 and 615 AAF squadrons to be sent to France, still equipped with Gladiators.

He also agreed to consider the possibility of further reinforcements if the safety of the BEF was seriously threatened, and if Fighter Command strength had moved closer to the minimum required for the defence of Great Britain. Dowding saw no value in committing valuable fighter units to France when enemy air activity over the Western Front was posing little threat to British troops. During the first autumn of 1939 and into early winter, Luftwaffe activity was restricted to local reconnaissance and isolated bombing raids, with rarely more than two or three aircraft. The Luftwaffe was busy re-equipping and resting after the Blitzkrieg campaign in Poland.

During the spring of 1940, 87 Squadron visited the Blenheim squadron at Toul-Rosieres, but the weather was still bitterly cold. There were no hangars at the airfield and starting the Merlins

A Hurricane Mk I of 607 Squadron re-fuelling and re-arming in France in 1940 after converting from antiquated Gladiator biplane fighters. (*P. H. T. Green collection*)

Winston Churchill, as First Lord of the Admiralty, inspecting an RAF Guard of Honour in France in 1940. (*Author's collection*)

could often take up to three hours, often with the ground crew using hand cranks on each side; maintaining the aircraft was a formidable challenge. With each aircraft, the pilot and ground crew worked closely together, with a bond developing with each Hurricane as if it had a personality of its own. The squadron returned to Lille Seclin when warmer weather began to develop.

By now, 1 Squadron was at Vassingcourt, 73 Squadron at Rouvres, and 85 and 87 Squadrons at Lille Seclin, operating occasional patrols or scrambles. The major problem they faced was the grass surfaces of the French airfields, which were poorly drained, and with the arrival of winter, they became waterlogged due to rain and snow. However, Hurricanes with their wide track rugged undercarriage were rarely unable to operate due to the state of the airfields.

The first Hurricane victory against the Luftwaffe was against a Dornier Do 17P reconnaissance aircraft, which was shot down by Pilot Officer Peter Mould of 1 Squadron in Hurricane L1842 over Toul on 30 October. This Hurricane confirmed the type's ruggedness when in further combat against a He 111 on 23 November. Led by Flt Lt George Plinston, three Hurricanes intercepted a He 111 at 20,000 feet between Verdun and Metz and all three attacked the enemy aircraft. Sergeant 'Taffy' Clowes was flying L1842 and just as he broke away from the combat, six French Moranes were diving down to engage. One collided with Clowes's Hurricane, removing an elevator and half of the rudder. The Hurricane made a forced landing back at Vassingcourt, but was repaired on site and Clowes only suffered a few bruises.

The French airfields often had poor surfaces due to inadequate drainage, which may have resulted in this 87 Squadron Hurricane Mk I ending up on its nose with a broken Watts propeller. It is also possible it was damaged in combat as the guns have obviously been fired with no fabric doped over the gun ports. (*Author's collection*)

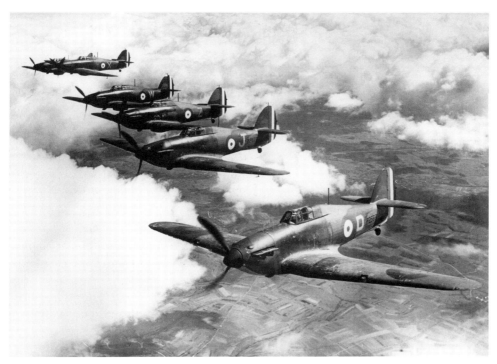

Two flights of 73 Squadron Hurricane Mk Is fitted with three-blade propellers, including P2569:D and P2575:J flying over France in early 1940. These aircraft feature the tail stripes on the rudders instead of the fin in the style of the French Air Force. (*IWM photo*)

Flying Officer (Fg Off.) 'Cobber' Kain opened the score for 73 Squadron on 2 November when he shot down a Do 17P from 27,000 feet, believed to be the highest altitude combat to date.

In the first few days of June, Cobber Kain was due to come home to Britain from Echemines near Paris having finished operational flying. He decided to do one more flight in celebration on 7 June, beating up the airfield at too low an altitude, did two slow rolls, attempted a third at too low a speed, and crashed, being instantly killed. He had achieved a total of seventeen victories to date.

The first victory for 85 Squadron was on 21 November when Flt Lt Richard Lee, flying L1898, shot down a He 111 into the sea off Boulogne and in the same month Flt Lt Robert Jeff achieved the first success for 87 Squadron when he shot down a He 111 over Hazebrook.

The first RAF pilot to experience combat with a Bf 109 was Peter Ayerst of 73 Squadron, who was on standby in his Hurricane cockpit, when he saw a red flag waved by a French Army unit on the side of the airfield. The enemy aircraft was a Do 17 approaching the airfield, which on seeing the defending Hurricane turned back and was lost to view when he entered cloud. As he turned for home, Peter saw a formation of nine aircraft below, and when he was closer, realised they were Bf 109s, giving the tail end one a quick burst and claiming it

The first victory for 85 Squadron in France was claimed on 21 November 1939. Included in the combat training in France were mock gas attacks on the airfields. (*IWM photo*)

as damaged. After that, Peter dived straight down from 18,000 feet as he was flying by then over Germany, and without armour plate was vulnerable to fire from the rear. Flying through scattered cloud, he attracted a further eighteen Bf 109s and dropped down to low level, leading the enemy fighters through a flight of French fighters, who claimed nine Germans. It was probably the first major air battle of the war, and Peter landed at a French airfield, his engine stopping due to lack of fuel.

Only three days into the Blitzkrieg on 13 May, Billy Drake of 1 Squadron was shot down on 13 May 1940. He was flying in a formation of four Hurricanes at 18,000 feet when he realised that his oxygen supply was not working. On his way back to base at 10,000 feet, he saw three Do 17s without any escort and shot one down. Positioning behind the formation leader, there was a sudden explosion in his aircraft from a Bf 110 right behind setting his aircraft on fire. Just before releasing the canopy, Billy turned the Hurricane upside down and baled out—the flames on the underside of the wing. Landing safely but injured, Billy was in a French hospital for about a week; his injuries included two bullets in the leg, one in the back, with cannon shell splinters also. His wounds were operated on without anaesthetics. Following his discharge from hospital, he returned to Britain to teach new pilots fighter tactics.

The days were very long for the squadrons operating from Britain during the Battle of France. They were required to get up at around 3 a.m., have breakfast, take-off in the dark, fly inland across the French coast, and land at a rudimentary French airfield. The pilots received no instructions; they refuelled the aircraft themselves and hand started them in turn without any assistance from the French. They would spend the entire day operating with no assistance, begging food from local farmers. At the end of the day, they departed overhead of Le Havre across the English Channel, reaching Biggin Hill at around 9.30 p.m. to 10 p.m. following a meal and then to bed.

Having been deployed on 12 May to Rochford (Southend) from North Weald, 151 Squadron was finally in combat south of Dover when two Bf 109s were engaged. One was probably destroyed, but it could not be confirmed in the heat of battle. As the enemy advances drove rapidly forward, Churchill offered the support of ten more fighter squadrons—one of which was 151 Squadron and moved to Martlesham Heath on 13 May, with daily deployments to Abbeville on 17 May and Vitry-en-Artois on 18 May, returning to Manston that evening when the French airfields became untenable. While at Abbeville on 17 May, eleven Ju 87s were claimed for no losses to 151 Squadron; Teddy Donaldson claiming two confirmed and one unconfirmed. On 18 May, Teddy led nine pilots of 151 Squadron to Vitry, where the aircraft were refuelled and prepared for the next sortie. While this was going on, more than twenty Bf 109s attacked another Hurricane squadron providing cover against the Luftwaffe bombers. The Hurricanes were launched at around 3.40 p.m. to engage a pair of He 111s that had overflown the airfield. Three more He 111s appeared, one of which went down in flames. The leader then led a line astern attack on about twelve Bf 110s, one of which exploded in mid-air, another had the tail shot off, a third had an engine blow up before crashing into a field, and a fourth was abandoned by the crew when it caught fire.

The squadron was again caught on the ground at 6.30 p.m., when six Do 17s made a low-level attack that destroyed twelve Hurricanes on the ground, but fortunately no damage to 151 Squadron aircraft. The airfield at Vitry suffered two more bombing attacks that day, but at 7.30 p.m., much to everyone's relief, the pilots departed for Manston. The ground crews had to make their own way back with the retreating Allied troops before the airfield was overrun.

Following the departure from Vitry, 151 Squadron, while still based at North Weald, used Manston as its forward base for operations over France, providing support for RAF bombing raids. No. 151 Squadron was again in action on 22 May, with six Ju 87s destroyed out of the twenty-four bombing St Omer.

Tragedy struck on 25 May when two pilots from 151 Squadron, Flt Lt Ives and Fg Off. Bushell, collided in mid-air. Bushell spun out of control into the sea, while Flt Lt Ives managed to belly land on the beach. Two days later, Ives was manning a gun on board a ship when it was sunk by torpedo. The enemy boat then machine-gunned survivors in the water—only twenty-four of the original 500 on board survived and Ives was one of those killed. This action changed the pilots' attitude towards the Germans, who up until then had been considered 'rather decent chaps'.

On 27 May, Belgium formally surrendered and the evacuation of Allied troops across the Channel began. No. 151 Squadron joined other RAF units attempting to stop the Luftwaffe bombers reaching the beachhead, and destroying the rescue ships. Operation Dynamo, as the evacuation was termed, was expected to recover some 45,000 men from the beachhead by the Royal Navy, but with the help of anything that would float, a third of a million men were saved over nine days. Civilian-operated shallow draft boats joined the evacuation on 29 May. Much of the aerial combat took place at higher altitudes or away from the coast to shield the remnants of the BEF, which led many troops to believe they had been abandoned by the RAF. The Luftwaffe was bombing the troops and ships with devastating results, but it was not widely known that only a fraction of the enemy bombers reached their targets.

Contact with enemy aircraft was sporadic in the earlier stages of the evacuation, with few confirmed results despite both 151 and 56 Squadrons operating over Dunkirk. However, on 29 May a Bf 110 was claimed, followed by Bf 109s and He 111s being engaged, with a decoy Ju 88 shot down. The following day, two of 151 Squadron's pilots were shot down into the Channel by Bf 109s, but both pilots were picked up. On 30 May, twelve Hurricanes of 151 Squadron took off from North Weald to link up again with 56 Squadron, but after two patrols there was no contact with the enemy.

On 31 May, The London Gazette announced the award of the DSO to Teddy Donaldson in recognition of his leadership during the Battle of France. With four enemy aircraft credited to him, his final total came to ten and a half confirmed, with many more unconfirmed or damaged enemy aircraft.

On 4 June, with operation Dynamo at an end, two days' leave was granted in rotation to the battle-weary pilots. For most of the nine-day period they had been in the air for around six hours a day, flying three and sometimes four sorties over the evacuation beaches and Channel. Fighter Command as a whole had flown some 2,750 sorties providing cover for the beleaguered army, allowing 338,226 men to be rescued to fight another day.

Flying Officer Gerry Edge was on patrol with 605 Squadron when they engaged a formation of twenty-plus Ju 87s heading for the coast. Edge closed on one and shot it down with his number two destroying another, then Edge shot down a third. With the sky suddenly empty, Edge climbed to 8,000 feet when he saw another formation of thirty to forty Ju 87s some 2,500 feet above. Pulling up into a vertical climb, as he approached he fired into the undersides of a Ju 87 from a distance of around 20 feet. The Hurricane stopped and went into a tail slide, diving away and recovering at a little over 1,000 feet above the ground. Turning for home, Edge saw a Ju 87 with its rear gunner firing at a column of refugees on the ground. Edge approached behind the Stuka, with his final one-second of ammunition was enough to down the enemy aircraft.

The last of the initial batch of 600 L-series Hurricanes had been completed at Brooklands by the end of September, with the next batch of 300 following on directly. The new batch featured Merlin III engines driving either de Havilland or Rotol three bladed-propellers, although the first eighty retained fabric-covered wings. These aircraft were allocated with some urgency to replace the earlier versions with the four Hurricane squadrons in France, which still used Merlin IIs driving the Watts propeller.

Meanwhile, it was one of the new aircraft, flown by the 111 Sqn Ldr Harry Broadhurst (later Air Chief Marshal Sir Harry Broadhurst) commanding 111 Squadron, then based at Acklington, who achieved the unit's first aerial victory. Flying N2340 on 29 November, Broadhurst shot down a He 111 into the sea off Newcastle. This was the period of what was

What must be a posed photo of an 87 Squadron scramble in France in March 1940, as the Hurricanes would normally be dispersed around the airfield. The nearest Hurricane is L1774 LK-D:87 Squadron, and all bar one of the aircraft have the Watts two-blade propellers. Hurricane LK-L is fitted with a three-blade Rotol propeller. (*Author's collection*)

known as the 'Phoney War' with the Germans making probing attacks and Britain preparing for the anticipated Blitzkrieg, but with no major engagements.

The war really started for Dennis David with 87 Squadron on 10 May 1940, when he brought down a He 111, followed by a Do 17.

An hour later, on his third sortie of the day, the squadron attacked a formation of four Heinkels, and destroyed two of them. The hectic day continued with the need to return to base as quickly as possible after combat to refuel and rearm. Dennis flew six sorties that day and spent nearly seven hours in the air. In the early days, the Luftwaffe bomber crews flew without escort due to the supreme confidence gained from the Spanish Civil War and the invasion of Poland where they had had full aerial superiority, but this did not last for long.

The next morning, the six Hurricanes of the sadly reduced 87 Squadron was called to defend a tented Army hospital that was being attacked by some forty Ju 87 dive bombers. The squadron destroyed fourteen aircraft, with Dennis also claiming a Do 17. With his ammunition gone and fuel running low, Dennis turned for base feeling that a worthwhile victory had been achieved, but then saw a new wave of some 150 enemy bombers starting another raid—available RAF numbers were not sufficient to defend against the onslaught.

The pilots soon learned never to fly in vulnerable tight formations, but operate in weaving pairs as the experienced Luftwaffe pilots did. RAF pilots also learned to get close to their targets to ensure making a kill, and Dennis had his eight wing-mounted machine guns aiming at a fixed spot of 167 yards (153 m) rather than the usual 250 yards (229 m) to get greater concentration of fire. The Hurricane ammunition could be used up in one burst of fourteen seconds, which made short, two-second bursts more effective. The rigid wings made the Hurricane an excellent gun platform; Dennis gained all twenty-one of his victories in the type.

As the spring of 1940 approached, Hitler decided to safeguard his vital stocks of Swedish iron ore by protecting the shipping routes from the port of Narvik in northern Norway. The initial move was a rapid invasion of Denmark, which had no modern aircraft in its air force, and the country was occupied in one day on 9 April, allowing its airfields and harbours to be used for operations against Norway. German forces made simultaneous attacks in Norway, capturing Narvik and making landings in large numbers in Oslo and other cities including Kristiansand, Bergen and Trondheim, with the vital airfield at Stavanger being captured, all on the same day.

Britain was able to react fairly quickly to the growing German occupation of Norway, since plans had already been forming for an occupation of Narvik when the enemy attacked. Now, faced with a major campaign that required support from the Norwegian army in central Norway, British forces were totally inadequate for the tasks required. Nevertheless, landings were made on the coast of central Norway between 15 and 18 April with the intention of moving north towards Narvik, and then south to link up with the Norwegian army north of Oslo.

Air cover was initially provided by 263 Squadron equipped with Gladiators that were delivered aboard the aircraft carrier HMS Glorious, with the only airfield being the frozen surface of Lake Lesjaskog. The British landing forces were rapidly contained by the Wehrmacht, while the Luftwaffe attacked the Gladiators on the lake. Despite strenuous efforts to meet the attacking German aircraft, 263 Squadron was overwhelmed and ordered to destroy its aircraft and be ready to evacuate Norway by early May. One of the wrecked Gladiators sank to the bottom of the lake was later salvaged and preserved at the Royal Air Force Museum, Hendon.

Britain then reverted to its original plan to capture Narvik, sending 263 Squadron, re-equipped with more Gladiators, plus 46 Squadron with Hurricanes under the command of Sqn Ldr Kenneth Cross (later ACM Sir Kenneth Cross), to provide aerial cover for the ground forces.

Eighteen Hurricanes were loaded aboard HMS Glorious at Greenock on 10 May, and set sail for Norway. Although the type had never been launched from a carrier before, the Hurricanes were flown off and landed at Bardufoss and Skaanland on 26 May, with the Gladiators then based at Skaanland and the Hurricanes operating from Bardufoss.

Soon after arrival, pilots from 46 Squadron carried out a number of reconnaissance flights to familiarise themselves with the area around Narvik, but it was the Gladiators that were in action first, destroying a number of German aircraft attacking the port. On 28 May, two of the Hurricanes successfully destroyed a Junkers Ju 88 over Tjelbotn, and in the evening the squadron shot down a pair of Dornier Do 26s flying boats about to disembark alpine troops, one aircraft made a forced landing near Narvik, with the crew and ten troops on board being taken prisoner.

A Hurricane Mk I of 46 Squadron being loaded aboard ship at Greenock in May 1940 for the short and unsuccessful Norwegian campaign. (*RAF Museum photo*)

With German forces advancing from the south, both RAF squadrons were active every day during the first week in June with at least twenty-eight German aircraft destroyed, in both combat and accidents, for the loss of two Hurricanes in combat and two as a result of accidents; one pilot was wounded and returned home. On 3 June, it was apparent that the British position at Narvik was untenable as Luftwaffe attacks became stronger due to their use of captured Norwegian bases, and the decision was made to make another evacuation from Norway.

The Allied forces began embarking on the long and hazardous journey home. Their departure was protected by patrols from both RAF and FAA pilots defending against enemy air attacks on the approaches to the harbour at Narvik. On 7 June, German attacks on the port increased, and 46 Squadron was called into action against He 111s three times. At the end of the day, the squadron was ordered to destroy its surviving Hurricanes and board the ship in the harbour. Although neither Cross nor any of his pilots had landed aboard a carrier previously, he requested permission to fly the ten serviceable Hurricanes out to Glorious, which was nearby, calling for ten volunteers to make the landings.

After being granted permission, all the pilots who had volunteered added an extra weight in the tail to move the centre of gravity aft for a landing without an arrester hook, and at 6 p.m., the first three pilots took off and landed successfully on the carrier. At 6.10 p.m. and 6.15 p.m., two of the pilots were returning from a patrol over Narvik and engaged four Heinkels—two were claimed as shot down and the other two damaged. On 8 June, the seven remaining serviceable Hurricanes, led by Sqn Ldr Cross, took off at 12.45 a.m. and landed safely aboard the ship. Four were destroyed at Bardufoss, while squadron personnel boarded the MV Morning Star in Narvik and left for home. Throughout the morning and early afternoon of 8 June, Glorious sailed westward with its escort of two destroyers, HMS Acasta and HMS Ardent moving out of the range of shore-based bombers, unaware that a much greater hazard lay ahead.

At 4 p.m., the lookouts on the German battle cruisers Scharnhorst and Gneisenau spotted the carrier's smoke. Closing to a range of 28,000 yards, they opened fire well beyond the range of the carrier's defences. The destroyers made straight for the battle cruisers and attempts were made to launch a Swordfish strike, but within a very short time the enemy shells had set the carrier on fire, the vessel taking on a heavy list. At 5.20 p.m., the order was given to abandon ship, and twenty minutes later the carrier turned over and sank. Some sixty hours, later a Norwegian fishing boat located life rafts containing three officers and thirty-five men. In addition to five men rescued by a German flying boat and taken prisoner, they were the sole survivors from the carrier. Among the rescued officers were Sqn Ldr Cross and Flt Lt Jameson, who landed on the Faroe Islands. The loss of one of Britain's few aircraft carriers, together with 1,515 men of the Royal Navy and RAF, was a major blow that made the loss of the ten Hurricanes insignificant by comparison.

To prevent a German invasion of strategically important Iceland following the occupation of Norway, 98 Squadron was based at Kaladarnes from August 1940 and equipped with Fairey Battles. With the USA taking over responsibility for the defence of Iceland in July 1941, 98 Squadron was tasked with providing air cover for the withdrawal of British forces, and four Hurricane Mk IIAs were shipped in crates from 47 MU in Britain. At the end of the month, 98 Squadron returned to Britain, leaving behind the four Hurricanes, which allowed 1423 Flight to be established.

The initial four Hurricane Mk IIAs of 1423 Flight were used for the air defence of Iceland from July to December 1941. (*Author's collection*)

By this time, the first North Cape convoys to Russia were forming up in Britain and it was decided to strengthen the air defences in Iceland to help protect them from enemy air attack. As a result, five more Hurricane Mk IIAs were shipped to Reykjavik. On 28 August, a reconnaissance He 111 was spotted and chased by a Hurricane but escaped into cloud, as happened with subsequent contacts. Although it was clear that the Luftwaffe was engaged in spotting convoys sailing to Russia, the Hurricanes had no contact and 1423 Flight was disbanded. Its aircraft returned to Britain in December 1941.

Almost a month before the end of the Norwegian campaign, on 10 May, the Germans commenced their advances in the West, when the Wehrmacht was unleashed against Holland, Belgium, Luxembourg, and France. The plan was to outflank the defensive Maginot Line from the north and drive an armoured wedge through to the English Channel, isolating the BEF and dividing the French army, before turning south towards Paris.

By this time, the majority of RAF squadrons in France had changed bases, although 1 Squadron was still at Vassincourt, and planning a move to Berry-au-Bac. Number 73 Squadron had moved to Reims Champagne, 85 Squadron was still at Lille Seclin, and 87 Squadron had moved to Senon under French control.

Both 607 Squadron at Vitry-en-Artois and 615 Squadron at Abbeville were in the process of converting from Gladiators to Hurricanes and were not fully operational, each retaining about a dozen biplane fighters. Together, the six squadrons had a reported total strength of ninety-six Hurricanes on 10 May.

No. 85 Squadron later received improved Hurricane Mk Is in France with the Merlin III engine and three-blade propellers. VY-H is ready to depart with the pilot on standby in the cockpit at Lille with another Hurricane overhead. (*IWM photo*)

Hurricane Mk Is of 87 Squadron at Lille-Seclin in March 1940 during a practice gas attack. (*IWM photo*)

With reports reaching London in the early morning of the advancing German attacks, Dowding ordered three more Hurricane squadrons to France, Nos 3, 79, and 504, to reinforce the Air Component, and 501 Squadron to add support to the AASF. By that evening, 3 Squadron had arrived at Merville, 79 Squadron at Mons-en-Chausee, and 501 Squadron at Betheniville.

Two days later, 504 Squadron landed at Vitry-en-Artois, but the moves were marred when a transport aircraft bringing remaining pilots from Tangmere crashed on landing at Betheniville, killing three and injuring six. All ten squadrons were regularly engaged by the enemy as Luftwaffe aircraft operated over and ahead of the savage fighting on the ground. Number 501 Squadron, despite the shortage of pilots, claimed the destruction of fifteen German bombers and three Messerschmitt Bf 110 fighters for the loss of three aircraft and two pilots in its first two days in France. On 12 May, 3 Squadron claimed eight enemy aircraft without loss.

Despite their numerical superiority, German bomber losses were high during the first few days of the offensive because of poor tactics. The twin-engined Bf 110s were tasked with protecting the bombers, while the more effective Bf 109s were to protect the enemy ground advances from air attack. The Bf 110s were unable to provide adequate protection to the bombers due to limited manoeuvrability, allowing the Hurricane pilots to achieve considerable success against the Heinkels and Dorniers.

As the Allied armies were beaten back by relentless German blows, there were greater demands on the Battles and Blenheims to attack key communications points to slow the enemy advance.

No. 79 Squadron was sent to Merville in France on 10 May 1939, and AL-K is being prepared for starting with the ground battery starter plugged into the aircraft. (*RAF Museum*)

The Hurricane Mk Is of 504 Squadron were deployed to France in May 1940 to increase the defences of the Air Component of the BEF. They were initially based at Vitry-en-Artois, and L1944 was on the squadron strength. (*Peter Green collection*)

Hurricane Mk Is of 501 Squadron were deployed at Bethenville on 10 May 1939 as part of the AASF and are seen dispersed on a typical French airfield. (*RAF Museum photo*)

It was in these operations, which for the Battles were practically suicide attacks, when the heaviest losses occurred despite attempts by the Hurricanes to provide protection.

The fates of the Belgian Air Force and its Hurricanes is also very much part of the early stages of the Battle of France.

There was an agreed plan between the Allies and Belgium that if there was a German attack on the country, the BEF would move forward and take up a defensive line alongside the Belgian army. However, there was no warning of the German advances that drove rapidly across the Belgian countryside, leaving the BEF fighting in the open against the Wehrmacht armoured thrust that had a momentum which was impossible to slow.

In addition to Hurricanes, the Belgian Air Force had about eighty vintage Fairey Fox light bomber biplanes, some twenty Fairey Battles, twenty-three Fiat CR.42 biplane fighters, and twenty Renard R-31 reconnaissance aircraft. Although this represented a fairly large force, only the Hurricanes could effectively match the modern Luftwaffe aircraft.

There is no doubt that given a chance, Belgian aircrews would fiercely defend their homeland, and the Luftwaffe therefore devised a series of devastating pre-emptive attacks on Belgian airfields.

By the end of 10 May, sixty-seven Belgian aircraft had been destroyed on the ground in raids made a great deal easier for the enemy attackers by the Belgian's failure to disperse their aircraft around the airfields, instead leaving them tidily lined up ready for rapid destruction.

Queen Elizabeth of Belgium reviewing the pilots and Hurricanes of the Belgian Air Force in 1939. These aircraft are all specified to the early Mk I standard, with Merlin IIs driving the Watts two-blade propellers. (*Brussels Air Museum photo*)

Belgian-built Hurricane Mk I H-10042 at Schaffen-Diest in 1940, one of the few assembled by Avions Fairey. (*Brussels Air Museum photo*)

Even heavy maintenance on the Hurricanes was undertaken outside in primitive conditions. (*Brussels Air Museum photo*)

The sole Rotol Hurricane was destroyed at Liege-Bierget in March 1940 when attempting a forced landing. (*Brussels Air Museum photo*)

Part of the ill-fated line-up of Belgian Air Force Hurricanes, which were rapidly destroyed by the Luftwaffe attack on 10 May 1940 at Schaffen-Diest airfield. (*Brussels Air Museum photo*)

Following the Luftwaffe attack on the Belgian Air Force, many of the Hurricanes were badly damaged or written off. No 24 was tipped up on to its nose. (*Brussels Air Museum photo*)

A wrecked Belgian Air Force Hurricane after the attack against the line-up on Schaffen-Diest Airfield on 10 May 1940. (*Brussels Air Museum photo*)

A further twenty aircraft, including half the serviceable Hurricanes, were destroyed in the air. On the second day, out of fifteen Battles that attacked a pontoon bridge at Maastricht, only five aircraft survived. On 12 May, a formation of almost all the surviving Hurricanes was attacked by a Staffel of Bf 109s, which shot down three, including the first victory for Hauptmann Adolf Galland, who would later achieve many victories and attain a high rank in the Luftwaffe. The Wehrmacht's unchecked advances through Belgium were largely down to the failure to destroy key bridges and in spite of the enormous sacrifices of British and French light bomber attacks.

The swift German advances across Belgium and Holland meant that RAF Hurricanes were not ordered forward from their bases in France, so that when they were required to escort the light bombers they were at the extreme of their endurance. When they could be spared from escorting the AASF squadrons, the Hurricanes flew patrols over the British forces and achieved excellent results. On 11 May, 87 Squadron twice attacked large formations of Ju 87 Stuka dive bombers, one near Brussels and the other at Tongres, claiming the destruction of ten for the loss of two aircraft and pilots.

Allied casualties were heavy during the first three days; twelve Hurricanes were lost and seven pilots killed. In anticipation of heavier losses to come, Dowding authorised a further thirty-two Hurricanes and pilots be sent to France on 13 May, bringing the two ex-Gladiator squadrons up to strength and replacing losses in the other squadrons. However, on the

Hurricane Mk I H39 was the only Belgian Air Force aircraft fitted with a three-blade Rotol propeller. This aircraft was one of the few Hurricanes built under licence in Brussels by Avions Fairey. (*Brussels Air Museum photo*)

following day, German bombers increased their attacks on RAF airfields in France, which made it essential to move from base to base to escape destruction by the Luftwaffe raids and avoid capture by the advancing ground forces.

Unfortunately, these continual redeployments were the major cause of aircraft losses as the ground crews with the skills, spares, and tools to maintain them could not always keep pace with the changes of bases. If an aircraft landed with battle damage and no ground crew were available, it would have to be abandoned, even though ground crew often repaired damaged aircraft quite rapidly. Many Hurricanes were burned where they had landed, while others were left in the hope that the ground crew would arrive in time for repairs to be made, but this did not often happen.

Another problem was that even at a rudimentary level there was no command and control. It was not economic for the pilots to fly standing patrols due to fuel shortages, and if they had then they were vulnerable to attack when they landed. Otherwise, there was little warning of an enemy attack, so pilots were on constant readiness awaiting the first signs of a raid in the hope that they would be scrambled in time and without any prior warning.

No. 1 Squadron survived in France intact for five weeks after 10 May by continually moving from one base to another. The squadron edged along the Channel coast until returning to Northolt on 18 June. Not only was it able to keep ahead of the advancing German ground forces, but it kept from being attacked from the air by constant changing of bases and maintained the necessary logistics to remain operational. The Air Component Hurricane squadrons suffered the most, although 85 Squadron claimed twenty-nine enemy aircraft in the first nine days of the German assault while at Merville, but they lost six pilots and aircraft, with reinforcements used up elsewhere. Attempts were made to combine its survivors with 87 Squadron, which had also suffered heavy losses, but both squadrons were withdrawn to Britain; 85 Squadron on 22 May, and 87 Squadron on 24 May.

There was constant pressure from Churchill, the French government, and the British Air Staff for Dowding to commit more Hurricane squadrons to France and what was obviously a lost cause. He resisted strongly, pointing out that the campaigns in France and Norway had drained the home defence squadrons by one-third of their fighter strength, and 40 per cent of their pilots, which silenced his critics. The extraction of the remainder of the BEF from France would create even more fighter and pilot losses.

On 21 May, German Panzers arrived on the Channel coast near Abbeville, isolating about half a million British, French, and Belgian troops to the north with their backs to the sea. They were threatened all around, especially when the enemy's armed columns turned north towards Boulogne and Calais. Fortunately for the Allies, Hitler was influenced by the chief of the Luftwaffe, Hermann Göring, who persuaded him to halt the armoured advances to conserve troops for the remaining battles in France and instead allow the might of the Luftwaffe to attack the apparently doomed and cornered Allied armies in north-east France.

Planning for the evacuation of the BEF under Operation Dynamo had begun on 19 May. AVM Charles Blount, commander of the Air Component, brought his headquarters back to Hawkinge above the cliffs in Kent and working with AVM Keith Park, commander of 11 Group covering the south-east of Britain, co-ordinated the provision of air cover for the BEF in France, initially using Hurricane and Lysander units still in the country.

When the final evacuation was ordered to commence on 26 May, most of the RAF squadrons were recalled from the Pas-de-Calais, although only about half their strength remained airworthy. At Merville alone, some twenty Hurricanes had been abandoned with attempts made to disable them by setting fire to the rear fuselages. The Hurricanes of 607 and 615 Squadrons had mostly been transferred to the regular units where they were of greater value, but many of the Gladiators were returned safely. The Lysander squadrons (apart from No. 13, which had lost all its aircraft) were able to return to Britain, with the surviving personnel from 13 Squadron making it home on 29 May. Both 213 Squadron and 601 Squadron had sent detachments to Merville for a few days from 17 May, but were able to return to England.

From then on, all fighter operations across the Channel came under the control of 11 Group, also bringing into action Spitfire and Defiant squadrons from other Groups to complement the Hurricanes. The aim was to provide defensive cover over the evacuation at least by day, with all available Kent-based Hurricane squadrons ordered to attack motorised columns on the Cambrai–Arras road. To maintain a more rapid reaction, many of the Hurricane squadrons were sent over to French airfields on a day-to-day basis until all had been overrun. Despite criticism by BEF troops of the apparent lack of air cover by the RAF over the beaches, German army commanders were reporting that for the first time since 10 May, the RAF had achieved air superiority over the battle on the ground.

No. 87 Squadron Hurricane Mk I L2047 looking battle-weary and on its nose, probably due to the poor surface of the French airfields. This Hurricane had been fitted with a Merlin III driving a three-blade propeller. (*Author's collection*)

Hurricane Mk I VY-G:85 Squadron about to take-off in France, with the tented accommodation behind. (*RAF Museum photo*)

On the first day of the Dunkirk evacuation, Park's 11 Group had seven Hurricane squadrons available, together with nine Spitfire squadrons, ready for their first major combat, and 264 Squadron and its Defiants. The latter had been decimated once the Luftwaffe realised that the turret fighter had no forward armament and a blind spot on its rear undersides. Until Luftwaffe tactics became clear, Park deployed one fighter squadron at a time over Dunkirk and was able to cover the evacuation continuously during daylight hours. At least one squadron of Hurricanes and another of Spitfires was kept on instant standby should there be a large-scale attack.

Unfortunately, the Luftwaffe was able to attack the embarkation area and surrounding troop concentrations with more than 220 bombers, supported by some sixty Bf 110s and a number of Bf 109Es. Within forty-eight hours, this enemy force had been reinforced by around 120 of the deadly Ju 87 Stuka dive bombers and more than another 100 Bf 109Es. On 27 May, a lighter Luftwaffe fighter escort allowed RAF fighters to claim about sixteen bombers with a further dozen damaged for the loss of four Hurricanes and four Spitfires. The enemy bombers were able to bomb Dunkirk, but only two ships were destroyed. Park hoped that if there was not a substantial numbers of Bf 109s escorting the bombers, RAF fighter cover could be increased to two squadrons on patrol in an effort to destroy more of the bombers. On 28 May, fewer bombers attacked the beachhead due to poor weather at their bases and only four were claimed, but the increased strength of Bf 109Es resulted in wasteful fighter-to-fighter combat with claims for nineteen German fighters, although thirteen RAF fighters were shot down with the loss of eight pilots.

With the availability of a fresh Spitfire squadron as well as 111 Squadron's Hurricanes, Park began to authorise patrols of four fighter squadrons to help overcome the vast numerical advantage of the enemy fighters now, in effect, operating from their home soil. The RAF fighter squadrons operated as pairs and on one occasion, three Hurricane squadrons and 264 Squadron's Defiants were faced by about eighty Bf 109Es defending a Stuka attack. With favourable odds the RAF fighters claimed twenty-two enemy aircraft, including fifteen by the Defiants. Four Hurricanes were lost and many more returned to base with battle damage, but the preoccupation with escort fighters had allowed the dive bombers to reach Dunkirk, where five ships were sunk.

Fortunately, bad weather reduced enemy air activity on 30 May, allowing for more than 140,000 men to be repatriated since the start of Operation Dynamo. The Luftwaffe concentrated its Ju 87s against ships where they were most effective, and when the weather improved on 1 June they were up in strength, penetrating the RAF fighter cover by arriving between patrols. As a result, three destroyers loaded with troops were sunk. There was further combat on 2 and 3 June, but casualties were kept to a minimum by ships crossing the Channel under cover of darkness.

Early on 2 June, a Luftwaffe attack consisting of about 120 aircraft was met by five RAF fighter squadrons, which kept the enemy bomber crews so busy defending themselves that little damage was inflicted on the ships still in the port. This was the last major German raid; the Luftwaffe sent over small groups of Ju 87s and Ju 88s that attempted to sneak through gaps in the RAF fighter cover. Caught on their own, the Stukas proved to be very vulnerable.

Soon after midnight on 4 June, the evacuation of the stranded British and French troops came to an end, leaving a considerable amount of equipment for the enemy. A total of 338,226 troops were rescued from France, with about 25,000 French troops left behind. During the nine days of Operation Dynamo, 135 Hurricanes, Spitfires, Defiants, and Blenheims were lost, and eighty-four pilots listed as killed, missing, or taken prisoner.

However, there were still British army AASF units in France along with RAF Hurricanes and a few remaining Battles. The army units were moving west through northern France ahead of the German advances, looking for a port from which they could escape. To help the remaining reduced RAF presence provide air cover, 17 and 242 Squadrons were sent to France—the former based at Le Mans from 8–16 June before departing rapidly for the Channel Islands and then back to Britain two days later. No. 242 Squadron based at Châteaudun was ordered to withdraw with all its pilots and aircraft from Nantes back across the Channel, arriving at Coltishall on 18 June. The last three Hurricane squadrons to leave France were the personnel of 1 Squadron, who were evacuated from St Nazaire on 18 June, leaving their aircraft behind; 73 Squadron, which destroyed its aircraft by fire at Nantes and escaped via St Malo on 17 June; and 501 Squadron, which was tasked with providing air cover for troops departing from Cherbourg on 19 June while flying from Jersey, returning to Britain by 20 June with eight Hurricanes.

The cost of the Battle of France and the fighting in the Low Countries had been high, with the loss of 949 RAF aircraft, including 477 fighters, of which 386 were Hurricanes. While

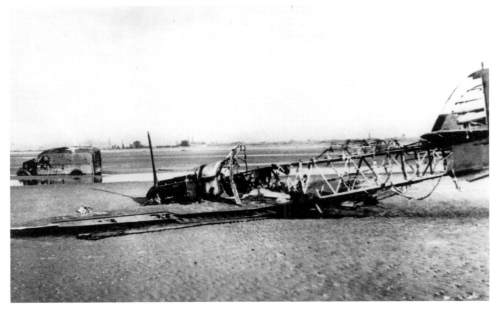

A RAF Hurricane abandoned on the beach at Dunkirk after the withdrawal of the BEF in June 1940. It is believed that this is the Hurricane that became buried in the sand and later reappeared to be salvaged for restoration as a warbird. (*Brussels Air Museum photo*)

fighters could be replaced as more and more factories were established to build Hurricanes and Spitfires, the loss of experienced pilots was more serious. Almost 200 pilots were killed, seriously wounded, missing, or taken prisoner—twenty-nine of which were squadron and flight commanders, and all but around forty were peacetime regulars since the training process had not been able to add many pilots in the short time of the battle. Fighter Command was faced with training new pilots with the skills they would need in combat and the leadership abilities to defend against the full weight of the Luftwaffe, which was beginning to establish bases in France facing across the Channel to Britain.

It would be four hard years before the Allies were able to return in strength to France. In the words of Prime Minister Churchill: 'The Battle of France is over. I expect that the Battle of Britain is about to begin'.

6

The Battle of Britain

T HE FRONT LINE for the air defence of Britain had originally been anticipated as being across the North Sea towards East Anglia. It had not been foreseen that the Germans would attack France and the Low Countries and bring their troops close to Britain across the English Channel. This brought the front line to Kent, Surrey, and London, all of which were within range of the Luftwaffe bombers escorted by fighters. Fortunately, Britain had been making preparations for the Second World War by increasing the air-defence strength of the RAF and FAA.

In April 1933, Air Chief Marshal Sir Edward Ellington was appointed Chief of the Air Staff, and Air Marshal Sir Hugh Dowding was Air Member for Supply and Research. The two of them were advocates for air defence against enemy bombers while many other senior officers and Government ministers believed that the bomber would always get through and therefore invested heavily in RAF Bomber Command. The major part of the RAF defence budget was allocated to the bomber squadrons, but in April 1938, the Government accepted Scheme L as sponsored by Sir Thomas Inskip, Minister for the Co-ordination of Defence. This plan allowed RAF strength to reach 1,352 bombers and 608 fighters by April 1940. This support for an improved priority for fighters gave the RAF an increased strength that proved so critical in 1940. Between 1935 and 1937, the combined strength of the RAF and FAA increased from ninety-one to 169 squadrons and, in effect, the doubling of aircraft available to 2,031. Unfortunately, some 80 per cent were obsolete and required urgent replacement by modern monoplane fighters like the Hurricane and Spitfire to match the performance of the new generation of combat aircraft in service with the Luftwaffe.

Not only was there a need for the new generation of fighters, but there was an urgent requirement for aircrew to operate them effectively in combat. Many pilots were volunteers from the British Commonwealth and other Allied countries, and 1,700 Short Service Commissions were granted, with an additional 800 NCO pilots accepted. To cope with the training of the additional aircrew, the Flying Training Schools (FTS) were increased from six to eleven, but it took a year to train a pilot to fly, let alone operate in combat. In due course, an Empire Air Training Scheme was set up, but the burden fell on the fighter pilots trained with the Auxiliary Air Force and the Volunteer Reserve in the interim.

There were some forty-two Reserve Flying Training Schools (RFTS), the majority equipped with de Havilland Tiger Moths to teach the basic flying syllabus, and in 1938, the basic flying training was supplemented by the Government-sponsored Civil Air Guard, which allowed the established civil flying clubs to train men and women between the ages of sixteen and sixty to provide a pool of pilots for non-combat flying, such as the delivery of service aircraft to the squadrons. With the declaration of war in September 1939, all civil flying ceased and the Civil Air Guard was disbanded. Once the Empire Air Training Scheme was established, pilots were given basic training overseas uninterrupted by the weather or hazards of enemy aircraft.

Bob Foster was a young pilot who finished his training at Sutton Bridge on 18 July 1940 having completed forty to fifty hours, including formation flying in simulated attacks, which were useless when it came to air fighting. His instructor was called Smallwood, who later reached the rank of Air Chief Marshal Sir Basil Smallwood with the obvious nickname of 'Splinter'. As a young regular career flying officer, he survived a week flying patrols over France in May, and was then posted to instruct on Hurricanes. When Bob's posting came through he lived in London and was posted to Edinburgh, while there was a Scotsman on the same course posted to Kenley. They both went to the station commander to see if they could exchange postings, but Bob was later pleased he said no. The Scotsman only survived a few weeks before being killed, while Bob was able to gain another forty flying hours, making a total of ninety, before being posted to Croydon in the thick of the Battle.

In 1936, what had been known as the Air Defence of Great Britain was replaced by four functional commands: Fighter, Bomber, Coastal, and Training. Air Marshal Sir Hugh Dowding was appointed Commander-in-Chief of Fighter Command and quietly took up residence at Bentley Priory to the north of London in July 1936.

One of his first tasks was to create four operational groups for the defence of different parts of Britain, and with his staff he began to set up a new direction system to provide control of the fighters when the enemy were attacking.

One of the greatest defence aids was the secret radar chain set up along the east and south coast of Britain to detect potential attacks by hostile aircraft. This system was supplemented by civilian volunteers of the Observer Corps, whose duties were to track and identify enemy aircraft strengths, heights, and direction once past the radar screen and over Britain. Having been alerted by the radar, and with the information provided by the Observer Corps, Fighter Command was able to deploy its defending fighters to gain as much advantage as possible over the enemy.

Radar was a key to success in the Battle of Britain as it gave advanced notice of enemy raids. In 1935, secret experiments had been conducted in what was known as Radio Direction Finding (RDF) both in Britain and Germany, unknown to each other, although the German experiments were less successful. In Britain, a committee was set up in 1934 under the chairmanship of Sir Henry Tizard to investigate various means of defence against air attack. Robert Watson-Watt, a senior scientist at the National Physical Laboratory (NPL), identified

Air Chief Marshal Sir Hugh Dowding. (on the right) escorting HRH King George VI and Queen Elizabeth on a visit to the HQ Fighter Command on 6 September 1940. (*IWM photo*)

three areas of research covering the complementary requirements of the reflection of radio waves, radio communications with the fighters to direct them to potential targets, and a coded signal transmitted from the Allied aircraft to differentiate from friend and foe (IFF). Tizard had established a reputation for having a very good knowledge of the needs of the services and was able to identify practical military applications. Among the many projects backed by him was the Barnes Wallis Bouncing bomb and Frank Whittle's jet engine. Watson-Watt had become superintendent of the NPL in 1933 and working with his assistant, Arnold Wilkins, a paper was prepared entitled 'The Detection of Aircraft by Radio Methods', which formed the basis of his proposal to the Tizard Committee.

Tests were made initially in May 1935 with the transmitters mounted on 70-foot masts, and in 1936 the development team moved to Bawdsey Manor on the east coast of Suffolk. Radio waves were transmitted and reflected off aircraft, which were then returned to the base station where they were identified on a cathode ray tube. This gave an opportunity for the scientists to work with the visiting civil servants and RAF officers to better understand the requirements and therefore devise solutions. In 1936, Biggin Hill was selected for a series of tests to explore the problems of linking the radar warning, as RDF had come to be known, to a hostile attack for the defending fighters. Teams of ground controllers using plotting tables were able to produce a rapid indication of the converging courses which would guide the defending fighters to an interception. Following the success of the experiments, a network

AVM Keith Park, OC 11 Group, in his personal Hurricane in which he flew around the stations under his command. He was the only Group commander who flew regularly in a modern RAF combat aircraft, while at the same time being very supportive of his people.

of what was known as Chain Home radar stations were set up along the east and south coast from Scotland around to the Isle of Wight. In addition, Chain Home Low radar stations were set up to detect low-flying aircraft. From this stage, the Observer Corps would then take over the observation of the enemy formations.

The four operational groups created within Fighter Command were 11 Group headed by AVM Keith Park in the front line defending the south-east areas of London, Kent, Surrey, Essex, and parts of Hampshire and Suffolk. Supporting 11 Group to the west was 10 Group commanded by AVM Sir Quintin Brand, which was responsible for the defence of Wales and the South West; 12 Group to the north of London commanded by AVM Trafford Leigh-Mallory with responsibility for the defence of the industrial Midlands up to Yorkshire; and finally, 13 Group commanded by AVM Richard Saul covering the defence of the north of England, Scotland and Northern Ireland.

Each of the Groups were divided into sectors, which were controlled by sector stations and supported by other airfields and satellites where aircraft could be dispersed. The sector stations were responsible for the tactical control of fighter defences within their area and to provide additional reinforcements to 11 Group when required. Each sector station was equipped with its own control room and had comprehensive maintenance facilities, as well as accommodating the relevant personnel to operate and defend from enemy attacks.

No. 245 Squadron, based at Aldergrove in Northern Ireland, was responsible for the air defence of Belfast and the surrounding area. The squadron began to receive Hurricane Mk Is in March 1940 at Acklington, moving to Drem on 12 May, and Turnhouse on 5 June 1940. The squadron moved to Aldergrove on 20 July 1940, where it remained for the remainder of the Battle. These six Hurricanes of 245 Squadron with P3762 DX-F nearest were with the squadron late in 1940. (*Author's collection*)

Air Chief Marshal Sir Hugh Dowding was the architect of Fighter Command and had been working on its development since 1936. Sometimes known as 'Stuffy' Dowding, he could be a difficult man to work with, and as well as having the Luftwaffe as his enemy he also had to contend a number of enemies within the Air Council. With the unrealistic belief by many members of the Air Council that the bomber would always get through to its target, Dowding's Fighter Command was seen as the 'Cinderella' service with less resource dedicated to it. It was Dowding's task to overcome this belief and he answered operationally to ACM Sir Cyril Newall, the Chief of the Air Staff (CAS) and the Air Council, and politically to Winston Churchill and the War Cabinet. There were times during the Battle of France when Dowding had to reject the political wish to send reinforcements to France, which would have resulted in a fatal reduction of Britain's air-defence capability. As it was, many experienced aircrew were lost while the aircraft factories were able to replace the fighters with more Hurricanes and Spitfires.

Fortunately, Dowding was a man with a formidable personality, a sharp tongue, and he could be very direct in correspondence. However, with his staff of men and women who clearly worked as hard as he did, Dowding was polite and very supportive if someone had a promising idea. When necessary he would stand up for his principles with other authorities, however high. Dowding was very demanding of his staff, but had a great sense of justice that earned him the respect of his colleagues. He often considered suggestions that conflicted with accepted views. He did not see the need to persuade opponents that they were wrong, or even compromise with them. He gained the nickname 'Stuffy' in his thirties, but 'Maverick' would have been more appropriate. Although not of a jovial disposition, he could be very entertaining away from work and had a keen sense of humour.

Dowding's service as head of Fighter Command was due to be completed by the end of July 1939, with his replacement to be Air Marshal Sir Christopher Courtney. Unfortunately, A. M. Courtney was injured in an air accident from which it would take time to recover, and Dowding was allowed to remain in the service until he reached the age of sixty, although not necessarily in his current role. However, Newall confirmed that Dowding should continue in his existing appointment until at least the end of March 1940. The day before he was due to retire on 30 March, Newall asked Dowding to stay on until 14 July, but there was no decision as to who his successor would be. A further extension was then allowed until the end of October, but Churchill finally came to the rescue and confirmed Dowding as the chief of Fighter Command, which was approved reluctantly by Newall and Sir Archibald Sinclair, allowing Dowding to have some security in fighting the enemy.

Dowding's task was to defend Britain against enemy air attacks through the summer months and into the autumn when the weather would make an invasion across the English Channel impossible. When the good weather returned in the spring of 1941, Fighter Command would be stronger and the Army would be re-equipped and ready to defend the country. The speed of the German advances across the Low Countries and northern France had been so rapid, that the considerable logistical support for an invasion of Britain would take time to establish. Meanwhile, Hitler spent the pleasant summer weather on holiday, touring some of the First World War battle sites.

Dowding's main adversary was the flamboyant Hermann Göring, commander of the Luftwaffe, as well as a leading member of the Nazi Party and Hitler's designated successor. It was not until 21 July that Göring called together his senior commanders to prepare plans to achieve air superiority in preparation for the planned invasion. Hitler ordered that a major air assault be mounted from 5 August, codenamed Eagle Day, with 15 September the target date for the start of the invasion of Britain, codenamed Operation Sealion.

The Luftwaffe order of battle in July 1940 included 2,800 aircraft, of which some 760 were Bf 109 fighters, against a RAF strength of about 700 Hurricanes and Spitfires. Not only was the Luftwaffe at greater strength, but the German pilots were generally better trained and had gained battle experience in the Spanish Civil War.

The Battle of Britain officially lasted from 10 July until 31 October 1940. The Luftwaffe combat fleet in July included 1,300 bombers, of which over 300 were dive bombers, plus 1,050 fighters, including 250 of the vulnerable twin-engined Bf 110s. Dowding had 450 Hurricanes and 300 Spitfires, of which around 600 were combat ready, supported by a number of inferior Blenheims and Defiants. To defend against the expected massed Luftwaffe attacks, Dowding practised an air reserve strategy that made use of tactical reserves and used individual squadrons as the largest practical fighting unit, therefore ensuring that there was always a challenge to enemy attacks. This policy preserved RAF resources and denied the Luftwaffe the opportunity to destroy large numbers of defending fighters in any particular engagement.

Once it was realised that the main enemy attacks would come against the south-east of England, nearly half the fighter force of twenty-one squadrons was allocated to Park in 11 Group distributed around seven sectors. Brand's 10 Group had ten squadrons in four sectors, Leigh-Mallory's 12 Group had fourteen squadrons in six sectors, and Saul's 13 Group had fourteen squadrons in six sectors, although many of the northerly based units were in training or resting from combat.

The group commanders were responsible for the conduct of operations in their areas, with Park's 11 Group the most demanding. The New Zealander Keith Park had been Dowding's deputy at Bentley Priory from July 1938 until taking over the 11 Group HQ at Uxbridge in April 1940. Park was also the only Group head to fly his own modern fighter, a Hurricane, which he used to communicate with his squadrons and keep up to date with progress.

The priority was to destroy enemy bombers before they hit their targets. However, because the German front line was just across the English Channel, the Luftwaffe could provide fighter cover. When radar detected raids forming up and approaching, it was important to concentrate the defences against the bombers while trying to avoid fighters, the Luftwaffe

The Hurricane could absorb a great deal of combat damage and still bring its pilot back home. (*Author's collection*)

Squadron Leader J. W. C. Simpson DFC was the commanding officer of 245 Squadron at Aldergrove. Here he shows his score of enemy aircraft on the aircraft door. (*Author's collection*)

Ground crew. ('Erks') installing an oxygen bottle in a Hurricane during July 1940. The bags over their shoulders carry their gas masks. (*Author's collection*)

often sending over fighter sweeps to lure the RAF fighters into the air. In these battles the Hurricanes were concentrated wherever possible on the bomber formations, with the Spitfires giving top cover and intercepting enemy fighters.

The experience of air-to-air combat in France, where many of the squadrons were led by First World War combat veterans, forced the commanders to improvise a more flexible approach to combat. The set First World War 'follow-the-leader' approach was too vulnerable, and a more loose formation of finger four was more practical. Bob Doe believed it was best to go straight into attack without waiting to get into position, which did not give the enemy time to think. He believed his success was that he had been trained as a bomber pilot and the only gunnery he had experienced was from the rear turret of an Anson, which had given him the basics of deflection shooting. In a dogfight it was shooting that mattered rather than the flying. The Hurricane was sturdy, reliable, and a steady gun platform, allowing Doe to claim fourteen-and-a-half victories during the battle.

The month of rest while the German war machine prepared for the invasion was helpful for the RAF to rebuild some of its strength, train more pilots, and evolve new tactics. On 1 July 1940, British home territory was invaded for the first and only time when the Germans occupied the Channel Islands. By this time, the Fighter Command Order of Battle was 30 squadrons in 11 Group, of which seventeen were equipped with Hurricanes and eight with Spitfires. No. 12 Group had eleven squadrons, three equipped with Hurricanes and eight with Spitfires; and 13 Group had seventeen squadrons, nine with Hurricanes and six with Spitfires.

Ground crew checking a Merlin in a Hurricane at the time of the Battle of Britain. (*Author's collection*)

Little had changed at the practical commencement of the battle; 10 Group had three Hurricane and four Spitfire squadrons. Many of the squadrons in the more remote locations were veterans from the Battle of France and were using the time to bring in and train replacement pilots for combat. However, 1, 32, 79, 85, 501, 615 Squadrons, and a number of other combat-experienced units, were part of 11 Group ready to use their skills to defend London and the South East from attack.

The pilots with the greatest experience were distributed among the key sector airfields of Biggin Hill, Kenley, North Weald, and Northolt to help develop and test new tactics among the less experienced pilots.

The majority of Fighter Command squadrons were equipped with Hurricanes, which outnumbered all the other aircraft types combined. This was also true within the strategically placed 11 Group, although it was not just numbers but the state of readiness that was critical. The serviceability rate of the Hurricanes was around 75 per cent, even though about 100 of the aircraft had seen combat in France. Spitfires had been operational over Dunkirk and had an availability rate of 72 per cent. Although the Spitfire was more advanced than the Hurricane, it did require specialist engineering support, while the more rugged Hurricane was more readily available for combat. The Hurricane could absorb battle damage better, and when damaged could rapidly be returned to operations with basic repairs. Its wide track

No. 85 Squadron began to take delivery of Hurricane Mk Is at Debden from September 1938 and moved to France on 9 September 1939 at the outbreak of war. A return was made to Debden on 23 May 1940, and then the squadron moved to Croydon on 19 August, followed by Castle Camps on 3 September, and then to Church Fenton two days later. (*IWM photo*)

Probably as many Hurricanes were damaged in accidents as combat. Hurricane Mk I P2754 YB-W:17 Squadron at Debden on 27 June 1940. (*RAF Museum*)

undercarriage allowed for operations from primitive forward airfields, as well as landing back at their own bases after they had been bombed. Although the Hurricane was slower than the Spitfire and soon to be outperformed by Luftwaffe fighters, it was a well-established, tried and tested fighter with good manoeuvrability.

John Ellacombe found that the Hurricane had very good visibility, with a large rear-view mirror above the windscreen. Twice he saw Bf 109s in his mirror, did a flick roll, and the enemy aircraft would end up in front. One was so close that John hit it in the radiator before pulling out and shooting it down into the sea.

The main fault with the Hurricane was the location of two of its three fuel tanks, with the most vulnerable ones being on either side. Once the wing root fuel tanks caught fire, the flames would spread rapidly along the dope- and fabric-covered wooden rear fuselage. An additional hazard for the pilot was the open space between the thick wing root and the fuselage where the air could flow through the gun ports to feed the flames and take them directly from the wings to the cockpit floor. The fire would erupt suddenly from the cockpit floor and envelop the pilot from all sides—hopefully, he would be able to abandon the aircraft safely without too serious burns to himself and his parachute.

Among the new tactics developed was one by Sqn Ldr John Worrall, commanding officer of 32 Squadron. He opened an attack with a head-on charge, which had the effect of breaking up the enemy bomber formations. A less gung-ho approach was adopted towards the end of the battle whereby the combat unit was a pair of aircraft with the number two covering the

A Hurricane being re-armed and refuelled between sorties during the Battle of Britain. (*Author's collection*)

No. 32 Squadron started re-equipping with Hurricane Mk Is at Biggin Hill in October 1938, moving to Wittering on 25 May 1940 until returning to Biggin Hill on 4 June. The squadron moved to Acklington for rest and training on 27 August 1940. Hurricane Mk I P3522 GZ-V:32 Squadron was dispersed to Hawkinge on 31 July 1940. (*Author's collection*)

leaders tail. The RAF had a total of 905 fighters available for the defence of Britain, including Hurricanes, Spitfires, Defiants, and Blenheims—the latter two types were largely outperformed by the Luftwaffe. Among the immediate reserves held at MUs were ninety-two Hurricanes and, should the need be dire, a further thirty-eight single-seat fighters including Gladiators, which were with Group fighter pools and station flights.

Pilot numbers were critical following the losses in France of so many experienced aircrew. There was a total of 1,103 pilots listed with the squadrons, but only 820 were combat ready as the remainder were being trained up to the right standards by the squadrons. The Operational Training Units (OTUs) were producing about twenty new Hurricane pilots every week, but because the newer, more capable Hurricanes were issued to the operational squadrons, the OTUs were having to use the earlier war-weary aircraft with Merlin IIs, the Watts propeller, fabric-covered wings, and the basic ring-and-bead gun sight, while the operational pilots had a much more effective reflector gun sight. As a result, the novice pilots were familiar with the broad handling of the Hurricane, but had to learn to fight with the aircraft when they joined a squadron. In many cases, the new pilots probably only had about ten hours on type when posted to an operational squadron, which put a greater responsibility on the experienced pilots, who in addition to taking the aircraft into combat also had to spend time training the new intakes. Fortunately, much of this training was achieved on so-called rest postings away from 11 Group where the demands of combat were reduced.

Peter Ayerst, having had experience of the fighting in France, was posted to the Hurricane OTU at Sutton Bridge, with another at Aston Down. When another was opened at Hawarden

Hurricane Mk I SW-E:253 Squadron taxiing by the heavily camouflaged hangars at Northolt on 19 April 1940. (*P. H. T. Green collection*)

near Chester, some of the instructors were posted there as a nucleus. On 14 August, when flying was finished and the aircraft dispersed around the airfield, an aircraft appeared overhead at 8.30 p.m. being fired upon by AA (anti-aircraft) guns as it bombed nearby RAF Sealand. Three of the instructors put on their flying gear and took off, Peter being the youngest and least experienced. The other two had shots at the He 111, followed by Peter, which resulted in the bomber going down and making a crash landing in a field. The crew were taken prisoner.

Other pilots did not have the luxury of attending an OTU. Bill Green had about five or six hours in Hurricanes, mainly ferrying to Northolt and Hornchurch, as the battle continued all around. He flew a Hurricane to Gravesend on 19 August where he met the CO of 501 Squadron, who asked how Bill was getting on. When he found out how many hours Bill had accumulated, he said he would get him trained quicker and to report back to Gravesend that night. Having arrived, Bill went to bed and was woken at 4 a.m.; within ten minutes, he was walking to the flight line as green three to cover the rear end of the squadron. Flying with the ace Ginger Lacey, he was told that when Lacey turned to the right, Bill was to turn left, but when this happened he lost the squadron. He found his way back to Hawkinge, and so began his operational career.

Hurricane Mk I L2124 SD-H of 501 Special Reserve Squadron at Tangmere. The squadron formed with Hurricane Mk Is at Filton in March 1939 to provide air defence for the aircraft and aero-engine factories in Bristol. However, the squadron was moved to Tangmere on 27 November 1939 in preparation to provide reinforcements in France from 10 May 1940. A return was made to Croydon on 26 June 1940, with moves to Middle Wallop on 4 July, Gravesend on 25 July, Kenley on 10 September, and back to Filton on 17 December 1940. (*RAF Museum photo*)

A Hurricane Mk I of 229 Squadron being refuelled and prepared for the next sortie. No. 229 Squadron began to receive Hurricanes at Digby in March 1940. The squadron moved to Wittering on 26 June 1940, Northolt on 9 September, and returned to Wittering on15 December 1940. (*IWM photo*)

The aim was for each squadron to have a minimum strength of eighteen operational pilots, but in practice it was often less during the battle. The situation became critical in early September when pilot losses were equivalent to two squadrons every day. The training courses at the OTUs were so reduced that the pilots were learning to operate their aircraft from their first sortie, making them more vulnerable to being shot down. Fortunately, the RAF pilots were generally able to bale out of their damaged aircraft over friendly territory, whereas the Luftwaffe crews were over hostile territory and if they survived were soon taken prisoner.

The Luftwaffe commenced hostilities against Britain in early July 1940 with a small number of probing attacks along the eastern and southern coasts of England to test the reaction of the defences. Göring had tasked the Luftwaffe with denying the English Channel to Allied shipping, which was so vital to the country's survival, as well as discouraging the Royal Navy from using its bases from Dover to Plymouth. The enemy attacks on shipping in the Channel were made with the devastating Ju 87 Stuka dive bombers together with Do 17 bombers, giving the Luftwaffe crews experience of operating over water, and hopefully tying up RAF pilots on defensive convoy patrols.

Having regrouped and trained new pilots at Church Fenton, 87 Squadron moved south to Exeter on 5 July, as part of 10 Group, just in time for the start of the Battle of Britain. Dennis

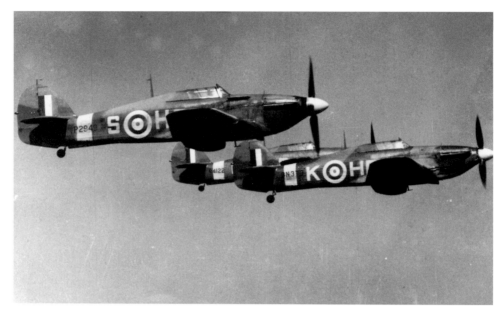

A flight of Mk I Hurricanes of 239 Squadron, with P2949 HB-S:239 Squadron nearest the camera. (*P. H. T. Green collection*)

Squadron Ian 'Widge' Gleed DFC, OC 87 Squadron, leading his squadron in Hurricane LK-A 'Figaro' from Exeter on a detachment to Bibury in September 1940. (*Author's collection*)

Armourers carefully feeding the 0.303-inch bullets into the port wing of a Hurricane at Debden during the Battle of Britain. (*RAF Museum photo*)

David was still with the squadron and realised that the Luftwaffe had changed their tactics following the Battle of France, with the bombers always escorted by fighters. This meant that the pilots had to get the bombers quickly before the Bf 109s were on their tails. The tactics of going for the leading aircraft by the RAF pilots caused serious Luftwaffe casualties, particularly to their experienced leaders, which became unsustainable.

The first actual attack on a convoy was on 7 July when the ships were approaching the Isle of Wight with 145 Squadron on standing patrol. They claimed one Do 17P, and soon after 43 Squadron took over and accounted for a further Do 17P, followed by a kill by 601 Squadron. A total of seven German bombers were claimed during the day for the loss of one Hurricane and five Spitfires, mainly to Bf 109s. While the enemy bombers were attacking the convoys, free-ranging Bf 109s were able to catch the Hurricanes and Spitfires when they were most vulnerable, either returning to base short of fuel or just getting airborne for the next patrol.

On the second day, every effort was made not to send RAF fighters on convoy defence if there was a chance that German free rangers were likely to be encountered. However, with the Luftwaffe units based along the Channel coast of France, even if the radar did not detect any attackers they could be rapidly deployed.

Hurricanes claimed two bombers, one each off the coasts of Sussex and Yorkshire, but two Hurricanes and two Spitfires were lost together with their pilots. During the first ten days of combat, Hurricane pilots claimed thirteen bombers, seven fighters, and one reconnaissance aircraft for the loss of eight aircraft and five pilots, one of whom was Sqn Ldr Joslin, the commanding officer of 79 Squadron.

Hurricane Mk I P3221 SO-K:145 Squadron at Westhampnett in July 1940. The squadron began to receive Hurricanes at Croydon in March 1940, moving to Filton in 10 Group on 9 May. The squadron then moved to Tangmere the next day and arrived at Westhampnett, the Tangmere satellite, on 23 July. The squadron moved to Drem for a rest on 31 August 1940 and returned to Tangmere on 9 October 1940. (*RAF Museum photo*)

No. 43 Squadron first received Hurricane Mk Is at Tangmere in December 1938 and operated from Acklington in 12 Group from 18 November 1939, and Wick from 26 February 1940. The squadron returned to Tangmere on 31 May 1940 until retiring to Usworth on 8 September, where Hurricane Mk I NQ-G:43 Squadron headed the flight line. (*RAF Museum photo*)

F/O Whitney and ground crew of a 601 Squadron Hurricane Mk I at readiness at Exeter during the Battle of Britain. The squadron started taking delivery of Hurricane Mk Is at Tangmere in February 1940. A move was made to Middle Wallop on 1 June, before returning to Tangmere on 17 June. The squadron moved to Debden on 19 August and back to Tangmere on 2 September. The next move was to Exeter on 7 September, and finally to Northolt on 17 December 1940 after the Battle of Britain was over. (*RAF Museum photo*)

No. 79 Squadron started to re-equip with Hurricane Mk Is at Biggin Hill in November 1938, moving to Manston on 12 November 1939 and back to Biggin Hill on 8 March 1940 before going to France on 10 May 1940. The squadron returned to Biggin Hill on 21 May 1940, going to Digby six days later, before returning to Biggin Hill on 5 June. No. 79 Squadron moved to the advanced airfield of Hawkinge on 1 July 1940, but withdrew to Sealand on 11 July and Acklington two days later before returning to Biggin Hill once again on 23 August. The final move during the battle was to Pembrey in 10 Group on 8 September 1940. (*RAF Museum photo*)

A Hurricane Mk I of 32 Squadron being refuelled at Biggin Hill on 16 August 1940. (*IWM photo*)

The first Hurricane Mk Is were delivered to 56 Squadron at North Weald in April 1938, with the squadron moving to Martlesham Heath on 22 October 1939 until they returned to North Weald on 28 February 1940. A move was made to Digby on 31 May 1940, and then back to North Weald on 5 June; the squadron's Hurricanes were operating there in early July. The squadron moved to Boscombe Down on 1 September and then Middle Wallop on 29 November 1940. (*IWM photo*)

On 10 July, the RAF was involved in the heaviest combat to date when twenty-two Hurricanes of 32, 56, and 111 Squadrons, along with eight Spitfires of 74 Squadron, fought against a Luftwaffe force of Do 17s, Bf 110s, and Bf 109s over a convoy off the Kent coast.

This was the first time 111 Squadron used the head-on attack to break up the bomber formations.

Channel convoys continued to be targeted throughout July, with Hurricane pilots gaining some successes. Eight He 111s and three Bf 110s were claimed on 11 July by 145, 238, and 601 Squadrons for the loss of two Hurricanes, whose pilots were saved.

On 13 July, while protecting a convoy in the Channel, Hurricanes of 43, 56, and 238 Squadrons claimed two Do 17s, and one Ju 88, Bf 110, and Bf 109 respectively, albeit for the loss of three aircraft and pilots.

On 19 July, the Hurricanes of 111 Squadron went to the aid of the Defiants of 141 Squadron, which were being attacked by Bf 109s exploiting the Defiant's weak link of having no forward-firing guns. Only four Defiants escaped. Dover Harbour was attacked on 19 July by some fifty Ju 87 Stukas with escorts of about eighty Bf 109s. Spitfires from 41 Squadron were scrambled from Manston, and joined by Hurricanes of 501 Squadron from Hawkinge, four Stukas being shot down.

Since June, it had been realised that Bf 110s were vulnerable to Hurricanes when they formed a defensive circle on being threatened, each aircraft covering the tail of the other while they gradually orbited into cloud or back home. The Hurricane pilots could use their greater manoeuvrability to make attacks from various angles and avoid the forward-firing

No. 111 Squadron was responsible for the introduction of the Hurricane to the RAF when the first aircraft arrived at Northolt in December 1937. The squadron operated from Acklington, Drem and Wick before returning to Northolt on 13 May 1940 and moved to Digby on 21 May. On 4 June the squadron moved to Croydon, then Debden on 19 August, returning to Croydon on 3 September. A move was then made to Drem on 8 September. The squadron is seen refuelling at Wick in early 1940, and the nearest Hurricane, L2001 JU-B, was lost in a flying accident when it crashed and killed Sgt Pascoe on take-off from Hatfield. (*Author's collection*)

Hurricane Mk I N2479 of 56 Squadron at North Weald during 1940 when 'Sailor' Malan was the commanding officer. (*Author's collection*)

Some pilots of 111 Squadron in a posed 'readiness' scene at Acklington with Hurricane Mk I L1822 JU-K. (*IWM photo*)

Three Hurricanes at Tangmere being re-armed and refuelled during the Battle under the watchful eyes of S/Ldr Max Aitken, son of Lord Beaverbrook. (*Author's collection*)

guns of the Bf 110s. During the first month of combat over Britain, Hurricane pilots claimed eighty-seven enemy aircraft destroyed out of the overall total of 187, with forty Hurricanes lost and sixteen pilots killed.

Due to the pressures of combat and pilot fatigue resulting in unacceptable losses, a number of the active squadrons had to be withdrawn to less busy areas in the north of Britain.

This allowed for the training of replacement pilots while providing a defence against possible attacks from northern Europe, which was beyond the endurance of defending fighters.

Meanwhile, although the German aircraft losses were only about half of those of the RAF, by operating over hostile territory their aircrew losses were up to seven times greater than those of the Allies.

While Spitfire squadrons were struggling to maintain pilot strength, the Hurricane units were managing better. They were also boosted progressively by volunteers from the FAA and the training of Czech, Polish—the first unit, 302 Squadron, was formed at Leconfield on 13 July before moving to Northolt in September—and American volunteer pilots who later formed the Eagle Squadrons. Also, the first RCAF squadron was formed—No. 401 based at Middle Wallop, all flying Hurricanes. The overall front-line strength of Fighter Command was about 75 per cent of the numbers on paper, and the main battle was still to be fought and won.

By the summer of 1940, approximately 35,000 Polish airmen, sailors, and soldiers had escaped the Germans and made their way to Britain, making them by far the largest foreign military presence in the country. Of these, 8,500 were airmen, and the RAF realised the potential value of experienced men to fight the enemy, with the majority posted to Bomber Command or the RAF Volunteer Reserve.

P/O A. G. Lewis DFC and bar, was with 85 Squadron in 1940, and here clearly shows the strain of combat operations after returning from a sortie in a Hurricane. (*Author's collection*)

The pilots of 'B' Flight 85 Squadron taking a break at Castle Camps in July 1940. The Hurricane behind them features the metal plate used to shield the exhaust glow from the pilot when on a night patrol. (*RAF Museum photo*)

Hurricane Mk I P3700 RF-E:303. (Polish) Squadron at Northolt in early September 1940, which had been the mount of various pilots who had accounted for a number of enemy aircraft destroyed. The squadron had formed with Hurricane Mk Is at Northolt in August 1940 and moved to Leconfield on 11 October. (Polish Aircraft Archives)

In July, the RAF agreed to form two Polish squadrons, 302 and 303, with Polish pilots and ground crews, although the flight commanders and commanding officers were British. Many other experienced Polish fighter pilots were integrated in regular RAF squadrons.

The Polish pilots had gained a reputation for being fearless and inspired by hatred following the destruction of their homeland. Their experience of air warfare had taught them that the most effective way to destroy enemy aircraft was to open fire from close up, at a devastating near point-blank range. Despite accusations of recklessness, the losses of 303 Squadron were nearly 70 per cent less than other RAF squadrons in the Battle of Britain.

The 145 Polish pilots claimed 201 victories, with Sqn Ldr Urbanowicz of 303 Squadron the highest Polish scorer with fifteen victories, and Sgt Tony Glowacki one of only two Allied pilots to claim five Luftwaffe aircraft in one day—a feat he achieved on 24 August. In total, thirty Polish fighter pilots were killed in the Battle of Britain. There were also eighty-eight Czech airmen, who mostly flew Hurricanes, with 310 Squadron from July and 312 Squadron from September.

During the first week in August, the German forces consolidated their position in preparation for the anticipated assault on Britain. With the diversion of convoys away from the vulnerable English Channel to the western ports, and the departure of the Royal Navy warships away from the high-risk southern ports, the pressure was taken off the RAF fighter

Hurricane Mk I P3707 NN-A:310. (Polish) Squadron force-landed near Duxford after a mid-air collision with another Hurricane on 29 October 1940. No 310. (Polish) Squadron formed at Duxford on 10 July 1940 with Hurricane Mk Is, which were retained until they were replaced by Mk IIAs in March 1941. (*Author's collection*)

squadrons. This short lull in the fighting allowed some additional Hurricane squadrons to be formed, including the second Polish squadron, No. 303 at Northolt. With 11 Group becoming too large to control effectively, two of the western sectors were transferred to 10 Group covering the South West.

On 8 August, Luftwaffe attacks recommenced with orders to destroy the RAF in the air and on the ground in preparation for an invasion to be launched within a month. Göring was convinced that Fighter Command had been fatally weakened during July and sent bombers to attack the southern airfields and radar installations. As he was not anticipating heavy losses, he allocated the vulnerable, but accurate Stuka dive-bombers most often to the task, covered by a fighter escort of Bf 110s, which in turn required the protection of the shorter endurance Bf 109s. The Bf 109s were not able to stay in the target areas for long enough to be effective, leaving the Stukas vulnerable to high losses.

In early August, there was an attempt to move a trapped convoy of un-laden merchant ships from the Thames Estuary to load in ports in the west of Britain. The convoy was located by the enemy radar near Calais on 7 August and attacked by the usual combination of Stukas covered by Bf 110s and Bf 109s. RAF protection consisted of eighteen Hurricanes from 145, 238, and 257 Squadrons, plus 609 Squadron Spitfires. The RAF fighters dived through the fighter escort and shot down two Stukas before being engaged; a further Stuka, Bf 110, and three Bf 109s were claimed for the loss of three Hurricanes. Four of the ships were sunk and seven more damaged. This was followed by a second attack for which the Hurricanes of 43 and 145

Squadrons, who had a good position at a higher altitude and attacked out of the sun, claiming ten Ju 87s, four Bf 110s, eleven Bf 109s, and one He 59. Unfortunately, twelve Hurricane pilots were killed with fourteen aircraft lost, and by that evening only four ships were undamaged.

The earlier RAF tactics based on First World War experience proved ineffective for dog-fighting, but Dowding was reluctant to make changes during the battle itself as he thought it might upset known standards. However, in many cases it was done for him; an example being the South African, Sailor Malan, who abandoned the RAF standard rules and was a very experienced pilot leading Spitfires of 74 Squadron. He developed ten rules of engagement in fighter combat, which have stood the test of time:

1. Wait until you see the whites of their eyes. Fire short bursts of one or two seconds only when the sights are definitely ON.
2. While shooting think of nothing else, brace the whole of the body; have both hands on the stick; concentrate on the ring sight.
3. Always keep a sharp lookout.
4. Height gives the initiative.
5. Always turn and face the attack.
6. Make the decisions promptly. It is better to act quickly even though the tactics are not the best.
7. Never fly straight and level for more than thirty seconds in the combat area.
8. When diving to attack always leave a proportion of the formation above to act as top guard.
9. Initiative, aggression, air discipline and teamwork are words that mean something in air fighting.
10. Go in quickly—punch hard—get out!

To achieve the best results, squadrons were organised in three sections of four, allowing the fours to split into pairs, with the squadron being the largest practical formation.

Luftwaffe tactics changed on 11 August to flying formations from the Thames Estuary to the Dorset coast hoping to catch RAF fighters in transit or on patrols. Park's 11 Group controllers provided support to these vulnerable formations, adding Spitfire squadrons with plenty of fuel and ammunition as reinforcements. On this day, there was a major raid on Portland and more than seventy fighters were put in the air from both 11 and 10 Groups to protect the harbour and the fighter airfields at Warmwell and Tangmere. Hurricanes of 1, 87, 145, 213, 238, and 601 Squadrons were joined by the Spitfires of 152 and 609 Squadrons over Weymouth Bay and met the enemy fighters ahead of the bombers. The Luftwaffe tactics were successful; sixteen Hurricanes were shot down with the loss of thirteen pilots—145 Squadron lost a further four aircraft. Hurricanes claimed eighteen aircraft with the death of three senior bomber force officers, resulting in the fighters being ordered to stay close to the bombers, which limited their freedom of attack against the RAF fighters.

Allied radar was having increasing success at detecting the build-up of enemy raids as they formed up over the French coast, allowing RAF fighters to be scrambled early and gain a height advantage. The coastal radar stations therefore became priority targets for the Luftwaffe, and on 12 August four Bf 110s attacked the radar installations at Dover, Rye,

No. 1 Squadron received its first Hurricane Mk Is at Tangmere in October 1938 and was moved to France on 9 September 1939. A return was made to Northolt on 18 January 1940, and the squadron moved to Tangmere on 23 July 1940. A rest move was made to Wittering in 12 Group on 9 September 1940 where Hurricane Mk I P3395 JX-B was put in a typical blast pen. A return to Northolt was made on 15 December 1940. (*IWM photo*)

Hurricane Mk I P2829 LK-G:87 Squadron at Debden in 1940 on jacks during maintenance. (*P. H. T. Green collection*)

A Hurricane Mk I of 213 Squadron being re-armed at Biggin Hill on 9 June 1940. The squadron began to receive Hurricane Mk Is at Wittering from January 1939 and moved to Biggin Hill on 9 June, then to Exeter on 18 June, Tangmere on 7 September, and Leconfield on 29 November 1940 after the battle. (*IWM photo*)

Pevensey, and the English Dunkirk, damaging three of them. This allowed a fleet of German bombers to form up over France while the RAF was relatively blind—an advanced guard of which bombed the fighter airfields at Lympne and Hawkinge. The main raid was identified late by Ventnor radar as it approached the Isle of Wight and the formations split into two at the last minute, heading for Portsmouth and Ventnor radar itself.

Brand and Park ordered forty-eight Hurricanes of 145, 213, and 257 Squadrons into the air, together with ten Spitfires of 266 Squadron. The RAF squadrons attacked in waves to spread the risk. They were able to attack the circling Bf 110s while the AA guns around Portsmouth fired at the Ju 88 bombers. The escorting Bf 109s were too far away to provide protection, enabling the Hurricanes to shoot down ten Ju 88s over Portsmouth, while 615 Squadron Hurricanes shot down two of the Bf 109s before they could come to the aid of the German bombers.

The total Luftwaffe losses were eleven Ju 88s, five Bf 110s, and four Bf 109s, but 145 Squadron lost three more pilots and Hurricanes, bringing the squadron casualties since the start of the month to eleven pilots killed and thirteen Hurricanes lost. There was no alternative but to withdraw the squadron survivors to Drem in Scotland for a rest and to train replacements.

Meanwhile, Portsmouth dockyard had been severely damaged and Ventnor radar was out of operation for three days. The Germans mistakenly assumed that when a radar station had

Three Hurricanes of 257 Squadron on finals to land at Debden during the battle. No. 257 Squadron began to equip with Hurricane Mk Is at Hendon in June 1940, moving to Northolt on 4 July, Martlesham Heath on 5 September, and North Weald on 8 October 1940. (*Author's collection*)

Hurricane Mk Is of 615 Squadron taking off from Northolt in October 1940. The squadron exchanged its Gladiators for Hurricane Mk Is at Le Touquet in April 1940 and withdrew from France to Kenley on 22 May 1940. The squadron moved to Prestwick on 29 August 1940, and moved back into 11 Group at Northolt on 10 October 1940. (*Author's collection*)

been taken out of operation it would not come back on line. Fortunately this was not true, and they were rarely out of action for more than a day or so.

Although Stukas had suffered heavy losses in early August, they were deployed again in strength in preparation for the planned invasion. It was hoped that to have the greatest effect in overwhelming Fighter Command defences, the Ju 87s would be launched in three separate Luftflotten from bases as far apart as Norway and the Brest peninsula. For this attack to work successfully, the weather had to be perfect. The day earmarked was 13 August, although the main raid was delayed until the afternoon. Some bombers had already taken off unescorted in the morning and could not be recalled. Therefore, instead of a co-ordinated attack, a number of less effective isolated raids were launched, including one that severely damaged Eastchurch airfield. Five Do 17s were shot down by Hurricanes, one of which was an experimental version with 151 Squadron armed with a pair of 20-mm cannons fitted under the wings.

In the afternoon, the main enemy force of over 300 aircraft crossed the Channel along a front 40 miles wide, passing over the English coast to the west of the Isle of Wight. At the same time, Bf 109s, which were at the extreme of their range, went on free chases in an attempt to attract RAF fighters. The Bf 109s had to return to base before interception and had alerted the RAF controllers to the attack.

Hurricane Mk I V7434 DZ-R:151 Squadron in a dispersal at Digby sometime in 1940. This aircraft was piloted by P/O I. S. Smith when he shot down a He 111 at Chapel St Leonards on 2 October 1940. The squadron began to receive Hurricane Mk Is at North Weald in December 1938 and moved to Martlesham Heath on 13 May 1940 in preparation for a move to France four days later. No. 151 Squadron returned from France at Manston after only one day and went to North Weald on 20 May before being dispersed to Stapleford on 29 August 1940. The squadron flew to Digby on 1 September 1940 where it remained for the remainder of the battle. (*Peter Green collection*)

Hurricane Mk I N2359 YB-J:17 Squadron ready for departure from Debden during August 1940, with P/O Stevens in the cockpit. (*RAF Museum photo*)

Brand of 10 Group was able to scramble seven squadrons of over ninety fighters from Warmwell, Exeter, Middle Wallop, and Tangmere to counter the incoming raiders. On crossing the coast, the enemy formations split into three. One group flew up the Solent towards Southampton. A number of Ju 88s in the second formation attempted a raid on Portland, but the Hurricanes of 213 and 601 Squadrons destroyed three of the escorting Bf 110s, which caused the Ju 88s to jettison their bombs and head for home. The third element made for the airfields at Warmwell and Middle Wallop, but with the escorts already departed the damage was minor.

Later in the afternoon, the final raid of the day involved forty Ju 87s escorted by free-ranging Bf 109s struck at RAF Detling, causing extensive damage and casualties, including sixty-seven dead. It was fortunate the station was not part of the Battle of Britain defences as twenty-two aircraft were destroyed, as well as the operations block, hangars and three messes. On this rather uncoordinated day, both air and ground defences claimed fifteen German bombers, six Ju 87s, fifteen Bf 110s, and nine Bf 109s. Fighter Command lost twelve Hurricanes, with three pilots killed and three badly injured, and one Spitfire was lost.

The following day, Hurricane pilots claimed two He 111s, two Ju 87s, and four Bf 109s for the loss of four aircraft. There was a slight rearrangement of the Fighter Command defences when the Hurricanes of 238 Squadron moved to St Eval in Cornwall to cover the Western Approaches, and their place was taken at Middle Wallop by the Hurricanes of 249 Squadron, which moved from Church Fenton in 12 Group.

Some of the Hurricane pilots of 601 Squadron in the mud at Exeter during the battle; the squadron badge on the white of the fin flash. (*Author's collection*)

In a fight with Bf 109s, Hurricanes could always out-turn them, but to escape the enemy fighters would push their nose down and dive away to safety as the Daimler Benz engines used fuel injection rather than carburettors. The Merlins of the Hurricanes and Spitfires used SU carburettors that, went put into negative g by pushing the nose down, forced the fuel to the top of the float chamber. This starved the engine, which lost power for a critical two or three seconds. If the negative-g continued, the carburettor flooded and drowned the supercharger with an over-rich mixture that could shut down the engine completely, which was not helpful in a fight to the death.

The problem was overcome by a very simple stop-gap solution known as 'Miss Shilling's orifice', named after a bright thirty-one-year-old engineer who, while working at RAE Farnborough, introduced a simple flow restrictor in the form of a small metal disc like a plain washer. The restrictor was made to allow the fuel needed for maximum engine power, usually used in dogfights, allowing the pilots to go through quick negative g without loss of power. Miss Shilling travelled around the RAF fighter bases with a small team fitting the restrictors, giving front-line squadrons priority.

In order for the invasion of Britain to progress before the arrival of unpredictable autumn weather, the main German assault had to commence immediately. Dowding and his squadrons were as ready as they would ever be to meet the onslaught; the Luftwaffe aircrew were uneasy as bomber losses to the RAF defenders were high with the aircraft vulnerable to fighters not adequately protected by the Bf 109s and Bf 110s. The German fighter pilots were unnecessarily restricted by having to fly close escort to the bombers, which in turn made them vulnerable to Fighter Command, and their endurance was insufficient to provide a full protection throughout the bomber actions. The Ju 87s were proving vulnerable to sustained air defence, which they had never experienced before, and were taking heavy losses.

Thursday 15 August was designated Adlertag ('Eagle Day') by the Germans. There was to be a concerted attempt to destroy the RAF Fighter Command in the air and on the ground by targeting airfields. Attacks were planned not from just France, but also Scandinavian bases against the north of Britain, but these would be far beyond the range of escorting fighters.

The first airfield targeted was Hawkinge, Kent, at around midday, when a force of around fifty Ju 87s, supported by Bf 109s, attacked. The initial defence was by 501 Squadron with Hurricanes, which claimed two Stukas, but lost two aircraft to the Bf 109s. Three more Stukas were destroyed by Spitfires—other Ju 87s causing considerable damage at Lympne—but no aircraft were caught on the ground at either airfield.

Up until this time, 11 and 10 Groups had borne the brunt of the defence. It now fell to the squadrons to the north to take their share, even though some were on a 'rest'. A force of over sixty He 111s, with an escort of twenty-one Bf 110s, was detected coming across the North Sea towards the Firth of Forth. At around 50 miles out, turning south towards Newcastle and Sunderland, the force was successfully intercepted by eighteen Hurricanes from 79 and 605 Squadrons, plus Spitfires from Drem and Acklington. The Luftwaffe lost eight He 111s, of which four were shot down by Hurricanes, and seven Bf 110s—three destroyed by Hurricanes. The RAF broke up the raid and turned the remainder home with no bombs dropped and no losses to Fighter Command.

Another incoming raid was detected approaching the Humber and a dozen each of Hurricanes and Spitfires from 73 and 616 Squadrons were scrambled from Leconfield and Church Fenton. The enemy attack turned out to be an unescorted formation of Ju 88s from Aarlborg in Denmark. Their target was Driffield, where ten Whitley bombers were destroyed on the ground. As the Ju 88s departed they were intercepted by fighters—Hurricane pilots claimed five and Spitfire pilots two, with a further two so badly damaged that they later crashed. Once again there were no losses to Fighter Command. With the fighting of the RAF in the south, the Germans obviously did not expect any squadrons to be deployed in the north.

In the south, a major attack on Martlesham Heath put it out of action for two days; three of the defending Hurricanes from 1 and 17 Squadrons were shot down by the Bf 109 escort. A further raid started building in the South East, with some ninety Do 17s escorted by approximately 130 Bf 109s detected approaching Deal, and supported by sixty Bf 109s on free range over Kent. There were already twenty-four Hurricanes and twelve Spitfires airborne and directed towards intercepting the enemy, with another forty-plus Hurricanes scrambled from Croydon and Biggin Hill to provide additional support. The bomber formations were so well-protected that only two Do 17s were shot down and the formation split into two, with one group seriously damaging the Short Bros aircraft factory at Rochester and the other attacking the airfield at Eastchurch.

Meanwhile, two more raids were in progress over southern Britain with some sixty Ju 88s attacking Middle Wallop and Worthy Down at around 6 p.m. Portland was again bombed,

No. 17 Squadron began to re-equip with Hurricane Mk Is at North Weald in June 1939. The squadron operated from Debden and Martlesham Heath until May 1940, when it was posted to France, before returning to Debden on 19 June 1940, moving to Tangmere on 19 August and back to Debden on 2 September. These are the Hurricanes of 17 Squadron at Debden on 25 July 1940, with the pilot's parachute on the tailplane of the nearest aircraft. (*IWM photo*)

this time by forty Ju 87s escorted by twenty Bf 110s and sixty Bf 109s. These raiders were driven off by around fifty-six Hurricanes from 43, 87, 213, 249, and 601 Squadrons, as well as twenty-four Spitfires from 234 and 609 Squadrons.

The final raid of the day worth mentioning was on Croydon Aerodrome and conducted by fifteen Bf 110s and eight Bf 109s, catching 111 Squadron just as they were taking off. The Hurricanes of 32 Squadron based at Biggin Hill were quickly on the scene and attacked the enemy despite considerable damage and casualties around the airfield. The Bf 109s had to depart due to a lack of fuel, leaving the Bf 110s in a defensive circle allowing the Hurricanes to pick them off.

On this important day for German strategy, when around 70 per cent of Fighter Command pilots were in combat at least once and some units flew up to four combat sorties, Luftwaffe losses were sixty-four aircraft. Hurricane pilots claimed forty-one victories, Spitfires sixteen, and the remainder by the other defences. RAF losses in the air amounted to seventeen Hurricanes, with seven pilots killed, and two taken prisoner in France—plus eleven Spitfires destroyed. For the first time, the German high command had to admit that they had not destroyed Fighter Command and probably never would break the air defence of Great Britain. Adlertag was to prove a decisive failure in the battle.

Although serious damage had been inflicted on ports, airfields, and aircraft factories by enemy bombing, Fighter Command had been able to meet all the threats from one end of Britain to the other. The enemy's belief that all the fighter defences were only concentrated in the South East proved a costly mistake, with the loss of many experienced Luftwaffe aircrew that day. However, the enemy air attacks continued the following day with a further fifty Luftwaffe aircraft shot down—nineteen claimed by Hurricane pilots, twenty by Spitfires, and the remainder by the ground defences. The targets continued to concentrate on RAF airfields and RAF losses continued to rise, with eleven Hurricanes destroyed and four pilots killed, including the first American volunteer, who was with 601 Squadron. Ten Spitfires were destroyed with the loss of another four pilots.

One noteworthy engagement on 16 August involved three Boscombe Down-based Hurricanes of 249 Squadron led by Flt Lt James Nicolson, who approached an enemy raid building up over Gosport.

Just as they attacked some Bf 110s, they were bounced by Bf 109s from behind, and the Hurricanes were set on fire. While one pilot baled out, Nicholson pressed home his attack on a Bf 110 before baling out with extensive burns to his face and hands. Both pilots were fired upon by the ground forces while they descended under their parachutes, killing the other pilot, but Nicolson survived despite being shot as he landed. After a long stay in hospital to recover from his injuries, he was awarded the Victoria Cross, the only Fighter Command VC, but sadly he was to be killed later in the war in Asia.

While a F/Lt with 249 Squadron, Wing Commander Eric J. B. Nicholson gained the only Fighter Command VC following combat on 16 August 1940. No. 249 Squadron was equipped with Hurricane Mk Is at Leconfield in June 1940 and moved to Church Fenton on 8 July, followed by Boscombe Down on 14 August 1940, where F/Lt Nicholson was based when he earned his VC. The squadron moved to North Weald on 1 September 1940. (*Author's collection*)

John Grandy, Nicolson's CO, recommended him for a DFC, and during this period 249 Squadron moved from Boscombe Down to North Weald on 1 September 1940. The award was supported by Wing Commander Victor Beamish on 26 October, eleven weeks after Nicolson was shot down. Two days later, with the recommendation in front of him at 11 Group HQ, AVM Keith Park made an exceptional decision from among the award recommendations that came to him daily. He stated that Flt Lt Nicolson showed exceptional courage and disregard for the safety of his own life by continuing to engage the enemy after he had been wounded and his aircraft was burning. For this outstanding act of gallantry and magnificent display of fighting spirit, he recommended Nicolson for the immediate award of the Victoria Cross. Six days later, the recommendation was endorsed by Dowding, which was gazetted on 15 November 1940.

During the engagement, Nicolson's Hurricane was hit by three cannon shells—the first shell came through the canopy and sent splinters into his left eye that almost severed his eyelid and blinded him with blood. The second shell hit the gravity fuel tank, setting the aircraft on fire. The third shell tore off his right trouser leg. After shooting the enemy Bf 110 down into the sea, Nicolson was only successful with his third attempt to bale out. He pulled the rip-cord and pretended to be dead to avoid being shot at by other German aircraft. On reaching hospital, Nicolson was given twenty-four hours to live due to extensive third-degree burns and cannon wounds, but after three months convalescing he learned that he had been awarded the VC. He was reported to have commented, 'now I'll have to earn it'.

Following a relatively quiet day on 17 August, radar detected the approach of more major attacks the next day. The enemy objective was to make heavy attacks along the south coast to overwhelm the RAF defences. Like before, the airfields were the primary targets, with Biggin Hill and Kenley singled out for a major attack by a large force of He 111s, Ju 88s, and Do 17s supported by free-ranging Bf 109s. Ten Hurricanes were destroyed on the ground at Kenley, with five that managed to take off intercepted by Bf 109s. Despite standing patrols ordered to cover the airfields, both Croydon and West Malling were hit again—the latter was not yet operational—and remained out of action during the battle due to continued bombing.

A formation approaching the Isle of Wight was tasked with the destruction of Poling radar and the airfields at Thorney Island, Gosport, and Ford. Hurricanes of 43 and 601 Squadrons were in a good position to cover the attack on the radar station, destroying five Stukas while Spitfires of 234 Squadron attacked the Bf 109s, although the radar was put out of action for a week. A further thirteen Ju 87s were shot down by Spitfires of 152 and 602 Squadrons, with total enemy losses that day reaching sixty-six aircraft, of which Hurricane pilots claimed thirty-two, Spitfires twenty-nine, and other defences the remainder.

Including those on the ground, Fighter Command lost thirty-six Hurricanes with eight pilots killed, as well as six Spitfires with one pilot lost. Fortunately, Hurricane stocks were available to replace the lost aircraft and seven of the damaged aircraft were repaired and returned to service. However, the main problem was the loss of pilots, who were becoming harder to replace.

The losses to the Luftwaffe were causing even greater concern. The Ju 87 Stuka was proving to be too vulnerable, with nearly 25 per cent destroyed and 136 aircrew killed—a rate of attrition that would mean the Stuka force would cease to exist by mid-September. As a result, they were withdrawn from any operations where fighter defences were likely to be encountered. The slow-flying Bf 110s were also suffering unacceptably high losses, with eighty-six having been shot down in a period of ten days with the loss of many experienced aircrews. Therefore, the role was changed from vulnerable escort to fighter bomber, leaving the Bf 109s to operate on free-ranging sorties.

Despite the ferocious battles from 8 to 18 August and exaggerated claims for RAF losses, the Luftwaffe was unable to detect any weakening in the Fighter Command defences. The destroyed aircraft were continually replaced by factories working around the clock. More volunteers came from the FAA and surviving Fairey Battle pilots were retrained to operate Hurricanes. Dowding hoped that if losses did not exceed the average rate for July until the middle of August then it would just be possible to hold the Luftwaffe back until the poorer autumn weather set in.

Sunday 18 August was a typically warm, sunny summer's day with little cloud over Britain. At 12.45 p.m., as the Operations Room staff at Kenley was changing over, a high degree of German activity was detected by radar. With the threat growing rapidly, the Kenley-based Hurricane 615 Squadron was scrambled along with Spitfires of 64 Squadron.

Soon after 1 p.m., a force of nearly sixty enemy aircraft crossed the south coast in two waves split between medium and high altitude. While the Observer Corps tracked these formations, a force of nine Do 17s crossed the coast near Beachy Head below radar coverage,

The pilots of 615 Squadron receive a briefing at Northolt before the next operation. (*J. G. Millard photo*)

flying at around 50 feet above the ground and heading towards their target of Kenley. On reaching the North Downs, the aircraft climbed up the steep slope passing over Caterham. Meanwhile, a dozen 111 Squadron pilots were strapped in their Hurricanes waiting to be scrambled by the Kenley controllers. When it became clear that Kenley was the target, six Hurricanes were scrambled, soon followed by the rest of the squadron.

The initial instructions were to climb to 20,000 feet, but when it was realised how low the enemy was, they were progressively brought down to intercept at 50 feet. The Do 17s separated into three groups of three aircraft as the first contact was made by 111 Squadron, who broke away as the airfield defences were approached. When the Dorniers approached the airfield, they fired their guns and, as the leading aircraft came over the airfield boundary, a Hurricane was taking off towards them. Avoiding a collision, the pilot pulled round in a tight right turn. The hangars, station buildings, runways and dispersals were all targeted with bombs and gun fire. Three of the four Warren Truss girder hangars were destroyed, and bombs fell on the hospital block and around an adjacent shelter where the medical staff had taken cover. The pilots of the three leading Do 17s were approaching the northern boundary when they were confronted by a line of rockets trailing steel cables; one of the aircraft was caught but managed to break free. Another damaged Do 17 hit another cable and was brought down, hitting a tree and cottage, while the Hurricanes pursued the remaining escaping Dorniers.

The burning hangars were used as target markers for a formation of high-altitude Do 17s, while others continued on to bomb Croydon. One Do 17 was shot down near Biggin Hill by a 111 Squadron Hurricane pilot, and two more fell into the Channel with engine failure. No. 111 Squadron lost three Hurricanes with one pilot killed and another badly injured. No. 615 Squadron had some success with the high-flying raiders, with claims for a He 111, Ju 88, and a Bf 109 for the loss of two Hurricanes and two damaged with one pilot killed. In addition to the wrecked hangars, the station HQ and hospital were ruined, while some barracks and the Sergeant's Mess were damaged.

Considering that over 100 bombs were dropped on Kenley airfield and the surrounding area, casualties were not that substantial. One officer and eight RAF personnel were killed, with eight others, including a WAAF, injured. One soldier was killed and two others injured. Ten aircraft, including six Hurricanes from 615 Squadron, had been destroyed, and six more, including two Hurricanes and a Spitfire, were damaged. Of the nine Dorniers from the special low-level unit, four failed to return to France and two more crash-landed.

Kenley was fully operational the next day, with the runways repaired and communications restored. The operations room was later moved off-base to a disused butcher's shop in Kenley.

With a period of bad weather between 19 and 23 August, air combat was reduced sufficiently for redeployment of some RAF squadrons. Meanwhile, the Luftwaffe was taking the opportunity to reorganise and replace lost aircrew, with the operational priority still being the destruction of RAF airfields and fighter production. Bf 109s were released from close support and allocated into large formations with the object of destroying Fighter Command in the air and on the ground. This was the move most feared by Dowding and his Group and Sector commanders.

The new pattern of Luftwaffe attacks commenced on 24 August with the key Spitfire station of Hornchurch one of the main targets. The front-line airfield at Manston was attacked by twenty Ju 88s and the overall losses of Defiants were so great that they were withdrawn from day fighting. Manston was badly damaged, with seven men killed, the bombs hitting many buildings and the landing area, destroying a number of aircraft. As a result of this raid, non-essential personnel were evacuated. When Winston Churchill visited the station on 28 August, it was barely operational—it was still marked with craters and unexploded bombs.

North Weald was another target, but the Hurricanes of 151 Squadron were able to scramble in time to claim four He 111s. The enemy lost eighteen aircraft during the day, with ten Hurricanes shot down and two pilots lost. Spitfires went after the Bf 109s and claimed four for the loss of six aircraft, but no pilots were killed.

The next day, Fighter Command did not take the bait of large formations of free-ranging Bf 109s, choosing to keep the squadrons grounded in readiness for the later bombing attacks—the major target of which was Warmwell. During the day, a further fourteen enemy aircraft were destroyed by Hurricanes for the loss of eight aircraft and five pilots, while Spitfires accounted for seven enemy aircraft. No. 32 Squadron had been so reduced in strength that it was withdrawn north for a rest and re-equipment. With ten pilots killed, nine wounded, and one taken prisoner in just two days, Fighter Command had lost the equivalent of two squadrons.

On 26 August, while Fighter Command losses continued to rise the damage to ground installations was reduced. A total of fifteen Hurricanes were shot down for the loss of one pilot, as well as nine Spitfires destroyed with three pilots lost and nine pilots wounded. German losses amounted to thirty-four aircraft with the loss of all the crews either killed or taken prisoner.

There had also been conflict between Park in 11 Group and his neighbour to the north, Leigh-Mallory, who headed 12 Group and whose main sector station was Duxford, with Fowlmere close by. Whenever Park's airfields north of London were being attacked, he called on 12 Group to provide protection. However, Leigh-Mallory, supported by Douglas Bader, believed that the best method of attack was in large numbers of aircraft in the form of a wing. It took so long for the wing to get airborne and form up that generally by the time they arrived over the airfields the enemy had long departed for home, leaving airfields heavily damaged. It was difficult to co-ordinate a wing as it was made up from a mix of Hurricane and Spitfire squadrons, and their endurance was reduced due to the time taken to form up. Although the Duxford Wing made high claims of enemy aircraft destroyed, this was not supported by evidence of wreckage on the ground. Leigh-Mallory preferred to destroy the Luftwaffe raiders after the bombs had been dropped, which somewhat defeated the concept of protecting RAF airfields.

With more bad weather on 27 August, operations were quiet. On the following day, an attack was detected approaching the Thames Estuary, splitting into two with Eastchurch and Rochford as planned targets. Assuming that Kent-based fighters would go after the departing bombers, a number of free-ranging Bf 109s flew in over Kent with many dogfights breaking out. A total of twenty-eight enemy aircraft were shot down, fifteen of which were Bf 109s.

Hurricanes of 32 Squadron return from combat on 15 August 1940, with ground crews indicating safe passages for landing around unexploded bombs. (*Author's collection*)

Hurricane Mk I V7203 T:242 Squadron at Cranwell in late 1940 was flown by Douglas Bader. The squadron began to equip with Hurricanes at Church Fenton in February 1940 and moved to Biggin Hill on 21 May, before going to France on 8 June for ten days. The squadron then went to Coltishall and moved to Duxford on 16 October 1940. (*Peter Green collection*)

Six Hurricanes were shot down, with one pilot killed, and seven Spitfires were destroyed with the loss of four pilots.

Heavy fighting continued on 29 August with fighter versus fighter combat resulting in nine Bf 109s being destroyed for the loss of six Hurricanes and three Spitfires. To try and reduce these wasteful losses, Fighter Command attempted to avoid engaging the enemy fighters, and concentrate instead on the bombers. Hurricanes of 1, 56, and 242 Squadrons intercepted a raid by He 111s north of London after the escorts had turned for home due to lack of fuel. A section of four Hurricanes, led by Sqn Ldr Tom Gleave, was vectored towards what was believed to be a large bomber formation, but on emerging through the cloud it turned out to be an enemy formation of about ninety Bf 109s. Gleave managed to shoot down at least three Bf 109s, but his three colleagues were shot down, two of whom were killed. At the end of the day, the RAF claimed sixteen bombers, of which twelve were shot down by Hurricanes, and six Bf 110s and sixteen Bf 109s all claimed by Hurricane pilots. Allied losses included nine Hurricanes destroyed with six pilots killed.

The vital sector station of Biggin Hill was first attacked on 18 August, but sustained little damage. However, a second raid was more damaging. The defending fighters, which included Hurricanes from 32 Squadron, were outnumbered by five to one, but claimed three enemy aircraft for the loss of six Hurricanes with one pilot killed. This resulted in the squadron being moved for rest to Acklington after nine years at Biggin Hill.

No. 87 Squadron received Hurricane Mk Is at Debden in July 1938 just before 85 Squadron. No. 87 Squadron moved to France on 4 September 1939 and returned to Debden on 22 May 1940. A move was then made to Church Fenton in 12 Group on 24 May, and then to Exeter in 10 Group on 5 July, with detachments to Hullavington and Bibury. (*Peter Green collection*)

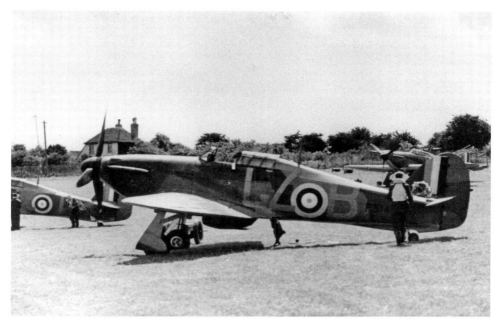

Hurricane Mk I P3144 LZ-B:32 Squadron at readiness during the Battle of Britain at the 11 Group airfield of Hawkinge on 31 July 1940. (*P. H. T. Green collection*)

No. 32 Squadron was at that time the highest scoring squadron in Fighter Command with 102 enemy aircraft claimed destroyed for the loss of three pilots killed and one taken POW.

Over the next two weeks, German bombers continued to reduce the station to rubble, and all personnel remained busy keeping the airfield operational. Then, on Friday 30 August, there was a major raid that almost knocked it out altogether. The first raid, at around midday, cratered the landing area and damaged surrounding residential properties. Then, at 6 p.m., nine Ju 88s attacked at low level from the south. The attack, which lasted for thirty minutes, destroyed most of the remaining buildings and many others were deemed unsafe. A total of sixteen 1,000-lb HE bombs were dropped—six scoring direct hits within the technical site, and all utilities including phones were cut. Tragically, a WAAF shelter was hit directly, killing many of the women inside. Total casualties on the ground were thirty-nine killed and twenty-six wounded.

There was no time to make repairs as the station was hit again the next day both at 1 p.m. and 5.30 p.m. The hangars were further damaged and the operations block received a direct hit that collapsed its concrete roof onto the operations table. On 1 September, more bombs were dropped from high altitude and few buildings were still standing. The operations room was moved to a temporary dispersed site and later relocated to a more permanent location until the end of the war. The airfield was only capable of operating a single squadron with the most basic facilities and most of the aircraft were dispersed. Biggin Hill shared with Hornchurch the dubious honour of being the most bombed airfield in Fighter Command.

German pressure continued to build. Fighter Command suffered a bad week beginning with 31 August, on which Hurricane squadrons suffered twenty-four losses—the equivalent of two operational squadrons. Reinforcements were rushed from the north of Britain from squadrons that had been rebuilding and training in order to help defend against attacks on sector airfields such as Biggin Hill, which was put out of action twice, as well as the Vickers factory at Brooklands where there were many casualties. Detling was hit again, and the weapons store was hit at Eastchurch, resulting in the demolition of many surrounding buildings. During this dreadful week, 107 Hurricanes were shot down in addition to seventy-one Spitfires and the total loss of fifty-five pilots and seventy-eight seriously wounded. This loss rate was equivalent to the loss of one squadron of pilots and two squadrons of aircraft per day. In the face of this onslaught, fatigue was affecting the experienced pilots and many of the replacement pilots lacked capability due to inadequate experience.

John Ellacombe was one of the RAF pilots shot down on 31 August when flying his third sortie of the day. He was attacking a Ju 88 when the rear gunner fired and hit the gravity fuel tank with a tracer, which immediately burst into flame. Immediately, Ellacombe pulled the canopy back, undid the straps and baled out, falling well clear of the enemy fighters before pulling the parachute rip-cord. He landed in Essex with burns and no trousers. However, on the final part of the descent, a Home Guard soldier fired two shots that fortunately missed Ellacombe, who shouted: 'Don't shoot, I am British!' The soldier came up and was very apologetic, taking John to a farmhouse from which he was taken to Southend General Hospital, where he recovered.

While Flt Lt James Nicholson was recovering from his wounds received on 16 August, 249 Squadron moved from Boscombe Down to North Weald to relieve the battle-weary 56 Squadron on Sunday 1 September. The pilots of 249 Squadron took over the Hurricanes of 56 Squadron, which were fitted with VHF radios, and 56 Squadron pilots took the 249 Squadron aircraft back to Boscombe Down. The commanding officer was Sqn Ldr John Grandy, who later became Marshal of the Royal Air Force Sir John Grandy. Having settled into their quarters at North Weald, the pilots were on standby to scramble the next morning. There were four operations during the day, which saw a number of Do 215s and Me 110s claimed for the loss of two Hurricanes, but the pilots were safe.

There was a major bombing raid on North Weald on 3 September. The squadron was scrambled at 9.45 a.m. and landed an hour later for an immediate refuel, which was achieved in ten minutes. Very soon after take-off, the alarm went and a broadcast over the loudspeaker called for everyone to take cover. One of the pilots remaining on the ground was George Barclay, who stood at the entrance of the air-raid shelter, watching the AA fire. Almost immediately, a formation of approximately twenty-five German bombers flew directly overhead at 17,000 feet, at which point George went into the shelter as they unleashed their payload. Some 250 bombs were dropped; the noise was unbearable and it seemed certain that at least one would hit the shelter. After the terrifying ordeal, George emerged from the shelter to an aerodrome enveloped in a vast cloud of smoke and dust, with the hangars on fire and the sound of ammunition exploding. Despite the whole site being covered with bits of anti-personnel bombs, casualties were light and only three killed. Although the squadron was in the air they were too late to engage the enemy, and once the fires were put out damage was fairly light—the mess was untouched, and half the aerodrome unserviceable, with some delayed action bombs scattered about.

A major change came from the Luftwaffe on 7 September when Göring ordered a raid of about 1,000 aircraft against London instead of airfields. His intention was to attract all the remaining RAF fighters into the air where he hoped they would be destroyed. The formations were split between the north Kent coast and along the south coast, and within fourteen minutes of the raid being detected, all Fighter Command squadrons within a 70-mile radius of London were airborne and ready to intercept. A total of twenty-one squadrons, including Hurricanes of 43, 46, 73, 79, 111, 242, 249, 253, 257, 303, 310, 504, 605, and 607 Squadrons, were airborne and expecting to protect airfields. They had to be diverted rapidly against the first bombing raid when it was realised that London was the target. By this time, the first bombs had fallen on London Docks and the bombers were chased by the Duxford Wing as they headed for home.

Meanwhile, 11 Group fighters were heading for the enemy formations approaching from the south, resulting in one of the biggest air battles of the war involving approximately 1,250 aircraft and lasting just thirty minutes. The Duxford Wing—with 43, 240, and 310, Squadrons—was in the process of forming up when it was attacked by a mass of Bf 109s, losing fifteen Hurricanes in twenty minutes.

With London Docks burning fiercely, the final toll in the air for the RAF during the day was twenty-nine Hurricanes and fourteen Spitfires with the loss of seventeen pilots, including two squadron commanders and three flight commanders. German losses amounted to fifty-two aircraft, including twenty-six fighters.

This change of strategy by the Luftwaffe to bomb London, later often at night, gave Fighter Command the respite it so desperately needed to replace the depleted squadrons in the front line with rested units from in the north. Had the attacks on the airfields continued at the

Hurricane Mk I P2874 AF-F:607 Squadron at readiness with the ground crew during 1940. (*P. H. T. Green collection*)

previous rate, Fighter Command would have had to face the option of withdrawing to airfields beyond the range of the Luftwaffe escorting fighters, which would leave the south-east of England virtually undefended. The rate of RAF pilot losses was becoming unsustainable at the prevailing rate with the loss of the equivalent eleven squadrons in the first two months of the Battle, which was greater than the number of new squadrons brought into action since the beginning. Many experienced pilots had been killed or injured and new pilots had to learn the rules of combat if they were to survive. Luftwaffe losses had also been high, but they had more trained pilots to start with, and could more readily withstand a war of attrition.

With the start of the Blitz, particularly at night, Britain was largely undefended. Some of the more experienced squadrons, including 87 Squadron, were tasked with attempting to defend Bristol and Cardiff from their Exeter base. The sorties were a complete waste of time as it was impossible to find the enemy by visual contact in the dark. Ground control was more effective, but even when hitting the enemy slipstream the pilots could see nothing, despite the risk of amid-air collision. The situation did not improve until night fighters with AI radar were available.

Flying Hurricanes at night was hazardous. A complete, country-wide blackout gave no sense of horizon and no guiding lights for the take-off; many of the experienced pilots were killed. Once airborne the pilots had to rely on very basic instruments, and directions to their patrol line were indicated by tiny glim lamps set out at a predetermined location, setting a new heading for a certain number of minutes to reach the patrol area. After patrolling for around thirty minutes, pilots had to find their way back to base.

However, the German leadership believed that Fighter Command was all but destroyed and on 15 September, the Hardest Day, now known as Battle of Britain Day, the Germans launched another massive attack on London. Fighter Command had been able during the previous week to restore its strength and was able to win a resounding victory. For the loss of twenty Hurricanes, including seven pilots killed, and seven Spitfires destroyed with three pilots lost, the Luftwaffe lost thirty-six bombers and twenty-three fighters with 163 aircrew killed or taken prisoner. The RAF was obviously still a potent fighting force, and therefore Hitler abandoned any idea of invading Britain until at least the following spring. Naturally, Hitler did not inform Britain of his decision, so the country was still on full alert, but the attacks were confined mainly against British cities at night, which although less accurate were more difficult for the fighters to detect without effective Airborne Interception (AI) radar.

The defending RAF air and ground crews had been lead to believe that the Germans were going to invade on 15 September, but because of secret Ultra interceptions the Government knew it was not going to happen. The RAF continued to fight strongly against the Luftwaffe into November, still thinking the invasion was possible. If such a situation had been made public, it would have compromised Britain's knowledge of the German codes, which had been breached at the top secret Bletchley Park establishment.

Dowding realised that the Luftwaffe no longer had the capability of launching major raids by day, although some were attempted. On 27 September, some 120 Hurricanes and Spitfires intercepted a raid over Surrey and Sussex and another large raid on the Bristol Aircraft factory at Filton was intercepted by five of the 10 Group squadrons. German losses amounted to fifty-four

Hurricane YB-S:17 Squadron shows battle damage to the inboard section of the starboard wing and also has the metal plate on top of the nose to reduce exhaust glow for the pilot during night operations. (*RAF Museum photo*)

aircraft with ten Hurricanes destroyed and another five RAF pilots killed, with eighteen Spitfires lost with ten pilots killed. The next day the Luftwaffe shot down eleven Hurricanes and five Spitfires for the loss of only ten enemy aircraft. Luftwaffe day-bomber attacks decreased further during October, apart from some isolated high flying Bf 109 nuisance raids dropping 550-lb bombs at random over London which were generally too high to intercept in time. The only raid by the Italian Air Force based at the time in Belgium was on Harwich and was intercepted by the Hurricanes of 17, 46 and 257 Squadrons. The inexperienced Italians in their biplane fighters were easily outperformed and lost ten aircraft with no losses to Fighter Command.

No. 249 Squadron, still operating from North Weald, were in action on the Hardest Day. Their first scramble was at 11.30 a.m., with a climb through cloud to 16,000 feet. George Barclay preferred to fly with the canopy open as it gave a better view. Cruising above the clouds, about eighteen enemy bombers were sighted, which they set out to engage. Barclay followed three Hurricanes for a head-on attack, but decided to go for a beam attack on the leader and nearly collided with the lead Hurricane. He broke away to avoid a collision, diving down through the formation. The attack was fairly successful, with Barclay opening fire on full deflection and letting the Do 215 fly into the bullets. The escorting Bf 109s were kept busy by Spitfires above, so Barclay made a quarter-attack that resulted in the bomber breaking away from the formation with the engines idling as it glided down. It was then intercepted by eight Hurricanes at around 3,000 feet below Barclay, and on landing he claimed a probable destroyed.

Barclay continued by climbing for a further attack, but by then the bombers were too far away so he dived down through the clouds to return to base from over the lower Thames. He noticed how painfully cold his hands were because they were pushed right into the gloves—it was much better if the gloves were only worn loosely.

The squadron was scrambled again at 2 p.m., joining 46 Squadron beneath the cloud. Enemy fighters were sighted above the squadron's position soon after reaching 16,000 feet, which usually meant the approach of bombers. The controller gave the call sign 'Ganer Leader' to look to the right, and spotted about twenty Do 215s at the same height as the Hurricanes.

The squadron went into a beam attack, with some pilots going after some Heinkel 111s in the second wave, which were behind the Dorniers, with a third wave further behind. After Barclay's attack, a Do 215 dropped behind the formation and a parachute emerged from underneath, but he was too busy to watch for what happened so claimed it as damaged. The Dorniers then jettisoned their bombs and broke up, some diving for cloud cover whereas others stayed just above the clouds. George dived after one Dornier, giving it a four-second burst of fire that resulting in a flash of bright flame as the enemy aircraft went into the clouds, later claimed as probably destroyed. The next Dornier, skimming across the cloud tops, was shot at down to a range of about 30 yards. With Barclay running out of ammunition, he followed the enemy aircraft through the clouds when the Dornier gently nosed over at 7,000 feet and plummeted vertically into the ground close to a bungalow.

All the 249 Squadron aircraft returned safely with ten confirmed victories, the same number of probable victories, and more damaged. It was the most successful day since the squadron had formed in May.

On 27 September, Pilot Officer George Barclay successfully destroyed a Bf 109, and his combat report covered the action. He was flying as Red 1 when he saw some Bf 109s about 400 feet on his port side—there was no definite attack in squadron formation. He chased a Bf 109 that dived very steeply. He had to use boost throttle to catch up with the 109. He lost the enemy aircraft in haze and its camouflage against the ground, but it suddenly climbed vertically out of the haze. He closed to about 150 yards and fired four bursts almost vertically at the 109 before going down almost vertically, firing two more bursts from the beam at the e/a. The damaged e/a poured glycol coolant, the cockpit roof flew off and the pilot baled-out successfully as his aircraft crashed in a farm south-west of Ashford. The victory was confirmed by another pilot who had been following Barclay.

As a result of his combat successes during the Battle of Britain, Barclay was recommended for the Distinguished Flying Cross (DFC) by his station commander, Wing Commander Victor Beamish, on 8 November 1940. The recommendation was approved by the AOC No. 11 Group Air Vice-Marshal Keith Park, and by Air Chief Marshal Sir Hugh Dowding, Commander-in-Chief RAF Fighter Command. George had been credited with four-and-a-half confirmed destroyed enemy aircraft and probably six others.

Victor Beamish was an ex-Cranwell cadet and pre-war Rugby International player. He did not lead from behind a desk but participated in flying on almost every operation as a freelance. From being station commander at North Weald, he was appointed commander of the Kenley Wing as Group Captain on 25 January 1942. He was awarded the DSO on 23

Some of the pilots and ground crews of 615 Squadron. (with their mascot) gather around a Hurricane Mk I at Northolt in October 1940. (*J. G. Millard photo*)

September 1940, the DFC on 22 October, and a bar to his DSO on 2 September 1941. He lost his life leading Kenley's Wing when he was shot down on 28 March 1942. He had flown seventy-one combat operations, with three confirmed victories and three probables. He was also awarded the AFC, and a road in a development on the Kenley Aerodrome technical site is named Victor Beamish Avenue in his memory.

On the last day of September, the Luftwaffe mounted another serious raid of 200 aircraft in the morning, which only reached Maidstone before being turned back by eight squadrons in 11 Group. To the west, a further 100 German aircraft were repulsed.

In the afternoon, two raids totally 200 aircraft were involved in combat over Kent. The day ended with the highest daily Luftwaffe fighter losses of the entire Battle of Britain, which consisted of forty-three aircraft against RAF losses of nineteen aircraft.

Defeat of the Germans in the Battle of Britain did not destroy the Luftwaffe, but it did halt the German invasion. Hitler turned his attentions to Operation Barbarossa—the opening of a second front against his former allies in Russia. This was probably the most disastrous German miscalculation of the Second World War, but Britain was left attempting to intercept the enemy night-bomber raids with black-painted Hurricanes and Defiants, groping around in the dark in the hope of spotting an enemy aircraft caught long enough in the glare of searchlights.

Almost half the RAF pilots who had been in the service before the war had lost their lives in the Battles of France and Britain, in addition to many other overseas volunteers, reservists, and raw recruits. The top-scoring Allied pilot was a Czech, Sergeant Josef Frantisek of 303 Squadron, with claims for seventeen enemy aircraft during the Battle of Britain, but sadly he was killed in combat on 8 October 1940.

At the end of the battle on 31 October 1940, a total of 278 Fighter Command pilots had been killed, with 256 wounded, 305 missing in action, and forty-seven taken prisoner. In the following offensive actions from 1941 by Fighter Command over occupied Europe where the fighters were over enemy territory, the pilot losses were even greater.

After the battle, Hurricanes continued to operate from Britain, but were adapted from air defence to ground attack. No. 175 Squadron based at Warmwell was equipped with Hurricane Mk IIBs from 3 March 1942 until April 1943 that were armed with the more destructive 20-mm cannons. Soon after being declared operational, the squadron was tasked with a firepower demonstration against stationary army vehicles and dummy soldiers on Salisbury Plain near the deserted village of Imber. Invited to the demonstration was an audience of military personnel. The weather on 13 April 1942 was dry and sunny, but with a haze reducing the visibility for the pilots. Six Hurricanes of 175 Squadron made low-level approaches to the targets with two achieving good results, but tragically the sixth Hurricane mistook the grandstand where the visitors were gathered and opened fire, killing twenty-five Army personnel, including Brigadier Grant Taylor, the most senior officer to lose his life. A total of seventy-one others were injured to varying degrees, but this unfortunate incident did not prevent the Hurricanes from adopting new roles with great effect in other theatres of the Second World War.

The commanding officer, Squadron Leader Peter Townsend, in the centre with stick after being injured, with the pilots of 85 Squadron at Church Fenton in October 1940. (*IWM photo*)

7

Sea Hurricanes and Naval Operations

With the Battle of Britain over, the next major challenge was the Battle of the Atlantic. Britain being an Island country and not self-sufficient for food and raw materials, required a regular supply of materials by sea, as is still the case today. Hitler therefore ordered increased air and U-boat attacks on Allied shipping in an effort to starve Britain into submission. It was therefore necessary to devise an effective protection for North Atlantic convoys bringing vital supplies to Britain. Before the German invasion of Norway in April 1940, the established trade routes were threatened by a few U-boats and surface raiders, with any air attacks confined to the Channel and along the east coast of England, allowing Atlantic convoys to approach around the north or south of Ireland into the Irish Sea. With the fall of France in June 1940, Germany controlled the entire European coastline from the Arctic Circle to the Pyrenees.

Although the Germans had not produced any long-range strategic heavy bombers, the Fw 200 Condor airliner was adapted for maritime patrol and attack, much like the later RAF Nimrods, but the basic airframe was not very robust. One of the Condor bases was at Bordeaux, and in the first two and a half months of operations from August 1940, these converted airliners sank nearly 90,000 tons of Allied shipping, alongside losses due to U-boats. Condors were able to operate at 1,000 miles out over the Atlantic, which was far beyond the range of Britain's shore-based fighters. Normal patrols were flown at 2,000 feet at 190 mph seeking out easy targets such as lone ships or stragglers from convoys. The small number of RN aircraft carriers available were busy with combat duties, with none available for the mundane but vital task of convoy protection.

Once the Condor had been selected for long-range maritime patrols, ten military versions were ordered, six of which were fitted with defensive armament and bomb racks. The Condors entered service with I/KG 40 on 1 October 1939 flying armed reconnaissance sorties to cover the invasion of Norway. An improved version of the Condor was then produced with a forward-firing 20-mm cannon fitted in the forward section of a ventral gondola, complemented by a rearward-firing 7.9-mm machine gun in the rear of the gondola. Further armament included forward- and rear-mounted 7.9-mm machine guns in the nose and tail. These guns were for air-to-surface attacks and not air-to-air defence. The weapons load consisted of six 250-kg (551-lb) bombs or two underwing mounted aerial mines. Even though Condors were not fitted with a bomb sight, by attacking ships from abeam at low level they could hardly miss. Despite their success against surface shipping, production was not increased significantly, and the ones in operation suffered from serviceability problems including structural failures while manoeuvring violently due to their poor structural strength.

Air Commodore Donald Stevenson, the Director of Fighter Operations at the Air Ministry, was concerned that not enough was being done by the Admiralty to protect Britain's life-line convoys on the Western Approaches. The Condor was a major threat, although it was vulnerable to air attack, it was not a robust military design and had only been produced in small numbers. Stevenson persuaded Air Chief Marshal Sir Charles Portal, the recently appointed Chief of the Air Staff, to call a conference on 12 November 1940 to discuss fighter protection of the Allied convoys. Included in the invitation list were Admiral of the Fleet Sir Dudley Pound; the First Sea Lord Admiral Tom Phillips, with the Chief of the Naval Air Services and the commanders-in-chief of RAF Fighter and Coastal Commands. Out of this conference came two immediate actions: RAF bombing raids would be made on the Condor base at Bordeaux and manufacturing facilities at Bremen, and the merchant ships would have improved anti-aircraft defences.

What was required were high-performance fighters capable of intercepting the Condors at their extreme range, and although aircraft carriers were a logical answer, the losses of the Courageous and the Glorious in the early part of the war and the demands of the Mediterranean theatre resulted in none being available for convoy escort duties. During discussions, it was suggested that selected merchant ships should be fitted with radar to detect the raiders and some should be fitted with a catapult to launch two or three fighters against an attack. These fighters would be expendable if land was beyond the range of the aircraft, and the pilot would have to abandon and hope to be picked up by one of the ships he was protecting.

With Condors continuing to sink Allied shipping in the Atlantic, it was suggested that the convoys be routed from the north-west around Northern Ireland where the Condors would be at the limit of their range from their bases in Norway and France. The convoys would then be timed to pass through the danger zone under the cover of darkness and within the protection of land-based fighters after dawn. This proved impracticable, resulting in a new interest being taken in catapult-launched fighters.

A suitable platform for launching the fighters had to be found. Their ample deck space made the tankers the most obvious choice, but they did not have the forward speed of at least 10–12 knots to allow for a successful launch, depending upon the headwind.

While causing considerable damage, the bombing of the main Condor base at Bordeaux had little effect on the fortunes of convoys. As a short notice stop-gap, the catapult-training ship HMS Pegasus sailed on 9 December carrying two Fulmars, but they had inadequate speed to be effective. With pressure from Churchill to come up with an answer to the air defence of

Sea Hurricane Mk IA Z4852, powered by a Merlin III engine and configured for CAM ship operations with catapult spools but no arrester hook. (*Peter Green collection*)

convoys, the decision was taken in principle on 30 December 1940 to convert a number of merchant ships. These were known as Catapult Aircraft Merchant Ships, or CAM ships, which would be an integral part of the convoy when in the danger zone and would carry cargo. While the CAM ships were being adapted, four auxiliary naval vessels—the Ariguani, the Maplin, the Patia, and the Springbank—were fitted with catapults and known as Fighter Catapult Ships (FCS), each carrying two expendable fighters, with one ready to go on the catapult and the other held in reserve. These ships would only be used within the danger zone and would not carry any cargo. They would escort outgoing convoys to the western limit and then pick up the incoming convoys, taking an average of seventeen days on dedicated convoy defence.

After considering a number of aircraft types, the Hurricane was selected as it was the most robust and, with the aftermath of the Battle of Britain, there were supplies available from Fighter Command, which had taken delivery of more Spitfires. Three pilots were usually allocated to each ship, and after launch and hopefully interception of the raider, they would either have to fly to the nearest land if they were close enough or abandon the aircraft close to a ship in the hope of being picked up before succumbing to exposure. The ideal launch method was established as a simple catapult propelled by banks of 3-inch rockets.

On 6 March 1941, Churchill proclaimed that the Battle of the Atlantic had begun with defensive action taken against both U-boats and Condors. The CAM ships were afforded the most urgent priority. Within three months, four FCSs and the first CAM ship, the Michael E, were ready for operations. The original plan was for some 200 CAM ships, but the logistical problems, such as the number of pilots, aircraft, and Merlin engines from both sides of the Atlantic, were insurmountable with all the other priorities to consider.

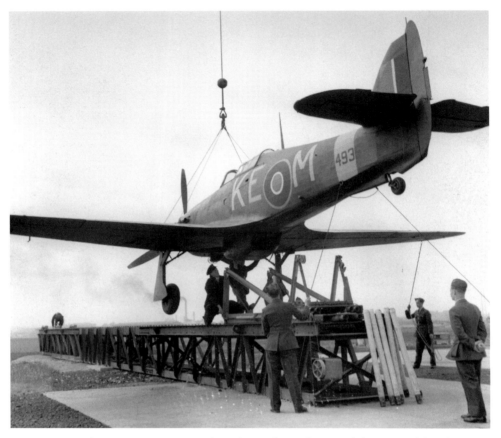

Sea Hurricane Mk IA Z4936 KE-M:MSFU being lowered onto the catapult for a ground-based training launch. The rockets have yet to be fitted to the carrier. (*IWM photo*)

The effectiveness of the concept was still to be proven, so the total number to be produced initially was reduced to thirty-five, with any expansion to await successful results. The FCSs were to be used on the Britain–Gibraltar route, with the CAM ships initially allocated between Britain and the eastern seaboard of North America. This ensured the quickest delivery of Canadian-built Hurricanes and enabled the CAM ships to provide protection for as long as possible.

CAM ships required at least 85 feet of clearance from the bow to the foremast to accommodate the catapult. The ships generally selected were large freighters in excess of 9,000 tons with the freight capacity fully utilised. Even with maximum utilisation of the CAM ships, the pilots and crews were unlikely to spend more than thirty days annually on convoy duties, allowing time for loading, repairs, maintenance, training, and leave. With catapult trials having been completed on land, sixty Merlin III-powered Hurricane Mk Is had been allocated to convoy protection by the end of March. The fitting of catapults to ships had started, and the modified Hurricanes, which did not need arrester hooks as they would not be landing

Sea Hurricane Mk IA V6756 of MSFU being loaded aboard CAM ship *Empire Tide* with the pilot in the cockpit ready to retract the undercarriage. The second Hurricat is waiting its turn on a lighter. The wartime censor has removed the ships in the background. (*HSA photo*)

back on deck, became known as Hurricats. The major changes were the local reinforcement of the airframe and the fitting of catapult spools. A new organisation was formed at Speke, Liverpool, known as No. 9 Group Fighter Command to control the operations of the new Merchant Ship Fighter Unit (MSFU), which consisted of thirty-five ship detachments.

The provision of air defence for the convoys was very much a combined services operation. The RN was responsible for the operation of the FCS and the RAF was responsible for CAM ship duties. On the CAM ships, the maintenance was undertaken by RAF sea crew consisting of a fitter, rigger, armourer, and radio-telephone operator in addition to the pilots. The RN provided the fighter direction officers (FDOs) to guide the pilot to the target and assist with the recovery, together with radar operators and torpedo men to service the catapult. The Army were responsible for manning the anti-aircraft guns on board, all the service men being volunteers.

Finally, the crews of the CAM ships were civilian merchant seamen. The RAF pilots were in command of the service team, but the captain was in charge of the ship. This could sometimes cause difficulties with overall responsibilities. The pilots had to be experienced and capable of operating aggressively after long periods of inactivity. In addition, they had to be good sailors to withstand the rigors of the North Atlantic at its worst. However, the FAA pilots for the FCS were not volunteers, and a number were posted to the specially formed 804 Naval Air Squadron (NAS) together with their FDOs and support team based at Sydenham, Belfast.

Sea Hurricane Mk IA V6756 L:MSFU being prepared for launch, although the undercarriage is still to be retracted. (*Peter Green collection*)

MSFU Sea Hurricane ready for launch from catapult of CAM ship with undercarriage retracted. (*Author's collection*)

The Hurricats were launched at close to 3.5 g, creating a deafening noise and flame and a recoil that required the ship's crew and structure to be protected during launch. The pilot forced his head back against the padded headrest with his right elbow wedged into the hip to avoid involuntary pull-back as the aircraft accelerated forward. Owing to the rotation of the propeller, the Hurricat had a tendency to swing to port on take-off, and it was longitudinally unstable at the slow launch speed. The aircraft was prepared for take-off with one-third starboard rudder, one-third flaps, and both the elevator and trim tabs neutral. The heavy aircraft tended to drop after launch in a light wind, but care had to be taken not to try to climb until well above the stalling speed, particularly with a fully loaded operational aircraft. This was particularly noticeable in ground-based training at Speke where there was no advantage of wind over the ship's deck and ground clearance was only 6 feet. As a precaution during land-based training, the undercarriage was kept down. At sea, the catapults were mounted about 40 feet above the water, giving much more time to recover into the launch headwind.

There was, of course, the problem of the best way to recover the pilot. Previous experience of ditching fighters at sea suggested that it would go straight down, and the Hurricane, with its large under-fuselage radiator air-scoop, had the worst reputation of all with a tendency to flip over immediately on its back on impact, trapping the pilot in the cockpit. It was therefore decided that the most effective drill was to abandon the aircraft close to the convoy at around 2,000 feet, trimming to slightly tail heavy, and to fall out after inverting the aircraft. The intention was to be pointing away from the convoy, but to land as close as possible to the designated pick-up ship.

MSFU Hurricane Mk I mounted on the catapult of CAM ship *Empire Tide*. (*Author's collection*)

Once training was completed, individual teams led by a pilot were despatched to the appropriate west coast port where Hurricanes were loaded from the dock-side fully assembled. During the lift, the pilot was in the cockpit to retract the undercarriage before the aircraft was lowered on to the catapult. The breakdown of responsibility for these operations on the CAM ships, as referred to earlier, was a complex issue. The MSFU crews signed the ship's articles as supernumerary officers or deck hands, coming under the jurisdiction of the captain and having civilian identities in neutral ports. It was the captain's decision to launch the aircraft as he needed to turn into wind, but it was the pilot who decided if the conditions were suitable to fly.

The first launch at sea in the operational trials was made by Fg Off. H. J. Davidson, who was the first pilot to be posted to MSFU and it was his first ever launch. He joined the SS Empire Rainbow, the first of the CAM ships, at Greenock on the Clyde on 31 May 1941. She steamed down the river at 10 knots into a 2-knot headwind; the Hurricat blasted off the catapult and the port wing dropped beneath the bows of the ship, staggering into a left turn. When the aircraft next appeared to observers on the bridge it was 100 yards ahead low down. The port wing touched the water, but the aircraft recovered and eventually climbed away at a right angle to the ship to the great relief of the pilot and everyone on board, Davidson landed safely at Abbotsinch.

Following an analysis of the take-off, it appeared that the pilot had not selected the 30 degrees of flaps and the proper rudder correction to prevent the swing to port. Only eleven of the thirteen rockets had ignited and a cover plate had blown off and hit the tailwheel, which may have slowed the take-off. After further tests by a Farnborough test pilot, a drill was introduced to ensure the throttle friction nut was tightened to avoid loss of power at launch. Despite his interesting first take-off in hardly suitable conditions, Davidson was not held to blame, and on 8 June, he sailed on the Empire Rainbow to Nova Scotia. By the end of the month, there were six CAM ships on convoy protection duty.

Meanwhile, the FAA crews from 804 NAS on the FCSs had already been operating since January 1941 (with the Pegasus as the first ship) in the danger zone and without the inactivity of spending many weeks off watch as their FAR counterparts in the CAM ships had. They returned to the base at Sydenham more frequently, got to know their colleagues better, and served on RN ships with less confusion of their responsibility. The pilots of 804 NAS generally flew individually, and never as a squadron. Being RN ships, the FCS did not carry any cargo, but their holds were filled with empty oil drums to facilitate buoyancy in the event of damage to the hull.

Banana boats were selected for conversion as they were faster than the average cargo boats and made launching of aircraft less hazardous. Three of the four—the Springbank, the Ariguani, and the Maplin—went into service in May, all equipped to carry Fulmars apart from the Maplin, which was equipped with Hurricats.

With the trials of the Michael E, a Sea Hurricane Mk IA was loaded aboard for her maiden voyage and, because there was a shortage of RAF pilots for the trip, FAA pilot Sub-Lieutenant Birrell was chosen having been one of the twenty-five Navy pilots who served in the Battle of Britain. He had his first ground training catapult launch from Gosport in a Hurricane,

F/Lt D. R. Turley-George, left, and P/O C. Fenwick on board CAM ship *Empire Tide* for convoy PQ17. (*Author's collection*)

A flight of 804 NAS Hurricane Mk Is flying over Strangford Lough. By John Scott. (*Author's collection*)

A pair of CAM ships on an arctic convoy with the Sea Hurricanes ready for launch. (*Author's collection*)

followed by a Fulmar launch from Farnborough. His first ship launch proved to be challenging as only half the rockets fired, but he was able to make a safe landing at Sydenham. The ship sailed from Belfast on 28 May ready to join a convoy, but no Condors came within range, resulting in the Hurricat not being launched. However, the ship was sunk by a torpedo from a U-boat outside the Condor range after the convoy had dispersed, but Birrell and his crew survived to join another CAM ship.

Even though Hurricats had little surplus speed to catch the Condors, they did prove to be a deterrent. Their best chances of success was either from a head-on attack or abeam in an attempt to kill the enemy pilot. Any attack from the rear or below was unlikely to be successful due to the heavy defensive armament and armour plating, while hitting one engine was unlikely to stop the aircraft as it had three more available. Forced to maintain a safe distance rather than leading an attack, the Condor crews tended instead to become spotters for the U-boats.

Of the FAA-manned FCSs, the Maplin alone was ready for her maiden voyage, carrying two Sea Hurricanes and three pilots on 9 May. The Hurricanes gave a better performance than the Fulmars, which could barely catch up with the Condors even under ideal conditions. Unfortunately the Hurricanes supplied were obviously considered expendable, while some had already seen service in the Battle of Britain and gave poor performance as they were not in the best condition. By the beginning of July, twenty-five Sea Hurricane Mk IAs had been delivered to MFSU and sixteen CAM ships had sailed, but without any launches.

The FCS HMS *Maplin* converted from a banana boat on convoy protection. By John Scott. (*Author's collection*)

After an uneventful first trip, HMS Maplin saw more action on her second voyage. Sailing from Halifax Nova Scotia in mid-July—with two Hurricats and Lt R. W. H. Everett, Sub-Lieutenants C. W. Walker, and J. E. Scott as pilots—the ship was painted pale pink for camouflage. On 18 July, as recounted in an illicit diary kept by John Scott, while Bob Everett was at readiness in the cockpit, a Condor began to orbit the convoy closer than usual. It then flew off, but suddenly another Condor was seen approaching at low level and closing fast. Bob was fired off the ship and turned into position for a head-on attack and, just as he was about to fire, the Condor lost a section of its starboard wing, shot off by the anti-aircraft gunners aboard HMS Norman Prince. The attacker crashed into the sea for the loss of all on board. Fortunately, Bob Everett had sufficient fuel to fly for just under two hours to St Angelo by Lough Erne near Donegal Bay where he was able to make a safe landing.

Bob Everett rejoined the ship for its next voyage on the Gibraltar run. John Scott was present again, but Dickie Mancus replaced Cecil Walker. During the return voyage to Britain, they were escorting Convoy SL 81 from Sierra Leon—the RN escort warships being the St Albans, the Campbeltown, and the Wanderer.

At 2 p.m. on 2 August, Bob Everett climbed into the Hurricat cockpit for his spell of standby duty with the Maplin about 450 miles from Land's End. There was no hope of reaching land if launched. After about ten minutes, a suspected U-boat was detected, followed by a Condor in the distance acting as a contact plane. Soon after the first Condor departed back to base, a second one was spotted approaching the convoy. With the Hurricat ready to go

The point of no return—a Sea Hurricane Mk IA being launched on a training flight from a CAM ship. (*IWM photo*)

Everett started the engine while the ship turned into wind. With the engine at full power, he gave the signal to launch and was catapulted off over the bow. A tail chase then started with the Hurricat slowly gaining on the Condor from the starboard side. The rear gunner began to fire at Everett, who at 244 mph still could not get abeam to the enemy, with shots now coming from the nose guns. Although Everett still had not gained enough distance to get abeam to the Condor, the problem resolved itself when the pilot pulled sharply to port, almost losing the Hurricat, and then turned back on his original track, presenting an ideal target. Everett held his fire until a range of 200 yards, aiming for the cockpit, but there appeared to be no effect as he dropped astern and used the last of his ammunition. To make matters worse, his windscreen became obscured with oil where one of the gunners had hit his engine. Looking out at the Condor, he saw that it was still flying but losing oil from one of the engines. There followed a glow of fire that erupted, causing one wing to drop and the aircraft to crash into the sea.

By this time, Everett was at 200 feet and about 40 miles from the escort with engine trouble. He managed to climb to 2,000 feet to get a bearing and flew back to the convoy where unknown to him, two of the escorts were busy depth charging U-boats. As he approached, HMS Wanderer put about to recover him, and he prepared to bale out about half a mile from the ship. He rolled the aircraft over to fall clear, but when he was halfway out, the nose jerked up instead of down, forcing him back into the seat. After a second unsuccessful attempt he decided to risk ditching, stalling on to the surface with the tail down, but true to reputation the aircraft sank instantly. Struggling out of the cockpit, he fought his way to the surface and was picked up by a boat lowered from the Wanderer. For destroying the first Condor by Hurricat, Bob Everett was awarded the DSO. Ironically, while ferrying a Hurricane from Belfast to Abingdon on 26 January 1942, he was killed when his aircraft fell into the sea off Anglesey.

While the FCSs were under RN control, there were often difficulties between the RAF crews and the Merchant Navy command of CAM ships, although the Condor threat had diminished due to the protection of the Hurricats. The MFSU crews were subject to the regulations of the Merchant Shipping Act under the captain's direction, but the captain had no powers under the Air Force Act. As time went on, relations improved considerably, especially when the pilot and his team adapted to the captain's personality.

Three months after the sailing of the first CAM ship, a total of thirty-nine pilots and 164 men had been trained at Speke, with thirty-five CAM ships in commission. Although there was a continuing shortage of pilots, no North Atlantic convoy escorted by a CAM ship had been successfully attacked from the air. The whole CAM ship programme was reviewed with the possibility of withdrawing them and replacing them with FCSs under RN control, but it was believed they provided an effective deterrent despite tying up valuable pilot resources. In contrast, the route from Gibraltar was suffering losses from the combination of Condors and U-boats due to there being too much action for the FCSs to cover.

The second launch from HMS Maplin by 804 Squadron was by Cecil Walker on 2 September. He was catapulted against a Condor, which eventually flew away damaged after jettisoning its bombs. The Condor probably survived because the machine gun of the Hurricane was too light and cannons would have been more effective. The aircraft performance would have been much improved if it had been a Merlin XX-powered Hurricane Mk II. Walker was able to successfully abandon his aircraft after an hour of combat flying and was soon picked up from the sea.

With the loss of the surviving Fulmar-equipped FCSs to enemy action in September and October, only the Maplin was left, and it was adapted to carry a third Hurricat in reserve. On 19 September 1941, the decision was made to transfer six CAM ships to the Gibraltar route, putting them in the danger zone for fourteen days—seven out and seven back. Each ship had two pilots allocated and a pool was established at Gibraltar with three Hurricats and three pilots from the MSFU. The first of the Gibraltar-bound CAM ships, the Empire Gale, sailed on 3 October, and a week later the last of the thirty-five CAM ships went into service—the remainder being allocated to the North Atlantic convoys.

It was not until 1 November 1941—after five months of escort duties—that the first operational launching was made from a CAM ship by George Varley. There was a U-boat alert about 550 miles off the Irish coast and a Condor was spotted ahead of the convoy flying at about 1,000 feet. Varley was launched off the Empire Foam and chased the Condor, which by then was starting to attack the convoy with bomb doors open. Spotting the approaching Hurricat, the Condor pilot broke off his attack and made for nearby cloud cover, where Varley lost contact. Thinking that this aircraft might be a decoy, he came back down below the cloud and flew around for about two hours without any other enemy contact. Varley was unable to jettison the cockpit emergency side panel, and after trying a number of times to get out, he climbed over the side and walked along the wing until he fell off. He was picked up rapidly by an escort ship and put in a hot bath fully clothed to recover from the effects of exposure.

CAM ships were just as vulnerable to U-boat attacks as other ships and there was nothing the Hurricanes could do in defence, but for the first three months there were no losses. Then, on 19 September and 2 October, two CAM ships were hit by torpedoes but without loss to the MSFU personnel. On 3 October, the Empire Wave was sunk with the loss of two MSFU men and another severely injured; the survivors remaining in an open boat for fourteen days before reaching Iceland in very poor condition.

Owing to the cold weather and corrosion caused by salt water, it was not easy to keep the vulnerable Hurricats serviceable during heavy winter storms. However, by the end of 1941, many of the Condors had been transferred to other duties thanks to the deterrent effect of the Hurricats, although if the Hurricats were removed the Condors would return. There was pressure for the crews to be allocated to more active duties, and there was also a need to protect the convoys to Russia. On 3 January 1942, the operation of CAM ships with the North Atlantic convoys was suspended and some of the ships converted back to cargo configuration. Convoy protection continued on the Gibraltar route, and the MSFU organisation was retained pending developments, which gave time for reorganisation and training.

On 3 March 1942, convoy protection by CAM ships on the North Atlantic resumed, and on 28 March the decision was made to deploy CAM ships to the notorious Murmansk route to protect the supply of material to Russia. The first CAM ship to join this route was the Empire Morn, which sailed with convoy PQ15 from Hvalfjörður on 26 April. Despite an attack by torpedo-carrying He 111s, which succeeded in sinking three ships in the convoy, conditions were too bad to be able to risk launching the Hurricats. Not only did the pilots not have immersion suits to protect against exposure in the water when they had to abandon the aircraft, it was also too cold to sit in the aircraft cockpits at readiness. In an attempt to mitigate the enemy attacks, the convoys to Russia were usually phased in pairs sailing from both ends, Iceland and Russia, simultaneously.

The second pair of convoys were PQ16, sailing eastward from Iceland, and QP12 departing westward from Murmansk. PQ16 was allocated the CAM ship Empire Lawrence, while fifteen ships in QP12 included the Empire Morn as escort, sailing on 21 May under the protection of land-based Russian fighters. PQ16 was ready at Hvalfjörður on the same day, and under the cover of poor weather, the two convoys gradually converged.

By 25 May, when out of range of the land-based Russian fighters, the conditions had improved and favoured an enemy air attack on QP12. Reconnaissance aircraft were spotted in the distance, bringing the MSFU crews to five minutes' readiness. John Kendal was in the cockpit when two torpedo-armed Ju 88s appeared and the decision was made to launch the Hurricat. He initially went after the BV 138 reconnaissance floatplane as it presented the easiest target, but although Kendall could hear directions from the ship he was having difficulties with his radio transmissions. When the BV 138 took cover in cloud, Kendal went after one of the Ju 88s, hitting it in both engines and causing it to crash into the sea. Kendal then went after the other Ju 88, BV 138, and Condor, but all appeared to have departed for home. It was then time to abandon the Hurricat, but when he climbed to a safe height, the aircraft was lost to view due to the low cloud. Within a short while, the pilotless Hurricat was seen diving from the cloud followed immediately by Kendal, whose parachute was unopened. About 50 feet above the water, it began to deploy, but was only half out before the pilot hit the sea. Although the badly injured Kendal was quickly picked up, he died shortly after from his injuries—the first MSFU pilot to shoot down an enemy aircraft. His death had not been in vain as QP12 reached its destination in Iceland without losing any ships.

Meanwhile, Al Hay was at readiness in his Hurricat cockpit as PQ16 approached hostile territory when six Ju 88s appeared too suddenly for a launch. When the ship's radar identified four He 111s carrying torpedoes the Hurricat was launched. Hay chased after the last He 111, setting the starboard engine on fire, but the straggler caught up with the formation despite the damage and Hay attacked the second aircraft in the formation, believing that the one he had already hit would be unlikely to survive. While firing at the rear of the cockpit of the enemy, Hay's aircraft was hit in the glycol tank, obscuring his windscreen, and was then was hit in the leg. Out of ammunition and with an engine about to stop, he abandoned the Hurricat successfully and was picked up after six minutes in the water. Thanks to the confusion caused by Hay, although there were a number of near misses, no ship in the convoy was hit.

The Germans were determined to stop the convoys and, on 27 May, the Empire Lawrence was hit by two bombs that caused serious damage and the order was given to abandon ship. In the next wave of attacks by Ju 88s, the magazine was hit and the ship sank rapidly, but Al Hay was among the survivors. Three other ships in the convoy were lost in this action, but twenty-eight out of the original thirty-five ships entered the Kola Inlet on 30 May with just under three-quarters of the cargo intact.

Even in summer, the conditions between Iceland and Russia were far from pleasant. In addition to both sides having to contend with appalling weather, at that latitude at the time of year gave almost continuous daylight, making the convoys vulnerable to around the clock attacks by U-boats, bombers, and torpedo aircraft. Although the enemy was able to often inflict heavy losses to the convoys, their own resources were stretched to the limit by the harsh operating conditions especially when they suffered damage. For a crew ditching in the sea there was no chance of survival since rescue was impossible. Despite this, attacks were often pressed home without regard to the defences, although the Hurricats were a definite deterrent. During August 1942, the Russian convoys were reduced with priority given to Operation Pedestal, which was the vital supply of Malta, while some CAM ships continued to provide convoy protection in the Bay of Biscay.

In September, Churchill ordered the resumption of the convoys to Russia. The first left Loch Ewe on 2 September 1942—convoy PQ18 joining up with some American ships off the west coast of Iceland as a total of forty merchant ships set sail for Russia. This was the largest convoy to date, with the largest escort including the CAM ship Empire Morn in addition to the American lend-lease escort carrier Avenger for the first time. The Avenger carried a complement of twelve Sea Hurricane Mk IIBs of 802 Squadron together with three Swordfish biplanes, all on the flight deck. The Swordfish were used for reconnaissance, and both they and the Hurricanes had the luxury of being able to land back on the deck. This ship stayed with the convoy until the main escort took over the defence of the returning east-bound convoy QP14 in the Barents Sea. The protection of the CAM ship Hurricats would therefore not be required until after the Avenger departed, covering the west-bound convoy. Additional protection was provided by two squadrons of Hampden torpedo bombers operating from Russia to defend against surface warships, and a squadron of Catalina flying boats was also based in Russia for long-range reconnaissance. Losses from the predatory U-boats soon commenced, with the convoy also coming within range of the Luftwaffe on 15 September. The Avenger was the primary target, the enemy torpedo bombers using what was known as the 'Golden Comb' formation approach with a massed attack in line abreast of some forty He 111s releasing two torpedoes each, straddling the convoy. The only chance of survival was for the entire convoy to turn to face the onslaught of about eighty torpedoes, hoping to present less of a target. Not surprisingly, a quarter of the convoy was sunk in one day, but the Avenger survived.

During a similar attack the following day, Hurricanes were launched from the carrier. Not only did they help break up the attack but they shot down five enemy aircraft over the convoy and a further nine damaged aircraft were written-off on their return to base. Such was the intensity of the defending anti-aircraft guns that three Hurricanes were shot down by 'friendly fire', but all the pilots survived.

On 16 September, the Avenger and the main escort departed and were replaced the next day by four Russian destroyers. Enemy attacks followed, but the hostile aircraft were at the extremity of their endurance. The Hurricat on the CAM ship was ready to launch with Jackie Burr in the cockpit, waiting for the torpedo bombers in the wake of the dive bombers, but conditions were not suitable for a launch and the torpedoes missed the ships. Jackie Burr was just about to be replaced by John Davies, but before he could get out of the cockpit another attack rapidly developed and the Hurricat was launched. As he turned after take-off, fifteen Heinkels were seen approaching in an attempted 'Golden Comb' attack, but Burr approached the formation head-on and forced one of the bombers to crash into the sea. He used his remaining ammunition against another He 111, which flew over the convoy with both engines smoking and fell into the icy water. At least two other He 111s were damaged badly enough that they would be unlikely to reach their base, and Burr continued to fly around the convoy to deter any further attacks even though he had run out of ammunition. He therefore decided to save the Hurricane and set out for Archangel at the extreme of his endurance. With only a rudimentary map for navigation and a distance of 230 miles to fly with about 60 gallons of fuel, he arrived safely with 4 gallons of fuel remaining—the equivalent of six minutes flying time.

There were no more torpedo attacks on convoy PQ18, and twenty-seven of the total of forty ships arrived safely in Russia with their cargos intact. Unfortunately, Avenger did not last very long. She was commissioned on 2 March 1942, but was sunk on 15 November the same year by U-155 west of Gibraltar.

Following the introduction of CAM ships on the Arctic convoys in May 1942, the MSFU reached its operational peak with a total of twenty-nine ships on three different routes. At the end of July, the decision was made to withdraw the CAM ships from the North Atlantic route, and eight were withdrawn from service. The numbers were further reduced to thirteen ships by the end of the summer—eight on the Gibraltar route and the remaining five with the Russian convoys. As winter approached, and with it impossible weather conditions on the Arctic route, the CAM ships were withdrawn and the pilots trained for deck landings from the escort carriers. The new organisation became eight ship detachments with a pool of two in reserve at Gibraltar consisting of thirty-eight pilots, ten FDOs, and 182 crewmen. A total of fourteen Sea Hurricanes were allocated to the CAM ships, with ten more Mk Is at Speke for training.

On 1 November 1942, Fg Off. Norman Taylor was aboard the Empire Heath on the Gibraltar run when a Condor was sighted approaching the convoy with the CAM ship as its target. Taylor was rapidly launched, but he had difficulty seeing the attacker as he was flying straight into a low sun. Despite this, he managed to gain on the Condor and fired his guns despite heavy return fire. After a burst from close quarters, the Condor reared up in a climb, apparently towards some cloud, and Taylor was able to fire at the cockpit area. Before achieving the safety of cloud, the Condor pitched forward in a dive, hitting the sea with the loss of all on board. Taylor then abandoned his Hurricat, but had difficulties in the water as he was a non-swimmer. He was safely rescued and for this successful combat he was awarded the DFC to add to his earlier DFM.

With the Allied invasion of North Africa in November 1942, the CAM ship's responsibilities were extended to Casablanca and Algiers. The first CAM ship convoy escort duty to North Africa left Britain on Christmas Eve in 1942 and arrived at Algiers on 7 January 1943. In early March 1943, the CAM ships were withdrawn from Arctic convoy protection, and with new escort and merchant aircraft carriers entering service, the MSFU was disbanded on 15 July. Some CAM ships were lost earlier; the Empire Morn was withdrawn from the Arctic convoys, but struck a mine off Casablanca in April 1943 and was abandoned. However, the ship did not sink, and was reboarded and towed into port. The Empire Eve was hit by a torpedo on 18 May while in the Mediterranean and was abandoned before sinking.

The last two CAM ships in service, the Empire Darwin and the Empire Tide, left Gibraltar on 23 July 1943 escorting Convoy SL133. While many of the Condors had been transferred to other duties during the winter, they returned in the spring with a change of tactics to bombing in formation from a minimum altitude of 9,000 feet, which made them more difficult to engage. The CAM ship crews were extra vigilant, despite being on the way home to an uncertain future. After a number of Condor sightings, one was seen approaching the convoy at 500 feet on 28 July, and 'Jimmy' Stewart was catapulted off from the Empire Darwin to attempt an intercept. Meanwhile, two more Condors began to bomb from a higher level, with a near miss on the other CAM ship. Stewart attacked the low-level Condor until his guns jammed, but he had dealt a fatal blow and the aircraft fell into the sea. He then climbed toward the other Condors and helped to put off their attack. By this time, a catapult fault had been repaired on the Empire Tide and its Hurricat was launched with Paddy Flynn in the cockpit, who went after another low-level Condor, only to receive damage from the enemy guns. Closing for the kill, his ammunition ran out and the damaged Condor limped away with an engine on fire and losing height, later confirmed as destroyed. Both pilots returned to the convoy and abandoned their aircraft successfully to be picked up by the escorts.

The next day, the convoy was again bombed from high level, but no serious damage was sustained. The value of having more than one CAM ship protecting a convoy had been demonstrated on this final voyage, but it was not possible to restart up the MSFU. Of the total of thirty-five CAM ships that entered service, twelve were lost to enemy action. Eight operational launches resulted in six successful Hurricat interceptions of Condors, and the deterrent effect of the Hurricats were successful in reducing losses to Allied merchant shipping. Despite the hazards involved, the operations were by no means suicidal, as only one pilot lost his life during combat.

Hurricanes were also used in the more conventional role on traditional aircraft carriers. When war broke out the Royal Navy had only six carriers, HMS Courageous, Glorious, Furious, Argus, Hermes, and Ark Royal, and by the time Italy entered the war, there were only four left—the Courageous was sunk early in the war and the Glorious was sunk during the withdrawal from Norway.

These carriers were generally equipped with vintage 1930s biplane fighters pending the arrival of the Fulmar during 1940. Following the successful—albeit, in the event, wasted attempt to save the 46 Squadron aircraft on HMS Glorious, the Hurricane was obviously suited to deck operations, although it required some adaptation. Although spools had already been fitted for the catapult operations, the rear fuselage would need to be restressed for arrester hook retarded landings. With a reluctance to delay production of Hurricanes by introducing

Hurricane Mk Is of 260 Squadron RAF on HMS *Ark Royal* at Gibraltar in 1941 ready to reinforce the air defence of Malta. (*RAF Museum photo*)

major modifications to the airframe, it was not until March 1941 that a Canadian-built Mk I was fitted with an A-frame arrester hook and rear fuselage strengthening was ready for trials at Farnborough. This aircraft, P5187, had already been fitted with the catapult spools as a Mk IA and with the arrester hook it became the prototype Sea Hurricane Mk IB. After successful trials, further low-hour Sea Hurricane Mk IAs and some Hurricane Mk Is were converted from May 1941, with about120 Mk IBs completed by October, which also included a small number of Hurricane Mk IIAs and IIBs, as well as some Canadian Hurricane Mk Xs, XIs, and XIIs with eight- or twelve-gun wings. In addition, about 100 Merlin III-powered Sea Hurricane Mk IBs were fitted with four 20-mm cannon-armed wings to become the Mk IC. Although this armament was heavy for the 1,030-hp Merlin-powered Sea Hurricane, it was still faster and more manoeuvrable than the Fulmar.

Sea Hurricanes were intended for use on RN fleet carriers, with Mk IBs replacing Fulmars and entering service with 801 NAS on HMS Argus and Eagle, 806 NAS on HMS Formidable, 880 NAS on HMS Avenger, and 885 NAS on HMS Victorious. The Mk IC began to enter service with the FAA in January 1942 with 801, 802, 803, 880, 883, and 885 Squadrons—a few with fitted with tropical filters for operations in the Mediterranean and tropics.

A number of Mk IBs equipped with tropical filters were flown to 889 NAS in the Western Desert via the Takoradi route across Africa. With the supply of the beleaguered Maltese becoming urgent in 1942, seventy Merlin XX-powered Sea Hurricanes were converted, starting in March, to Hurricane Mk IICs, and brought up to full naval standard with naval radios, catapult spools, and arrester hooks. A number were also converted during their build at Langley.

The Hurricanes of 802 NAS aboard the escort carriers HMS *Biter* and *Avenger* in relatively benign sea conditions on an Arctic convoy protection in August 1942. (*IWM photo*)

No. 803 Squadron FAA Sea Hurricane Mk I V7816:K was one of the aircraft based at Ramat David from June 1941 to March 1942. (*FAA Museum*)

Sea Hurricanes of 801 NAS on board HMS *Victorious* in late 1942 being refuelled and sheltered behind windbreaks. (*Author's collection*)

Deck operations with Sea Hurricane Mk IA after landing and rapidly moving out of the way to allow for following arrivals. (*Author's collection*)

When Italy entered the war on 10 June 1940, German forces were already in control of North Africa, threatening Allied-held Egypt and supply routes through the Suez Canal. Malta was a strategically vital Allied base but suffered badly from enemy air attacks and resupply had become critical. As a break from Arctic convoys, a major effort was put into the Mediterranean theatre, with HMS Argus sailing from Gibraltar on 2 August carrying a dozen Hurricane Mk Is, which were flown off the deck without difficulty by RAF pilots and arrived in Malta for the defence of the island.

The major action involving Sea Hurricanes was Operation Pedestal in August 1942, which involved taking vital supplies from Gibraltar to Malta during the build-up of Mediterranean forces in preparation for the Battle of Alamein.

The convoy consisted of just fourteen merchant ships, including the vital oil tanker Ohio, with a strong RN escort force consisting of four carriers, HMS Eagle, Furious, Indomitable, and Victorious, with the Furious carrying Spitfires for the defence of Malta and therefore unable to operate any naval fighters.

There were also two battleships, seven cruisers, and twenty-four destroyers. On board the carriers were thirty-nine Sea Hurricanes of 880 NAS on the Indomitable, 801 NAS on the Eagle, and 885 NAS on the Victorious, in addition to thirty-one Fulmars and 804, 806, 809, and 884 NAS with Martlets.

Not long after the start on 11 August, and just as the Spitfires were taking off from Furious, some of the destroyers were refuelling when disaster struck. A nearby U-boat fired a salvo of torpedoes, four of which hit the Eagle, which sunk within eight minutes. A total of thirty aircraft were lost aboard the carrier, and four Sea Hurricanes which were airborne at the time landed instead on HMS Indomitable and Victorious. The convoy had to contend with up to 200 Luftwaffe aircraft, plus 300 Italian aircraft based in Sicily, Sardinia and mainland Italy.

Sea Hurricane Mk IC V6741 with arrester hook and armed with four 20-mm cannons of the type used on the Malta convoys in 1942. (*Peter Green collection*)

Sea Hurricanes of 885 NAS on board HMS *Victorious* with *Indomitable* and *Eagle* astern at the commencement of Operation Pedestal. (*FAA Museum*)

Sea Hurricane Mk IA being manhandled on the deck of HMS *Furious* ready for launch to Malta. (*Author's collection*)

Sea Hurricane 7-Z of 880 NAS in an idyllic setting. (*FAA Museum*)

The ultimate Sea Hurricane Mk IIC NF717 powered by a Merlin XX and fitted with the full naval standard equipment including four-20mm cannons. (*RAF Museum photo*)

The first air attacks began to develop on the evening of 11 August, but the approach of darkness prevented the carrier based aircraft from intercepting the attackers, although a number of the bombers were shot down by the ship's anti-aircraft guns. The next day there were four attacks on the convoy, and the second one was intercepted by the Sea Hurricanes which broke up the formations, although one merchant ship was sunk. While the Victorious was recovering some of the Sea Hurricanes of 885 NAS, two Italian fighter bombers broke away from the circling formations and dived at the carrier, each releasing a 1,100-lb bomb, one hitting the bows and the other shattering on the armoured flight deck, neither affecting the operation of the ship or aircraft. The third attack on 12 August involved about 100 enemy aircraft, including a formation of Ju 87s targeting the Indomitable, which was hit by three 1,100-lb bombs and two near misses. Once again the armoured deck saved the ship, but she could no longer operate aircraft, and her Sea Hurricanes in the air at the time landed safely on the Victorious, which was the only carrier still in operation with a crowded deck and hangar of forty-seven fighters and nine torpedo bombers.

With a carrier, destroyer, and one merchant ship lost, the convoy passed into the Sicilian narrows where the naval escort had to turn back to Gibraltar due to there being insufficient room to manoeuvre in defence of the convoy. This left the merchant ships at the mercy of U-boats, torpedoes, mines and more aircraft attacks, which contributed to the loss of two cruisers and eight merchant ships. The five surviving merchant ships, of which three were damaged (including the Ohio), delivered enough supplies to sustain the Island. In addition to the thirty-five aircraft lost when the Eagle was sunk, there were eight more FAA aircraft lost in combat, while the enemy losses totalled thirty-one aircraft.

Sea Hurricanes of 800 NAS preparing for departure from HMS *Unicorn* in 1943. (*Peter Green collection*)

Sea Hurricanes of 800 NAS on board HMS *Unicorn* in the spring of 1943. (*FAA Museum photo*)

The landing of British and American forces in Algeria and Morocco against the Vichy French, known as Operation Torch was the final major operation in the Mediterranean involving Sea Hurricanes. The supporting force of carriers for the landings was the largest brought together so far during the war. They comprised four Royal Navy fleet carriers—HMS Formidable, Victorious, Furious, and Argus—carrying thirty-five Martlets, forty-five Seafires, and seven Fulmars, and three Royal Navy escort carriers consisting of HMS Biter, Dasher, and Avenger, with forty-two Sea Hurricanes.

One American fleet carrier held fifty-four Wildcats, while a further fifty-seven were shared across four American escort carriers. In addition, the combined carrier force embarked with thirty-five Albacores, fifteen Swordfish, twenty-seven Avengers, thirty-six Dauntless aircraft, and seventy-eight USAAF P-40s.

While American forces were allocated to landings on the Atlantic coast in French Morocco at Casablanca, the British Task Force 'H' and the British Central and Eastern Task Forces supported the British and Americans landings at Oran and Algiers. To simplify the identification of British and French aircraft, as the American gunners were not familiar with these types, all ship-borne fighters were marked with the American star. The Sea Hurricanes were mainly involved with support of the American landings at Oran, which started on 8 November when the Biter launched three Swordfish to drop leaflets on the port urging surrender. Eight

Sea Hurricane Mk IA roaring down the deck of HMS *Furious* on departure for Malta with another aircraft ready to follow behind. (*Author's collection*)

Albacores were launched from the Furious to bomb the local airfield, but they were pursued by French Dewoitine D.520 fighters that shot down the vulnerable biplanes. The Dasher and the Biter launched twelve Sea Hurricanes—the pilots shooting down five French fighters for the loss of two Sea Hurricanes, which the pilots were able to force-land along the coast. The loss of life on both sides was totally unnecessary and was not repeated, but Sea Hurricanes from the Dasher and the Biter, with Seafires from the Furious, maintained covering patrols around Oran for the next two days, including an attack on French artillery, before the French at Oran surrendered on 10 November.

As mentioned previously, the escort carrier Avenger was torpedoed by U-155 on 15 November, exploding immediately and sinking rapidly with the loss of almost the entire crew and the compliment of Sea Hurricanes, making it the largest single loss of the entire operation.

This was the last major use of Sea Hurricanes from carriers. The type was gradually phased out and their place taken by later versions of the Seafire, Martlet, Hellcat, and Corsair. The escort carriers were used more commonly in confined waters to support landings, where there was a greater risk of meeting enemy land based fighters. The Sea Hurricane, in its ultimate form as the Mk IIC, had a top speed of 316 mph at 17,000 feet and was no match for the latest Luftwaffe fighters entering service in early 1943. Although Sea Hurricanes operated in other theatres of the Second World War they did so from land bases, which will be covered separately.

A less than perfect landing by a 824 NAS Sea Hurricane on HMS *Striker* on 13 June 1944. (*FAA Museum*)

A Sea Hurricane Mk IIC, with 20-mm cannon armament, starting its take-off run aboard HMS *Striker* with a pair of Swordfish ready to follow. (*IWM photo*)

Sea Hurricane Mk IICs of 835 NAS, including NF700:7-T, on board HMS *Nairana* were the last in operational service with the FAA. (*FAA Museum*)

The FAA of the Royal Navy (RN) also operated Hurricanes in a variety of Fleet support and training duties. No. 700 NAS were traditionally the unit to introduce new aircraft types to FAA service, and when service trials were completed, the squadron was allocated a permanent identity with the crews who were responsible for working up.

No. 700 NAS was initially formed at RNAS Hatston on 21 January 1940 by amalgamating the Catapult squadrons, which acted as a pool for all catapult aircraft embarked on battleships and cruisers. After disbanding on 24 March 1944, it reformed on 11 October 1944 at RNAS Donibristle as a Maintenance Test Pilots Training School, moving to Worthy Down, Middle Wallop, in November 1945, and Yeovilton in April 1946. Among the aircraft used by the squadron were the Hurricane Mk IIC in May 1945 and the Sea Hurricane Mk IIB from August to September 1945.

No. 702 NAS operated Sea Hurricane Mk IBs from 10 May to July 1942 with the task of operating a pair of Hurricats from the Maplin, but disbanded two months later.

No. 727 NAS was formed at Gibraltar on 26 May 1943 and some RAF Hurricane Mk IICs were loaned to the squadron between August 1943 and August 1944 to undertake dummy fighter attacks for training Allied armies. No. 728 NAS was one of the FAA long-term Fleet Requirement Units (FRU), forming at Gibraltar on 1 May 1943 and operating two Hurricane Mk IICs from May 1944 until January 1945.

No. 731 NAS formed at East Haven on 5 December 1943 for Deck Landing Control Officer training, and among the aircraft used were Sea Hurricane Mk IBs from December 1943 to June 1944.

Sea Hurricane Mk I of TTU at Gosport in early 1939. (*FAA Museum photo*)

A line abreast formation of Sea Hurricane Mk Is, with V6541 nearest. (*IWM photo*)

Sea Hurricane Mk IA N2631 of the type operated from CAM ships. (*FAA Museum*)

No. 748 NAS formed at St Merryn on 12 October 1942 as a Fighter Pool squadron providing refresher flying. Among the aircraft used were Hurricane Mk Is, Sea Hurricane Mk IBs, and Sea Hurricane Mk IIC from October 1942 until February 1944.

No. 759 NAS was formed at Eastleigh on 1 November 1939 as a Fighter School and pool squadron initially equipped with Skuas, Rocs, and Sea Gladiators. A move was made to RNAS Yeovilton on 16 September 1940 where Sea Hurricanes were supplied from June 1941 until March 1944. In April 1943, it became the Advanced Flying School, and in May, there were sixty-six Sea Hurricanes among Spitfires, Fulmars, and Masters.

No. 760 NAS formed at Eastleigh on 1 April 1940 as Fleet Fighter Pool No.1, moving to Yeovilton on 16 September 1940 and equipped with Sea Hurricane Mk IBs and IICs, disbanding on 1 November 1944. While based at RNAS Inskip, Hurricane Mk IIs were used for training in ground attack using 20-mm cannon and RP. At that time, the RPs could be unreliable, resulting in hang-ups with the rocket not firing when the button was pressed. The safety drill was to switch off all relevant circuits and point the aircraft out to sea for fifteen minutes, at the same time informing Inskip on the radio. If nothing happened after fifteen minutes, a return to the airfield was made. On one occasion, having run through the standard drill, one 60-lb concrete warhead RP hung-up about half a mile off Fleetwood—the hung-up rocket launched in the direction of the town. Calling Inskip, the pilot advised of what had happened, suggesting the local police were contacted to see how many casualties had been caused. After landing in a state of acute concern, there were no reports from the police. After waiting for an hour, there was still no news or trace of 60-lb of concrete somewhere in the middle of Fleetwood at high velocity.

Sea Hurricane Mk IA with exhaust shields for night operations. (*Author's collection*)

Sea Hurricane V7438 YI-C:759 NAS for training at Yeovilton. (*FAA Museum photo*)

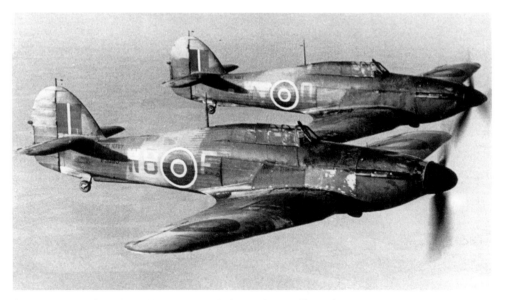

Sea Hurricane Mk IB P3090 W8-F:760 NAS. (*Peter Green collection*)

Sea Hurricane KI-F:766 NAS after a forced landing aboard HMS *Ranger* in the autumn of 1944. (*FAA Museum photo*)

Sea Hurricane Mk IBs of 768 NAS in the hangar deck of HMS *Argus* in August 1943. (*RAF Museum photo*)

Sea Hurricane Mk IB M2-K:768 NAS being pushed back to the stern of HMS *Argus* in August 1943. (*RAF Museum photo*)

Sea Hurricane Mk IB M2-H:768 Deck Landing Training Squadron on finals to land aboard HMS *Argus* in August 1943 with the A-frame arrester hook lowered. (*IWM photo*)

Sea Hurricane Mk IB being refuelled on board HMS *Argus* ready for the next sortie with 768 Deck Landing Training Squadron in August 1943. (*IWM Museum*)

During training with 768 NAS, there were often less than perfect arrivals with Sea Hurricanes on board the training carrier HMS *Argus*. (*Author's collection*)

No. 766 NAS formed at Machrihanish on 15 April 1942 as a night ALT (Attack Light Torpedo) Course, with Swordfish moving to RNAS Inskip and becoming part of No. 1 Operational Training Unit (OTU) operating some Sea Hurricane Mk IICs from November 1944 to March 1945. No. 768 NAS was formed at RNAS Arbroath on 13 January 1941 as part of a Deck Landing Training School, initially with Swordfish—the practical, training being mainly on HMS Argus. Sea Hurricane Mk IBs and IICs joined the unit from September 1941 until March 1944, which served at Machrihanish from 1 March 1943, Ayr from 29 September 1943, and Abbotsinch from 19 January 1944.

On 1 January 1941, 770 NAS reformed at Donibristle as a FRU, moving to Crail on 1 June and Dunino on 29 January 1944. Hurricane Mk IICs arrived in June 1944 and remained until April 1945, with a move to Drem on 25 July 1944.

On 24 May 1939, 771 NAS was formed at RNAS Portland as a FRU with Swordfish and Walrus aircraft. On 28 September 1939, it was based at Hatston and moved to Twatt on 1 July 1942, with Hurricane FB IICs arriving in May 1944 until April 1945.

No. 772 NAS was formed on 28 September 1939 at RNAS Lee-on-Solent as a FRU. Its activities included target towing, height finding, photography, and radar calibration. Hurricane Mk IICs arrived in June 1944 until April 1945. On 27 May 1944, 772 NAS put into the air as many aircraft as possible for a dummy attack on the Fleet in preparation for the planned invasion of Europe.

No. 775 NAS was formed at Dekheila on 25 November 1940 as a FRU for target towing. A fighter flight was formed in September 1943 with Fulmars, and Hurricanes were part of the equipment from May 1944 until January 1945.

No. 776 NAS was formed at RNAS Lee-on-Solent on 1 January 1941 as a FRU, with fourteen Hurricanes arriving in March 1944 until April 1945, with the headquarters at Speke. No. 779 NAS was formed at Gibraltar on 1 October 1941 as a FRU for target towing, with Sea Hurricane Mk IICs from June 1944 until April 1945, and disbanding on 5 August 1945.

No. 781 NAS formed at Lee-on-the-Solent on 20 March 1940 as a communications unit, with duties increasing to include both training and refresher flying. Among the aircraft on charge were Sea Hurricane Mk IBs and IICs from November 1942 to February 1945.

No. 787 NAS formed at Yeovilton on 5 March 1941 as a Fleet Fighter Development Unit equipped with Sea Gladiators, Sea Hurricane Mk IAs, IBs, and IICs, from March 1941 until September 1944. Sea Hurricane Mk IAs and IICs also served with 787Z Flight from November 1943 to June 1944.

No. 788 NAS formed at China Bay on 16 February 1942 as the Eastern Fleet TBR (Torpedo Bomber Reconnaissance) pool. It was initially equipped with Swordfish, but all six aircraft were destroyed by Japanese raids on Ceylon on 5 April 1942. The squadron regrouped and moved to Mombasa on 24 June to become a FRU with a number of aircraft including Sea Hurricane Mk IBs and Hurricane Mk IIBs from August until November 1942.

No. 789 NAS formed at Wingfield on 1 July 1942 as a FRU with aircraft including Sea Hurricane Mk IBs from July 1942.

No. 791 NAS formed at RNAS Arbroath on 15 October 1940 as an Air Target Towing Unit and operated Sea Hurricane Mk IAs, IBs, and IICs from December 1943 to January 1944. It disbanded on 10 December 1944.

No. 792 NAS formed at RNAS St Merryn on 15 August 1940 as an Air Target Towing Unit and among the aircraft in its arsenal was Sea Hurricane Mk IA Z7162 in May 1944.

No. 794 NAS formed at RNAS Yeovilton on 1 August 1940 as a TTU (Target Towing Unit), moving to Angle on 1 July 1943 with the new title of Naval Air Firing Unit, which operated sixteen Sea Hurricane Mk IIBs until October 1943.

The final FAA second-line unit to operate Hurricanes was 795 NAS, which formed at Tanga on 24 June 1942 as the Eastern Fleet Fighter Pool initially equipped with Martlets and Fulmars, with Sea Hurricane Mk IBs from December 1942 until January 1943. It disbanded on 11 August 1943.

8

Hurricanes on the Offensive

APART FROM THE Channel weather becoming less conducive for an invasion of Britain, and the removal of invasion landing craft from the Channel ports, there was no clearly defined end of the Battle of Britain. The Luftwaffe continued the Blitz of London and other British cities, mostly at night, and in many cases continued the destruction after many of the buildings had been raised to the ground. Ken Tempest, during his training at the Mount Batten Centre, was incensed at the continued destruction of Plymouth, with bombs raining down every night using the existing fires as target markers.

Meanwhile, Hitler had ordered the Luftwaffe to prepare for the invasion of the USSR, which he believed would be an easy conquest, and moved his armies to attack his former ally. Operation Barbarossa commenced with a massive onslaught against Soviet bases on 22 June 1941.

Meanwhile, Sholto-Douglas and Leigh-Mallory managed to organise the eventual retirement of Dowding and the posting of AVM Park to 23 Group Training Command. The two men responsible for winning the Battle of Britain were formally removed on 18 December 1940. Dowding was given a Barony in 1943, and Park found that RAF Training Command were still using the discredited pre-war fighter tactics, which he was able to correct before returning to active command in the Middle East in 1942. Sholto-Douglas took over as head of RAF Fighter Command, with Leigh-Mallory leading 11 Group, the reason for his appointment being that he was seen as an offensively-minded leader who demanded, 'attack, always attack'.

Once appointed, Leigh-Mallory introduced wing-size fighter sweeps into France known as rodeos, and when accompanied by bombers to provoke enemy fighters, they were known as circus operations. The first offensive sortie was made on 10 January 1941, with an attack by six Blenheims on Forêt de Guînes near Bordeaux. The escort consisted of 108 fighters, with the Hurricanes of 249 and 56 Squadrons as close escort, flying in the somewhat hazardous position below the bombers to stop the enemy fighters coming up from underneath. With

No. 239 Squadron formed at Hatfield on 18 September 1940 as an Army Co-operation squadron equipped with Lysanders. It flew Hurricane Mk Is and IICs from Gatwick between January and May 1942. The squadron moved to Abbotsinch on 3 May 1942 to convert to Mustangs. Hurricane Mk I W9232 was powered by a Merlin III engine. (*Author's collection*)

the bombers briefed to attack from 7,000 feet (2,133 metres), the Hurricanes were flying at 5,000 feet (1,524 metres), which was the worst height due to the vulnerability to ground-based defences. The top cover Spitfires were well clear of any hazards at 15,000 feet (4,572 metres).

The attack was led in by Bader. Eventually, Tom Neil was down at 800 feet (244 metres) crossing the French coast on the way home, and on return he reported to the intelligence officer that it was a pretty useless trip—the other pilots were pretty incensed about the whole operation. Bader was totally irresponsible, his philosophy was: 'Me first, I'm next, and anything left I'll have'. He caused so many problems in the POW camp when he was shot down that the other inmates were delighted to see him moved out to Colditz Castle. He had a batman at Colditz to look after his legs, but when the batman was given permission to go home on medical grounds, Bader refused to let him go.

Tom Neil, like many of the other pilots, were not fans of Douglas Bader. He had the image of a gutsy man, but to his fellow pilots he was a menace. He caused the loss of more pilots by doing the wrong thing at the wrong time than anyone else of that rank and influence. When Fighter Command went on the offensive, the first rhubarbs were undertaken in the cover of cloud to attack unimportant targets in France on which the pilots ran into swarms of defending fighters who should not have been there. Bader's own wing had already done the morning raid that alerted the enemy and raised a hornet's nest of Luftwaffe defenders ready for the later wave of fighters on ground attacks.

No. 315. (Polish) Squadron was formed at Acklington on 21 January 1941 and was allocated to the defence of Liverpool from March until moving to the Polish squadron base at Northolt in July 1941, when it was soon operating rodeos across occupied Europe. The pilot of Hurricane Mk I V7538 PK-O:315 Squadron is standing by his aircraft while based at Speke during the defence of the Liverpool area. (*P. H. T. Green collection*)

Sholto-Douglas briefed a group of pilots at Martlesham Heath: 'We have to take this to the enemy now. We can't let things just lie down'. The purpose was to bring the Luftwaffe into the air, but the poorer performance Hurricanes were simply shot down for the loss of many experienced pilots.

With its thick wing and rugged construction, the Hurricane was never going to match the speed of the Spitfire, but its performance could be improved by fitting a more powerful Merlin—the first step being the 1,260-hp Merlin XX that led to the basic Hurricane Mk II and gave the initial Hurricane Mk IIA a maximum speed of 342 mph at 17,400 feet, which was still about 20 mph slower than the Spitfire.

An increase in endurance was also desirable, and the first trial installation of long-range wing-mounted external fuel tanks was tested on Hurricane Mk I P3462 in May 1940. The first practical use of external 44-gallon auxiliary fuel tanks was on delivery flights, starting in September 1940, across Africa to Egypt known as the Takoradi route. The tanks were not stressed for combat or jettisonable.

While providing for the fitting of additional fuel tanks, Hawker also developed a universal wing that could be fitted with eight or twelve Browning machine guns—these aircraft were designated Mk IIA Series 2 and remained in front-line service until mid-1941. The authorisation to go ahead with production of the twelve-gun wings was received in November 1940, and a request for the provision for bomb racks followed. The first Mk IIA Series 2 Hurricanes were with 46 Squadron at Digby, 303 (Polish) Squadron at Leconfield and 605 Squadron at Croydon by the end of 1940, and with eight more Fighter Command squadrons by the spring of 1941.

In February 1941, the first Mk IIBs, albeit without the bomb rack modifications, were delivered to 56 Squadron at Duxford, 242 Squadron at Martlesham Heath (still commanded by Douglas Bader), and 249 Squadron at North Weald.

By the middle of 1941, Hurricane Mk IIAs and Mk IIBs were operational with twenty-four squadrons in Britain, with the first Hurribombers reaching the squadrons in May and working parties from the MUs wiring the wings and fitting bomb carriers to allow the carriage to hold a pair of 250-lb bombs.

In late May, the Hurricane Mk IIB production line at Langley was beginning to turn out aircraft fitted with tropical filters, with the first reaching Malta in June, where they were issued to 185 Squadron. Due to the aircraft at Hal Far being busy on air defence duties, the bomb racks were not fitted for about a year when the Island moved from defensive mode onto the offensive.

With the improved performance of the Hurricane Mk IIB, the type was a good match for the Bf 109E, but by the time it was widely in service in northern Europe in the spring of 1941.

The superior Bf 109f was entering service with the Luftwaffe—the shortcomings of the Hurricane, particularly the ineffectiveness of the 0.303-inch Browning machine gun against the increased German armour.

Hurricane Mk II Series 2 Z2521 from the fifth production batch armed with eight wing-mounted machine guns. (*HSA photo*)

Hurricane Mk IIA Z2515 in February 1942. (*RAF Museum photo*)

Hurricane Mk I V7826 with fixed 44-gallon long-range fuel tanks under the wing and the tropical intake under the nose for operations in the Middle East. (*HSA photo*)

No. 615 Squadron arrived at Kenley from Northolt with Hurricane Mk Is on 16 December 1940 and exchanged them for Mk IIAs in February 1941. The squadron undertook fighter sweeps over the Channel and moved to Valley on 21 April 1941. Hurricane Mk IIA Z2703 KW-M:615 Squadron in a Kenley dispersal was presented to the RAF by the Borough of Croydon. (*IWM photo*)

Hurricane Mk IIA Z3451 in March 1942 for small bomb underwing carrier development at A&AEE March 1942. (*IWM photo*)

Hurricane Mk IIB BN114 with 500-lb bombs development in March 1942 at A&AEE. (*RAF Museum*)

When 615 Squadron moved to Valley on 21 April 1941, it was tasked with convoy and shipping patrols over the Irish Sea with Hurricane Mk IIBs. The squadron moved to Manston on 11 September to fly rangers and rhubarbs before being posted to Asia in March 1942. (*RAF Museum photo*)

Merlin XX-powered Hurricane Mk IIC KZ466 armed with four 20-mm cannons in April 1943. (*RAF Museum photo*)

The machine guns were only effective in ground attack against soft skinned targets such as trucks and troop concentrations. Camm had been pushing for the more effective cannon armament since 1936 and it was not until in February 1940 that approval was given for a trial installation of four Oerlikon 20-mm cannons to be fitted in a pair of damaged metal Hurricane wings. The guns supplied were a fairly old naval version, but it was shown that they could be accommodated within the wings with a small blister fairing on the upper surface. Provision was made for the assembly and removal of the guns, the barrels of which protruded forward of the wing leading edge, by adding access panels aft of the wing rear spar. Using a spare development aircraft, the installation was flown for the first time on 27 May, with the preliminary handling, performance, and reaching a top speed of nearly 300 mph at 12,800 feet being of great interest. As a result, sanction was given to make an installation on the first available Merlin XX-powered airframe on the Langley production line.

This aircraft, V7360, was completed in great secrecy and first flown from Langley on 10 July, from where it was immediately delivered to the A&AEE at Boscombe Down for a series of six-gun firing flights. With adjustments made following the trials, V7360 was delivered to 151 Squadron at North Weald in September for evaluation under combat conditions. However, as this squadron had just been withdrawn for a rest tour, the cannon Hurricane was passed to 46 Squadron where the aircraft suffered combat damage on 7 September, and it was repaired at a MU. The next record of this Hurricane was when Philip Lucas took the aircraft on a gun-bay heating test flight, by which time this Hurricane was referred to as the Mk IIC prototype.

Hurricane Mk IIC prototype Z2905, armed with four 20-mm cannons and carrying 88-gallon fixed ferry tanks under the wings in February 1942. (*IWM photo*)

Meanwhile, intensive development had been carried out at the armament establishments and companies in the development of an aircraft cannon in Britain. Instructions were given to Hawker to repair thirty sets of damaged metal wings for the installation of twelve batteries of drum-fed Oerlikons, twelve belt-fed Chatellerault, and six sets for Hispano Mk I 20-mm cannons. There had been some difficulties with the drum-feed Oerlikon, and the other two cannons were under development for the Typhoon. These modified wings were fitted to aircraft on the Langley and Gloster production lines as the guns were made available, and by the end of February, eleven development Hurricane Mk IICs were flying. Three were already on test at Boscombe Down, where the performance was recorded at 336 mph at 16,600 feet at an AUW of 8,100 lb. The Oerlikon cannons achieved initial approval by the end of March, by which time the first forty production Mk IICs were being prepared at MUs for the Fighter Command squadrons—the first to receive the new Oerlikon-armed aircraft being 3 Squadron at Martlesham Heath, and 257 Squadron at Coltishall commanded by Bob Stanford Tuck. The first Mk IICs with Chatellerault ammunition feeds were delivered to 46 Squadron at Sherburn-in-Elmet at the end of April with the intention being to fly them to the Middle East in May, but the plans were cancelled. Following the removal of tropical filters, the aircraft were issued to 87 Squadron at Charmy Down led by Sqn Ldr Ian Gleed. The first Mk IICs to serve in the Middle East were with 229 Squadron in the Western Desert during September.

A reported total of 4,711 Hurricane Mk IICs were produced, which was more than any other version, with production ending in September 1944. This version was initially operational

An armourer loading belt-feed 20-mm-linked cannon shells into the port wing of a Hurricane Mk IIC. (*Author's collection*)

in Britain on offensive daylight attacks and night-fighter patrols over Britain and intruding across the Channel into Northern France. The original load was a pair of 250-lb bombs under the wings, but by 1942 the aircraft had been cleared to carry two 500-lb bombs. To provide extended endurance, the Hurribombers often carried underwing 44-gallon drop tanks into combat, and when flying on long-range ferry flights, such as the Takoradi route across Africa to Egypt, they could be fitted with a pair of 88-gallon ferry tanks.

While waiting for the development of an effective night fighter, the Beaufighter was equipped with Airborne Interception (AI) radar following the Battle of Britain. Hurricanes were increasingly used for night patrols seeking out the lone enemy raider that may be illuminated by a searchlight. Unfortunately, they met with little success, with far more losses to the RAF defenders than enemy aircraft destroyed due to the ease of getting lost and having to bale out or crashing on landing.

During the Blitz of London, from 7 September 1940 for fifty-five nights, among the Hurricane units sent aloft at night were 73 and 85 Squadrons. The pilots of 73 Squadron, flying from Castle Camps, found conditions over London extremely hazardous and suffered greater losses from the anti-aircraft gun barrage firing blindly than any victories gained.

A Hurricane Mk IIC armed with four 20-mm cannons. (*Author's collection*)

No. 3 Squadron introduced Hurricane Mk IIBs and IICs at Martlesham Heath from April 1941, moving to Stapleford Tawney on 23 June, and then Hunsdon on 9 August until re-equipping with Typhoons in February 1943. These six Mk IICs were armed with four 20-mm cannons each. (*IWM photo*)

S/Ldr Stanford Tuck DSO, DFC and bar, the commanding officer of 257. (Burma) Squadron, in the cockpit of his Hurricane Mk II at Coltishall. (*Author's collection*)

Hurricane Mk II night-fighter P2792 LK-A:87 Squadron being flown by W/Cdr Gleed from Coltishall on 6 February 1941. (*IWM photo*)

Hurricane Mk IIC Z3888 fitted with a pair of underwing 44-gallon fuel tanks and armed with four 20-mm cannons. (*RAF Museum photo*)

During the Battle of Britain, 85 Squadron specialised in night-fighting against enemy raiders; the black-painted Hurricane Mk I VY-X here is on standby at Debden. (*IWM photo*)

S/Ldr Peter Townsend, who achieved the first squadron success at night against a Do 17 on 25 February 1941, leading 85 Squadron on a patrol from Kirton-in-Lindsey in late 1940. The squadron operated Hurricane Mk Is from September 1938 until April 1941, briefly flying Havocs until converting to Mosquito NF.IIs at Hunsdon in August 1942. (*Author's collection*)

No. 85 Squadron, later to become a full-time night-fighter unit equipped with AI-equipped Mosquitos, flew more hours at night from November 1940 until January 1941 than any other day or night fighter squadrons in 11 Group, yet their first success was not until 25 February when the CO, Sqn Ldr Peter Townsend, intercepted a Do 17.

In an attempt to reduce the hazards from the anti-aircraft guns, a system named Fighter Nights was introduced in November 1940, which consisted of a height band being defined for use by single-seat fighters that no guns would fire into or two-seat fighters to fly within. This certainly reduced losses among Hurricane squadrons, but less than 10 per cent of enemy raiders flew within these arbitrary bands, which made the chance of a Hurricane pilot detecting a Luftwaffe bomber were fairly slim. Despite this, seven hostile bombers were shot down by Hurricanes during the Fighter Nights, which continued until the summer of 1941 when the Blitz ceased. Hurricane squadrons were allocated to night-fighter operations during the Blitz, including 87 Squadron based at Colerne covering the night defence of the Bristol area and South Wales, as the Luftwaffe did not just concentrate the night-bombing to London.

A number of the existing Hurricane day fighter squadrons were allocated to night duties, with others formed specially for night fighting. As an example, 96 Squadron was formed out of 422 Night Fighter Flight, which had been on the night defence of London and was allocated to the night defence of Liverpool in December 1940, which had already suffered nine heavy bombing raids.

Hurricane Mk IIC HL864 LK-?: 87 Squadron fitted with 44-gallon underwing fuel drop tanks, with P/O F. W. Mitchell standing on the wing. No. 87 Squadron re-equipped with Hurricane Mk IICs at Charmy Down from June 1941 and also operated from Colerne, with detachments to St Mary's until leaving for North Africa on 2 November 1942. (*IWM photo*)

No. 151 Squadron at Wittering operated Hurricane Mk IICs from June 1941 until January 1942 on the night defence of the industrial Midlands of England. Hurricane Mk IIC V6931 DZ-D:151 Squadron was at Wittering during 1941. (*RAF Museum photo*)

No. 151 Squadron, now fully recovered from the activities in the Battle of Britain, was equipped with a mixture of Hurricane and Defiants at Wittering to cover the approach of raids from German bases in Holland against the industrial Midlands, achieved its first night victory when a Do 17 was shot down on 15 January 1941. Two Polish units joined the night defences—306 Squadron in February and 308 Squadron in March—with the latter destroying a Ju 88 over Coventry during an early sortie. They were joined in the defence of Coventry by 310 (Czech) Squadron.

No. 255 Squadron, based at Kirton-in-Lindsey as part of the defence of the East Coast ports and the Midlands, used its Hurricanes to claim six enemy bombers over Hull on 9 May 1941—the highest score by any night fighter squadron during the Blitz. In Northern Ireland 245 Squadron, which had been busy during the Battle of Britain, added night patrols to its normal day operations, with the first confirmed victory being on 13 May 1940 when Sqn Ldr John Simpson, DFC and bar, shot down a Do 17Z over the Irish Sea.

No. 253 Squadron was tasked with the night air defence of the naval base at Scapa Flow from Skaebrae in the Orkneys when the squadron arrived with its Hurricanes in February 1941. As the spring of 1941 approached, the remaining Hurricane night-fighter squadrons converted to the more suitable Douglas Havoc twin-engined night fighter, but the Blitz ended in May when Göring withdrew his bombers from France and the Low Countries to prepare for the assault on Russia, which began the following month.

No. 306 was the third of the Polish fighter squadrons when it formed at Church Fenton on 29 August 1940 with Hurricane Mk Is. These were operated by the squadron until April 1941 when Mk IIAs replaced the earlier aircraft at Northolt. The squadron was tasked with night patrols from May 1941, gaining the first victory against a He 111 on 10 May. The squadron also flew escorts to Blenheims and converted to Spitfires in June 1941. Among the aircraft dispersed at Church Fenton was Mk I V7118 UZ-V:306. (Polish) Squadron, with parachutes on the wings and the Polish insignia on the rear fuselage. (*IWM photo*)

No. 96 Squadron reformed at Cranage on 16 December 1940 with Hurricane Mk Is in the night-fighter role for the defence of Liverpool, P3712 ZJ-J being an example. The squadron operated Defiants from March 1941 until May 1942, with some Hurricane Mk IICs from September 1941 until January 1942. (*RAF Museum photo*)

No. 310. (Czech) Squadron was formed at Duxford with Hurricane Mk Is on 10 July 1940 ready to participate in the Battle of Britain. The squadron re-equipped with Mk IIAs in March 1941 with eight-gun wings for the night defence of Coventry. Here an example is being serviced inside one of the Belfast hangars at Duxford. The squadron moved to Martlesham Heath on 26 June where some Mk IIBs were added to the squadron, leaving for Dyce on 20 July, and began to re-equip with Spitfires in October. (*Author's collection*)

No. 245 Squadron re-equipped with Hurricane Mk Is at Leconfield in March 1940 and was based at Aldergrove from 20 July during and after the Battle of Britain. One of their aircraft was W9200 DX-?, flown by S/Ldr John Simpson, who claimed an enemy bomber off Northern Ireland on the night of 7–8 April 1941, bringing his score to eleven aircraft. The squadron converted to Hurricane Mk IIBs in August 1941 and moved to Chilbolton on 1 September. (*RAF Museum and Author's collection*)

Hurricane Mk Is of 245 Squadron at Aldergrove in Ulster for the defence of the Belfast area in May 1941 before converting to Mk IIBs in August 1941. (*P. H. T. Green collection*)

After operating with Hurricane Mk Is within 11 Group during the Battle of Britain, 253 Squadron began to convert to Mk IIBs in July 1941 at Skaebrae. Hurricane Z3971:SW-S heads the line-up of Hurricane Mk IIBs being prepared for an operation in the defence of Scapa Flow. The squadron also operated Hurricane Mk IIAs and IICs, leaving for North Africa in November 1942. (*RAF Museum photo*)

This brought London and the other major targets of the German bombing respite having suffered tremendous damage. However, it had failed to defeat Britain. Official German records confirm 307 bombers lost on night raids, of which anti-aircraft guns claimed around one-third. Although it was not possible to confirm exactly how many could be credited to Hurricane pilots, it was believed to be between sixty and eighty aircraft, with the remainder being claimed by Defiants, Blenheims, and later Beaufighters. The Hurricanes were only an interim solution pending the availability of the dedicated night fighters with AI radar to guide them to their targets—the Beaufighters in service by the end of the Blitz with their radar were helped by the very efficient ground-controlled interception system.

A far less effective use of Hurricanes in night fighting was with the Turbinlite flights, later to be designated squadrons. An idea to detect enemy bombers appearing to have some chance before the availability of AI radar was to fit a powerful searchlight into the nose of a twin engine bomber with an interim AI system and accompanied by a single-seat fighter. The principle was for the target to be tracked using the AI and, when in position behind the raider, illuminate it with the light and allow the fighter to move in for the kill. The aircraft most commonly used for this work were a Turbinlite Douglas Havoc converted bomber accompanied by a Hurricane. The Havoc was fitted with a General Electric-developed airborne searchlight in the nose; a carbon arc lamp requiring 1,400 amps at 105 volts powered by very high discharge batteries that allowed four illuminations of thirty seconds before being recharged at a local power station.

The Havoc was fitted with formation-keeping lights to assist the accompanying Hurricane to maintain contact, the Havoc approaching to within 3,000 feet of the target when the code 'hot' was passed to the fighter pilot. When the Havoc was positively locked on, the code word 'boiling' was passed to the pilot and the fighter would drop 300 feet and open up on full power ahead of the Havoc. When the Hurricane was about 900 feet behind the enemy, the Havoc would turn on the light, illuminating the target for the fighter. The major weakness was that as soon as the target pilot was aware of the light, he would take violent evasive action that was impossible for the Hurricane pilot to follow having lost his limited night vision in the glare of the searchlight.

Despite the system being successful in making a considerable number of contacts, only one enemy aircraft was claimed as destroyed, with one probable and two damaged. The answer was clearly to concentrate development on higher performance aircraft, such as the Beaufighter and Mosquito, with their own AI radar and guns fitted. All eight Turbinlite flights operated a flight of Hurricane Mk IICs allocated from the night fighter squadrons, and while the majority operated Hurricanes from September 1942, the first to form was 1453 Flight at Wittering in July 1941.

No. 1455 Flight was renumbered 534 Squadron on 7 July 1941—the remainder of the flights gaining squadron status in September 1942. The final operational patrols were in October and all eight squadrons had disbanded by 1 February 1943. This was long after effective dedicated AI radar-equipped night fighters were in service from May 1941, even before the first Turbinlite flight had been formed, which begs the question why such an ineffective system was persevered with for some year and a half.

Hurricane Mk IIBs of 245 Squadron co-operated with Turbinlite Havocs while based at Middle Wallop in early 1942. (*Author's collection*)

With Hitler's attack on the Soviet Union in June 1941 relieving the pressure on Britain, Churchill pledged support for the new ally and plans were made to supply war materials by convoy via the North Cape route to Archangel and Murmansk. In addition to catapult-launched Hurricanes being used for the air defence of these convoys, a major part of the early cargoes were Hurricanes for the defence against air attack of the disembarkation ports, as well as training the Russians to operate and maintain the aircraft. The RAF therefore shipped two squadrons of Hurricane Mk IIAs and IIBs on the North Cape convoys for use by the Russians. These were 81 Squadron, which formed at Leconfield with Hurricane Mk IIAs on 28 July 1941, and 134 Squadron that had formed there the previous day. With the ground crews embarked on SS Llanstephan Castle in one of the early PQ convoys, the pilots and Hurricanes from the two squadrons were loaded aboard HMS Argus on 12 August and arrived at Vaenga near Murmansk on 1 September. As additional convoys sailed for Russia, further crated Hurricanes for the Soviet Air Force were shipped, increasing the threat to the Luftwaffe and requiring the two RAF squadrons to provide active air defence as well as their training role.

When taking off from HMS Argus, RAF Hurricanes had six of their twelve guns removed to reduce weight, but they were declared operational on 12 September. The additional guns were landed at Archangel, and when they arrived at Vaenga, the blast tubes were missing resulting in Russian engineers having to make replacements.

Despite this, 81 Squadron was in action on the first day when five Hurricanes intercepted five Finnish Bf 109Es escorting a Luftwaffe Hs 126. Hurricane pilots claimed three Bf 109s and damage to the Hs 126 reconnaissance aircraft with the loss of one RAF pilot killed. Soon after, a Bf 110 was damaged and three more Bf 109s were shot down during the afternoon. Both squadrons remained in action during September, with No. 81 claiming the most successes.

No. 81 Squadron reformed at Leconfield from 'A' Flight 504 Squadron with Hurricane Mk IIBs on 28 July 1941 and left for Russia aboard HMS *Argus* on 12 August. The squadron arrived at Vaenga on 7 September, and with its task completed returned to Britain in November and re-equipped with Spitfires at Turnhouse. (*Author's collection*)

No. 134 Squadron reformed at Leconfield on 28 July 1941 from a nucleus of 17 Squadron with Hurricane Mk IIBs and was shipped aboard HMS *Argus* on 12 August to Vaenga to become part of 151 Wing with 81 Squadron. Hurricane Mk IIB Z3768 49-FK on dispersal soon after arriving at Vaenga with a flight of Hurricanes overhead. (*IWM photo*)

No. 151 Wing at Vaenga, consisting of 81 and 134 Squadrons, operated Hurricane Mk IIBs for the air defence of the port installations around the North Cape, as well being responsible for the training of pilots and ground crews in the Soviet Air Force. In the harsh climate, the conditions were somewhat primitive. (*Author's collection*)

A 134 Squadron Hurricane Mk IIB being prepared for departure from Vaenga on another training sortie.

A Hurricane Mk IIB of 151 Wing at Vaenga fitted with a rather inappropriate tropical filter, which would have reduced the performance in such harsh conditions. (*P. H. T. Green collection*)

Hurricane Mk IIBs of 151 Wing at Vaenga prepare for take-off on another air defence operation. (*P. H. T. Green collection*)

A 151 Wing Hurricane Mk IIB on dispersal in the harsh conditions at Vaenga in Russia. (*P. H. T. Green collection*)

On 17 September, 81 Squadron was escorting a Soviet bomber raid when eight Luftwaffe Bf 109s attacked—two were claimed by RAF pilots. Four Russian fighters attacked the Hurricanes, fortunately without causing any damage.

No. 81 Squadron was again on Soviet bomber escort duties on 26 September when they were attacked by nine Finnish Bf 109Fs, but three were claimed as shot down. On 6 October, 134 Squadron caught a Luftwaffe bombing raid on Vaenga claiming two shot down—one probable and two damaged.

By the end of October, some sixty Hurricanes had been assembled for the Soviet Air Force from the aircraft shipped in from MUs in Britain. Pilots of the two RAF squadrons commenced training the local pilots on the operation of the aircraft. On 28 October, 134 Squadron handed over its aircraft to the Soviet Air Force—the personnel embarked on board for return to Britain, and No. 81 Squadron personnel followed a month later. It was estimated that some 2,952 Hurricanes were supplied to the Soviet Union from both Britain and Canada, including sixty Mk IIDs and thirty Mk IVs.

In addition to the majority shipped by sea, some were delivered by rail from surplus stocks with MUs in the Middle East via Iran. There are no detail records of Hurricane service with the Soviet Air Force, but wastage was very high due to a lack of spares and trained ground crew to correct even the simplest repairs, resulting in the aircraft being abandoned or scrapped on site.

In the late summer of 1941, a dedicated night fighter version of the Hurricane was developed with an AI Mark V radar mounted in a fairing similar to the 44-gallon fuel tank under one wing, with a fixed 44-gallon fuel tank under the other wing as balance. The associated aerials were mounted on the outer wing surfaces. No. 245 Squadron had Hurricane AI radar-equipped Mk IICs issued in September 1942; one flight flew from Angle in South Wales, but with no success due to the lack of enemy aircraft.

Lt Col. B. F. Safanov was one of the first Soviet Hurricane aces, but he was killed in action in May 1942. (*Author's collection*)

Some Hurricane Mk IICs with four 20-mm cannons, 44-gallon drop tanks, and tropical filters, were shipped overland by rail from Iran taken from surplus RAF stocks for the Soviet Air Force. (*P. H. T. Green collection*)

This Hurricane Mk II with the Soviet Air Force was converted locally into a two-seat artillery spotting aircraft. (*P. H. T. Green collection*)

With the Luftwaffe abandoning its daylight offensive against Britain by the end of October 1940, Air Marshal Sir William Sholto-Douglas, who succeeded Dowding as head of Fighter Command, began to plan an offensive using Hurricanes against German targets in occupied France. The main purpose of these attacks was to raise the morale of the British people, who were experiencing endless night-bombing attacks, by reversing the six-month old defensive posture to one of offensive operations. As the operations developed, a number of well-defined attacks were created, some based on the Luftwaffe attacks during the Battle of Britain.

The smallest form of attack was with no more than four fighters and later fighter-bombers known as a rhubarb, which were normally authorised at station level. These aircraft would go after targets of opportunity, such as enemy road vehicles, trains, river transport, and aircraft on the ground.

The rodeo was similar, but carried out with a full squadron level, and in addition to targets of opportunity, enemy airfields were also targeted as planned events. The largest form of offensive was organised at Group level, known as a ranger, which would consist of three or four squadrons as a wing from sector stations, and occasionally for a heavy attack could involve two or three wings—the aim being to draw enemy fighters into the air when they may have been overwhelmed by greater numbers of RAF aircraft.

There were also armed bomber escorts, with the bombers more likely to attract the attention of enemy defending fighters; a circus, when the aircraft were going for targets of opportunity; and a Ramrod where the bombers had a specific target such as a railway junction, airfield, ports, and other military concentrations.

Anti-shipping attacks, which had the additional hazard of encountering dedicated flak ships sailing along the French coast and entering or leaving port, were known as roadsteads. As it became imperative to increase offensive operations to deny the use of the English Channel by enemy shipping blockade runners, Operation Channel Stop was instigated.

There was a less informal air defence of coastal drifters fishing in the North Sea, which had gone largely unmolested during the Battle of Britain either by German ships or aircraft. However, towards the end of the Battle of Britain, some spiteful attacks had been made against these vulnerable and unarmed fishing vessels, as a result of which the Admiralty requested help from Fighter Command. What was known as the Kipper patrols were set up from late October 1940 whereby Hurricane squadrons based along Eastern Britain protected the fleet. Among the units involved were 257 Squadron based at Coltishall, 258 Squadron at Acklington, and 310 (Czech) Squadron from Dyce at Aberdeen. Only one enemy aircraft was claimed during these patrols, but a number were deterred by the presence of Hurricanes providing protection to this important source of food for Britain.

The Hurricane's rugged construction was more suited to the ground-attack duties than the Spitfire, but the latter was more effective in providing top cover while the Hurricanes went in at low level to create the maximum surprise on these hazardous missions.

One of the first Hurricane units to introduce the offensive across the Channel was 249 Squadron based at North Weald, two of whose pilots flew a rhubarb in Hurricane Mk Is over Boulogne on 29 December 1940.

257 Squadron take off from a snow covered Coltishall led by S/Ldr Tuck. (*Author's collection*)

No. 601 Squadron flew rhubarbs and circuses with Hurricane Mk Is from January 1941, but after suffering heavy losses converted to Mk IICs from March while based at Northolt. (*RAF Museum photo*)

In January 1941, 601 Squadron, which had moved from Exeter to Northolt, flew half a dozen rhubarbs and two circuses, but when they suffered heavy losses of seven aircraft destroyed or written-off in accidents with four pilots missing, it was realised that the older Hurricane Mk Is were vulnerable to offensive action, particularly in low-level combat. In March, the squadron began to receive Hurricane Mk IICs. During a typical rhubarb on 22 May with the improved Hurricanes, two 601 Squadron pilots operating from the advanced base at Manston, claimed a Ju 52/3m transport as a probable, but were then set upon by a pair of Bf 109Es, one of which the Hurricane pilots shot down into a wood, while the other departed without attacking.

The first Hurricane wing was formed at Martlesham Heath when 605 Squadron arrived in February 1941 and were joined by 17 Squadron. Both squadrons were equipped with Hurricane Mk IIAs, ready to take part in rangers. However, this did not last long as both squadrons were due for a rest; 17 Squadron had been in action in the south since the Battle of Britain, 605 Squadron went to Ternhill in March, and 17 Squadron to Castletown in April.

Other Hurricane squadrons gradually began to take the offensive, with 257 Squadron based at Coltishall commencing rhubarbs from March along the Dutch coast. No. 258 Squadron, which reformed at Kenley with Hurricane Mk IIAs on 22 April, began rhubarbs along the French coast in May, but lost four pilots while claiming three Bf 109Es.

No. 71 Squadron, the first American volunteer 'Eagle' Squadron, formed at Church Fenton on 19 September 1940 and received Hurricane Mk Is in November, replacing them with

Hurricane Mk II V6564 DT-A:257. (Burma) Squadron being refuelled at a snowy Coltishall ready for another strike sortie. No. 257 Squadron operated Hurricane Mk IIs from April 1941 until September 1942, when the squadron was re-equipped with Typhoons. (*IWM photo*)

No. 71. (Eagle) Squadron formed at Church Fenton on 19 September 1940 with Hurricane Mk Is as the first American volunteer squadron—before the USA entered the Second World War in December 1941. (*IWM photo*)

No. 71. (Eagle) Squadron replaced the Hurricane Mk Is with Mk IIAs at Martlesham Heath in April 1941, moving to North Weald on 23 June where offensive patrols were flown over occupied Europe. (*Author's collection*)

Mk IIAs at Martlesham Heath in April 1941, and moving to North Weald on 23 June. Before converting to Spitfires in August, 71 Squadron flew twenty-eight rhubarbs, five rodeos, nine circuses, three ramrods, as well as convoy patrols around the Thames Estuary, the first victory being a Bf 109F over Lille on 21 July. In June, 312 (Czech) Squadron arrived at Kenley with Hurricane Mk IIBs and was soon involved in circuses, claiming the destruction of two Bf 109Es and two Bf 109Fs, but with three pilots missing. No. 312 Squadron was posted to Martlesham Heath on 20 July from where it flew convoy patrols until moving to Ayr and converting to Spitfires. No. 317 (Polish) Squadron exchanged its Hurricane Mk Is for Mk IIBs at Fairwood Common in July 1941, claiming Bf 109Es during a circus on 10 July before moving to Exeter on 21 July and converting to Spitfires in October.

No. 247 Squadron flew its first rodeo from Predannack, Cornwall, in August 1941 with Hurricane Mk IICs over the airfield at Morlaix in France.

The first two Canadian Squadrons, 401 and 402, had formed at Digby on 1 March 1941 initially with Hurricane Mk Is, but after training changed to Mk IIAs in May. No. 401 Squadron converted to Spitfires in September 1941, while 402 Squadron moved to Martlesham Heath on 23 June, which had Hurricane Mk IIBs by then. The pilots had undergone training for the fighter-bomber role with the Air Fighting Development Unit at Duxford to allow the aircraft to be modified to carry two 250-lb bombs on underwing racks. No. 402 Squadron moved briefly to Ayr before operating from Rochford, Warmwell, and Colerne, where they converted to Spitfires in March 1942.

F/O 'Red' Tobin was one of the American volunteer pilots with 71. (Eagle) Squadron. (*Author's collection*)

No. 121 Squadron formed at Kirton-in-Lindsey on 5 May 1941. It was the second of the three American volunteer. (Eagle) squadrons and used Hurricane Mk Is for training, which were replaced by Mk IIBs in July. The squadron moved to Digby on 28 September, undertaking convoy patrols off the East Coast. A move was made back to Kirton-in-Lindsey on 3 October for conversion to Spitfires. (*Author's collection*)

No. 312. (Czech) Squadron formed at Duxford on 29 August 1940 with Hurricane Mk Is. On 29 May 1941, the squadron moved to Kenley where it re-equipped with Hurricane Mk IIBs and participated in circuses, losing three pilots. Ground crew pose in front of Hurricane DU-C of 312 Squadron in a Kenley dispersal during the spring of 1941. (*Author's collection*)

No. 312. (Czech) Squadron moved to Martlesham Heath on 20 July 1941, with Hurricane Mk IIBs flying convoy patrols until moving to Ayr on 19 August to convert to Spitfires. Hurricane Mk IIB Z3588 on dispersal ready for the next sortie. (*Author's collection*)

No. 331 Squadron was the first Norwegian fighter squadron. It formed at Catterick on 21 July 1941 with Hurricane Mk Is for training. These were replaced by Mk IIBs in August, with the squadron based at Castletown and Skaebrae for the air defence of Scapa Flow as well as shipping and convoy patrols. The squadron saw little action and converted to Spitfires in November 1941. (*Author's collection*)

No. 401 Squadron formed at Digby on 1 March 1941 from the renumbering of 1 Squadron RCAF. The squadron was initially equipped with Hurricane Mk Is, but replaced them with Mk IIAs in May and converted to Spitfires in September. P/O J. Small and Sgt G. B. Whitney scramble to their Hurricane Mk IIBs of 401 Squadron at Digby on 24 July 1941. (*Author's collection*)

No. 402 Squadron was initially equipped with Hurricane Mk Is for training and formed at Digby on 1 March 1941 by renumbering No. 2 Squadron RCAF. The Mk Is were replaced with Mk IIBs in June 1941 when a move was made to Martlesham Heath. A pilot is seen during the training programme scrambling towards his Hurricane Mk I with the ground crew ready. (*Author's collection*)

The ground crew running up the Merlin engine of Hurricane Mk IIB Z3658 YC-N:401 'Ram' Squadron RCAF at Digby on 24 July 1941. (*The Public Archives of Canada*)

Hurricane Mk IIB BE485 AE-W:402 Squadron with a pair of 250-lb bombs under the wings. No. 402 Squadron moved to Martlesham Heath on 23 June 1941, from where it operated offensive patrols. (*IWM photo*)

After being based at Martlesham Heath, 402 Squadron moved briefly to Ayr, and then to Southend on 19 August 1941, followed by a move to Warmwell on 6 November where conditions were somewhat primitive. S/Ldr R. E. Morrow DFC, CO of the squadron, waits while the 250-lb bombs are loaded onto Hurricane Mk IIB BE417 AE-K:402 Squadron at Warmwell in early 1942. The squadron moved to Colerne on 4 March when it converted to Spitfires. (*Author's collection*)

By the late autumn, sixteen Hurricane squadrons were flying regular sweeps along the French, Belgian, and Dutch coastlines. They suffered heavy losses to the newly introduced Luftwaffe Fw 190 As, which was around 80 mph faster than the Hurricane Mk IIB. It was therefore decided to discontinue the fighter sweeps and rhubarbs and rodeos, with the Hurricane Mk IIs reverting to the fighter role by day.

Meanwhile, many Hurricane Mk IIBs had been at the MUs during the summer and modified for the fighter-bomber role to operate as bombers in circuses and ramrods with Spitfire Mk VBs as escort. The Hurribomber operations commenced on 30 October with 607 Squadron flying from Manston and dropping 250-lb bombs on a transformer station near Tingry, followed by 402 (Canadian) Squadron attacking the airfield at Berck-sur-Mer.

In addition to the already described Hurricane night-fighter operations during and after the Battle of Britain, Fighter Command began to investigate the use of Hurricanes for the night-intruder role to intercept some of the Luftwaffe bombers returning to their bases close to the French coast. No. 87 Squadron was the most experienced in night flying, having operated at night throughout the Battle of Britain with some success.

Two flights of 87. (United Provinces) Squadron Hurricane Mk IICs, which were based at Charmy Down in 1942 and specialised in night-intruder sorties, armed with four 20-mm cannons. (*Author's collection*)

In June 1941, 87 Squadron exchanged its Hurricane Mk Is for Hurricane Mk IICs while based at Charmy Down, where they had the dual role of defending the Bristol area at night against enemy attack, and conducting night intruding operations against Luftwaffe bomber bases in Brittany. Hurricane Mk IIC BE500 LK-A:87 Squadron with the commanding officer, S/Ldr Denis Smallwood, in the cockpit. (*Charles E. Brown photo*)

The squadron exchanged its Hurricane Mk Is for IICs at Charmy Down in June 1941, with detachments at St Mary's in the Scilly Isles having the dual task of defending the Bristol area against enemy night attack and intruding at night over Luftwaffe bomber bases along the French coast—in particular the He 111 path-finding unit at Vannes in Brittany. The twin tasks kept the squadron busy with their successes increasing steadily until it was sent to North Africa in November 1942. The Hurricane Mk II made an ideal intruder, especially when fitted with a pair of underwing drop tanks.

When weather conditions appeared suitable for Luftwaffe night-bombing raids, a pair of Hurricane intruders would take off from their base at dusk to arrive over the enemy airfields about one hour after dark to detect if the flare paths were being lit as that signified planned bomber operations.

The RAF intruders would then report back at base what airfields were operating, allowing two or more intruders to depart and intercept the returning enemy bombers at the end of their sorties. By coming in close to the enemy bomber at the top of the descent to the flare path, the Hurricane pilot could make out the dim shape of the aircraft and a short burst from the 20-mm cannons would cause the bomber to crash on to the runway threshold. Among experts at night intruding was 1 Squadron, whose role changed from daylight sweeps to training for night-intruder operations from March to July 1941.

Two flights of 87 Squadron Hurricane Mk IICs, led by S/Ldr Dennis Smallwood, in overall black finish for night intruding and armed with four 20-mm cannons. The squadron left for North Africa in November 1942. (*Charles E. Brown photo*)

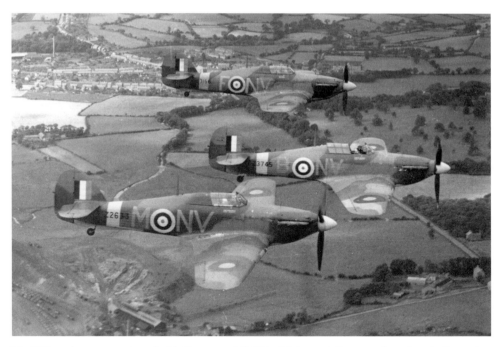

No. 79 Squadron was equipped with Hurricane Mk IIBs at Fairwood Common from June to December 1941; Z2633:NV-M, Z3745:NV-B and Z3156:NV-F being examples. The squadron moved to Baginton and left for India in March 1942. (*IWM photo*)

No. 247. (China-British) Squadron was equipped with Hurricane Mk IICs at Exeter from August 1941 to March 1943, when the squadron converted to Typhoons. The squadron was tasked with night intruders—its first confirmed victory a He 111 destroyed at night in September 1941. The squadron also operated rhubarbs, and in May 1942 was flying roadsteads at night against enemy shipping. Hurricane Mk IIC BD936 ZY-S:247 Squadron was painted in the overall matt black finish and armed with four 20-mm cannons. (*IWM photo*)

No. 1 Squadron's role changed from daylight operations to night intruders from March to July 1941 with Hurricane Mk IICs at Tangmere—the first success being three He 111s destroyed in one night on 4 May. Two flights of 1 Squadron Hurricane Mk IICs fly an echelon to starboard still in daylight camouflage and armed with four 20-mm cannons. (*RAF Museum photo*)

On 4 May 1942, a Hurricane Mk IIC was able to claim three He 111s destroyed in the circuit to land in one sortie. The pilot was the Czech Flight Lieutenant K. M. Kuttelwascher operating from Tangmere. He eventually claimed eighteen enemy aircraft shot down on intruder operations until posted to 23 Squadron Mosquitos, where he never encountered another enemy aircraft.

Although Hurricanes were vulnerable to the growing menace of the Fw 190 As, the RAF continued to make offensive daylight attacks over occupied France during the winter of 1941 to 1942. Hurricanes increasingly took part in bombing attacks in the Mk IIBs and IICs. Operations were stopped for long periods at a time due to bad weather, which was when the German Navy decided to sail the battle cruisers Scharnhorst and Gneisenau with the cruiser Prinz Eugen from Brest to the comparative safety of home ports in Germany. Although the breakout had been expected, the convoy was covered by bad weather and not detected until 12 February as it approached the Straights of Dover. Among the RAF and RN responses were 3 and 607 Squadrons, with four aircraft detachments at Manston. Although Hurricanes would have little effect on the capital ships, four Hurricanes of 607 Squadron took off at 12.30 p.m. to attempt to attack some of the escorts. The aircraft were vectored too far south of the main group, but located a flak ship that was set on fire by one of the pilots, who failed to return to base.

On 16 February, 402 Squadron RCAF based at Warmwell was ordered to attack a small convoy of minesweepers off Brittany. After refuelling at Perranporth, they set of south, with six Hurricane Mk IIBs each carrying a pair of underwing 250-lb bombs escorted by Spitfires.

No. 3 Squadron, with Hurricane Mk IICs, was among the RAF response to the German battlecruisers detected in the English Channel on 12 February 1942 when they tried to break out from Brest. The squadron had received Hurricane Mk IICs in April 1941—BD962:QO-Q being an example—and were based at Martlesham Heath, Stapleford Tawney, and Hunsdon before converting to Typhoons in February 1944 at Manston. (*Author's collection*)

No. 402 Squadron RCAF was based at Warmwell from 6 November 1941 until 4 March 1942 with Hurricane Mk IIBs. Sgt I. J. Eady and Sgt B. E. Innes in front of a Hurricane Mk IIB of 402 Squadron with underwing 250-lb bombs at Warmwell on 9 February 1942. (*Public Archives of Canada photo*)

Flying at low level of around 50 feet, the Hurricanes located the enemy ships, which turned out to be four heavily armed destroyers that had been escorts to the capital ships four days earlier, and were returning to their base at Brest. By this time, there was no option but to attack; the Canadian pilots headed for the ships, one of which was hit twice and another by one bomb to take heavy damage, but they reached their destination safely. All the Hurricanes were undamaged and returned to base, with one making a crash landing.

Under Lord Louis Mountbatten, the Chief of Combined Operations, a plan was developed to seize and hold a major German-occupied French port for a short period to prove it was possible, and to gather intelligence from prisoners and captured material while assessing the enemy's response. The raid would hopefully give a morale boost to troops back on the offensive for the first time since the Dunkirk withdrawal, and give backing to US and British commitment assured to Stalin.

On 19 August 1942, the Allied Combined Operation was planned at Dieppe, and Fighter Command—led at this time by Air Marshal Leigh-Mallory—was responsible for the protection and support of the troops landing, and the cover of the ships to and from the beaches and offshore. It was expected that this operation would attract a heavy response from the Luftwaffe remaining in France, so Leigh-Mallory decided to see how the newly introduced Typhoons and Spitfire IXs would perform against Fw 190 As in combat. In addition, most of the Hurricane and Spitfire squadrons were deployed in a number of roles, with eight Hurricane squadrons to bomb the enemy positions at Dieppe just before the first assault troops landed until the last ships were back out of range of the massive coastal gun batteries. Leigh-Mallory stated:

> We are going to attack Dieppe. The army are going to land. They're a brigade of troops. They're going to walk into the town and show the Germans how we can invade when the time comes. There are a lot of guns placed around. I have told the light bombers from Bomber Command that I don't need them. I want to take out all the defences with my Hurricanes and my Hurricane fighter-bombers. I don't mind losing 50 per cent of them.
>
> I don't want Bomber Command. This is going to be a Fighter Command operation.

Aircraft losses during the ill-fated raid were heavy, partly due to the superiority of the new Luftwaffe Fw 190 over even the Spitfire Vs, let alone the cannon-armed Hurricane Mk IICs. Leigh-Mallory's command lost ninety-seven aircraft in action, but claimed ninety-six enemy aircraft destroyed, thirty-nine probables, and 145 damaged. In fact, the Luftwaffe lost forty-eight aircraft and thirteen pilots. The RAF lost forty-seven pilots and a further seventeen taken prisoner.

The Dieppe disaster did not affect Leigh-Mallory's career; he became C-in-C Fighter Command in late 1942—in time to plan the Air Component for the D-Day landings.

Hurricane operations at Dieppe were flown under an enormous umbrella of Spitfires providing protection from the Fw 190 As and Bf 109Fs, which only got through when the Hurricanes were not in action. Among the twenty-one Hurricane units in action in the Tangmere Sector was 43 Squadron, which started the day at readiness at 4 a.m., reverting to thirty-minute availability after 5 a.m. for a total period of twelve hours. During this period, the squadron flew forty-eight sorties to Dieppe consisting of four complete squadron trips—the highest of any squadron in the sector.

No. 43 Squadron was the first of five squadrons to attack the gun positions on the beaches and the buildings on the west side of the harbour from 5.15 a.m. These were the primary beaches for the Allied landings and were heavily defended by both light and heavy flak, as well as machine guns. It was the task of the Hurricane pilots to bomb the coastal defences and set up a smokescreen under which the assault troops could make their initial attack. In the two initial attacks, hits were recorded on a number of installations, but out of the dozen aircraft with 43 Squadron that went into the attack, only five returned home unscathed at 6.20 a.m. One pilot was posted missing; another baled out but was picked up by air-sea rescue; and another Hurricane was so badly damaged in the wing that the pilot had to make a wheels-up landing at Tangmere.

No major objective of the raid was achieved. A total of 3,623 men were killed, injured, or taken prisoner out of the 6,086 mostly Canadian troops who landed. The RAF lost eighteen Hurricanes compared to forty-eight aircraft lost by the Luftwaffe, and the RN lost thirty-three landing craft and one destroyer. However, lessons were learned that influenced the preparations for the Allied landings in North Africa and D-Day in Normandy.

Among the many RAF aircraft in action during the Dieppe raid was Tangmere-based 43 Squadron with Hurricane Mk IICs, which made forty-eight sorties on 19 August 1942. The squadron operated Mk IICs at Tangmere from December 1941 until moving to Kirton-in-Lindsey on 1 September 1942 in preparation for going to North Africa. Here the squadron's Hurricanes are lined up at Tangmere in August 1942. (*RAF Museum photo*)

One of the minor objectives of the Dieppe raid had been to gather intelligence on the performance of the German radar station on the cliff top east of Pourville using a RAF radar specialist with eleven Canadians as his bodyguard. The team failed to gain entry to the radar installation due to heavy defences, but the radar specialist was able to cut the telephone lines into the building, resulting in the Germans having to resort to radio transmissions that could be intercepted, allowing Britain to gain important knowledge of enemy radar stations along the Channel coast.

The Typhoons proved ineffective in dogfights and two were lost on the Dieppe operation due to structural failure of the rear fuselage. However, the aircraft was redeveloped in the ground-attack role, for which it proved most effective, and the Hurricane fighter-bomber squadrons were to provide the experience for the introduction of the new aircraft into RAF service.

While the 20-mm cannon-armed Hurricane Mk IIC was a great improvement in destructive effect, the rugged airframe was obviously capable of packing an even greater punch and perhaps penetrate heavy armour. Late in 1941, as part of a broader programme of weapons trials with various aircraft types, Hurricane Mk IIA Series 2 Z2415 was fitted with three unguided rocket launchers under each wing. Although there were no recoil forces from the rocket launch, this particular Hurricane already had a strengthened wing from terminal velocity diving trials during 1941, and the stronger wing was believed to be required to withstand high-g manoeuvres during combat. This aircraft, together with two more similarly modified Hurricanes, was delivered to Boscombe Down soon after.

Hurricane Mk IIA Z2415 was used at the A&AEE at Boscombe Down for rocket-firing trials during February 1942. (*P. H. T. Green collection*)

Although unguided rocket projectiles (RP) were lacking in accuracy for small targets, a salvo ripple fired in four pairs with 60-lb explosive warheads had an effect equivalent to a broadside from a cruiser.

However, at low level, the explosion of the warheads could be a hazard to the launch aircraft, and on anti-shipping attacks it was found to be just as effective to fire inert RP phased for some to hit the superstructure, while others hit the water and went through the side of the hull below the waterline. This method of attack was later developed to great effect with the Mosquito FB VIs against surface shipping. During the trials, it was found that the rockets were not very accurate when fired from low level, but a rocket attack was found to be more accurate if they were launched in a steep dive. Following the trials, there was some delay introducing the weapons into service due to the RN claiming a higher priority for the use of rocket attacks against shipping in 1942, and the commanders of Fighter Command were not convinced regarding the accuracy of the weapons. Despite the slow introduction of RP, this form of weapon was to continue in use by the RAF right into the jet age alongside the 20-mm cannon.

Against more compact armoured ground targets, both Rolls-Royce and Vickers had been developing 40-mm cannons since 1939 to be fitted to fighter aircraft. The challenge was to develop a gun with the calibre of the Bofors light anti-aircraft gun, with weight reduced and compact enough to be fitted to an aircraft. By 1941, enough progress had been made to allow a trial installation in a fighter, and the Hurricane was selected as it was already able to cope

Hurricane Mk IID KZ320 at Langley armed with a pair of faired Vickers S 40 mm anti-tank cannons. (*Author's collection*)

with up to twelve machine guns or four 20-mm cannons, and was believed to be capable of having a pair of 40-mm cannons fitted. In early May 1941, instructions were given to the Hawker design office to design modifications to allow installation of a pair of the Vickers S cannons to be mounted under the wings of Hurricane Mk IIA Series 2, Z2326.

Two of the Browning machine guns were retained to assist in the aiming of the big guns, and modification of the aircraft commenced on 30 May at Langley with the first pair of guns delivered two weeks later. The maiden flight of what was to become the prototype Hurricane Mk IID was on 18 September, with the guns unfaired, and the aircraft was delivered to Boscombe Down the next day for preliminary trials. After a brief period at Farnborough, the aircraft returned to Langley for the installation of the Rolls-Royce belt-fed 40-mm cannons, but these were rejected after a major failure as the guns were bulkier and carried less rounds than the Vickers S with fifteen each.

Additionally, more comprehensive weapons trials were carried out at Boscombe Down from February 1942, with four initial Mk IIDs fitted with guns enclosed in a low-profile fairing to reduce drag. The first ninety-two production aircraft were delivered to the MUs with standard armour protection of the Mk IICs, but from July armour protection was increased by 368 lb, resulting in the maximum AUW increasing to 8,540 lb. The first unit to receive Hurricane Mk IIDs in Britain was 184 Squadron, based at Colerne, on 1 December 1942, which was specially formed to undertake service trials with the new armament and develop appropriate tactics.

Hurricane Z2326 was originally built as a Mk II and converted to the prototype Mk IID with a pair of underwing-mounted 40-mm Vickers S cannons, making its maiden flight in this configuration on 18 September 1941. (*Author's collection*)

Hurricane Mk IV KZ198 armed with two 40-mm Vickers S cannons, powered by a tropicalised Merlin 27 driving a Rotol R S 5/11 four-blade propeller for operations in the North African desert. This version of the Hurricane was operated on its first rhubarb on 23 July 1943. (*Author's collection*)

The RP-armed Hurricane Mk IID was fitted with additional armour plate around the Merlin engine. The type was first issued to 184 Squadron at Colerne on 1 December 1942 for service trials. (*Author's collection*)

During these trials it was found that to penetrate armour effectively Hurricanes had to approach the target at very low level to achieve effective destruction—aiming was facilitated by firing the tracer ammunition from the two machine guns. When larger scale trials were made in Exercise Spartan in March 1943, very poor results were experienced, in contrast to the outstanding successes with the Hurricane Mk IIDs of 6 Squadron in the Western Desert. As a result, operations against armour by the Mk IIDs were generally abandoned and the aircraft used with great effect against alternative types of target.

The first operational units to receive the Mk IIDs was 164 Squadron at Middle Wallop from February 1943, and 137 Squadron at Rochford in June. Both became operational very quickly, although it was Hurricane Mk IVs fitted with Vickers 40-mm 'S' cannons that operated the first rhubarb on 23 July.

Hurricane Mk IV was a basic Mk IIA powered by a Merlin XX featuring a universal wing that could be fitted with eight or twelve machine guns, pairs of 250- or 500-lb bombs, drop tanks, ferry fuel tanks, RP, and any other external stores. However, both RP and the installation of the 40-mm cannons caused more wiring and plumbing than was practical within the wing structure, while still ensuring the continual operation and maintenance of whatever system was fitted. An example could be a fault caused by battle damage, which may not have been

Hurricane Mk IV LB774, armed with a pair of Vickers 40-mm S cannons in June 1943. This aircraft went on to serve with 6 Squadron in support of the 8th Army in North Africa. (*RAF Museum photo*)

The Hurricane Mk IV was fitted with the universal wing that could be armed with eight or twelve machine guns, and carry two 250-lb or 500-lb bombs and other external stores. Hurricane Mk IV KX877, powered by a Merlin XX engine, was photographed officially in April 1943. (*RAF Museum photo*)

Hurricane KX405 was built as a Mk IV with tropical radiator and converted to the Mk V prototype powered by a Merlin 32 driving a four-blade propeller. This aircraft was armed with a pair of Vickers 40-mm S cannons and was used for development trials at Langley, where it was photographed, and the A&AEE at Boscombe Down. It was later converted back to the Mk IV standard. (*Author's collection*)

detected until a role change was made for an urgent operational sortie. In 1941, Hawker suggested a universal wing for Hurricanes that would be capable of carrying various stores without alterations to the armament wiring and fuel plumbing, avoiding the necessity of changing wings. Although there was little interest by the Air Ministry, Rolls-Royce suggested the development of a long-life Merlin, which with wider tolerances would be unaffected by dust and sand, although the logistics of servicing a different engine in the Middle East would add difficulties to the existing stretched supply situation.

The whole emphasis with Hurricanes changed to improving its performance in hot climates. Rolls-Royce offered the new 1,280-hp Merlin 27 designed for operation in higher ambient temperatures and giving optimum power at lower altitudes, but still being capable of intercepting enemy aircraft at higher altitudes.

Work on the earlier Mk IIE stopped, and Hurricane Mk II KX405, which was powered by a Merlin 32 with a four-blade Rotol propeller until Merlin 27s were available and fitted with a pair of Vickers 'S' 40-mm cannons and additional armour protection, emerged as the prototype Mk IV. First flown by Lucas on 14 March 1943, it was replaced by a more representative Mk IV prototype, KZ193 which was flown by Lucas on 23 March powered by a Merlin 27 driving a Rotol three-blade propeller.

Hurricane Mk V KZ193, with a tropical radiator and armed with two 40-mm Vickers S cannons made its first flight on 23 March 1943 and was delivered to the A&AEE for weapons trials. It was then converted to a Mk IV and served with 164 Squadron at Warmwell as FJ-O where it was used on anti-shipping strikes. (*IWM photo*)

This aircraft was fitted with full engine and radiator armour for protection in ground attack, 40-mm cannons and ammunition, and was flown with full fuel at an AUW of 8,189 lb. All development trials were carried using KZ193 with delivery to Boscombe Down for service trials, including performance with alternative underwing stores and asymmetric loads. Full service clearance was achieved on 1 June which allowed the aircraft to carry pairs of 250- and 500-lb bombs; two, four, or eight 3-inch RP; one or two anti-armour 40-mm cannons; and one or two 44-gallon fuel drop tanks. The 88-gallon ferry fuel tank was the only store not to be carried asymmetrically.

Although mainly destined for tropical operations, the first Mk IVs joined Mk IIDs with 164 Squadron at Colerne in May 1943, and 137 Squadron at Rochford added Mk IVs to their Mk IIDs the following month, replacing Westland Whirlwinds. Other British-based RAF units to fly Mk IVs were Nos 63, 184, 186, and 309 (Polish) Squadrons, while in the Middle East, 6 Squadron acquired the reputation as the flying can-openers with their high success rate against armour around the Mediterranean theatre, North Africa, Palestine, and the Balkans. In Burma, 20 and 42 Squadrons used the Mk IVs with effect against the Japanese. A total of 524 Hurricane Mk IVs were built at Langley, and in addition to service with ten RAF front-line squadrons, others served with eleven second-line units, including mainly anti-aircraft co-operation units.

Hurricane Mk IV fitted with the launch rails for a pair of underwing large 'Long Tom' RP for test firings in 1945. (*Author's collection*)

Hurricane BP173 was originally built as a Mk IIB and delivered to 47 MU at Sealand on 1 April 1942. It was returned to Hawkers and modified to a Mk IV as the first RAF fighter to be armed with rockets. It was delivered to the A&AEE on 29 July 1942 for RP trials with four unguided missiles under each wing. Hurricane Mk IVs were issued to 137 Squadron in June 1943 and first saw action over Holland on 2 September 1943. (*Author's collection*)

No. 174 'Mauritius' Squadron was formed at Manston from a nucleus of 607 Squadron on 3 March 1942. Its role was bombing intruders on shipping, industrial units, and airfields by day and night. It was one of the Hurricane squadrons in operation Jubilee, the attack on Dieppe, but lost five pilots, including the Free French commanding officer. (*Author's collection*)

Hurricane Mk IIB BN795 *Our John*, which was issued to 174 Squadron and is seen at Odiham with its pilot F/Lt J. R. Sterne DFC, on 1 April 1943. This was one of three Hurricanes presented to the RAF by the mother of W/Cdr John Gillan DFC, who was killed in action on 29 August 1941 while flying Spitfire V W3715. As OC 111 Squadron, S/Ldr Gillan had been responsible for the introduction of the Hurricane to the RAF. No. 174 Squadron converted to Typhoons in April 1943. (*Author's collection*)

With the considerable additional weight of armour and loads of underwing stores, the Mk IV was less popular with pilots due to the loss of the control crispness experienced with the earlier examples. However, it was even more rugged than the earlier marks, with a high level of durability in demanding ground-attack and anti-armour roles. It could also operate from very rudimentary strips, which would have been no use to more sophisticated fighters.

Returning to the first rhubarb by 137 Squadron on 23 July, four Mk IVs with the squadron flew to the advanced base at Manston. The aircraft departed at 1.10 p.m. on a highly successful operation crossing the Belgian coast, after which a goods train was attacked using the 40-mm cannons; the locomotive was completely destroyed. Following this, two more freight trains were attacked and the engines destroyed, but considerable light flack was encountered. Next, an army vehicle was destroyed, and a small train damaged and brought to a halt. Finally, two barges were badly damaged before the Hurricanes returned safely to Manston at 3 p.m.

Rockets were introduced by 184 Squadron with Hurricane Mk IVs operating a roadstead from Manston on 28 June. Escorted by Typhoons in close support, four Hurricanes were airborne at 4.30 a.m. and met with the escort as planned. Just off the Dutch coast, a convoy of four ships was encountered and initially attacked by Typhoons with cannon fire, drawing the flak from the Hurricanes that attacked after the Typhoons. As a result, two ships were sunk, another beached on fire, and the fourth ship damaged, with one Hurricane being lost.

The destructive power of the RP was so high that they replaced the 40-mm cannons in northern Europe by the end of 1943, and the Hurricane Mk IV was withdrawn from operations as it was inferior in performance to the similarly armed Typhoon. No. 186 Squadron began to take delivery of Typhoons in November, followed by 137 and 164 Squadrons in January 1944, and 184 Squadron in March.

Hurricanes had been in operational service in north-west Europe for four years in the defensive role, followed by offensive operations that helped to counter the German capability to hold back the Allied invasion of Europe in June 1944.

No. 286 Squadron was formed at Filton on 17 November 1941 for Army Co-operation duties with Hurricane Mk Is—L2006:Y being an example. The early Hurricanes were complemented by Hurricane Mk IICs from April 1942, with the last Mk I withdrawn in June 1943. The squadron was disbanded at Weston Zoyland on 16 May 1945. (*RAF Museum photo*)

9

Hurricane Training and Support Units

WITH THE SHORTAGE of both men and Hurricanes at the start of the Second World War, the pilots received their flying training initially on Tiger Moths or Magisters, and for those destined to fly fighters, they would move on to more advanced trainers such as the Miles Master or North American Harvard before being posted to the operational squadrons. At this time, the novice pilot would make his first solo on the Hurricane, where they not only had to learn to fly the new type, but also how to operate the aircraft, including the use of the guns, combat tactics, scrambles, emergency procedures, and all the other challenges of a modern monoplane fighter. This process was not only wasteful on the operational squadron pilots' time, but did not give the inexperienced pilots the depth of what was required not only to stay alive, but to make a positive contribution to the battle.

Early on in the war, both 11 and 12 Groups of Fighter Command formed Group Pools when surplus Hurricanes became available from the production lines, giving the partly trained pilots a short operational conversion course on the aircraft they would be flying on their first squadron. As these pools confused the responsibilities between Training and Fighter Commands, a more formal arrangement was set up with the formation of No. 5 Operational Training Unit (OTU) in February 1940 at Aston Down in Gloucestershire, equipped with Hurricanes, Defiants, and Blenheims, which took over the training responsibility from No. 11 Group Pool at Andover. This was followed by 6 OTU at Sutton Bridge in March replacing 12 Group Pool equipped with Hurricanes, Masters, and Battles, as well as 7 OTU at Hawarden near Chester operating Hurricanes, Spitfires, and Masters. These three OTUs were renumbered 55, 56, and 57 OTUs, and later moved to more distant locations away from the enemy where training could continue unhindered by potential combat.

The initial equipment of these OTUs were early Hurricanes, which became available as the newer improved examples were delivered to the front-line squadrons. Therefore, the new pilots were learning on aircraft with the original wooden Watts propeller, fabric wings,

Hurricane Mk I R2680 after a crash landing with 56 OTU at Sutton Bridge on 20 June 1941. (*RAF Museum photo*)

During training, there were some unconventional arrivals, including this landing by Hurricane Mk I L1926, probably at 55 OTU at Aston Down. (*H. Lees photo*)

A flight of 55 OTU Hurricane Mk Is practise formation flying. (*RAF Museum photo*)

and the early gun site, but at least they were able to experience handling characteristics and fly some forty hours on Masters and Hurricanes covering the basic combat tactics and operational procedures.

The new pilots therefore arrived on the squadrons with increased confidence and could develop their skills in the combat environment where they would be flying. During the critical stages of the Battle of Britain, the shortage of pilots resulted in the newcomers arriving on their operational unit with up to twenty hours' flying experience on the Hurricane at the OTU, but it was better than the previous year when he had arrived with no prior experience.

The major second-line role with the Hurricane during the Second World War was operational training, which continued in Britain until 1944 when the last Hurricane OTU, No. 55, was disbanded at Annan in Dumfriesshire. In addition, there were Hurricane OTUs in the Middle East: No. 71 (ME) OTU based at Ismailia from 1941 for fighter and fighter-bomber training, followed by 74 (ME) OTU at Aqir in Palestine from 1942 for tactical reconnaissance training, which both disbanded in 1945. No. 73 (ME) OTU was based at Abu Sueir, and 75 (ME) OTU at Gianaclis (both in Egypt) from 1943 until 1944 and equipped with Hurricane Mk Is and IICs.

In Cyprus, No. 79 (ME) OTU trained with Mk IICs at Lakatamia from 1944 until 1945.

There were also three Hurricane OTUs in India for operational training RAF and Indian Air Force pilots to fight the Japanese. These units eventually received ultimate versions of the Hurricane, the Mk IV. In the ideal flying conditions of Africa, the Rhodesian Air Training Group was established with Hurricanes from 1942.

Hurricane Mk I P3039 PA-J:155 OTU. (*Peter Green collection*)

Canadian-built Hurricane Mk X AG162 EH-W:55 OTU from Aston Down. (*IWM photo*)

A pair of Hurricane Mk Is, including V6874 UW-E:55 OTU, after a ground collision at Grangemouth on 17 June 1942. (*Peter Green collection*)

Hurricane Mk II BP553 44-A:71 OTU Ismalia in 1944. (*Peter Green collection*)

In addition to training pilots to fly, Hurricanes were also used for the training of air gunners and the pilots of bombers in the techniques of defending themselves against enemy fighters. Initially, this training was by the operational squadrons during their rest tours, but to formalise the training, Bomber Defence Flights were created.

As both Bomber Command and later the 8th USAAF started to take the offensive across occupied Europe and Germany, there was a vital need to have an accurate weather forecast. Although a number of aircraft were deployed on weather reconnaissance duties, it was the Middle East where Hurricanes were first used in this role when 1413 Flight was based at Lydda in Palestine—the Hurricanes replaced by Gladiators in August 1943. One of the characteristics of the region was the rapid development of violent tropical storms, and the initial aircraft were combat-worn Hurricane Mk Is operating with detachments at Aqir, Damascus, and Rayak.

With the expansion of weather flights, specially adapted Hurricane Met Mk IICs were issued. The aircraft was unarmed and fitted with a psychrometer on the starboard side of the fuselage below the cockpit, which was used to measure humidity. Normal operations were two sorties a day climbing to between 30,000 and 35,000 feet. Among the other weather units were 1412 Flight at Khartoum, 1414 Flight at Mogadishu and Eastleigh in East Africa, and 1415 Flight at Habbaniya in Iraq. Hurricanes continued in this role until September 1945, when 1413 and 1415 Flights received Spitfires and the other Middle East flights disbanded.

On the home front, Hurricanes equipped 518 (Weather Calibration) Squadron based at Aldergrove in Northern Ireland alongside Halifaxes from September 1945 until October the following year to cover the western approaches. Further south, 521 (Weather Calibration) Squadron operated Hurricane Mk IIC flights from Docking, Langham, and Chivenor from August 1944 until November 1945.

Hurricanes were allocated to the mundane but important task of calibrating ground defence radars, particularly the AMES Type 1(CH) system, which had a range of over 100 miles but under certain atmospheric conditions could be prone to spurious signals. The first of a number of special calibration units to be formed to help identify actual targets was 116 Squadron at Hatfield on 17 February 1941, which was initially equipped with Lysanders. The squadron moved to Hendon on 24 April and began to receive Hurricane Mk Is in November, which were eventually replaced by Hornet Moths and Tiger Moths at Heston from June 1942. During its period of service with Hurricanes, the squadron flew to assist the Royal Observer Corps and anti-aircraft gun defences, following which the pilots began work on the calibration of Chain Home Low (CHL) radars along the east coast, and continued in 1942 with CHEL (Extra-low) and Type 7 radars.

The other radar calibration unit was 527 Squadron, which formed at Castle Camps on 15 June 1943 with Hurricane Mk Is in addition to Hornet Moths and Blenheim IVs. From June 1943, Hurricane Mk IIBs began to arrive, with moves made to Snailwell on 28 February 1944, and Digby on 28 April. The Hurricanes remained with the squadron until July 1945, by which time the squadron was also operating a mixture of Spitfires, Oxfords, Wellingtons, and Dominies. The Hurricanes could be fitted with 44-gallon long-range fuel tanks and also flew detachments from Sutton Bridge and Coltishall providing calibration of CH Type radars around Britain.

No. 521. (Met) Squadron operated Hurricane Mk IICs from Langham between August 1944 and November 1945, making vertical assents to determine weather conditions. (*J. Rounce photo*)

No. 527 Squadron operating Hurricanes, including this Canadian-built Mk XII JS290, from Digby in 1944 and 1945 on radar calibration duties. (*RAF Museum photo*)

Before the start of the Second World War, ground-based anti-aircraft weapons were fairly basic and training was provided by regular RAF squadrons. A few miscellaneous units were formed in the late 1930s to provide target-towing aircraft, but with the massive wartime expansion there was a requirement to provide regular practice for Army and Navy guns on realistic targets, which resulted in a series of anti-aircraft co-operation (AAC) flights being formed. In addition, Hurricanes flew simulated dive-bombing and low-level attacks on ground troops and defended installations, as well as any other operations required for the training of ground forces. By the end of 1941, the flights had increased to squadron strength and were allocated numbers. The units concerned were 285 to 291 (AAC) Squadrons. No. 286 Squadron was formed at Filton on 17 November 1941 from 10 Group AAC Flight with a number of aircraft types—including Hurricane Mk Is, which were retained until June 1943, and Hurricane Mk IICs, which were added in April 1942 when the squadron was operating from Lulsgate Bottom and had detachments at a number of airfields in the West Country, The squadron disbanded at Weston Zoyland on 16 May 1945.

No. 285 Squadron formed at Wrexham on 1 December 1941 with Blenheim Is, Hudson IIIs, and Lysanders. It did not receive Hurricane Mk IICs until January 1944 at Woodvale, which were operated until 26 June 1945 when the squadron disbanded at Weston Zoyland. The squadron also flew Hurricane Mk IVs for a month from March 1944.

No. 287 Squadron was formed at Croydon on 19 November 1941 with Hurricane Mk Is, IIBs, and IVs, together with Blenheims, Hudsons, and Lysanders, with detachments around the 11 Group area. The Hurricanes were retired in March 1945.

No. 288 Squadron formed at Digby on 18 November 1941 from 12 Group AAC Flight and was equipped with Hurricane Mk Is until 1944. The squadron also operated Blenheims, Lysanders, and Hudsons throughout the 12 Group region.

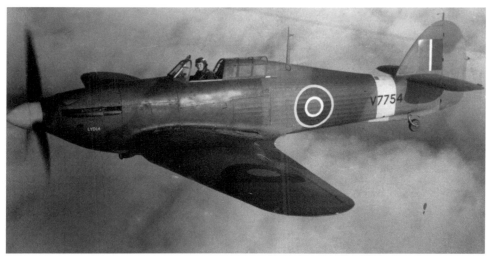

No. 289. (AAC) Squadron formed at Kirknewton on 17 November 1941 on anti-aircraft co-operation duties, Hurricane Mk I V7754 being one of its strength. The squadron disbanded at Andover on 26 June 1945. (*RAF Museum photo*)

No. 289 Squadron formed at Kirknewton on 17 November 1941 from 13 Group AAC Flight with Hurricane Mk Is, IICs, and IVs until 26 June 1945 when it disbanded at Andover, also operating a similar selection of aircraft as the other AAC units.

No. 290 Squadron formed on 1 December 1943 at Newtownards with Hurricane Mk IICs, which were retained until January 1945. Other types included Oxfords and Martinets.

No. 291 Squadron also formed on 1 December 1943, at Hutton Cranswick, with Hurricane Mk IICs and IVs—the latter being retained until the squadron disbanded on 26 June 1945—the last Hurricanes to be used in this AAC role.

For major combined operations, 516 Squadron was formed from 1441 Flight at Dundonald on 28 April 1943 using Hurricane Mk IIBs, until June 1943, with Lysanders, Mustangs, Ansons, and Blenheims. Hurricane Mk IIBs and IICs returned in December 1943 until the squadron disbanded on 2 December 1944. The squadron simulated low-level attacks on ground troops preparing for major assaults and participated in a number of assault exercises along the west coast of Scotland, laying smokescreens and making simulated strafing runs along the beaches.

By March 1944, vertical and oblique cameras had been fitted to Hurricanes in preparation for the D-Day landings in Normandy. Training continued until disbandment as there was little likelihood of any further major seaborne landings in Europe.

An important humanitarian task was performed in the safe recovery of downed aircrews in the sea and survivors from sunken ships by Air Sea Rescue (ASR) squadrons. Four of these units included Hurricanes in the varied fleets of specialist aircraft. In Britain, 276 Squadron was formed at Harrowbeer on 21 October 1941 and operated Hurricane Mk Is from November 1941 until January 1942, in addition to Lysanders and Walrus. No. 279 Squadron formed at Bircham Newton on 16 November 1941 with Hudsons, later flying Hurricane Mk IICs from February until September 1945. No. 284 Squadron was established at Hal Far in Malta with Walrus aircraft on 17 July 1943, later using Hurricane Mk IICs in the Italian Campaign from September 1944 until March 1945 when the squadron operated Warwicks until disbanding on 21 September 1945.

A less likely role for the single-seat Hurricanes was for communications. This was started by AVM Keith Park when, as commander of 11 Group, he flew around his squadrons to communicate first hand with his fighting team. In the case of 173 Squadron at Heliopolis in Egypt, Hurricanes were for the use of staff officers to units under their command when more conventional transport aircraft were not available. When 173 Squadron formed on 9 July 1942, Hurricane Mk Is were just one of many different types with the squadron, including Junkers Ju 52/3m, in February 1943. The Hurricanes were withdrawn in September 1943, having been used to carry urgent items such as films and prints from reconnaissance sorties to operational headquarters.

In 1944, the Air Despatch Letter Service was formed, based at Hendon, and equipped with around a dozen Hurricane Mk IICs to carry important despatches from Britain to France and Belgium following the invasion of Europe. The return flights were often used by the war correspondents to deliver their press reports. Initially, the loads were carried below the radio bay behind the cockpit, but as the volume of traffic increased, the material was carried in underwing containers adapted from fuel tanks. Once the Belgian capital had been liberated, the Belgian Communications Flight was formed in 1944, carrying urgent documents between London and Brussels using RAF-supplied Hurricanes.

Urgent mail and press materials were carried by the Air Despatch Letter Service. (ADLS) using adapted underwing canisters on Hurricane Mk IICs based from 1944 at Hendon. (*Author's collection*)

This. (ADLS) Hurricane Mk IIC with invasion stripes was being prepared for departure on a European airfield during 1944. (*Peter Green collection*)

Hurricane Mk IIC of ADLS in June 1944, with black-and-white invasion markings on the fuselage and wings to aid recognition. (*Peter Green collection*)

Hurricane Mk II MW339 DR-H:ADLS/1697 Flight at Northolt in 1946 was unarmed and fitted with mail canisters under the wings. (*Peter Green collection*)

10

Canadian Hurricanes

THE BRITISH COMMONWEALTH Dominion of Canada was a major contributor to the Allied effort during the Second World War. Not only did it build aircraft, in many cases under licence, but also supplying combat units in the air, at sea, and on the ground in the European, Middle Eastern, and Asian theatres while preparing for its own defence.

A major Hurricane production facility was created by the Canadian Car and Foundry Company (CC&F) at Fort William, Ontario, from 1939. The CC&F had been established in 1909 at Montreal as an amalgamation of a number of companies, its main business being the manufacture of buses and railway rolling stock. In 1911, the CC&F bought Montreal Steel works, the largest manufacturer of steel castings in Canada, and also the Ontario Iron and Steel Company, which included a steel foundry and rolling mill. The Fort William factory specialised in the production of buses and, towards the end of the First World War, a new factory was opened at Fort William, by then known also as Thunder Bay, which manufactured rail cars and ships, including minesweepers.

In an attempt to enter the aviation market, the CC&F built a small batch of Grumman G-23 fighters under licence, followed by the locally designed Maple Leaf I and II trainers, which were aimed at RCAF and private owner markets. The CC&F advised the Canadian Department of Transport in Ottawa of the plans on 12 June 1937.

The conventional welded-steel fuselage, empennage, and ailerons with wooden wing structure and fabric-covering, known as the Maple Leaf I, made its maiden flight from Fort William on 18 April 1938, but the programme was abandoned on 21 June due to inadequate performance. This was followed by the Maple Leaf II, which was a completely new design, albeit with the original fin and rudder. Construction was similar to the Maple Leaf I and power came initially from a 145-hp Warner Super Scarab engine. The prototype was first flown on 31 October 1939, but by this time the factory was busy building up Hurricane production; the Maple Leaf II prototype, together with two partly finished aircraft and all the jigs and tools with design information, were sent to Mexico where at least one of the incomplete airframes was completed in 1944.

In addition to producing their own trainer, the CC&F decide to develop a fighter. Although the Russian designer, Michael Gregor, was aware of the new monoplane fighters then in development, he believed that with careful design he could produce a high-performance biplane that was very manoeuvrable; the FBD-1 was designated as a fighter dive-bomber. The short fuselage was of stressed-skin construction with a retractable undercarriage. The unequal-span wings were of duralumin construction with fabric covering, and the upper wing had a gull form to allow the pilot good visibility. Power came from a 750-hp P&W R-1535 Twin Wasp Jnr, and the armament was a pair of 0.50-inch machine guns mounted on the upper-wing root. The prototype was first flown on 17 December 1938, but due to lack of performance and a number of deficiencies, the aircraft was put into storage and eventually destroyed by fire in 1945.

In 1936, the CC&F acquired the manufacturing rights for the Burnelli UB-14 twin-engined lifting fuselage high-wing monoplane airliner, but planned to build a larger CB-34 Wright Cyclone-powered version, which was not proceeded with due to the RAF orders for Hurricanes.

Canada was a major contributor to the Hurricane programme. The Canadian Car & Foundry Company produced over 1,400 aircraft for the RAF and home defence for the RCAF. RCAF Hurricane Mk XII 5658 of 127 Squadron was equivalent to the RAF Mk IIA, armed with eight 0.303-inch machine guns and was at Dartmouth Nova Scotia on 6 May 1943. (*Public Archives of Canada photo*)

In late November 1938, the CC&F were awarded a contract to produce forty Hurricanes to be built at the Fort William plant. The early aircraft had Merlin engines supplied by Rolls-Royce from Britain, together with de Havilland propellers and all British embodiment equipment. To ease the process into production, all castings and forgings were supplied from Britain to be machined by the CC&F, and all early British Merlin-powered aircraft had their engines fitted and were flight tested in Canada. During later production for the RAF, the airframes were shipped without engines, instruments, and armament, which was then installed in Britain. To ensure that the required standards were being achieved, randomly selected Hurricanes had a Merlin 'F'itted in Canada for flight testing, which was then removed to be used for further aircraft. Later Hurricanes were fitted with Packard Merlins, which were fitted before delivery.

The erection of tooling and preparations for production proceeded rapidly, and the first CC&F Hurricane, P5170, made its first flight on 10 January 1940 from Bishop's Field, Fort William, by Victor Hatton, who was qualified as an approved Air Ministry acceptance pilot.

Hurricane production generally proceeded well, partly due to the high priority placed upon the programme, but some problems did occur. In the summer of 1941, when there were delays in the supply of embodiment loan and other British-supplied equipment slowing production. When there was a shortage of de Havilland propellers, some had to be borrowed from Battle trainers and the blades shortened to fit. The following summer, delays were caused by faulty Merlins, which had to be returned to Packard for rectification. A total of 1,451 Hurricanes were delivered from CC&F production lines between the first one coming off the line in January 1940 and the last one in April 1943.

Canadian-built Hurricane Mk I 328 with the Test and Development Flight at Rockcliffe, Ontario, on 28 August 1939, fitted with a de Havilland three-blade variable pitch propeller. (*Public Archives of Canada photo*)

Hurricane Mk I 315 of 1 Squadron. (RCAF) with the two-blade wooden Watts propeller being run-up at Rockcliffe, Ontario, by S/Ldr E. A. McNab, the CO, on 6 September 1939. (*Public Archives of Canada photo*)

Some Canadian Hurricanes were adapted after delivery to the Sea Hurricane configuration with arrester hooks and catapult fittings; one batch of fifty was completed by the CC&F as Sea Hurricanes. Many of the Canadian Hurricanes were tropicalised before being sent to the Middle East and Asia.

The main versions of the Hurricane built in Canada were the Mk Is, Mk IIBs, and Mk IICs similar to the versions built in Britain. Canadian production also consisted of the Mk X, which was similar to the Mk I but powered by a Packard 28 engine; the Mk XI, which was the Mk X fitted with RCAF equipment; the Mk XII, which was powered by a Packard Merlin 29 and was otherwise similar to the RAF Mk IIB; and the Mk XIIA, which was similar to the Mk XII but fitted with eight-gun wings.

At least ten Hurricanes were lost during delivery to Britain, and the first to arrive for the RAF were just in time to participate in the Battle of Britain. It is believed that the first Canadian Hurricane to be lost in combat was P5208 of 601 Squadron, which was shot down on 31 August 1940, although the pilot survived the ordeal. There was no special allocation of Canadian Hurricanes to squadrons. The type was widely used, and a number were adapted for launching from the merchant ships and allocated to the FAA. Canadian Hurricanes were included in the aircraft supplied to the USSR, and many of the tropicalised versions were shipped to India for action against the Japanese. Most of the forty Hurricane Mk Is in the initial batch were shipped to Britain, followed by the majority of the 340 Mk Xs.

RCAF Hurricane XII at Rockcliffe, Ontario, on 16 September 1942. (*Public Archives of Canada photo*)

Canadian-built Hurricane Mk X AG122, powered by a Packard-built Merlin engine, was used by Rolls-Royce for engine development work. (*BAe photo*)

No. 1 OTU at Bagotville was responsible for the conversion and combat training with the RCAF Hurricanes. Hurricane Mk XIIs, including 5470:L, ready for the day's training on 31 July 1943, were fitted with the exhaust shield for night flying. As was common with many Canadian Hurricanes, no spinner fairing was fitted. (*Public Archives of Canada photo*)

Hurricane Mk XIIs of 1 OTU RCAF making a practice strafing run across the flight line at Bagotville on 19 November 1942. (Public Archives of Canada photo)

Back in Canada, with tension growing between Japan and the USA, the RCAF had requested an allocation of Hurricanes for home defence—particularly on the west coast—and although initially refused due to priorities in Europe, eighty aircraft were released. The RCAF later placed orders for 400 Hurricanes. These aircraft were primarily used for air defence on both the east and west coast, but no contact with the enemy was ever made.

No. 1 OTU was formed at Bagotville in Quebec on 6 June 1942 and was responsible for conversion and operational training of the RCAF pilots. Six squadrons were formed on the east coast with Hurricanes and Kittyhawks; 125 Squadron formed on 20 April 1942 at Sydney, Nova Scotia, equipped from the outset with Hurricane Mk Is and Mk XIIs. It was renumbered 441 Squadron at Digby on 8 February 1944 and equipped with Spitfires. No. 126 Squadron was formed at Dartmouth Nova Scotia on 27 April 1942 and operated Hurricane Mk XIIs exclusively throughout its existence.

The squadron flew its first mission on 11 July 1942, and the last on 13 May 1945, followed by disbandment on 31 May.

No. 127 Squadron formed at Dartmouth on 1 July 1942 equipped with Hurricane Mk XIIs and was renumbered 443 Squadron at Digby on 8 February 1944 with Spitfires.

No. 128 Squadron was formed at Sydney on 7 June 1942 and equipped with Hurricane Mk Is and Mk XIIs until it disbanded on 15 March 1944.

No. 129 Squadron formed at Dartmouth with Hurricane Mk XIIs on 28 August 1942 and disbanded at Gander on 30 September 1944.

No. 130 Squadron was formed at Mont Joli, Quebec, on 1 May 1942 with a mixture of Hurricane Mk XIIs and Kittyhawks, disbanding at Goose Bay on 15 March 1944.

Hurricane Mk XIIA BW850 BV-T:126 Squadron RCAF was based at Dartmouth. (*Photo Author's collection*)

Canadian Army Bren gun carriers training with Hurricane Mk XIIs of 127 Squadron RCAF at Gander in May 1943. (*Public Archives of Canada photo*)

A flight of Hurricane Mk XIIs: 547:B, 5497:Y, and 5459:Z, of 127 Squadron RCAF flown by F/O Paul Holden, and Sergeants A. R. Taylor and Mike Humphries ready for take-off from a snowy Gander on 16 December 1942. (*Public Archives of Canada photo*)

Hurricane Mk XII of 127 Squadron. (RCAF) being prepared for take-off at Gander on 14 August 1943. (*Public Archives of Canada photo*)

Hurricane Mk XIIs of 135 Squadron RCAF at Patricia Bay on 14 August 1943. (*Public Archives of Canada photo*)

There were three units on the west coast that flew Hurricanes. No. 133 Squadron formed at Lethbridge, Alberta, on 3 June 1942 with Hurricane Mk XIIs from July until March 1944, and also operated Kittyhawks and Mosquitos before finally disbanding at Patricia Bay, Vancouver, on 10 September 1945. No. 135 Squadron was formed at Mossbank, Saskatchewan, on 15 June 1942 flying Hurricane Mk XIIs from July until May 1944 in addition to Kittyhawks.

The first mission was flown on 9 November 1942 and the unit disbanded at Patricia Bay on 10 September 1945. The third west coast unit was 163 Squadron formed for Army co-operation at Sea Island, Vancouver, on 1 March 1943 with Bolingbrokes and Harvards. A conversion was made to Hurricane Mk XIIs in June 1943, and the squadron took on the fighter role on 14 October. The Hurricanes were replaced by Kittyhawks during November 1943 and the squadron disbanded at Patricia Bay on 15 March 1944. The only other RCAF Hurricane unit in Canada was 123 Squadron, which formed for Army co-operation training at Rockcliffe on 22 October 1941 with Lysanders, Grumman Goblins, and Hurricane Mk Is and XIIs. The Hurricanes were operated from November 1942 until October 1943, providing training in close support and reconnaissance for Canadian ground troops.

Hurricane Mk I of 1(F) Squadron RCAF flying over Vancouver BC on 3 April 1939. (*Public Archives of Canada photo*)

Ground crew undertaking maintenance on Hurricane Mk I 315 of 1 Squadron RCAF at Rockcliffe, Ontario on 6 September 1939. (*Public Archives of Canada photo*)

Ground crew winding the early inertia starter on 1(F) Squadron Hurricane Mk I 315 with the commanding officer, S/Ldr E. A. McNab, in the cockpit at Rockcliffe on 6 September 1939. This aircraft was still fitted with the Watts fixed two-blade wooden propeller. (*Public Archives of Canada photo*)

Hurricane Mk Is of 1(F) Squadron RCAF at Dartmouth on 12 November 1939. Four of the aircraft were fitted with the Watts fixed-pitch two-blade propeller, but the pair of nearer aircraft, 320 and 327, were fitted with the de Havilland variable pitch three-blade propeller. (*Public Archives of Canada photo*)

The Hon. Vincent Massey, Canadian High Commissioner, talking to Sgt Morris Hinam, who was supervising work by the ground crew on Hurricane Mk IIB YO-F:401 Squadron at Digby on 19 June 1941. (*Public Archives of Canada photo*)

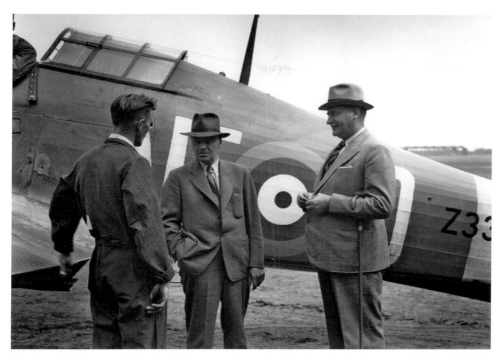

The Hon. C. G. Power and Hon. Ian Mackenzie talking to LAC Graham beside Hurricane Mk IIA AE-D:402. (Winnipeg Bears) Squadron RCAF at Martlesham Heath on 6 July 1941. (*Public Archives of Canada photo*)

The major Canadian contribution to the air defence of Great Britain was the Hurricane-equipped Digby Wing in Lincolnshire consisting of 401 and 402 Squadrons RCAF. No. 401 Squadron was originally formed as 1 Squadron RCAF and replaced its Siskins with Hurricane Mk Is at Calgary in February 1939. The squadron was mobilised at St Hubert, Quebec, in September and moved to Dartmouth, Nova Scotia, in November where it absorbed 115 (AuxAF) Squadron in May 1940. The squadron departed for Britain in June, joining 11 Group Fighter Command and arriving at Middle Wallop on 21 June. The squadron moved to Croydon in July and Northolt on 17 August, with the first victory claimed on 26 August against a Do 215. Before moving to Digby on 1 March 1941, the squadron claimed thirty enemy aircraft destroyed with eight probables and thirty-four damaged for the loss of ten Hurricanes and three pilots killed. On arrival with the Digby Wing, the squadron was renumbered 401 and equipped with Hurricane Mk Is until May, when they were replaced by Mk IIs. The Hurricanes were replaced by Spitfires in September.

No. 2 Squadron RCAF was formed from 112 (Army Co-op) Squadron RCAF at Digby on 9 December 1940 and was renumbered 402 Squadron as a Hurricane fighter-bomber unit on 1 March 1941 alongside 401 Squadron.

A move was made to Martlesham Heath on 23 June 1941—the first claim being damage to a Ju 88 on 18 September. The squadron was equipped with Hurricane Mk Is from March to May 1942, which were replaced by Mk IIAs until July, and IIBs from June 1941. The

Canadian-built Hurricane Mk X AG111 HK-G was operated by the Fighter Leaders School in 1942. (*IWM photo*)

squadron moved to Ayr in July 1941 and Rochford in August, where three enemy aircraft were claimed as destroyed and two damaged on 18 September. The final move with Hurricanes was made to Warmwell on 6 November 1941, followed by Colerne on 4 March 1942, where the squadron re-equipped with Spitfires.

As part of the Allied support in the Middle East, 417 Squadron RCAF formed at Charmy Down in Britain on 27 November 1941. The squadron was initially equipped with Spitfires, but when the squadron moved to Egypt in April 1942, Hurricane Mk IIBs and IICs were supplied from September 1942 until January 1943, by which time they had been replaced by Spitfires.

Three other Canadian squadrons operated Hurricane Mk IVs non-operationally for combat training before equipping with Typhoons to cover the D-Day landings and invasion of Europe: 438, 439, and 440 Squadrons.

No. 438 Squadron was originally formed as 118 Squadron RCAF at Rockcliffe on 13 January 1941 and was renumbered 438 Squadron at Digby on 10 November 1943. The squadron moved to Wittering on 19 December, and Ayr on 10 January 1944 where the conversion was made to Typhoons, although the Hurricane Mk IVs remained with the squadron until May 1944 during the conversion programme.

No. 439 Squadron was originally formed at Rockcliffe as 123 (Army co-op) Squadron RCAF on 15 January 1942 and was renumbered 439 Squadron at Wellingore on 1 January

Hurricane Mk XII 5624 for flight development of the ski-adapted undercarriage at Rockcliffe, Ontario, on 1 January 1943. The ski undercarriage was fixed with the wheel wells faired over, but the configuration was not adopted for service due to a reduction in performance. (*Public Archives of Canada photo*)

Although not modified in Canada, Hurricane Mk I 321 served with 1(F) Squadron RCAF, having originally been built in Britain as L1884. It was shipped back to Britain in 1940 and modified by F. Hill and Sons as the slip-wing Hurricane. The object of the trials was an attempt to provide temporary additional lift for a heavy weight take-off, with additional overload fuel for very long endurance direct flights to places such as Malta. The Hillson FH.40 Mk I, when it had reached its cruise altitude, would then jettison the upper wing. It was powered by a 1,030-hp Merlin 3 engine. The aircraft continued to fly from Boscombe Down until early 1944, long after the need to reinforce Malta had passed. (*BAe photo*)

1944. The squadron was moved to Ayr on 8 January to begin conversion on to Typhoons from February, retaining the Hurricanes until April.

No. 111 (F) Squadron RCAF formed at Rockcliffe on 1 November 1941 and was renumbered 440 Squadron at Ayr on 8 February 1944, operating Hurricanes for only a month until March when conversion was made to Typhoons. All three squadrons were disbanded at Flensburg on 26 August 1945 with their work having been completed.

Two RCAF Hurricanes, 1362 and 5624, were fitted with skis for trials on ice and snow. The modification used Noorduyn skis developed for the Harvard—installation on 5624 made by the CC&F at Fort William. The skis were non-retractable, the wheel wells were faired over, and the undercarriage hydraulic system was used to trim the skis. Test flights were made at Rockcliffe during February and March 1943, and although the installation was found to be satisfactory, the 11.5 per cent reduction in performance resulted in ski Hurricanes not being used operationally by the RCAF.

With the end of the Second World War, many of the Hurricanes were disposed of very rapidly, although the last one was not struck off charge until 1948. Many were sold for C$50 each, with quite a number surviving in museums and war-bird collections, including Sea Hurricane Z7015 with the Shuttleworth Collection in Britain.

11

The Mediterranean Theatre

T HE MEDITERRANEAN THEATRE consisted of a vast area stretching from Gibraltar to the Middle East, and from Greece to the desert warfare raging along North Africa. This created major logistical challenges for both the overstretched Allied forces as well as the Axis forces.

The small island of Malta was located in the middle of this theatre and was a strategically vital base for the Allies as it dominated the German supply lines from Italy to Rommel's army in the North African desert. Britain needed the important supply route through the Suez Canal from oil fields in the Middle East, and it was the German intention to occupy all of North Africa. This would not deny the Allies the oil supplies but ensure a regular supply of fuel for Germany. The only barrier to German success was the small garrison on Malta, which was within easy striking distance from enemy bases in the south of Italy. Meanwhile, Britain was facing an imminent German invasion from France just 20 miles of the English Channel, and the Luftwaffe was making every effort to destroy the RAF on the ground and in the air during the Battle of Britain.

There were times that Britain believed Malta was so exposed as to be indefensible. As a precaution, the HQ of the RN Mediterranean Fleet was moved from Valletta harbour in Malta to Alexandria in October 1939. Most of the 250,000 inhabitants lived within four miles of the Grand Harbour in Valletta and were subjected to the heaviest concentration of aerial bombing in history; defences on the island were practically non-existent. The RN maintained one ship and a few submarines, while the air defence consisted of six obsolete Gloster Gladiator biplanes with another six stored in crates at the time Mussolini declared war on Britain and France on 10 June 1940. Within hours of this declaration of war, Italian aircraft dropped the first bombs on the island on 11 June and were met by the legendary, but obsolete, Gladiators of the Hal Far Fighter Flight flown by volunteers, who were unable to gain any successes.

With the surrender of France on 25 June 1940, the French Navy was removed from the order of battle, giving the Italian Navy a greater balance of power against the Allies, which consisted of Britain and its Commonwealth as the USA had not yet become actively involved. In 1940, the conditions favoured an Italian naval assault on Malta, but they would only attack under favourable weather conditions and therefore missed the opportunity to dominate the middle of the Mediterranean and split the Allied forces between Gibraltar and Egypt.

Air power was chosen as the primary method of attack on Malta. On the first day, Italian bombers escorted by fighters bombed the dockyard at Valetta and the three airfields at Luqa, Hal Far, and Ta Kali, which were still under construction. The only defences were RN anti-aircraft guns. Most of the casualties were civilian and there was little damage to military installations.

Malta did at least have two early warning radar systems in operation, complimented by anti-aircraft guns and searchlights, against an Italian Air Force of some twelve squadrons of obsolete bombers, supported by three squadrons of antiquated fighters. However, against minimal air defences, the Italians had the upper hand of air superiority. On 20 June, 830 NAS, equipped with twelve Swordfish torpedo reconnaissance aircraft, attempted to defend against the first Italian night-bombing attack, but without success. The following day, two of the Gladiators were damaged in accidents, but the engineering officer was able to build one good aircraft out of the wreckage. On 22 June, a pair of Gladiators on patrol were able to claim the first Italian victim when an unescorted reconnaissance SM.79 was hit while flying over Valetta, crashing into the sea in full view of the cheering bystanders.

The priority for Hurricanes before Italy entered the war had been to deliver aircraft to Alexandria, but with the increased threat to Malta, a request was made to retain some Hurricanes to defend the island. The first three arrived on 13 June, with the ferry pilots departing the same day. Two more Hurricanes arrived on 21 June—this time the pilots remained—and six more arrived on 20 June using the overland route from Britain via France. However, six failed to arrive, and two were damaged on landing. By this time, Malta had more Hurricanes than Alexandria, so three were refuelled and flown on to Alexandria with a Blenheim escort. The five remaining Hurricanes had five pilots, and the first combat was on 3 July when Fg Off. John Walters shot down a bomber over the island. He was hit by Italian escort fighters; the aircraft was wrecked on landing, but he himself was unhurt.

Italian bombing attacks continued in the early part of July both on the island and against the RN Mediterranean Fleet, which had sailed from Alexandria to meet and protect two supply convoys on their way through the battle zone. On 10 July, Italian bombers arrived late over the island, but the fighter escort had to leave early due to a shortage of fuel and the Hurricane pilots were able to claim two bombers destroyed with no loss to the RAF. On 13 July, Flt Lt Peter Keeble was able to shoot down one of three CR.42 fighters during a dogfight, but was hit by one of the fighters and crashed, becoming the first RAF pilot to lose his life in the defence of Malta. By the end of the month, it was becoming impossible to keep the Hurricanes serviceable, and the air defence resorted to the three remaining Gladiators known as Faith, Hope, and Charity, although one was shot down on 29 July with its pilot badly burned.

It had become obvious that for the defence of Malta, more than a few Hurricanes would be required, and with the surrender of France the overland route ferry route was lost. The most practical method of reinforcing the island was to set sail from Gibraltar with an aircraft carrier and fly the fighters off at maximum range directly to Malta. In July 1940, 418 Flight was formed at Uxbridge consisting of one officer and seven sergeant pilots, all of whom had previous experience with the FAA but preferred to stay with the RAF. They collected Hurricanes from Hullavington and flew them to Abbotsinch near Glasgow, where they joined more Hurricanes ready for loading on HMS Argus. At this point, more RAF officers arrived, including Flt Lt D. W. Balden, the officer in command, who informed his colleagues that their destination was Malta.

HMS Argus sailed from Greenock on 23 July with a cargo of twelve Hurricanes and two Skuas heading for Gibraltar where the aircraft were assembled on deck and the spares loaded aboard a Sunderland flying boat. On 31 July, HMS Argus sailed from Gibraltar escorted by HMS Ark Royal and a number of other capital ships. The ships were finally near enough for the Hurricanes to depart at dawn on 2 August with the pair of Skuas used for navigation. All the aircraft arrived in Malta, covering the 380 miles in two hours and twenty minutes, but one Hurricane and one Skua were written-off on landing, although the crews were unhurt. To support these increased deliveries of Hurricanes, two Sunderlands flew in twenty-three ground crew, while also providing an air-sea rescue capability if required. Additional spares were delivered by submarine, but while the Hurricanes were being prepared for combat, two were wrecked on the ground by Italian bombers. The surviving aircraft with the Fighter Flight were merged with the newcomers to form a three flight 261 Squadron on 2 August with Flt Lt D. W. Balden promoted to squadron leader to take command.

Hurricane Mk I P3731 J:261 Squadron, which commenced operations in Malta on 16 August 1940. (*Author's collection*)

To defend against continual enemy night raids, an impromptu night-fighter section was formed. The first engagement was in the night of 13 August, when Fg Off. Barber shot down a SM.79, the first night-fighter victory of the war outside Western Europe. The rest of August was relatively quiet, although a CR.42 was claimed on 24 August and a Hurricane was damaged.

Early in September, the Italian Air Force acquired the first batch of fifteen Ju 87 Stuka dive bombers from Germany and based them at Comiso in southern Sicily, where they were not only a threat to Malta, but also Allied shipping passing through the Messina Strait. The first Stuka attack on Malta was by five aircraft on 4 September, followed by six more the next day and a further attack on 14 September, all without loss. The first Stuka was claimed by a Hurricane pilot on 17 September, with damage to a second, and a CR.42 fighter was shot down. The only RAF loss was a Wellington bomber on the ground at Luqa. On 25 September, three Hurricanes and two Gladiators were scrambled against an approaching raid and a C.200 was destroyed.

The following month was not much busier, with some C.200s on a reconnaissance sortie intercepted on 4 October with one shot down by a Hurricane. A night attack was made on 8 October when a 261 Squadron Hurricane claimed an Italian bomber with the aid of searchlights. This brought the total confirmed enemy aircraft destroyed by defending fighters to twenty-two aircraft, with a RAF Gladiator and Hurricane lost in combat. In a raid on 16 October, one C.200 was claimed damaged but had to be abandoned on arrival over an Italian airfield.

In early November, Italian air attacks resumed and a C.200 was claimed destroyed by a Hurricane on 2 November. A convoy carrying ground troop reinforcements departed Gibraltar on 7 November, arriving in Malta three days later, with a supply convoy leaving Alexandria at the same time, and five more Wellingtons arriving at Luqa on 8 November to take the RAF on the offensive against the Italians. When Malta-based reconnaissance aircraft located

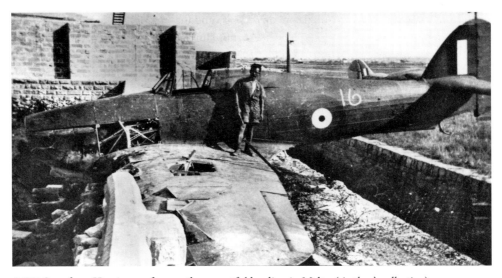

A 261 Squadron Hurricane after a rather eventful landing in Malta. (*Author's collection*)

the majority of the Italian fleet together in Taranto Harbour, a highly successful attack was made on the night of 11–12 November by FAA Swordfish torpedo bombers operating from HMS Illustrious, sinking many of the anchored warship fleet. Malta was attacked again on 12 November, with one reconnaissance C.200 shot down by a Hurricane.

In mid-November, HMS Argus sailed again from Gibraltar with another dozen Hurricanes and two Skuas on board. At dawn on 17 November, the first wave of six Hurricanes with a Skua escort started taking off for their 400-mile journey to Malta. It was anticipated that they would have about forty-five minutes of fuel reserves, but fifteen minutes was wasted forming up for the journey and the aircraft flew at 150 mph at 2,000 feet, which was not the most economic performance. The second group took off from the Argus an hour later, allowing the fleet to turn back to the comparative safety of Gibraltar. As the first group of aircraft continued, there was an unexpected change in the weather and they ran into head-winds. Despite accurate navigation and being met by an escorting Sunderland, two of the Hurricanes ran out of fuel and crashed into the sea with the loss of one pilot. The remaining four Hurricanes and the Skua landed safely in Malta with practically no fuel left.

The second wave was even less fortunate. They became hopelessly lost; one by one the Hurricanes ran out of fuel, ditching in the sea where all the pilots drowned. Only the Skua located land at the last minute and, damaged by gun fire, the crew made a forced landing on a beach in Sicily. This was a tragic loss of so many experienced pilots, a number of whom had achieved successes in the Battle of Britain. The four surviving Hurricanes and their pilots joined 261 Squadron to bring the air defence up to eight aircraft. With Wellington bombers taking up a lot of the space at Luqa, 261 Squadron moved to the civil airfield of Ta Kali on 20 November 1940, which then officially became an RAF base, and eight Hurricanes from the squadron were scrambled against an enemy raid on 23 November with indecisive results.

On 26 November, FS Dennis Ashton shot down a CR.42, but was then in turn shot down into the sea and killed by another CR.42.

With the arrival of another Allied convoy in Malta and the British Fleet active in the area, the Italians mounted an attack on 27 November, but Hurricanes were up and ready to meet the raiders. By concentrating on the bombers, Sgt Robertson claimed one SM.79 with no RAF losses. During the night of 18 December, during which there were a number of solo bombing raids, one enemy aircraft was successfully intercepted.

By the end of the year, the air defences had successfully fended off sporadic raids by the Italians. Malta remained a significant strike base providing harbour facilities for Royal Navy destroyers and submarines. RAF fighter pilots had claimed the destruction of thirteen bomb-ers, two Stukas, and sixteen fighters, with additional enemy aircraft shot down by the ground defences. Although there were days when there was little or no direct threat, the RAF air and ground crews were not able to rest. With Malta close to the main Axis supply route from Italy to North Africa, many enemy aircraft were detected in the vicinity, resulting in Hurricanes on alert being scrambled, even though there was little chance of engagement. Maintaining a constant state of readiness caused a great deal of wear and tear on the aircraft, pilots and ground crews. By the end of the year maintaining sixteen Hurricanes with four in reserve, plus the four surviving Gladiators was a considerable challenge for the personnel of 261 Squadron.

Hurricanes of 261 Squadron at Ta Kali in 1941 after an attack by Luftwaffe Bf 109s. (*Author's collection*)

With the start of 1941, the Battle of Britain had been won and the German invasion of Britain held off permanently, as it happened. The Allies were turning to the offensive, and the British Army in North Africa was advancing against Rommel's forces in Libya. However, the threat to Malta increased dramatically from 8 January with the arrival in Sicily of a large force of Luftwaffe bombers and supporting Bf 109s. The initial force consisted of some ninety-six bombers including He 111s, Ju 88s, and Ju 87 Stukas, with battle-experienced German pilots. By the end of the month, the force had increased to 141 aircraft with a much more offensive capability than the Italian Air Force, and their intention was to destroy the British garrison in Malta, which would allow freedom to supply weapons and materials to the Axis forces in North Africa.

The first enemy raid of the year on Malta was by the Italian Air Force on 9 January when 261 Squadron claimed two enemy aircraft for no losses. The British Mediterranean Fleet, Force H, was in action continuously between Gibraltar and Egypt, and an attack by Stukas on HMS Illustrious left it badly damaged on 10 January. Six bombs hit the ship causing heavy casualties, putting the flight deck out of action, and forcing the captain to withdraw to the Grand Harbour, Valetta, later the same day for urgent repairs. The ship made a very tempting target and attracted the first attack from the Italians on 13 January without any hits being scored, followed by another attempt three days later, which was deflected by the anti-aircraft guns. The Luftwaffe started to take an active interest on 16 January; a force of Ju 88s escorted by Bf 110s and Ju 87s covered by the Italian Air Force scored two direct hits on the carrier for the loss of four Ju 88s and one Ju 87 by the Hurricanes, with more damaged by the AA defences. The intensity of the Luftwaffe attacks was far greater than had been experienced previously from the Italian bombers.

In an effort to suppress the fighter defences, the airfields were bombed on 18 January in preparation for further attacks on the Illustrious, but Hurricanes and FAA Fulmars claimed seven Ju 87s destroyed for the loss of one Fulmar. The next day, the carrier was again the primary target for the Ju 88s and Ju 87s, with Hurricanes leading the air defence. There were total claims against the raiders of some forty aircraft, including sixteen to the AA guns, but there was a strong probability of over-claiming in the confusion. However, there were no direct hits on the Illustrious, although there was some additional damage caused by near misses.

With a short lull in the attacks, more RAF pilots arrived on 20 January—a number being experienced veterans of the Battle of Britain—and six more Hurricanes arrived on 29 January.

To supplement Hurricane deliveries to the Middle East by aircraft carriers, the old Imperial Airways' route from Takoradi across Nigeria and Sudan to Egypt was opened up for fighter deliveries. The initial deliveries had been on 20 September 1940 when five Hurricanes, escorted by four Blenheims, commenced overland deliveries. On 9 January 1941, forty Hurricanes departed from the decks of the Furious and the Argus to Takoradi and flew to Egypt from where the aircraft could be allocated to whichever area had priority. A total of thirty-eight Hurricanes arrived in Egypt, with eight leaving for Malta on 19 January for 261 Squadron, arriving in the middle of an enemy air attack. This brought the total strength of the squadron to twenty-eight Hurricanes, of which five were unserviceable. An additional six pilots arrived by Sunderland the next day, and HMS Illustrious was sufficiently patched up to depart on 23 January for Alexandria, after which she went to the USA for extensive repairs.

The pan-African delivery route could be hazardous and required precise navigation. Sometimes Hurricanes force-landed in the desert *en route*. (*Author's collection*)

To supplement the delivery of Hurricanes and other combat aircraft to the Middle East, an airfield was built at Takoradi in West Africa where aircraft could be delivered in crates, assembled, and flown across Africa to Egypt by the pilot who would operate the aircraft in combat. Hurricane Mk IIs here are being assembled and checked at Takoradi ready for their departure across Africa. (*Author's collection*)

Hurricane Mk IID DG626, with tropical filter and underwing ferry fuel tanks, with Sgt L. Davies at Takoradi prior to departure for Cairo. (*Author's collection*)

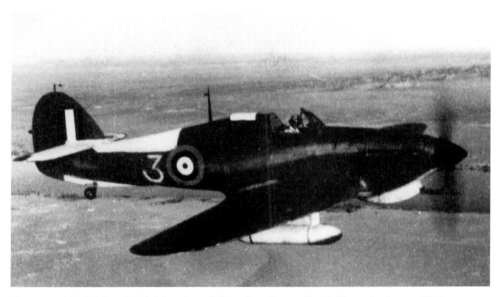

Hurricane Mk IIA Z4769 '3', flying from Takoradi to Fayour Road, Egypt, in August 1941, was one of forty Hurricanes delivered by this method. The aircraft had white paint on the rear fuselage and tailplane to assist in location in the event of a forced landing. (*Author's collection*)

A pair of Hurricanes, DG626:6 and Z4948:4, after ferry flight from Takoradi at Cairo awaiting delivery to operational units. (*Author's collection*)

Out of forty Hurricanes delivered overland from Takoradi to Cairo, thirty-eight arrived safely, but two made forced landings due to shortage of fuel or unserviceability. (*RAF Museum photo*)

Hurricane Z4380 of 261 Squadron at Ta Kali after a landing accident in 1941. (*Author's collection*)

On 26 January, two Hurricanes claimed a reconnaissance Ju 88, with an Italian fighter claimed in the morning of 1 February and a Ju 88 that evening. The airfields were again the target for the Ju 88 bombers on 3 February, with two claimed destroyed by the defending Hurricanes and Fulmars. Six Hurricanes were scrambled against a night raid on 8 February, with one He 111 claimed.

With the arrival of 7./JG26 in Sicily on 9 February, equipped with the latest Bf 109Es flown by combat-proven pilots, the Luftwaffe increased its threat considerably. The squadron's first appearance over Malta was three days later; 261 Squadron was scrambled against a bomber formation of Ju 88s but were surprised by the Bf 109s, losing two Hurricanes and another damaged. This sudden appearance of these more capable Luftwaffe fighters seriously affected the morale of the RAF pilots, many of whom were suffering from battle fatigue—particularly after recent losses. The Bf 109Es were encountered again on 16 February when six attacked 'A' Flight of 261 Squadron, destroying one Hurricane and damaging two others, although the pilots were safe.

Ju 87s returned on 23 February without the customary fighter cover, which made them very vulnerable to the defending fighters. One was shot down and another so badly damaged that the crew had to abandon it over the coast of Sicily. Two days later, one of four Bf 110s was shot down by a Hurricane, but during the afternoon, a Hurricane and pilot were lost during another engagement. The next day, Luqa was the target for a heavy bombing raid with Bf 109s as escort. Eight Hurricanes climbed above the Stukas to dive down with the Bf 109s following. Three Stukas were shot down, but three Hurricanes were destroyed with the loss of the pilots and a fourth Hurricane was damaged. Among the aircraft destroyed on the ground were six 148 Squadron Wellingtons, as well as extensive damage to the airfield buildings. Another major raid was met on 5 March with two Ju 88s, two Ju 87s, and one Bf 109 claimed as destroyed for the loss of one Hurricane and pilot. The next day, five replacement Hurricanes arrived from the stocks in Egypt, although one was destroyed the next day by a Bf 109. On 10 March, a night-flying Bf 110 was claimed by a 261 Squadron Hurricane.

A week later, further reinforcements arrived at Malta from North Africa consisting of seven Hurricanes with 274 Squadron, which were transferred to 261 Squadron ready for the next raid on 18 March by the Italians, who lost two CR.42s claimed by the Hurricane pilots. However, on 22 March, 261 Squadron suffered seriously during a German raid with five Hurricanes and their pilots lost in a battle between Ju 88s escorted by Bf 109s.

No doubt believing that the fighter defences had been seriously weakened, a major enemy attack developed, but Ju 87s, escorted by Italian C.200s, against an approaching convoy were met by fourteen Hurricanes. The RAF pilots claimed three Ju 87s for the loss of one Hurricane that the pilot successfully abandoned before it crashed. On 28 March, one Hurricane was shot down by Bf 109s, injuring the pilot. At the end of the month, 261 Squadron had thirty-four Hurricanes on strength, but not all were serviceable.

On 3 April 1941, significant reinforcements arrived when twelve Hurricane Mk IIAs were flown off HMS Ark Royal by a number of Battle of Britain-experienced pilots, going into action the next day. Two were shot down into the sea and the pilots killed by Bf 109s, although later in the day a Bf 109 was claimed. One of the surviving resident Hurricane Mk Is, V7101, was painted overall blue with all armament and armour plating removed and allocated to 69 Squadron for photo-reconnaissance duties. Additional fuel tanks were added to allow higher altitudes to be reached and to provide a longer endurance.

During the night of 11–12 April, 261 Squadron claimed a Ju 87, and on 13 April, Hurricanes on convoy escort duties spotted four Bf 109s, one of which was shot down into the sea by Ft Lt Mason. The other three retaliated, damaging one Hurricane, which was forced to ditch.

A new raid was detected building up over Sicily on 20 April. Two Hurricane Mk IIAs were sent to investigate initially, and a CR.42 biplane was soon shot down before Bf 109s joined the fight from above, diving through the formations, while another CR.42 was soon shot down. Two days later, while 261 Squadron Hurricanes were on patrol, they were alerted to enemy aircraft approaching, which turned out to be two Bf 109s, which damaged one Hurricane. The following day, Fg Off. Auger was shot down by a Bf 109 and parachuted into the sea, but drowned before the rescue boat could reach him.

On 27 April, news was received that HMS Ark Royal had left Gibraltar with twenty-four Hurricanes and twenty-six more pilots, many of whom were combat veterans. Each of the three waves of Hurricanes were launched with a Fulmar leading for navigation, and were met and escorted into Malta by three Marylands and a Sunderland. As the first wave arrived over the island, the Sunderland was attacked by the enemy after landing and sunk at its moorings. All but one of the Hurricanes landed safely. With both Luqa and Hal Far becoming crowded, Ta Kali became a permanent fighter base. In addition to Hurricane reinforcements, a detachment of six Blenheims arrived from 21 Squadron to replace the 148 Squadron Wellingtons, which were flown to Egypt. Malta was now moving from being a purely defensive force to having an active strike capability.

The German assault continued unabated, perhaps in the knowledge of the new arrivals, with Bf 109s returning in strength on 1 May and shooting down two 261 Squadron, Hurricanes injuring both pilots. The 69 Squadron modified photo-reconnaissance Hurricane made its first sortie on 4 May, and with the weight reductions was found to be able to operate regularly at 30,000 feet—although on one occasion it reached 36,000 feet and was somewhat unstable. On 5 May, Hurricanes damaged a Ju 88 badly enough for it to crash on return to base, killing the crew.

By early May, the situation in the Mediterranean Theatre was not very promising for the Allies. British ground forces had been driven back to the borders of Egypt by Rommel's army; the Balkans, including Yugoslavia and Greece, were under German control; and the invasion of Crete was imminent. A fast convoy left Gibraltar on 6 May to resupply British forces in Egypt in order to allow them to return to the offensive. The convoy was escorted by Force 'H' and carried tanks, motor transportation, and fifty-three crated Hurricanes. Meanwhile, the Mediterranean Fleet set out from Alexandria to meet up with the east-bound convoy at a rendezvous point south of Malta. At the appointed time, the island was under attack by He 111 bombers escorted by Bf 109s, one of which was shot down by a Hurricane. Meanwhile, the remaining Hurricanes were in a battle with the Bf 109s, resulting in the loss of three Hurricanes and another damaged. Just after dark, Hurricane pilots claimed a Ju 88 and He 111 destroyed.

As the convoy sailed into the Grand Harbour on 9 May, Ju 87s were ready to attack, but two were shot down by defending Hurricanes as they departed. The convoy, carrying 238 tanks and forty-three crated Hurricanes for the offensive against Rommel, finally reached Alexandria on 12 May after fighting its way through the Mediterranean. By this time, there were some fifty Hurricanes—mainly Mk IIAs and IICs—on Malta, allowing 185 Squadron to be formed from 'C' Flight of 261 Squadron on 12 May 1941 to share in the air defence of the island. The new squadron, led by Sqn Ldr Mould, was in action on 13 May with aircraft from 261 Squadron when they were attacked by Bf 109s. Two Hurricanes were destroyed and one pilot killed. This was the first time the Bf 109s had attacked in the fighter-bomber role over Malta.

On the next afternoon, both 185 and 261 Squadrons engaged a number of Bf 109s, but Fg Off. Hamilton, who had at least five claims against enemy aircraft, was shot down and later died from his wounds.

On 15 May, two 185 Squadron Hurricanes took off to provide top cover for 261 Squadron, but they were attacked by Bf 109s; Sgt Wynne died in a high-speed crash. Meanwhile, a SM.79 was claimed shot down by Fg Off. John Pain, and a Wellington was destroyed on the ground with three Beaufighters damaged. Between 12 and 15 May, the RAF lost five Hurricanes, with another four damaged, but with the German withdrawals from Sicily for the offensive on Russia, the Italian Air Force returned to the attacks against Malta.

At this stage, the Allied defence of Crete was about to begin. In preparation, further reinforcements were on their way from Gibraltar, consisting of HMS Ark Royal, HMS Eagle,

Hurricane Mk IIA Z2982 R:185 Squadron at Hal Far, Malta, in early 1942. (*P. H. T. Green collection*)

The carriers, HMS *Ark Royal*, HMS *Eagle*, and HMS *Furious*, left Gibraltar in mid-May 1941 with forty-eight Hurricanes of 213, 229, and 249 Squadrons, with 249 Squadron remaining for the air defence of Malta. Hurricanes on the deck of HMS *Furious* are being prepared for the ferry flight. (*Author's collection*)

and HMS Furious escorted by two battleships plus cruisers and destroyers. Although there were forty-eight Hurricanes on board the carriers, not all were for the defence of Malta. For the first time there were established RAF units on board, consisting of 213, 229, and 249 Squadrons, which had been ordered to prepare for service in the Middle East. As the new convoy approached Malta, Luqa came under heavy attack with a 261 Squadron Hurricane shot down—the pilot parachuted to safety and a Beaufighter burnt out on the ground.

No. 249 Squadron were told in April that they were to be sent to the Middle East, but their Hurricane Mk IIs were to be replaced with the much less effective Mk Is fitted with a pair of underwing extra fuel tanks that could not be jettisoned, giving an estimated total range of 1,020 miles (1,641 km). The Hurricanes were to make the journey via aircraft carrier, but the ground crew were to travel by ship around the Cape of Good Hope with the baggage—the two parties to be reunited in Egypt. The pilots and Hurricanes were loaded on HMS Furious, a converted 1918 battle cruiser, carrying three squadrons of aircraft in very crowded conditions. It took ten days to cross the Bay of Biscay to Gibraltar, where the Hurricanes were transferred to the larger Ark Royal, before heading for the Middle East with two more carriers and escorts of two battleships, half a dozen cruisers and supply ships, sailing through the dead of night, although the Germans knew exactly what was happening as they had a consulate two miles from Gibraltar.

This enormous force went through the Strait of Gibraltar on 21 May 1941, with the intention that the first aircraft would take off at dawn, when twenty-three aircraft were on the deck of the Ark Royal. The first flight of twelve Hurricanes was led by Butch Barton, and the following eleven were led by Tom Neil—the pilots had never launched from a carrier deck before. In the morning, the pilots were up at 4 a.m. and, following breakfast, climbed into the cockpits in the dark, rain, and a cloud base at around 800 feet (244 metres). With full fuel of 97 gallons, plus 88 gallons in the underwing tanks, it was 895 miles (1,440 km) to Malta, where the Hurricanes were allocated an airfield to land and refuel, before flying another 810 miles (1,303 km) at 100 feet above the sea to Mersa Matruh.

Tom Neil was second-in-command of 249 Squadron in May 1941 at twenty years old. He found the cockpits very crowded with little room to carry clothes, the total allowance being 30 lb of equipment to be carried in the otherwise empty ammunition tanks. Even the map case was full; the course instructions were stuffed down a crease behind the windscreen. Just after take-off, Tom Neil experienced a big bang caused by a cover over the guns on the port wing becoming partly detached and stood up at 45 degrees. Without rudder trim, Tom had to keep his foot hard down on the rudder to keep from going into the sea. He managed to climb high enough to circle the Ark Royal, but without proper control and overloaded with fuel, there was no option of landing back on the carrier.

As the remainder of the Hurricanes in Neil's flight took off they formed on him, but although he was the leader, they were to be guided by a Royal Navy Fulmar, which had a navigator in its crew, leading the Hurricanes to the Malta. They formed up behind the Fulmar, with Tom's right foot hard over to the right, the control column right over, the speed reduced to 160 mph (257 kph), he set off in the darkness, rain, and cloud. After flying parallel to the unseen North Africa coast in radio silence for an hour, the Fulmar inexplicitly gained speed, climbed into the cloud and left the Hurricanes. Neil was left with no maps and no course, having no idea where Malta was.

After circling with ten aircraft in formation, Neil had time to decide the course of action. Having been airborne for about an hour, he reckoned they had 800 miles (1,287 km) back to Gibraltar, plus an hour's flight, so just under 1,000 miles (1,609 km) to get back to Gibraltar. Turning around, they retraced their steps and after an hour spotted the wake of the fleet in the distance. The RN defences were alerted, thinking they may be under attack by torpedo bombers, and the ships scattered. When overhead the carrier, the deck crowded with aircraft was cleared and another Fulmar took off on a heading of the 580 miles (933 km) to Malta. Passing by some Italian-held islands, the Fulmar and Hurricanes went as fast as possible as they had no ammunition and could not defend themselves.

The weather became worse and the fuel levels decreased. After five hours and thirty-five minutes, Tom broke radio silence and said to the Fulmar crew that if they were not on the ground in five minutes, they would all be in the sea. At that moment the clouds lifted and Malta came into view, allowing the pilots to make for their designated airfields. Tom still had his numb leg jammed against the rudder, and on his final approach to Luqa, the defensive guns opened up at a bombing raid over the airfield. Tom then overshot and turned towards a nearby island, but decided to turn back to the airfield and landed among the black smoke from the fifty or sixty bombs dropped, coming to a halt with six gallons of fuel left in his tanks.

Tom was helped out of his aircraft and taken to an air-raid shelter where one of the pilots from the earlier flight told him that they were not going to the Middle East, but staying on Malta, with their Hurricanes going on to the Middle East and 249 Squadron taking over six battle weary Hurricane Mk Is of 261 Squadron, all in various states of disrepair. However, here were eight aircraft ready the next day for 249 Squadron, with 26 pilots, dividing the squadron into two and operating in morning and afternoon shifts. The first sorties started at 05.00, with the second shift at 13.00 hrs, operating alongside 261 Squadron. By the end of the first day, 249 Squadron was down to three serviceable Hurricanes, but the next day fortunately the Luftwaffe left for Poland and the Russian front, leaving the attacks on Malta to the less threatening Italian Air Force.

Operation Splice, the reinforcement of the assault on Crete, began on 21 May with the Hurricanes of 213 Squadron plus six from 229 Squadron taking off from the Furious led by a Fulmar for navigation. One of the 213 Squadron Hurricanes hit the sea after take-off and crashed.

Once arrived in Malta, the Hurricanes were turned around rapidly and departed for Mersa Matruh led by Beaufighters of 252 Squadron, but seven of 213 Squadron lost contact with their escort and returned to Malta. Meanwhile, HMS Ark Royal launched Hurricanes of 249 Squadron and despite being low on fuel, all arrived safely just at the start of another bombing raid.

No. 249 Squadron was based at Ta Kali, where 185 Squadron joined them with the surviving Hurricane Mk Is, making it the fighter base, and Luqa and Hal Far the bases for bombers and reconnaissance aircraft, as well as staging posts for aircraft en route to the Middle East.

Many of the new pilots had combat experience; their commanding officer, Sqn Ldr Barton, already had eight and a half victories to his credit. However, during their first readiness on 25 May, before 249 Squadron could become airborne, Bf 109s destroyed two Hurricanes on the ground and damaged three more. On 27 May, 249 Squadron was moved to Hal Far, and on the following night prevented several attacking force aircraft reaching their targets. By the end of the month, with the withdrawal of the Luftwaffe to the Russian Front, the RAF was able to achieve some level of air superiority, which made it possible to launch offensive operations against Sicily and German units in North Africa.

With reduced defensive fighter actions, it was not until 3 June that 249 Squadron recorded its first kill when Sqn Ldr Barton shot a SM.79 into the sea. With 46 Squadron scheduled to arrive shortly, led by Sqn Ldr 'Sandy' Rabagliati, 185 Squadron was allocated to night fighter defence. Including 46 Squadron and the aircraft left behind by 229 Squadron from previous deliveries, forty-three Hurricanes in total were despatched to Malta, led by Blenheims of 82 Squadron, all of which arrived safely. After exchanging their Hurricane Mk IIs for the remaining Mk Is on Malta, 229 Squadron departed the next day for Mersa Matruh. During the early hours of 8 June, Hurricanes of 249 Squadron claimed two Italian BR.20M bombers and another managed to return to base despite being badly damaged. With a radar alert of an approaching raid, 249 Squadron Hurricanes were scrambled, destroying two SM.79s. Malta had been experiencing active combat for a year, with total claims of 106 enemy aircraft shot down.

The wreckage of some of 249 Squadron Hurricanes at Ta Kali following a Luftwaffe Bf 109 raid in June 1941. (*Author's collection*)

Hurricane Mk IIB BG766 of 185 Squadron with underwing bombs in Malta. (*IWM Photo*)

Hurricanes of 249 Squadron at Ta Kali during the summer of 1941. (*Author's collection*)

A Hurricane Mk II of 249 Squadron, which crashed on arrival at Ta Kali after its ferry flight in August 1941. (*Author's collection*)

The first action for 46 Squadron was in the early morning of 11 June when seven Hurricanes were scrambled, shooting down one SM.79 into the sea for the loss of one Hurricane—the pilot posted as missing. The next day, eighteen Hurricanes from 46 and 249 Squadrons were scrambled early in the morning to intercept the Italian daily reconnaissance flight, and in a spirited fight one C.200 was shot down, but 249 Squadron had three aircraft hit with one pilot killed, a second parachuting into the sea, and a third crash landing at Safi. During the afternoon, a Cant floatplane and an escorting CR.42 were both shot down, but one Hurricane was lost with its pilot.

A further delivery of Hurricanes was made to Malta on 14 June with twenty-eight aircraft of 238 Squadron from the Victorious, and twenty more with 260 Squadron from the Ark Royal, all destined for combat in the North African campaign. However, five failed to arrive in Malta—three due to faulty navigation by the escorting Hudson and the other two due to lack of fuel. The majority of the aircraft left for Egypt over the next few days.

Owing to the success of the high-altitude reconnaissance Hurricane of 69 Squadron, it was joined by a second aircraft in mid-June, a modified long-range Mk II Z3053. On 18 June, a C.200 was badly damaged and crash-landed at its base, but one of the defending Hurricanes was lost with its pilot.

The rest of the month was busy for 46 Squadron, with combat on five days out of eight. At dawn on 23 June, Hurricanes went on the offensive and attacked a seaplane base at Syracuse. No. 46 Squadron led an attack on a SM.79 and thirty-six escorting C.200s—the SM.79 being damaged and two C.200s shot down with no RAF losses. During the afternoon, the new Hurricane Mk II reconnaissance aircraft located an Italian supply convoy on its way to Libya and called in an offensive strike, but no ships were sunk. Four days later, 46 Squadron intercepted a SM.79 escorted by twenty-four C.200s, with two of the latter shot down. Later, 46 Squadron claimed a further three C.200s, and on the same day, twenty-two more Hurricanes were flown off HMS Ark Royal, including some 20-mm cannon-armed Mk IICs. One went missing en route with the pilot taken prisoner, and another crashed on landing in Malta.

On 28 June, 46 Squadron was renumbered 126 Squadron, with a new 46 Squadron formed in the Middle East. On 30 June, the squadron moved from Hal Far to Ta Kali with some dispersals at the newly constructed Safi, where there was a dangerously narrow runway with anti-invasion devises along the border. During the first four days in July, five Hurricanes crashed at the difficult airfield.

The new 126 Squadron was in action on the first day of the move when six Hurricanes, including Mk IICs, shot down two C.200s. Also on 30 June, more Hurricanes arrived in Malta having flown from the decks of the Ark Royal and the Furious. Of the fifteen Hurricanes from Furious, the second departure crashed on take-off, killing the pilot and seriously injuring a number of aircrew, resulting in eight Hurricanes getting away whereas the final six could not be launched due to pilot injuries. A total of thirty-five Hurricanes reached Malta safely on this delivery.

Early on 4 July, a force of C.200s were detected approaching the island and were intercepted by four Hurricanes of 185 Squadron, with two shot down and three damaged. A pilot of 126 Squadron pilot was killed when he crashed on take-off from Safi into the sea.

Hurricanes bound for the defence of Malta lashed down on the deck of HMS *Ark Royal* on 27 June 1941. (*Author's collection*)

Hurricane Mk I V7803 safely airborne from HMS *Furious*, fitted with underwing ferry fuel tanks and the cockpit canopy open in the event of ditching after take-off. (*Author's collection*)

Hurricane Mk I V7563, fitted with underwing ferry fuel tanks and the tropical filter under the nose, departing HMS *Furious* for its ferry flight to Malta. (*Author's collection*)

During the night of 8–9 July, six SM.79s destroyed a Wellington on the ground, but one of the attackers was claimed by 249 Squadron. The next morning, a C.200 was badly damaged by a Hurricane of 185 Squadron, resulting in it crash landing on its return to base. Four Hurricanes from 126 and 185 Squadron returned to the offensive with an attack on the flying boat base at Syracuse, claiming six aircraft destroyed and four damaged. On 11 July, the Italians retaliated with a strong force of fighters at Hal Far. At least twelve Hurricanes were scrambled by 185 Squadron, claiming five Macchis damaged with no Hurricanes lost.

On 17 July, a large force of Italian fighters escorting a new reconnaissance aircraft, the Z.1007bis, was met by Hurricanes of 185 and 249 Squadrons. Two C.200s were shot down for the loss of one Hurricane. Another Z.1007bis with a heavy fighter protection appeared on 25 July and was again met by 185 and 249 Squadrons; the reconnaissance aircraft became a victim of 185 Squadron, while 249 Squadron claimed two of the escorting C.200s. In the early hours of 26 July, an attack was made by the Italian Navy to break through the harbour defences using boats packed with explosives. While the battle raged, cannon-armed Hurricanes from 185 and 126 Squadrons attacked four motor boats offshore and sank two, while two supporting C.200s were shot down for the loss of one Hurricane, from which Fg Off. Denis Winton baled out and climbed aboard one of the abandoned Italian motor launches. He was probably the only RAF pilot to capture an enemy warship single-handed.

A wheels-up landing at Ta Kali by Hurricane Z2827 M:MNFU in July 1941. (*Author's collection*)

By the end of July, the defending Hurricane pilots had been credited with twenty-one confirmed victories for the loss of three aircraft and two pilots killed during the month. The RAF on Malta now had fifteen Hurricane Mk Is and sixty Mk IIs in addition to the offensive capability provided by Beaufighters, Blenheims, and other types.

w At the end of July, the Malta Night Fighter Unit (MNFU) was formed at Ta Kali, commanded by Sqn Ldr George Powell-Sheddon, and equipped with eight Hurricane Mk IICs and four Mk IIBs. The aircraft operated in pairs and, aided by searchlights, claimed their first victory on 5–6 August with the destruction of two BR.20M bombers.

On 10 August, Sqn Ldr Rabagliati from 126 Squadron shot down a Z.506B, and after dark on 11 August, Italian bombers attacked Malta—one BR.20M was claimed by a Hurricane of the MNFU.

On 17 August, Hurricanes returned to Syracuse and destroyed two Z.506B flying boats, damaging four more. On the same day, a Hurricane of 249 Squadron shot a Ca.312 floatplane into the sea off Malta.

Two days later, C.200s approached the island and were met by 126 Squadron, who chased them back to Sicily, claiming four destroyed for no RAF losses. The last major engagement of the month came on 26 August when both 126 and 185 Squadrons were scrambled to intercept a formation of C.200s, with one claimed shot down for the loss of one Hurricane. The total RAF tally for the month stood at twelve victories for the loss of one Hurricane and pilot.

A Hurricane take-off crash at Ta Kali in August 1941, in which the pilot suffered two broken ribs. (*Author's collection*)

September began well; once again, 126 and 185 Squadrons met C.200s claimed the destruction of two fighters with no Hurricane losses on 4 September. That afternoon, another Italian attack was met by 249 Squadron with one C.200 shot down, but two Hurricanes were lost with their pilots.

There was a brief respite from day attacks, but the night-bombing continued—a Z.1007bis was shot down by a pair of MNFU Hurricanes on 5 September, followed by another during the night of 8 September.

On 9 September, fourteen Hurricanes arrived in Malta from the Ark Royal. Another twelve remained on board as there had been insufficient Blenheims for escort, and the next day the new delivery left for the Middle East. On 13 September, further Hurricanes flew in from the Ark Royal and the Furious, with twenty-three flying on to Egypt and the remainder remaining on Malta to bring the local squadrons up to strength and give some of the pilots a chance to rest. On 28 September, another supply convoy reached Malta, and to discourage attacks on the unloading of the ships in Valetta Harbour, 185 Squadron Hurricanes were fitted with bombs that were dropped on Comiso airfield. While six of the Hurricanes dropped over 5,000-lb of bombs, top cover was provided by six more aircraft from the squadron, and on 30 September, Comiso was hit again by fighter-bomber Hurricanes with one Hurricane lost.

The Malta garrison was now clearly on the offensive, sinking about one-third of all Axis supply ships to North Africa and diverting Luftwaffe bombing in Egypt to Sicily for convoy protection.

The Italians used C.202s over Malta for the first time at the beginning of October, which were intercepted by 185 Squadron Hurricanes. Sqn Ldr 'Boy' Mould was killed in action on 1 October.

On 7 October, 249 Squadron made a fighter-bomber strike on Gela station and Comiso, while the MNFU made a moonlight attack on railway installations in Sicily. Luqa was strafed by low-flying Macchis just before dawn on 14 October, with the Hurricanes of the MNFU, 185 and 249 Squadrons scrambled in defence. Fg Off. Barnwell, one of the most successful night-fighter pilots, was shot down and killed after destroying one raider.

With the arrival of the Blenheims of 18 Squadron on 13 October, 249 Squadron provided escort for a medium-level attack by the RAF bombers on the Syracuse seaplane base.

Two days later, two pilots of 249 Squadron went on a patrol with long-range fuel tanks fitted to seek out Axis troop carrying aircraft flying to North Africa; a single S.81 was located at low level and shot down. Meanwhile, 126 Squadron Hurricanes made another fighter-bomber attack on Comiso in the afternoon, and the next morning, a S.81 was shot down by a pair of patrolling 185 Squadron Hurricanes.

On 22 October, Italian C.202s made a strafing attack on Luqa, with one 249 Squadron Hurricane lost—the pilot baled out safely. An attack by Italian Z.1007bis escorted by C.202 fighters on the Grand Harbour on 25 October resulted in one bomber being so badly damaged by 185 Squadron Hurricanes that it crashed on landing. One C.202 was also shot down, although one Hurricane and pilot was lost. On the final night of the month, MNFU Hurricanes intercepted Italian bombers and claimed one BR.20M destroyed.

Offensive operations by Malta-based aircraft had caused major losses to Axis supply shipping over the previous three months, exceeding the rate of replacement ship construction, although it came at a cost of heavy losses to Malta-based Blenheim units.

With Tobruk still in Allied control, both the German and British forces were preparing for an all-out effort to decide who was to control North Africa. For the Axis to succeed in North Africa, the main priority was to crush Malta. The British offensive operations had included air and naval operations against convoys, air transport, and military targets in Italy and North Africa. RAF Hurricanes were used almost exclusively on ground-attack sorties over Sicily, with occasional interception duties. There were now adequate fighters and pilots for the air defence of Malta, as well as good stocks of fuel, ammunition, and food. The RAF strength exceeded the Axis forces in Africa.

On 8 November, 126 Squadron returned to the defensive against an Italian bombing raid in which one Hurricane was lost—the pilot baled out—for two enemy aircraft. On the following day, two 185 Squadron Hurricanes were deployed against enemy torpedo bombers attacking ships with Force 'H', one of which was lost.

A major RAF counter-offensive began on 12 November with a strafing attack on Gela airfield by 249 Squadron, during which the CO, Wg Cdr Brown, was killed. This was followed by a fighter-bomber attack on Comiso airfield by 249 and 126 Squadrons, with one Hurricane shot down and the pilot taken prisoner.

Reinforcements continued to be flown into Malta, allowing for the formation of 266 Wing comprising 242, 605, and 258 Squadrons with Hurricanes. The first two squadrons had some Battle of Britain veterans while the remainder of the pilots had recent combat experience. Nos 242 and 605 Squadrons were loaded aboard HMS Argus and HMS Ark Royal, while 258 Squadron Hurricanes were in crates aboard HMS Athene, and the ground crews of all three squadrons awaited departure from Gibraltar. On 12 November, thirty-seven Hurricanes took off from the carriers; all but three arrived safely and the three pilots were captured. The carriers were returning to Gibraltar to collect the next batch of Hurricanes when the Ark Royal was hit by torpedoes from U-81 on 13 November and sank with the loss of only one life. The remaining Hurricanes left at Gibraltar were redirected to Asia and later joined by 605 Squadron and a newly reformed 242 Squadron. The new personnel on Malta were integrated into 185 and 249 Squadrons.

On 21 November, the CO of 69 Squadron, Wg Cdr Downland, flew an unarmed Hurricane Mk II on a reconnaissance sortie over Sicily when he was attacked by a MC202 and had to bale out over the sea, but was later rescued.

The Italian air offensive continued to build. On 22 November, 126 Squadron provided top cover for 249 Squadron during an attack by Ju 87s with a strong fighter escort when one C.202 was shot down for no RAF losses.

November was a crippling month for the Axis supply convoys with 63 per cent of all cargo destined for Libya destroyed by both the Royal Navy ships of H Force and Malta-based RAF Blenheims; many of the aircrew were lost in the hazardous combat conditions. The enemy

Hurricane Mk IIB BG753 V:605 Squadron in Malta, January 1942. (*P. H. T. Green collection*)

therefore decided to move reinforcements from Sicily to Libya to support the North African campaign, particularly as bad weather would soon restrict the offensive on the Russian front and units could be spared for the Mediterranean offensive.

At the end of November, RAF fighter strength on Malta consisted of the Hurricanes of 126, 185, 249 Squadrons, and the MNFU, plus Hurricanes and Marylands with 69 Squadron for reconnaissance duties. For offensive duties, there were two detachments of Blenheim squadrons and three squadrons of Wellington bombers. An anti-shipping strike capability was maintained from the earliest days of the defence of Malta by two FAA squadrons of Albacores and Swordfish.

Early in December, MNFU was redesignated 1435 (Night Fighter) Flight under the command of Sqn Ldr Westmacott.

After a lull lasting a few days, Malta-based Hurricanes were back in action on 8 December when 185 Squadron shot down a S84 bomber without loss. The following day, Ju 88s were intercepted over an arriving convoy, and one was shot down by 126 Squadron. On 20 December, the Luftwaffe returned in force with Ju 88s escorted by Bf 109s, which were met by 249 Squadron over the Grand Harbour. One Ju 88 was shot down for the loss of two Hurricanes and pilots. On a repeat raid the next day, Sqn Ldr Rabaglian claimed a MC202, but two Hurricanes were lost with one pilot killed. On 23 December, another Hurricane and pilot was lost during an attack by Bf 109s over the Grand Harbour. In the week leading up to Christmas 1941, the Luftwaffe made twenty-five raids against Malta, many by Ju 88 bombers escorted by Bf 109s.

Graham Leggatt was scrambled with 249 Squadron from Luqa on 21 December in a very battle-weary Hurricane Mk I. Climbing to 12,000 feet (3,657 km), he spotted three Ju 88s in close formation heading for Malta. As Graham dived down to attack, he saw six Bf 109s in escort, which climbed to meet him when they spotted Leggatt approaching. While going around in circles, the Bf 109s hit Leggatt's Hurricane with a tremendous flash by his left leg, covering everything in a thick, black, hot oil, including his face and eyes. By this time, Leggatt was down to 3,000 feet (609 m) and made for home, crossing the coast in the hope of returning to Luqa. On selecting undercarriage down, he could see the wheels burning, and decided to climb over the side of the doomed aircraft. He looked up just in time to see the canopy open, and looking down, the ground was very close, taking about five seconds before landing. He was met by an army truck driven by a captain in the Hampshire Regiment who he had shared a couple of drinks with the night before, so they went off to continue where they had left off.

After a quiet Christmas Day, Luqa was attacked and the reconnaissance Hurricane of 69 Squadron, as well as other aircraft on the airfield, was destroyed. With regular night attacks by Ju 88s, 1435 Flight moved from Ta Kali to Hal Far to be closer to the action, and on 27 December, 126 Squadron shot down one Ju 88 during three daylight attacks, with 1435 Flight claiming another after dark.

With the end of the year, a 249 Squadron Hurricane was downed into the sea, but the pilot was rescued. This was followed by one of the heaviest attacks since the Luftwaffe's return to Sicily, with five scrambles during the day resulting in three major actions—the first raid being met by 185 and 242 Squadrons. Two Hurricanes and a pilot were lost in a mid-air collision, and during the second engagement, one Hurricane crashed and one Bf 109 was shot down.

In the third major raid during the day, two Hurricanes were shot down by Bf 109s during ground attacks on Luqa that destroyed fifteen aircraft, including nine Wellington bombers. The final attack of the year was on 30 December when Luqa, Ta Kali, and the docks were targeted by Luftwaffe bombers, who were met by 126 and 249 Squadrons with two Ju 88s destroyed.

Since hostilities had commenced in June 1940, Malta-based fighter pilots had been credited with 199 Axis aircraft of all types destroyed for the loss of forty-seven RAF fighter pilots, including one member of the FAA, and a further fifteen had been lost during the ferry flights. At least ninety Hurricanes had been lost in combat with many more destroyed on the ground. Although some Hurricanes were to continue in service in Malta during 1942, they were largely replaced by Spitfires, which took over the air defence of the island until Malta finally came through the hardships of a siege lasting.

In addition to playing an essential part in the air defence of Malta, Hurricanes were also in action in other parts of the Mediterranean theatre. Following Italian advances against Greece on 28 October 1940, the major part of British air support was provided by Wellington Bombers flying from bases in Malta and Egypt. On 19 November, the Gladiators of 80 Squadron were deployed to Trikkala in Greece, followed by the similarly equipped 112 Squadron at Yannina on 24 January 1941.

With the growing Italian threat, the potential German invasion of the Balkans, 33 Squadron was deployed to Eleusis with Hurricanes on 19 February. The primitive airfield conditions and inadequate support made it difficult to keep the aircraft serviceable, resulting in a move to the better airfield at Larissa during March. No. 80 Squadron received their first six Hurricane Mk Is on 20 February to begin the replacement of the antiquated Gladiators.

The German invasion of the Balkans commenced on 6 April with a devastating bombing attack on Belgrade, leading to a push into Greece and Yugoslavia. For air defence, the

A Hurricane of 80 Squadron on the rather basic airfield at Eleusis in Greece in 1941. (*Author's collection*)

Yugoslav Air Force (YAF) had thirty-eight Hurricanes among other types, of which around thirty Hurricanes were serviceable. The Luftwaffe concentrated their attacks on the airfields to destroy the opposition on the ground. The 51st Fighter Squadron YAF at Sarajevo had eighteen Hurricanes on strength, with 33rd and 34th Fighter Squadrons at Zagreb sharing a further twenty Hurricanes. With a rapid retreat from the advancing German forces, the Yugoslavs destroyed the Zemun factory, which deprived the YAF of replacement Hurricane aircraft and spares. The surviving aircraft only remained in action for a week; one or two escaped to Greece only to be destroyed soon after by Bf 109s.

Although the Greek government requesting all possible help, no further Hurricanes could be spared by the RAF. No. 112 Squadron, with a handful of Gladiators, withdrew to Crete on 16 April. Meanwhile, 208 Squadron was in the process of moving to Greece when the Germans invaded, but only had one flight of Hurricanes allocated to tactical reconnaissance for Army co-operation. By 19 April, the German forces had reached Larrissa, around 20 miles north-west of Athens, with 33, 80, and 208 Squadrons based at Eleusis for the protection of the capital and the harbour of Piraeus where Allied troops were being evacuated from. Five Hurricanes arrived from Egypt on 18 April, bringing the total of serviceable aircraft to twenty-two with seven more under repair, but the next day, a hangar was bombed and the Hurricanes under repair destroyed. A further three Hurricanes were lost in combat during the day in return for eleven enemy aircraft claimed destroyed.

The surviving Hurricanes of 33 and 80 Squadrons were combined on 20 April under the leadership of Sqn Ldr Pattle of 33 Squadron. That evening, while waiting to take-off, a large formation of Ju 88s attacked shipping in Piraeus Harbour, with three shot down for the loss of one Hurricane and pilot, plus two Bf 110s, two Ju 88s, and three Bf 109s for the loss of two more Hurricanes from which the pilots baled out. It was eventually determined that Pattle's remarkable total of victories was over forty enemy destroyed in the air, four shared kills, five destroyed on the ground, with six probables and five damaged—all during a period of just nine months. Seven of these victories were claimed while flying Gladiators and the remainder when flying Hurricanes.

'Pat' Pattle was a South African-born Second World War fighter pilot and flying ace who had destroyed five or more enemy aircraft in aerial combat. He joined the RAF in 1936 and was trained as a pilot in 1937, joining 80 Squadron based in Egypt on the outbreak of war in September 1939. In June 1940, Italy entered the war on the side of Germany, and Pattle began combat operations against the Italian Air Force, gaining his first victories during the Italian invasion of Egypt in September 1940. In December, General Archibald Wavell counter-attacked, destroying most of the Italian army, and taking more than 100,000 prisoners. After the Italian invasion, Pattle was sent with his squadron to Greece in November 1940, where he achieved most of his victories, claiming some twenty aircraft shot down. In March 1941, he was promoted to squadron leader. Following the German intervention, in fourteen days of operations Pattle claimed twenty-four to fifty victories, with five or more aircraft destroyed in one day on three occasions, which qualified him for ace-in-a-day status. Pattle's greatest success was on 19 April 1941 when he claimed six victories. The following day, while suffering from a high temperature, he took off against orders to engage German aircraft near Athens. He was last seen attacking a Luftwaffe Bf 110 before his Hurricane was set on fire and crashed into the sea, killing Pattle.

Another RAF fighter ace in the same battle was Vernon 'Woody' Woodward, the second-highest scoring Canadian pilot of the war. He was born in Vancouver, British Columbia, and joined the RAF as a pilot in August 1938. In June 1939, Woodward was posted to 33 Squadron in Egypt flying Gladiators; when Italy entered the war in June 1940, he claimed five kills and two probables before converting to Hurricanes. With a score of eighteen confirmed kills, four shared, two unconfirmed, three probables, and eleven damaged, he won his last victory in July 1941. He was posted to Rhodesia as a flying instructor, ending the war with a DFC and bar, and made a post-war career in the RAF until retiring in 1963.

The surviving eleven Hurricanes were flown to Argos on 22 April where they were joined by five more from Crete. In a subsequent German attack by forty Bf 110s, nine Hurricanes were destroyed on the ground, and at first light on 24 April, seven surviving aircraft were flown to Crete to provide cover for the last of the evacuating ships arriving from Greece. The Allied preparations on Crete had been slow, and with German forces now occupying all of Greece, the situation had become critical. The island was occupied by thousands of Allied troops who had been evacuated from Greece and were short of arms and equipment. There were only two basic airfields and a rudimentary landing strip, while the remnants of 33, 80, and 112 Squadrons consisted of fourteen Hurricanes and six Gladiators with a few FAA Fulmars. The Luftwaffe force against the defenders consisted of 430 bombers, 180 fighters, and around 600 transports. Enemy attacks commenced in early May against the northern ports, and on 14 May, the airfields of Maleme, Heraklion, and the strip at Retimo were targeted; seven Bf 109s were shot down for the loss of four Hurricanes together with other aircraft. Six more Hurricane replacement were supplied, but by 18 May only four remained operational, together with three Gladiators. The survivors were evacuated to Egypt the next day.

The main German assault on Crete started on 20 May. Twelve Hurricanes were deployed from Egypt to Heraklion to provide cover for the Allied evacuation, but two were shot down by 'friendly fire' from the Royal Navy, and four more were damaged during landing on the badly cratered airfield. The surviving six, supported by another six operating from Egypt fitted with long-range fuel tanks, provided cover until the end of the month when Crete finally fell. Losses on both side were heavy.

A few squadrons had converted to Spitfires in preparation for the invasion of Sicily on 10 July 1943, but 253 Squadron transferred its Hurricanes to night-fighter duties temporarily to provide some protection to the airborne forces in gliders and transports as they approached the landing zones in Sicily. The Hurricanes of 127, 213, and 274 Squadrons operated from bases in Cyrenaica, Egypt, and Cyprus in unsuccessful operations against German forces in the Dodecanese Islands in September and November, and some offensive sweeps were flown against German-occupied airfields in Crete.

Some Hurricane units were available for operations in the Italian campaign—particularly 6 Squadron, which had fully recovered from the fighting in North Africa (see Chapter 12) and arrived at Grottaglie in February 1944 equipped with Hurricane Mk IVs. The Hurricanes were normally armed with 40-mm cannons, which were later discarded, and four 3-inch rocket projectiles (RP)—the new role being to attack Axis shipping and ports on both coasts of the Adriatic.

Hurricanes burning on the ground during the German invasion of Crete in May 1941 after an air attack on an airfield. (*Author's collection*)

Hurricane Mk II HW798 AK-P:213 Squadron operated from Paphos in Greece in September 1943. (*Author's collection*)

With the destruction of Hurricanes on the ground in Crete, 213 Squadron provided air defence from Egypt during the Allied evacuation. The underside of the port wing was painted black to aid identification for allied guns. (*IWM photo*)

Hurricane Mk IIB HL795 V:274 Squadron, which served in Greece, Egypt, and Libya. (*RAF Museum*)

Hurricane Mk I P2544 YK- :274 Squadron in the Middle East during 1941. (*P. H. T. Green collection*)

With the retreat of the German forces later in the Second World War, Hurricanes returned to Greece—an example being a Mk IV armed with RPs under the wings preparing to take-off with an audience of Spitfire pilots. (*IWM photo*)

With the Allied advances during the Balkan Campaign, support was provided by Hurricane Mk IVs of 6 Squadron. LF498 lands at Tatoi in Greece in November 1944, the pilot responsible for the destruction of a rail bridge at Spuz. (*IWM photo*)

Hurricane Mk IVs of 351 Squadron Yugoslav Air Force being loaded with RPs ready for their next ground-attack operation. (*IWM photo*)

The squadron also hit the German headquarters at Durazzo on the Albanian coast on 29 March before moving north-westwards on 4 July to Foggia to cover the entire Yugoslav coastline. To cope with the greater endurance required in these operations, the Hurricanes carried a fuel drop tank under one wing and RPs under the other. During the five months of operations, 6 Squadron sank a 5,000-ton ship, twenty-one schooners, three ferries, and eleven other ships, in addition to severely damaging a further twenty-seven vessels.

No. 6 Squadron was temporarily transferred to the Balkan Air Force in August, joining 351 and 352 Yugoslav Squadrons, which had recently formed with Hurricane Mk IICs. No. 6 Squadron remained based in Italy initially and sent forward detachments to Nikšić, deep in Yugoslavia, to operate daily anti-armour patrols, while the two Yugoslav squadrons moved to the island of Vis in the Adriatic in October. For these operations, 6 Squadron Hurricanes were armed with four 25-lb armour-piercing—or four 60-lb semi-armour-piercing RPs, both of which were effective against enemy armour. The RAF squadron then moved to Prkos in Yugoslavia on 9 April 1945, where it remained until the end of the war in Europe. With just one week to go until the final surrender, the squadron operated RP-attacks against German troopships in the Gulf of Trieste, all of which raised white flags in surrender. No. 6 Squadron became the longest serving Hurricane unit, and in recognition of the skills of the pilots and the ruggedness of the aircraft in the anti-armour role, the unit adopted a red flying can-opener in a circle for its squadron badge, which is still carried by 6 Squadron RAF Typhoons.

The war in Europe finally came to an end. Hurricanes had first entered combat in the Mediterranean theatre when German forces invaded Yugoslavia on 6 April 1941. Four years later, the aircraft returned to the same country, which was devastated by the Nazi occupation.

12

The Desert Campaign

D URING THE SECOND World War, what was known as the North African Campaign took place from 10 June 1940 until 13 May 1943. It included campaigns fought in the Libyan and Egyptian deserts, in Morocco and Algeria (Operation Torch), and Tunisia. The campaign started with the Italian declaration of war on 10 June 1940, and on 14 June, British Army units crossed from Egypt into Libya and captured Fort Capuzzo. The Italians responded with an offensive into Egypt and the capture of Sidi Barrani in September 1940. The British Commonwealth forces staged Operation Compass, a counter-offensive in December 1940, which destroyed the Italian 10th Army, resulting in Rommel's German Afrika Korps being deployed to North Africa to reinforce the remaining Italian forces and prevent a complete Axis defeat.

Under the command of Rommel, by late 1940, German forces were well established in Libya. Their plan was to advance towards Egypt and the vital Allied strategic route through the Suez Canal. With planned advances throughout the Middle East, Germany would gain access to rich oil fields to fuel their war machine for future conquests and deny the energy to the Allies. The struggle to fight off the enemy was to last three years, with frequently moving fronts creating difficulties supplying and reinforcing both sides.

The rugged and adaptable Hurricane, operated by skilled pilots and maintained in difficult conditions by dedicated ground crews, played a vital support role in this area of conflict from its beginning to the Allies' ultimately successful end.

The first Hurricanes began to arrive in Egypt in August 1940 by sea and from East Africa to equip 274 Squadron.

No. 73 Squadron had arrived from Britain with Hurricanes, and more were supplied to 208 and 3 (RAAF) Squadrons, which converted from Lysanders on Army Co-operation duties. On 9 December 1940, General Wavell launched an attack on Italian ground forces; the Hurricanes were allocated to ground attack on troops and soft-skinned vehicles.

The first Hurricanes to reach Cairo were Mk Is with 274 Squadron, which arrived by sea in August 1940. The squadron reformed at Amriya on 19 August. The squadron initially had a mixture of Hurricanes and Gladiators and was commanded by S/Ldr P. H. Dunn. The aircraft were lined up and being made ready for flight at Amriya in November 1940, with P2544 nearest fitted with glare shields for night operations, and all have tropical filters. (*Author's collection*)

The Hurricanes of 73 Squadron supported General Wavell's attack on the Italian forces on 9 December 1940 with ground attack on troops and soft-skinned vehicles. Two of their Hurricane Mk Is are seen flying over the North African Desert. (*RAF Museum*)

Among the Commonwealth support for the North African Campaign was 3. (RAAF) Squadron with Hurricanes, including Mk I P3822, based at Amriya in March 1941. (*Author's collection*)

The 208 Squadron Hurricanes were initially tasked with the protection of the reconnaissance Lysanders, but with little sign of the Italian Air Force, they were diverted to tactical reconnaissance operations up to 50 miles behind enemy lines.

On 16 December, the last Italian troops were driven out of Egypt. Hurricanes of 33 Squadron attacked motor transport beyond the port of Bardia.

Although Hurricanes were required in other parts of the Mediterranean, particularly Greece, the dilution was resisted as although more aircraft became available, the conversion of the pilots from Gladiators took time.

Among the challenges was the formation of new squadrons, which required more than just aircraft and pilots but the full logistical support of spares, equipment, ground crews, and supplies. With the capture of Tobruk by the Allies on 22 January 1941, there were seven Hurricane squadrons in the Mediterranean and Middle East. By this time, both 208 and 3 (RAAF) Squadrons were based at Gambut in Libya, and from Egypt, 33 Squadron moved to Greece on 19 February, while 73 and 274 Squadrons were operational in the Western Desert from their base at Sidi Haneish. Further away, 1 Squadron (SAAF) was based in Khartoum, and 261 Squadron was committed to the defence of Malta.

Allied advances continued beyond Tobruk, with Benghazi taken on 7 February. However, the advance came to a halt the next day at El Agheila, and some Allied air and ground components were allocated to the abortive Greek campaign. As a result, when Rommel's Afrika Korps attacked a few weeks later, Wavell had insufficient troops and a weakened Air Component, resulting in a headlong retreat back across the desert.

The pilots of 33 Squadron helped to drive the last of the Italian forces out of Egypt in December 1940, and are seen relaxing by Hurricane Mk I V7419 NW:33 Squadron between operations. (*RAF Museum*)

A Hurricane having its guns test-fired in the gun butts during maintenance in the Middle East. (*IWM*)

Hurricane Mk I V7670 had been captured and flown by the Luftwaffe, but was recaptured by the Allies at Gambut in December 1941. (*IWM*)

No. 33 Squadron was posted to Greece on 19 February 1941, but later returned to Egypt where Hurricane Mk I V7419 was parked. (*RAF Museum*)

Some of the pilots of 73 Squadron in North Africa relax between sorties in front of a well-worn Hurricane. (*RAF Museum*)

Hurricane Mk I P2627 of 274 Squadron flying over the North African Desert in 1940. (*Author's collection*)

Hurricane Mk I TP-U:73 Squadron at Bu Amud, North Africa, around April or May 1941. (*Author's collection*)

In May 1942, 6 Squadron was re-assigned to the anti-armour role and equipped with Hurricane Mk IIDs armed with a pair of 40-mm cannons under the wings. Their operations commenced at the Battle of Alamein on 19 October 1942—the launch of Operation Supercharger. The nearest of the four Hurricane Mk IIDs is BP188 JV-Z:6 Squadron. (*IWM*)

With 73 Squadron sent back to Gazala West, and 274 Squadron still at the rear base of Sidi Haneish, the only air support available to cover the withdrawal were the two flights of Hurricanes with 208 and 3 RAAF Squadrons, and a flight of 6 Squadron issued with Hurricanes—the squadron having been used for short-range tactical reconnaissance. The issue of Hurricanes to 6 Squadron marked the commencement of a very significant association between Hurricanes and desert warfare. During the withdrawal, Hurricanes were operating far from their regular bases and, with the rapid German advances, were often landing at forward airstrips for fuel and rearming, only to find the ground crews had departed. As a result, some thirty aircraft were abandoned, their pilots seeking lifts back in retreating ground transport. However, Hurricanes continued to play a significant part in maintaining air superiority, with 73 Squadron destroying twelve Italian aircraft for the loss of two Hurricanes on 5 April during a running battle. A week later, 73 Squadron set up a detachment at Tobruk with Hurricane flights of 6 and 3 (RAAF) Squadrons, although enemy advances had already reached Bardia and Sollum, and also surrounded Allied forces in the port.

Axis forces made determined efforts to reduce the effectiveness of the port, dive-bombing with Stukas escorted by Bf 109s. The three defending units had eighteen Hurricanes and thirty-one pilots between them. On 21 April, four Ju 87s and a Bf 109 were claimed shot down, and the following day, the seven surviving Hurricanes of 73 Squadron claimed six enemy aircraft shot down in a combined attack by sixty Ju 87s and Bf 109s for the loss of one Hurricane. That evening, six surviving Hurricanes with 73 Squadron took off against an attack by some forty enemy raiders, destroying five for the loss of one Hurricane.

Hurricane Mk IIBs eventually replaced the Mk Is with 73 Squadron in North Africa. BD930 R:73 Squadron, featuring colourful unit markings on the fuselage, is being loaded on a 'Queen Mary' with the wings removed for repairs at a maintenance unit. (*RAF Museum*)

Hurricane Mk IID BP188 JV-Z:6 Squadron. (*P. H. T. Green collection*)

Armourers prepare a Hurricane Mk I of 260 Squadron for its next combat in August-September 1941. (*Author's collection*)

Hurricane Mk IID of 6 Squadron at Shandur, Egypt, fitted with a pair of 40-mm underwing cannons. There were often problems when firing both cannons together—firing one produced severe yawing, which made aiming difficult. However, when the guns worked well, they had a massive destructive power against Axis armour. (*Author's collection*)

On 23 April, 73 Squadron survivors withdrew to Sidi Haneish in Egypt, followed by the withdrawal of the last four pilots with 6 Squadron to Egypt on 8 May.

By this time, the stocks of Hurricanes in the Canal Zone had grown to more than 100 aircraft, and in June, General Auchinleck succeeded Wavell as the commander of Allied forces in the Western Desert, with Air Marshal Arthur Tedder in charge of the Air Components. With the failure of the relief of Tobruk and recapture of airfields in eastern Cyrenaica, preparations were made for a new offensive in the late summer. New pilots were trained by special Operational Training Units (OTUs), the first being 71(ME) OTU at Ismailia on 1 June, operating thirty Hurricane Mk Is and IIs, which within three months was training about forty new pilots every five weeks. In October, 74 OTU was formed at Aqir in Palestine, which took over the task of training Army Co-operation pilots, allowing 71 OTU to concentrate on the air-fighting and ground-attack roles.

Auchinleck launched his offensive, known as Operation Crusader, on 11 November across the Egyptian border into Libya, by which time Tedder had a significant force of Hurricanes

Hurricane Mk I Z4172 G:260 Squadron on final approach for landing with flaps down. (*RAF Museum*)

RAF pilots stationed in the Middle East were converted to flying Hurricanes initially by 71 OTU based at Ismailia. (*Author's collection*)

The pilot and ground crew of 260 Squadron Hurricane Mk I Z4172:G. (*Author's collection*)

The tank-busting Hurricane Mk IIDs of 6 Squadron operated in the North African Campaign from Egypt, through Libya, and into Tunisia from May 1942 until September 1943. (*Author's collection*)

with better trained pilots and equipped for desert warfare. Nos 6 and 208 Squadrons continued to operate one flight of Hurricanes on tactical reconnaissance with Lysanders, while 237 and 451 (RAAF) Squadrons were based in Egypt and operational in the Western Desert. Hurricane Mk Is, IIAs, and IIBs were used for air defence, with 33, 73, 94, and 260 Squadrons and 335 (Greek) Squadron in the process of forming. Hurricane Mk IIB fighter-bombers equipped 80 Squadron, while 30, 213, 229, 274, and 1(SAAF) Squadrons all used versions of the Hurricane Mk II on air-defence and ground-attack duties. No. 2 PRU operated up to five Hurricanes with other aircraft on photo-reconnaissance operations from Heliopolis.

Tactical reconnaissance Hurricanes were fitted with an additional radio, which allowed for communications with ground forces, and some had a vertical camera fitted aft of the cockpit with one or two of the Browning guns removed. The later Hurricane Mk IIC Tac R also had one or two cannons removed to accommodate a camera. The rare PR Hurricanes, of which there were no more than a dozen Mk Is with 2 PRU were modified in great secrecy at Heliopolis from January 1941, the first two fitted with a pair of f24 8-in cameras and another was fitted with one vertical and a pair of oblique F24 14-inch cameras in the rear fuselage aft of the radiator intake fairing. All armament was removed and additional fuel tanks were installed in the wings to increase endurance. Five more Hurricane PR Mk Is were modified in March in time for the Iraqi and Syrian campaigns. The PR Mk Is were followed by six PR Mk IIs—the first two were delivered to 2 PRU in December to support Operation Crusader.

With the launch of Operation Crusader on 11 January 1941, Hurricanes were in full support of the ground forces, including 237. (Rhodesia) Squadron with a pair of their Hurricane Mk Is taking off from a desert airfield. (*IWM*)

Hurricane Mk Is of 33 Squadron operating from the North African Desert airfield at Sidi Barami. (*Author's collection*)

Air defence for Operation Crusader was provided for by 94 Squadrons, seen on the ground here at El Gamil. (*Author's collection*)

The Hurricane Tac Rs were flown over the battlefield to obtain up-to-date information of enemy positions and strengths. Darkroom facilities could be rather rudimentary; the pilot here waits for the results before giving his report. (*Author's collection*)

The Hurricanes were believed to be capable of up to 350 mph and reach an altitude of 38,000 feet. An additional batch of about a dozen Hurricanes were converted between the end of 1942 and early 1943, mainly for issue to 3 PRU in India, but at least three were operated by a detachment of 680 (PR) Squadron in Libya as late as July 1944.

Operation Crusader caught the Axis forces by surprise just as Rommel was making preparations for the final assault on Tobruk. No. 33 Squadron provided air support against Italian ground transport behind enemy lines. When it began to look possible that Tobruk could be relieved, Rommel ordered two armoured Panzer divisions towards the Egyptian border, threatening the rear of the Allied forces and the forward landing grounds. Hurricane fighter bombers of 80 Squadron were sent to attack, but they were less effective against armour than they had been against soft-skinned vehicles.

With the pressure on the Tobruk garrison eased, a breakout was attempted on 26 November, supported by four Hurricane Tac Rs of 451 (RAAF) Squadron linking up with New Zealand forces approaching from the south-east. Rommel was now threatened with being cut off and began a withdrawal supported by an enlarged Luftwaffe presence, including a dive-bombing attack by Ju 87s on the Eighth Army. The Axis fighter cover was provided by hot-weather-adapted Bf 109F-4 tropical aircraft of JG 27 based at Cyrenaica, which had a performance of up to 380 mph at 20,000 feet. Fortunately, the aircraft were lightly armed with single 20-mm cannons and a pair of small machine guns.

No. 2 PRU provided photo reconnaissance for Operation Crusader, as well as a number of operations in the North African Campaign, flying unarmed Hurricanes. This aircraft has ended up in some soft ground with the starboard main wheel sunk in the sand. (*Author's collection*)

Unarmed Hurricane Mk IIB Z5132 2 PRU/680 Squadron on a desert airfield. (*P. H. T. Green collection*)

Air defence for Operation Crusader was also provided by 260 Squadron Hurricane Mk Is. Z4266 MF-E was a Mk I flown by an NCO pilot. (*Author's collection*)

Hurricane Mk IIB of 80 Squadron ready for another sortie, with the pilot ready room in the open air in mid-1940. No. 80 Squadron supported Operation Crusader with air defence and ground attack. (*IWM*)

Hurricane Mk IIBs of 80 Squadron were allocated to air defence and ground attack in Operation Crusader. A Mk IIB of 80 Squadron is being loaded with bombs for another ground-attack sortie at El Adam in 1942. (*Author's collection*)

No. 208 Squadron operated immediately ahead of the Allied advance and saw plenty of action. On 29 November, an unarmed Hurricane Tac R Mk I flown by Fg Off. P. T. Cotton was attacked by a pair of Bf 109Es and manoeuvred violently for around thirty minutes to evade the enemy fighters as they ran out of ammunition. Having escaped destruction, the overstrained Merlin engine failed on the way back to base, and the Hurricane force-landed 15 miles short of the airfield. The aircraft was subsequently recovered and repaired—Fg Off. Cotton was awarded the DFC.

Axis forces fell back to a pre-prepared defensive line at Gazala from which, after a three-day battle starting on 12 December, Rommel was able to extricate his forces once more.

By Christmas, the Eighth Army had advanced to Bengazi and captured all the Cyrenaican airfields at El Adam, Benina, Berka, Martuba, Gazala, Derna, as well as a number of the numbered temporary landing grounds. Due to the rapid advances by Allied troops, the supporting Hurricanes were unable to take full advantage of the forward airfields because of a lack of support, and were operating from bases well to the rear. The situation was corrected rapidly by Tedder, who ensured that each ground support unit was ready to move in and out of captured airfields at less than one-hour notice. In addition, RAF airfield construction units were ordered into newly captured airfields to repair runways and facilities without waiting for Army engineers, who were already fully occupied supporting the ground advance.

On 9 January 1942, the Allies captured and held El Agheila while support attempted to catch up with the advances. At this crucial time, Hurricanes destined for Egypt were diverted to South East Asia to defend against the Japanese attacks. Both 17 and 232 Squadrons had sailed from Britain on 12 December, expecting to reach Egypt by December, but were diverted to Asia—the former to Burma and the latter to Singapore—while 605 Squadron was split between Malta and Palembang in Sumatra.

Fortunately, Axis forces were also suffering from shortages of supplies and aircraft, partly because of the efforts of Malta-based aircraft destroying enemy supply ships during November and December, which prompted Hitler to order more Luftwaffe aircraft to Sicily to hopefully eliminate Malta as an Allied base. Despite continuous bombing of the Malta garrison the Island was not defeated and continued to deprive the Afrika Korps of vital supplies. Meanwhile, the support of German armies on the eastern front against Russia in harsh winter conditions required transport aircraft to provide supplies effectively—the same aircraft required to supply Rommel's army across the Mediterranean.

Despite this shortage of supplies, to prevent the Allies consolidating their position at El Agheila, Rommel launched a powerful frontal attack on 21 January supported by two days of dive-bombing attacks against Eighth Army units. Hurricanes and Tomahawks were grounded by torrential rain at Antelat, 100 miles to the rear, but 238 and 260 Squadrons had managed to reach El Gubba and Benina a few days before. When German armour broke through at El Agheila, the first 100 miles were covered in just over six hours, giving 33, 94, and 229 Squadrons with Hurricanes and 112 Squadron with Tomahawks just thirty minutes to escape before being overrun. Two unserviceable Hurricanes and four Tomahawks had to be abandoned as German shells began to fall, while the ground crews escaped with RAF armoured car companies.

The squadrons made their way back to Msus, 100 miles to the north-east, where the conditions were poor; stocks of both fuel and ammunition were soon depleted. Despite these problems, RAF Hurricanes alone destroyed more than 100 Axis vehicles in two days, and within another four days, the Hurricanes were withdrawn to Mechili, south of Derna.

Air Marshal Sir Arthur Coningham, commander of the Western Desert air units, ordered all RAF maintenance units to retire behind the Egyptian border to avoid the loss of the vital repair network. As a result, any forward-based aircraft with more than superficial damage had to be abandoned.

Sandstorms helped to make the fighting in Cyrenaica very confusing during the first week in February, grounding 33 and 238 Squadrons at Gambut. However, these weather conditions also prevented air attacks by the Luftwaffe, particularly Ju 87 Stuka dive bombers, which allowed the Eighth Army to attempt to consolidate a line of defence between Gazala and Bir Hakeim—in effect ending Operation Crusader, during which harsh lessons had been learned by both sides.

All the Hurricane units had been heavily involved in the fighting, often with significant success. Pilot losses had not been too high, but because it was outperformed in the air by the Bf 109Es, Hurricanes was much more effective in the ground attack role. Heavy fighting continued on the ground in Cyrenaica, with the Eighth Army attempting to withdraw with as much of its operational capability still intact as possible, to establish a new defensive line at Gazala.

Battle-damaged Huricane Mk IIAs, including Z4967 D:229 Squadron, *en route* to a RAF MU for repairs with the Pyramids in the background. No. 229 Squadron supported Operation Crusader with air-defence and ground-attack sorties. (*Author's collection*)

Four Hurricane Mk IICs were presented to the RAF by Lady MacRobert in memory of her three sons killed in action during the Second World War. All four Hurricanes were on the strength of 94 Squadron based at El Gamel in 1942—HL844 being named *Sir Alasdair*, while the others were *Sir Iain* HL735, *Sir Roderic* HL851, and *MacRobertsons Salute to Russia*. (*IWM*)

Hurricane Mk I Z4428 of the Air Firing and Fighting School after a forced landing at Bilbeis, Egypt, in February 1942. (*Author's collection*)

Meanwhile, Rommel held his forces against this line with his supply route from Bengazi and Tripoli reduced by around 100 miles, and the Allied supply lines increased by a similar amount.

Axis armour was still a major threat, which could not be countered effectively by air attack, although maintenance units in the Canal Zone had begun to modify some Hurricanes with underwing bomb racks to carry 250-lb bombs. Allied Army commanders made urgent requests for American M3 Grant and M4 Sherman tanks, while the RAF urged the rapid clearance of the Hurricane Mk II to carry more effective 50-lb bombs. While there were a number of reasons why it was not possible to clear the aircraft for operations in tropical conditions until later, an early batch of Hurricane Mk IID anti-armour ground-attack fighters were shipped to the Middle East armed with a pair of 40-mm Vickers S guns with an increased effectiveness against armour. In May 1942, 6 Squadron was designated to prepare for a change to the anti-tank role.

Rommel launched his offensive against the Gazala defensive line on 26 May, but the Allies had already been alerted to Italian armour moving forwards by a 40 (SAAF) Squadron Hurricane Tac R Mk II and were prepared. However, this proved to be a feint attack, as Rommel then brought forward two Panzer and one motorised divisions, outflanking the Eighth Army south of Bir Hakeim. By the next day, the enemy ground units were well to the rear of the Gazala line and had reached 'Knightsbridge' and El Adem. While the Free French Brigade continued to hold Bir Hakeim there was no danger of becoming encircled, and in turn the rear of the Panzer divisions became vulnerable. The Axis forces concentrated

Hurricane Mk I N2641 under maintenance in the open at El Ballah in 1941. (*Author's collection*)

The Hurricane Mk IIBs of 238 Squadron were operational in Egypt and Libya from May to October 1942 as Operation Crusader was driven back by Rommel's forces. Hurricane Mk IIB BP166:KC-J was on the strength of 238 Squadron in North Africa. (*RAF Museum*)

Work in progress in the open on the Merlin and propeller at Kasfareet MU in 1941. (*Author's collection*)

their attention on the destruction of Bir Hakeim by attacking with the 90th Light Division from the east, and on 3 June, Coningham switched the Hurricane Mk IIDs from fighting at 'Knightsbridge' to attacking enemy ground forces at Bir Hakeim. In support were Kittyhawk bombers and Tomahawks in ground attack, while other Hurricanes dropped supplies in canisters to the defenders.

The fierce battle continued for nine days, with Allied fighters operating against both Axis air and ground forces. The vulnerable Ju 87s suffered many casualties, and BF 109F pilots found themselves up against tougher opposition when 145 Squadron was deployed in their first desert air battle with Spitfire Mk VCs. Hurricanes, in the anti-armour role, were able to destroy about a score of German tanks, but needed more time and training to evolve the best tactics to counter the armoured threat. By 10 June, it had become obvious that without strong Allied artillery support, the Free French would no longer be able to hold their positions at Bir Hakeim, and about 2,000 men were ordered to withdraw, escaping to the east overnight.

Rommel's victory had not been as decisive as it seemed. The Axis campaign was based on gaining adequate fuel supplies with the capture of Tobruk by 1 June, but the objective was not achieved until 21 June. The nine days that Bir Hakeim was held by the defenders avoided an Allied rout and allowed for a costly fighting withdrawal by the Eighth Army, with Hurricane fighters providing top cover for the anti-armour Hurricanes in action against hostile ground forces.

On 18 June, 6 Squadron, with Mk IIDs armed with a pair of 40-mm cannons, attacked an armoured column of tanks and half-tracks at Sidi Rezegh, leaving eighteen vehicles destroyed

A convoy of RAF transports, taking Hurricanes to an MU for repair and salvage, takes a break in the North African Desert. The aircraft being transported include one each from 229 and 73 Squadrons. (*IWM*)

for no loss. During June, 73 Squadron continued with air defence against Bf 109Fs, claiming seven victories for the loss of five pilots, one of which was the CO, Sqn Ldr D. H. Ward. The following month, while operating from Burg-el-Arab in Egypt, the squadron destroyed a further twenty-three enemy aircraft for the loss of another six pilots. The squadron was then withdrawn from the direct battle to recover and was allocated to the night defence of the Suez Canal with Hurricane NF Mk IICs.

By early July, Commonwealth forces were withdrawn far into Egypt behind a line running from a small place called Alamein, just over 60 miles west of Alexandria. General Bernard Montgomery 'Monty' had now assumed overall command of the Eighth Army, assisted by Tedder, who began to strengthen the desert air forces by creating new units, and re-equipping and retraining the men. The RAF constructed a further thirty-three desert airstrips on which, together with the existing established airfields, eighty-four squadrons were based. The single-engined fighter units consisted of sixteen squadrons of Hurricanes, plus seven of Kittyhawks, six of Spitfires, one of Tomahawks, and three USAAF squadrons of P-40 Warhawks.

Peter Ayerst served in both the Battle of France and, after duties as an instructor, the latter part of the Battle of Britain, in which he shot down a He 111 in August 1940. In July 1942, he was one of twenty pilots posted to the Middle East. Arriving in Cairo on 22 September, he was allocated to 33 Squadron flying four 20-mm cannon-armed Hurricane Mk IICs.

Hurricane Mk Is were used for the night defence of the Canal Zone, W9291:M being an example. Without AI radar, they were not very effective. (*IWM*)

The squadron was part of the RAF force supporting the 8th Army providing air cover for 'Monty's' ground forces. The battle line was 30 miles (48 km) long at El Alamein—from the Mediterranean coast down to the Qattara Depression, where the ground was so soft, that any vehicle would sink straight down. Hurricane patrols were at around 10,000 feet (3,000 metres) over the troops for an hour at a time before being relieved by another squadron. Ju 87s regularly attempted to dive-bomb the ground troops, starting from around 8,000 to 9,000 feet (2,400 metres–2,700 metres) with a Bf 109 escort above. One squadron was allocated against the dive bombers and another against the fighters; if the raid was particularly heavy, four squadrons would operate in pairs.

Peter Ayerst was credited with two victories on 9 October: a Bf 109 and a Storch while on a strafing operation against two or three enemy airfields at the Dhaba, about 60 to 70 miles (96 to 112 km) to the west of the Alamein line. There were freak weather conditions on the German side, with torrential rain water-logging the airfields. All four squadrons in the Wing took part—33, 213, 238, and 1 (SAAF) Squadrons—flying ten miles out from the coast before turning due west until they could see Dhaba to the south where there was an escarpment. Aircraft could be seen on the ground as all four squadrons spread out, and tents could be seen on the straight in approach. As Peter approached, he saw a tent about 300 feet (91 metres) above sea level, and when the flap opened there was a soldier with shaving soap all over his

Hurricane Mk IIC HL887 AK-W:213 Squadron armed with a pair of 20-mm cannons at El Alamein in 1941. The squadron provided ground attack and air defence for Operation Crusader. (*Author's collection*)

face. Peter gave a quick squirt of gun fire and continued to attack the airfield, destroying many aircraft on the ground. When fifteen Bf 109s jumped the Hurricanes, Peter took a hit behind the cockpit, but destroyed a Bf 109, a Storch, and one tent. Nine RAF pilots were shot down on that attack—six were able to return and the other three were lost.

At the opening of the Battle of Alamein on 19 October, Tedder fielded both the established and new Hurricane squadrons, all now equipped with the various versions of the Mk II. Tactical reconnaissance was the responsibility of 208, 451 (RAAF), 7 (SAAF), and 40 (SAAF) Squadrons, which were all based in Egypt and operated over the Western Desert. Hurricane Mk IICs and IIBs were issued to 274 and 335 (Greek) Squadrons respectively for ground-attack duties, and 6 Squadron were issued Mk IIDs specialised in anti-armour operations. Air Defence over the Eighth Army was provided by Hurricanes of 33, 80, 127, and 1 (SAAF) Squadrons, with offensive sweeps carried out by 213 Squadron. Patrols along the Mediterranean coast line were the responsibility of 889 (FAA) Squadron Sea Hurricane Mk ICs and Mk IIBs, while air defence of the Canal Zone was allocated to 94 and 417 (RCAF) Squadrons. No. 2 PRU continued to operate a number of types, including Hurricane PR Mk Is and IIs. Against this major air capability, the Luftwaffe introduced the newly improved Bf 109G 'Gustav', which suffered from a number of teething troubles, but when fully operational was more than a match for the Spitfire VCs, let alone the poorer performing but more rugged Hurricanes.

The pilot of a Hurricane Mk IIC is handed his orders for the next ground-attack sortie. (*Author's collection*)

Hurricane Mk Is of 213 Squadron were tasked with the night defence of the Suez Canal in 1941. (*Author's collection*)

Five of 94 Squadron's Hurricane Mk IICs in echelon to the right—the last three being presentation aircraft from Lady MacRobert. (*IWM*)

On the night of 23–24 October, Montgomery directed his artillery to commence a devastating bombardment of the Axis positions, supported during the initial softening-up period by the Desert Air Force flying hundreds of sorties against enemy airfields destroying Luftwaffe aircraft on the ground and reducing air cover for the Axis armies. No. 33 Squadron was heavily involved over the night of 23–24 October. Peter Ayerst flew two sorties that day—the first protecting the Army attack in the north; and on the second trip, Bf 109s attacked and Peter was able to damaged one.

On 27 October, the Luftwaffe sent twenty Ju 87Ds, with an escort of Bf 109Fs, in support of an attempted counter-attack by the 90th Light Division, which was met by twenty-four Hurricanes and sixteen P-40Fs with the USAAF 57th Fighter Group. Allied pilots claimed twenty-seven Bf 109s for the loss of three Hurricanes.

Hurricane Mk IIDs of 6 Squadron were in action from the start of the campaign, attacking enemy tanks at low level from their more vulnerable rear and breaking away by turning, rather than climbing, to avoid the anti-aircraft defences to which they were vulnerable at higher altitudes. On 24 October, 6 Squadron destroyed eighteen Axis tanks supported by 80 Squadron, which provided cover and attracted most of the hostile fire. By the end of the month, 6 Squadron had claimed forty-three tanks and over 100 other vehicles destroyed, but had lost nine pilots and Hurricanes, almost all from ground fire.

Having softened up the Axis defences, Montgomery launched Operation Supercharger on 2 November as the major breakthrough thrust. In a dawn attack, twenty-four Hurricanes and Spitfires engaged about twenty Ju 87s escorted by Bf 109Fs and later in the day, Hurricanes of 80 and 127 Squadrons intercepted a similar force. Allied claims were four Ju 87s and two Bf 109s shot down for the loss of four Hurricanes and four Spitfires.

By 4 November, Rommel's army was in full retreat and the Bf 109s were withdrawn from operations, giving the Desert Air Force complete air supremacy. Peter Ayerst flew two sorties when the Axis forces began their retreat. The first was a patrol of the front line, where thirty-plus Stukas and twenty-plus Bf 109s were encountered. A day later, Peter claimed a Bf 109 but was shot down by flak, resulting in a forced landing 5 miles (8 km) behind German lines. Ayerst stayed still after climbing out of the Hurricane, pretending to be dead, as the Germans were still firing at him. After dark, he heard a vehicle approaching, which turned out to be Australians, and Ayerst returned to his squadron three days later.

The Axis air defence was so reduced that during the advances on Benghazi, Coningham ordered Hurricanes of 213 and 238 Squadrons to the forward airstrip at Martuba, well to the rear of the retreating enemy ground forces. Photo reconnaissance confirmed that the airfield had been abandoned by the Luftwaffe, and the two squadrons took the enemy by surprise, destroying about 300 vehicles over a period of five days.

After the Allied 8th Army had won the great victory of El Alamein, the cannon-armed — Hurricanes of 213 and 238 Squadrons inflicted a heavy toll on the retreating Axis forces—the defending Bf 109s were ineffective due to their short range and the rapid movement of the German and Italian troops. Peter Ayerst was with 238 Squadron at Martuba, which was some 450 miles (724 km) behind enemy lines, where they stayed for four days, sleeping in the open with no cover about 150 miles (241 km) from the Germans to the north. Hurricanes began strafing the enemy on the coast road, the Germans having no idea where the Hurricanes were coming from, but after three days of constant attacks, they began to get some idea where they were based. On the fourth day, a recce aircraft was sent over, and it was noted that the Germans were preparing to attack, so the entire wing moved out of the area. While there, the wing destroyed large numbers of vehicles as they were nose to tail on the road, presenting a target-rich environment to simply flying down one way and then back, firing in both directions. Ayerst's last trip was on 16 November 1943.

The Afrika Korps was finally driven out of Africa on 8 May 1943; the tank-busting Hurricane Mk IIDs with 40-mm cannons had played a significant role in the victory.

On 8 November, the Allies commenced Operation Torch, which were landings against the Vichy French forces in Algeria and French Morocco, which forced the Axis forces face attack from both east and west. More aircraft were flown in from Gibraltar—among the first arrivals being Hurricane Mk IICs at Maison Blanche on the day of the landings. It was not known for sure whether the enemy were still in residence at the airfield, but fortunately it had been abandoned, and when operations starting the next day, a He 111 and Ju 88 were claimed destroyed.

On 13 November, the Hurricane Tac R Mk IICs of 225 Squadron arrived, as well as the Mk IICs of 253 Squadron also based at Maison Blanche. On 19 November, the build-up continued with the arrival of more Tac Rs with 241 Squadron; the Mk IICs of 32 Squadron, which arrived at Philippeville on 7 December; and 87 Squadron on 19 December.

Hurricane Mk IIC FT-S:43 Squadron at Maison Blanche, Algiers. The squadron was based there in support of Operation Torch from November 1942 until March 1943. (*RAF Museum*)

Hurricane Mk IIC of 241 Squadron at Euston Strip, Souk El Khemis, in May 1943 fitted with underwing fuel tanks for greater endurance on ground-attack missions in support of Operation Torch in Algeria and Tunisia. (*RAF Museum*)

A Hurricane Mk IIC of 241 Squadron being loaded with bombs and prepared for another sortie from Souk-el-Arba on 21 January 1943. (*IWM*)

Operation Torch, the Allied invasion of West Africa, commenced on 8 November 1942 in Algeria, providing a second front against Axis forces in North Africa. One of the first RAF units to arrive was 32 Squadron with Hurricane Mk IICs at Philippville, later moving to Maison Blanche, where the squadron was based in early 1943. Heavy rainfall in the desert turned the airfield surface into waterlogged mud, but operations continued from runways laid with PSP. (*Author's collection*)

Meanwhile, on the Eastern Front, owing to the loss of fourteen Hurricanes and seven pilots during some 300 sorties of Libya, the tank-busting 6 Squadron was temporarily withdrawn to undertake defensive patrols over Cairo and the Canal Zone using Hurricane Mk IICs. This gave time for replacement Hurricane Mk IIDs to be supplied and modified for action, including uprating the Merlin XX engines to give more power at low level equivalent to another 40 mph. The engine and radiator were given armour protection, and 6 Squadron was ready to return to battle in the Libyan Desert on 2 March.

As the advances from the west in Tunisia approached a climax, more Spitfires were becoming available, allowing a number of the air-defence Hurricane squadrons to re-equip with the higher performance fighter. However, Tedder, who had been appointed Air Commander-in-Chief Mediterranean Air Command, still had twenty-three Hurricane squadrons at his disposal, as well as thirty-four Spitfire squadrons and six USAAF units. Additional Hurricane units deployed since then start of Operation Supercharger were 32, 73, 87, 123, 134,237, 238, 241, 253, 336 (Greek), 3 (SAAF), and 41 (SAAF) Squadrons, all of which were involved in operations in the Western Desert.

Following Operation Torch and the eventual surrender of the Vichy French forces, the Axis forces initiated a build-up of troops in Tunisia to take the place of the withdrawn Vichy forces. By mid-November, Allied forces were ready to advance into Tunisia, but only at single-division strength as the British First Army under Lt General Anderson. By this time, the Axis forces had been increased by one German and five Italian divisions deployed from Europe, and the remoteness of Allied airfields from the front line gave the Luftwaffe clear air superiority over the battlefield.

A couple of pilots pose by Hurricane Mk IIC HV817 ET-C:73 Squadron at Maison Blanche soon after their arrival in November 1942 at the start of Operation Torch. (*RAF Museum*)

Two pilots in tropical kit stand by Hurricane Mk IIC HL973 RZ-G:241 Squadron, which was based in Algeria and Tunisia from November 1942 until January 1944. (*RAF Museum*)

The intensity of the hazardous bombing operations by Hurricanes can be seen with sixty-nine bombing sorties recorded on the side of Hurricane Mk IIC HL973 RZ-G:241 Squadron. (*RAF Museum*)

The Allies closed to within 19 miles of Tunis, but were pushed back into a stalemate during the winter when both sides built up their forces. By the beginning of March 1943, the Eighth Army had continued its advance westward along the North African coast to the Tunisian border, trapping Rommel's Afrika Korps between the two Allied armies. The Eighth Army bypassed the Axis positions on the Mareth Line in late March, and the strengthened First Army launched its main offensive in mid-April, which resulted in the collapse and surrender of the enemy on 13 May 1943, capturing over 275,000 prisoners of war. The Allied invasion of Sicily following two months later.

Although outclassed by newer fighters in air defence, Hurricane squadrons had been decisive in the anti-armour and ground-attack role, although losses of experienced pilots were high on these hazardous missions. The robustness of the aircraft made it resistant to battle damage and it was relatively easy to maintain in the harsh desert conditions.

Hurricanes operated in a number of other campaigns in the Middle East and East Africa, where the already scarce resource of RAF aircraft was stretched even further. In January 1941, Italians succeeded in taking British Somaliland in East Africa and were threatening the borders of both Sudan and Kenya, as well as Allied supply routes through the Red Sea. Included in the planned counter-offensive was 1 Squadron (SAAF), which had six Hurricanes in Khartoum at the start of the offensive on 17 January. The unit strength increased at the rate of around one aircraft per week, which were mostly ex-RAF Hurricanes from the battle in Europe. These battle-weary aircraft were overhauled locally by the unit's engineers. The

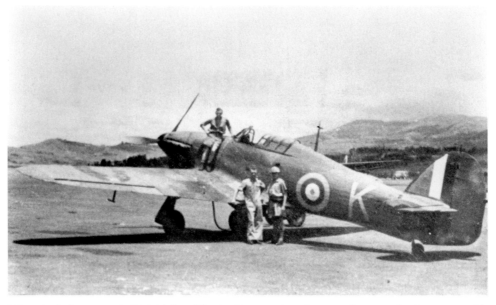

When the Italians occupied British Somaliland in January 1941, they were driven out by Commonwealth forces, supported by 3. (SAAF) Squadron, with Addis Ababa taken on 5 May. One of the aircraft was Hurricane Mk I 286 K:3. (SAAF) Squadron. (*P. H. T. Green collection*)

Hurricanes provided air support for the advancing ground forces, destroying ten enemy aircraft for no losses to Hurricanes. On 5 April, Addis Ababa was captured by the Allies. Three days later, Mussolini's colonial armies were defeated at Massawa; the surviving, tired Hurricane Mk Is were handed over to 94 Squadron in the Canal Zone.

Britain had been dependent upon oil reserves in the Middle East for many years and, particularly during the Second World War, one of the major sources was Iraq. Britain had a number of treaties with Iraq as well as access to considerable oil resources at Kirkuk and Mosul through the Iraq Petroleum Company (IPC), with pipelines running overland to the Mediterranean. As a result, there was a long-established and substantial British military presence in Iraq to protect the oil interests.

As the Italian forces were being defeated in East Africa, an Iraqi politician, Rashid Ali seized power in Baghdad. The RAF base at Habbaniya, 50 miles to the west of the capital was attacked by Iraqi troops on the night of 28–29 April 1941. The only aircraft available for the air defence of the base were trainers with 4 FTS (Flying Training School), but when fitted with bombs, it gave air superiority and the Iraqi forces withdrew overnight on 5-6 May.

On 13 May, the Iraqis returned with Luftwaffe air support, units of which had staged through Syria even though the country was occupied by British forces. Attacks were made by Bf 110s and He 111s, with RAF defence provided by Gladiators of 94 Squadron quickly reinforced by six Hurricanes from the Canal Zone. The first RAF air victory was a He 111 bomber shot down over the airfield on 20 May, with the rebellion finally crushed at the end of May.

During the Syrian Campaign in mid-1941, 213 Squadron were posted to Nicosia in Cyprus to provide air defence against Luftwaffe attacks from the Dodecanese Islands. A 213 Squadron Hurricane is being re-armed and prepared for the next sortie. (*IWM*)

Hurricane Mk Is of 213 Squadron taxi out for their next sortie from Nicosia in Cyprus. (*IWM*)

This skirmish highlighted the capability of the Luftwaffe to stage through Damascus to reach Iraq, which would also bring the enemy within range of the Canal Zone and threatened the accessibility of the Suez Canal. It was therefore decided to fortify Syria using ground forces and armour of the Australian, Indian, and Free French armies, with air support provided by Hurricane Mk Is of 80 Squadron and the Hurricane flight of 208 Squadron.

The advance of Allied forces into Syria commenced on 8 June and met stiff resistance from 100 Vichy French aircraft. With losses of half the FAA Fulmars providing protection for the Royal Navy ships off the landing beaches, the newly arrived 260 Squadron Hurricanes were brought in to provide additional air defence cover. The Vichy French were able to score some successes against RAF Blenheims and ground troops, but Allied air attacks on their bases forced a withdrawal northwards out of range of the RAF. With Allied advances and using long-range fuel tanks, all the French airfields came within range of RAF Hurricanes, which were able to destroy any French aircraft they could find both in the air and on the ground. Additional measures were taken against the possibility of a Luftwaffe attack from the Dodecanese Islands, by flying defensive patrols along the Syrian coast. Additional support came from 213 Squadron, which arrived in Nicosia, Cyprus, on 19 July with Hurricane Mk Is, which had not been adapted for hot weather operations and were replaced by more suitable Hurricane Mk IIAs the following month. The campaign finally ended with an Australian breakthrough of French defences south of Beirut.

As the Vichy French forces were being defeated in Syria, there were concerns about some aircraft of the French West African colonies when Vichy French Martin 167s carried out

Hurricane Mk IIB of 128 Squadron under maintenance at Sierra Leone from October 1941. (*Author's collection*)

Hurricane Mk IIB of 128 Squadron operating from Sierra Leone in 1941. (*IWM*)

Three ex-MEA Hurricane Mk Is were delivered to the CFS in South Rhodesia in 1944; T9531 had served with 317 and 80 Squadrons. This Hurricane survived until 1948–1949, but was then burned. (*Author's collection*)

reconnaissance flights over RAF Sunderland bases in Sierra Leone. To provide air defence, a Fighter Defence Flight was formed with six Hurricane Mk Is in early August, but these rather old aircraft were unable to catch up with the hostile air attacks. On 7 October, the flight was expanded into 128 Squadron and equipped with fifteen Hurricane Mk IIBs, discouraging the French flights by the improved performance of the RAF defending fighters. Following action in Operation Torch, the squadron was disbanded on 8 March 1943, and some of the aircraft were taken over by 1432 Army Co-operation Flight in Nigeria.

With its versatility and ability to adapt to a wide range of conditions, the rugged Hurricane saw action in many parts of Africa and the Middle East, although the squadrons and flights spread around the region were often equipped with elderly aircraft close to the end of their normal service life, demanding extra efforts on behalf of maintenance personnel. Supply lines south and east of the Mediterranean were stretched to the limits for both the Allies and Axis forces; without the gallant defence of Malta, it is doubtful whether the supply route to Alexandria could have been kept open. This allowed for the vital delivery of aircraft reinforcements not just to the North African Campaign, but all the other far flung areas of the war outside Europe.

13

The Asian Campaign

WITH THE GREAT distances from Britain, the Asian Campaign was more challenging to support, and the early defeat of Commonwealth forces in Singapore meant many of the records were lost in the resulting confusion. Following the dramatic Japanese attack on USA military installations at Pearl Harbor in Hawaii on 7 December 1941, which brought the USA into the Second World War, Japanese land forces attacked Kota Bharu in northern Malaya the next day. Just over a month later, Hurricanes were in action in Asia.

The first Hurricanes to arrive in Singapore were a number of crated Mk Is and Mk IIBs, with twenty-four pilots—including some of the spare air crews of 605 Squadron—on board a ship that had been diverted from the Middle East and docked on 3 January 1942. More Hurricanes arrived in Singapore via the Cape route on 13 January, with pilots and ground crews of 17, 135, and 136 Squadrons combined to form 232 Squadron, and joined by 258 Squadron, which was also diverted for the defence of Singapore. Once the crated Hurricanes were unloaded and assembly started, it was found that the guns had been packed with grease to protect them on the sea voyage, and it took several more days to prepare them for combat.

The initial Allied success was on 20 January, when a force of twenty-seven unescorted Japanese bombers was intercepted, with eight claimed shot down. However, when the enemy returned the next day with an escort of Mitsubishi Zeros, five Hurricanes were lost without any Japanese casualties. Although better armed and more robust than the Zero, the Hurricanes had been shipped from Middle East stocks and were fitted with tropical filters, which reduced performance and gave the larger number of Zero's clear air superiority.

By the middle of January, pilots and ground crews of 232, 242, 258, and 605 Squadrons had arrived in Singapore, and HMS Indomitable was on the way with forty-eight more Hurricane Mk IIAs and IIBs, also taken from Middle East stocks. To avoid vulnerability from enemy air attack, 242 and 258 Squadron remained at Seletar, and 232 and 605 Squadrons were dispersed respectively to Batavia in Java and Palembang in Sumatra.

Hurricane Mk I being serviced and protected against blast damage by a wall at Seletar in Singapore during January 1942. (*Author's collection*)

No. 232 Squadron with Hurricanes remained to cover the air defence of Singapore until forced to withdraw to Sumatra on 10 February 1942. (*Author's collection*)

Hurricane Mk II BE163, possibly of 258 Squadron, at Seletar after a landing mishap in January 1942. (*Author's collection*)

Hurricane Mk I under camouflage netting at Seletar, Singapore, in January 1942. (*Author's collection*)

No. 232 Squadron withdrew to a temporary airfield in Sumatra, but had to abandon the airstrip on 14 February after a Japanese paratroop attack. (*Author's collection*)

Japanese forces advanced rapidly down the Malay Peninsula towards Singapore with little advanced warning as the radar stations had been either overrun or dismantled to prevent them from falling into enemy hands. With only a few minutes warning of an air attack, Hurricanes were often engaged during the climb after take-off when they were at their most vulnerable. By 28 January, only twenty-one of the fifty-one Hurricanes delivered were still operational, and by the end of the month, 232 Squadron had only half its compliment of eight Hurricanes left for the air defence of Singapore. General Wavell, who had moved from the Middle East on 15 January to become the Supreme Allied Commander in the Far East, ordered all other units to withdraw.

During the first ten days of February, Hurricane pilots of 232 Squadron attempted to provide what air defence they could, even though on 8 February Japanese forces had landed on Singapore and shelled the airfields. The next day, six enemy bombers were claimed destroyed and fourteen damaged for the loss of one Hurricane and its pilot. The defence continued until the surviving 232 Squadron Hurricanes withdrew to Sumatra on 10 February, operating from a crude airstrip only 750 yards long. Five days later, the garrison of Singapore surrendered on 14 February, its leadership having become fragmented and without focus.

No sooner had 258 Squadron arrived in Sumatra, waiting on readiness on the first day, when Terence Kelly, a pilot with the squadron, heard some aircraft approaching. Expecting replacement Hurricanes, the pilots were surprised to see Japanese Navy Zeros diving to attack, strafing the RAF personnel on the ground. When Sumatra was invaded by the Japanese, 258 Squadron was ordered to strafe the invasion forces—the maximum number of Hurricanes available were fourteen. On their way to the target, the pilots, including Kelly, passed a formation of Hudsons going the other way, but the landing beaches were never located. The

Hudsons turned out to be Japanese transport aircraft, which dropped paratroopers around airstrip P.I, but as Terence did not have a radio, he was not aware. He, and Bertie Lambert, spotted some Zeros, one of which was claimed by Kelly, before both pilots returned to P.I, being told it was surrounded, and quickly made their way to airstrip P.II. On landing, Kelly found he only had two gallons of fuel left in his tanks.

One of the tasks for 258 Squadron was to seek out and strafe the Japanese invasion forces, which were travelling in barge trains with about six or eight in a row, with some 200 Japanese packed in each and only one defensive gun at the rear. When Terence Kelly was flying with an American, Art Donahue, they spotted a string of barges heading upriver in a straight line against the northern bank. Donahue and Kelly strafed the helpless soldiers with their twelve machine guns, diving from 1,000 feet, the bullets raking the barges from end to end, leaving large numbers of the undefended troops killed or injured. Kelly was later taken prisoner, and he found out that the Japanese were trying to identify who was responsible for the attack.

On 14 February 1942, only six Hurricanes were left with 258 Squadron, with many more pilots than aircraft. Kelly was one of the six who volunteered to stay—the other Hurricane pilots went to Colombo. The Hurricane was unable to out-turn the Zero, but it was more robust. The Zero had no armour plating, was lightly built, less powerful, and armed with two 20-mm cannons and two 7.7-mm machine guns, but it could climb faster.

When Sumatra was overrun by the Japanese, the surviving Hurricanes and their pilots retreated to Java. Kelly was taken prisoner and transported to Batavia, where his cruel treatment began.

The Japanese had never signed the Geneva Convention regarding the treatment of POWs, and Kelly spent seven months in Batavia, before spending two months on boats to Japan. The 1,000 prisoners were incarcerated in the ship's hold, which was 60 feet by 80 feet (18 m × 24 m) among the cargo of wet iron ore. The hold was soaking wet and riddled with rats, which made the prisoners ill with no medical attention. The prisoners were dressed for the tropics and headed for Japan in the winter. It was not long before prisoners suffered from diarrhoea, with the worst cases taken up on deck and thrown overboard to their death. The whole voyage lasted around five weeks. Out of 350, sixty-six had died by the time they reached Japan, with the illness continuing after arrival.

Kelly worked in a Japanese dockyard for more than three years located about 24 miles from Hiroshima on a hilly island without any direct view of the Japanese city. The prisoners saw many Allied bombing raids fly over—their island was also on the receiving end.

Then, one morning on 6 August 1945, one aircraft flew over. The prisoners were used to bombs falling and had no idea that the atomic bomb had been dropped on Hiroshima. Without the bomb, the Americans would have had to invade Japan, resulting in terrible casualties on both sides. There was no doubt among the POWs that if the A-bomb had not been dropped then the moment an invasion commenced, the prisoners would have been exterminated.

Meanwhile, airfields around Palembang were under threat. P.I was subjected to an air raid on 23 January followed by a paratrooper attack on 14 February. The destruction of Hurricanes on the ground resulted in all British and Dutch operations being transferred to P.II. The next day, Hurricanes escorted a force of Hudsons and Blenheims on a successful attack on a Japanese invasion force off the coast. Later in the day, Hurricanes destroyed a number of

Zeros on the ground at Banka Island. Although these attacks slowed the invasion, there were inadequate resources to consolidate the gains and the Japanese response was rapid and violent.

Following another Japanese attack, this time on P.II, there was a hurried and confused withdrawal to Java via Oesthaven, leaving behind all the spare Merlin engines and other support equipment. The airfield had still not been occupied by the enemy two days later when a party of fifty volunteers from 605 Squadron, led by Grp Capt. Gilbert Nicholetts, returned to recover all the spares and equipment.

By 18 February, eighteen Hurricanes out of twenty-five remained operational and were based in Java; 232 Squadron at Tjililitan; 242 Squadron at Bandung; 258 Squadron at Kemajoran; and 605 Squadron at Andir. The majority of the bomber force was based at Semplak, but was mostly destroyed on the ground by Japanese air attacks on 19 and 22 February. By 28 February, both 242 and 258 Squadrons had virtually ceased to exist, and the survivors were absorbed into the remaining two units. The next day, with only twelve Hurricanes still serviceable, all aircraft and personnel were amalgamated into 605 Squadron. On the same day, a combined force of Hurricanes, together with ten Dutch P-40s and six Buffalos, attacked an invasion force landing at Eretan Wetan. Although they caused many casualties, they were ultimately unable to stop the advances.

On 2 March, the pilots were unable to continue operations from Tjililitan due to constant enemy air attacks, which damaged the airstrip. The last two Hurricanes were destroyed on 7 March.

Of the original twenty-two pilots with 258 Squadron on 30 October 1941, eight were British, five New Zealand, four American, three Canadian, one Rhodesian, and one Australian. Of those, six were killed in action, plus one died from burns; three were killed in flying accidents; one died after the war from wounds received in action; and five became Japanese prisoners of war. Only seven survived to fight through the entire war.

British and Dutch fighters and bombers continued to attack Japanese invasion forces, but faced overwhelming odds. The Dutch army surrendered on 8 March. During this short but violent campaign against massive odds, the overall total of RAF losses stood at 435 aircraft with claims for 192 enemy aircraft destroyed—a grim testament to the intensity of the fighting. Over Singapore, Hurricane pilots claimed some 100 victories, but lost forty-five of their own aircraft. With the invasion of Java and Sumatra, less than 500 survivors of the four Hurricane squadrons made what escape they could, many reaching the shores of Australia, while others died at sea or were taken prisoner by the Japanese.

With Singapore and Malaya occupied, the Japanese forces began the conquest of Burma, which was strategically important as the route to India and included major supply routes to China along the Burma Road via Rangoon. The Japanese had experience in jungle warfare and continued to advance through the Malayan jungle and the Mergui Archipelago running along the Malay Peninsula.

Rangoon was bombed heavily on 23 December 1941, with the main attack on Burma following across the border from Thailand in mid-January. The only RAF air defence was 67 Squadron, with sixteen ineffective Buffalos at Mingaladon near Rangoon, while the only other air defence were twenty-one P-40s 650 miles to the north-east flown by an American Volunteer Group committed to defend the supply route along the Burma Road to China.

The Hurricane Mk IIAs of 17 Squadron arrived at Mingaladon near Rangoon, Burma, on 16 January 1942 for air defence. Five of their aircraft patrol above the clouds. (*Author's collection*)

India was also vulnerable to air attack and could not provide aircraft for air defence against advancing enemy. The first aircraft to come to the aid of the air defence of Burma was 17 Squadron, which left Britain bound for the Middle East on 12 November 1941 with Hurricane Mk IIAs, and was diverted to Asia en route, arriving at Mingaladon on 16 January 1942. They were joined by 135 Squadron with Hurricanes on 28 January and the personnel of 136 Squadron on 6 February, who were then sent to India to await more aircraft.

A further Japanese attack of considerable force was made on Rangoon on Christmas Day 1941, but there were still no Hurricanes available, although some defending P-40s were able to claim thirty-six enemy aircraft, despite poorer performance, by diving repeatedly through the enemy formations. Many of the Buffalos were destroyed on the ground during these attacks.

Finally, a batch of thirty Hurricane Mk Is and IIAs arrived in Rangoon as deck cargo from the Middle East, which were quickly assembled to be flown by the pilots of 67 Squadron, soon joined by 17 Squadron. Air Vice-Marshal Donald Stevenson, the Air Officer Commanding RAF Burma, sent Hurricanes and Blenheims to advanced bases in southern Burma to make strikes at Japanese bases in Thailand. During January, some fifty-eight enemy aircraft were claimed destroyed mainly on the ground at Bangkok, but with the Japanese invasion commencing during the second half of the month, all Allied advanced airfields were soon overrun. Meanwhile, Japanese air attacks continued on Rangoon and the surrounding area in an effort to gain air superiority over the RAF; the airfield at Moulmein to the east of the capital was captured on 30 January.

No. 67 Squadron operated Hurricane Mk IICs from Alipore and Chittagong from June 1942 to February 1944. Mk IIC RD-G:67 Squadron was used in the air defence of Calcutta in 1943. (*P. H. T. Green collection*)

A Hurricane Mk IIA of 17 Squadron at Mingaladon near Rangoon with the fabric burnt off the rear fuselage. (*Author's collection*)

On 5 February, Japanese forces crossed the Salween 80 miles east of Rangoon, and in a further three weeks were threatening the city's large port, which was vital to the resupply of Allied forces. The surviving twenty-four Hurricanes, plus four Buffalos, were ordered north with the pilots and ground crews of 17, 67, and 135 Squadrons to an airstrip at Zigon, 100 miles away. For three days, these fighters were employed on providing cover for the evacuation of Mingaladon and the forces around Rangoon, successfully stopping enemy aircraft from attacking roads to the north. The Japanese then split their advances into three prongs heading north—the most threatening for Zigon was the one advancing towards Mandalay along the Sittaung. By mid-March, the dozen surviving Hurricane Mk IIs of 17 and 135 Squadrons were withdrawn to Magwe with P-40s and some Blenheims of 45 Squadron. Six operational Hurricane Mk Is with 67 Squadron moved to the island of Akyab off the Burmese coast.

Hurricanes joined with Blenheims at Magwe, and on 20 March, 139 Squadron Hudsons flew a reconnaissance of the southern Burma airfields to determine the main enemy concentrations, and some fifty Mitsubishi Sally bombers were found at Migaladon. They were attacked the next day by ten Hurricanes and nine Blenheims—sixteen of the bombers being destroyed on the ground and eleven Oscars in the air. Two Hurricanes and two Blenheims were lost, but soon afterwards, sixteen Hurricane Mk IIBs and ten Blenheims arrived at Magwe as replacements from the Middle East. In retaliation to the RAF attack, over the next twenty-four hours Japanese made a devastating attack on Magwe with a force of some 200 aircraft, virtually destroying the airfield. The dozen surviving Hurricanes were moved to Akyab where all but one arrived on 26 March, and were back in the fight the next day against successive waves of Japanese bombers. Three of the Hurricanes were shot down and four more destroyed on the ground, making the RAF ineffective at both Magwe and Akyab.

Hurricane Mk IIAs of 135 Squadron joined 17 Squadron in the air defence of Rangoon on 28 January 1942, and later moved to Dum Dum, where Hurricane Mk IIB BM935 was based. (*P. H. T. Green collection*)

A Hurricane Mk IIA YB-L:17 Squadron making a low flypast at Red Road, Calcutta, after withdrawal from Burma. (*Author's collection*)

With the disorganisation of the remaining British ground forces in Burma, Stevenson withdrew what little was left for the defence of Calcutta and Ceylon, now known as Sri Lanka. The Japanese took Lashio on 29 April, Mandalay on 1 May, and Myitkyina on 8 May.

While the Japanese were advancing through Burma, Allied units had been progressively arriving in India to provide some air defence to the Royal Navy in Ceylon and the Bay of Bengal, where there was a major threat from enemy warships. On 6 March, HMS Indomitable arrived at Ratmalana in Ceylon, from Egypt, with Hurricane Mk IIBs of 30 Squadron and 261 Squadron, which arrived initially at Dum Dum, Calcutta, at the end of February, before moving on 6 March to China Bay in Ceylon. A totally new 258 Squadron was formed at Colombo from local resources, which was all part of Wavell's plan to defend the RN bases and shipping against the Japanese threat to control the eastern part of the Indian Ocean, where they were first reported on 4 April. During the next five days, twenty-three Allied merchant ships were sunk in the Bay of Bengal, fifteen of which were by carrier-borne aircraft.

On Easter Sunday, 5 April, Colombo harbour was attacked by about 125 enemy aircraft, but a pair of patrolling Catalina flying boats were able to radio a warning, allowing thirty-six Hurricanes of 30 and 258 Squadrons to take off, with six FAA Fulmars, to intercept the raid. The escorting Zeros were effective in defending the bombers, losing three Zeros, two Kates, and two Vals for the loss of fifteen Hurricanes and four of the more vulnerable Fulmars. Luckily, eight of the Hurricane pilots survived unhurt, and replacement Hurricanes were available from local stocks. The Japanese again attacked Ceylon on 9 April with a force of 129

No. 30 Squadron, with Hurricane Mk IIBs, was allocated to the air defence of RN assets in Ceylon, arriving on 6 March 1942. (*P. H. T. Green collection*)

A pair of 30 Squadron Hurricane Mk IICs flying over Ceylon on air-defence duties in 1942. (*Author's collection*)

Hurricane Mk IIB Z3826 ZT-A:258 Squadron having an engine run prior to rake-off in Ceylon in 1942. (*RAF Museum*)

aircraft targeting the airfields at Trincomalee and China Bay and were met by 17 Hurricanes of 261 Squadron and six more Fulmars from 873 NAS. This was a more successful defensive action with fifteen Zeros claimed shot down—twelve by the Hurricanes and the other three by the Fulmars. Eight Hurricanes were shot down, but six pilots were uninjured and three more Fulmars were destroyed. With most of the naval and merchant shipping withdrawn from the Bay of Bengal, the Japanese were able to concentrate their attacks on the Ceylon shore installations, causing widespread damage.

The Japanese naval task force consisted of five aircraft carriers, four battleships, three cruisers and eight destroyers, which was far in excess of all Allied warships in the Indian Ocean. There was insufficient air cover for Allied naval units, resulting in the loss of the Royal Navy aircraft carrier HMS Hermes, two cruisers, and two destroyers being sunk during the first ten days of April. The RN moved the main base facilities out of the immediate range of enemy attack, releasing the RAF from the air defence of naval assets.

Hurricane squadrons re-equipped in eastern India to prepare for the defence of Calcutta, with the Buffalo- and Mohawk-equipped 146 Squadron being re-equipped with Hurricane Mk IIBs at Dum Dum in May. Leaving Britain in March, 607 Squadron arrived at Alipore near Calcutta on 25 May, and in June equipped with the first Hurricane Mk IICs in the Asian campaign.

Operations on the Burma front by both sides were restricted by heavy summer rains that year, and Allied forces were still not strong enough to launch a major offensive against the Japanese as potential reinforcements were still active in the Western Desert of North Africa.

No. 146 Squadron was allocated to the air defence of Calcutta with Hurricane Mk IICs in December 1942. 'B' Flight is seen at Alipore, Calcutta, camouflaged by trees. (*Author's collection*)

Air Chief Marshal Sir Richard Pierse, the Air Officer in Chief, believed that the next enemy move would be against Calcutta. The task of the RAF was to build up the air defence to prevent heavy damage from bombers, and to demonstrate that the RAF still possessed a significant presence in the air. Additionally, there was still a need to maintain the air defence of Ceylon against further Japanese Navy attacks. By December 1942, the air defence of Calcutta consisted of Hurricane Mk IICs, all operated by 17, 67, 135, and 146 Squadrons, with further Mk IICs operated by 30 Squadron for the air defence of the ports in Ceylon. Hurricane Mk IIBs also equipped 258, 261, and 273 Squadrons. Tactical reconnaissance over the Burma front from Ranchi in Bihar was provided by 28 Squadron with Hurricane Tac R Mk IIBs, and in East Bengal, 79, 136, 607, and 615 Squadrons were mostly flying Hurricane Mk IICs on the air defence of Calcutta and offensive operations over Burma. In the event of an enemy attack on Calcutta, there were four operational day squadrons, and 146 Squadron by night to provide air defence, but when the first attack was made, it was by a small force at night, which caused panic among the civil population. Without airborne interception radar (AI) the Hurricanes were ineffective, so in January 1943, a flight of AI-equipped Beaufighters was deployed to combat the night threat.

Early in December, Wavell had made an abortive attempt to return to the offensive with a plan to establish a landing ground on the apparently lightly defended Akyab Island. However, the operation did not go to plan as due to delays with supplies the advance was held up, allowing the enemy to reinforce the island. In April, with the threat of some of the Commonwealth forces being cut off, a withdrawal was ordered to Cox's Bazaar.

Hurricane Mk IIC L-NA:146 Squadron being refuelled at Calcutta with the Australian pilot, Douglas St John, who retired as a G/Cpt RAAF in 1972. His sister was Lona. (*Author's collection*)

Many of the pilots of 30 Squadron were Canadians. P/O N. M. Scott; F/Sgt W. Thomson; and P/O Lloyd in front of F/Sgt Thomson's Hurricane Mk IIC *Dumbo* on the Arakan front on 21 July 1943. (*Public Archives of Canada*)

No. 258 Squadron formed at Colombo in March 1942, sharing the air defence of the RN assets with 30 Squadron. Some of their Hurricane Mk IIBs are dispersed at Kalemetiya in 1943. (*D. Nicholls via P. H. T. Green*)

Hurricane Mk IIB KZ353 of 28 Squadron was one of the aircraft operating Tac R missions over the Burma front in December 1942. (*Author's collection*)

Despite the failure of the plan, valuable experience was gained by the Hurricane pilots of 28, 67, 136, 607, and 615 Squadrons, who flew more than 150 sorties a day. Due to the effectiveness of the cannon-armed Hurricane Mk IICs against surface transport on the roads and rivers, the Japanese were forced to move under the cover of darkness. In addition to regular combat squadrons, 3 PRU operated a number of unarmed photo-reconnaissance Hurricanes—the unit had its beginnings in January 1942 when two Hurricanes were being ferried to Singapore but did not arrive before the surrender. The two pilots became based at Mingaladon, flying some twenty-five sorties over Thailand and Malaya before the aircraft were written-off. The pilots made their way to Calcutta, where they were joined by three others, one of whom was Flt Lt Alexander Pearson, who had been flying with 2 PRU in Egypt and was given the task of forming and leading 3 PRU.

Twenty-year-old Eric Batchelar flew his 17 Squadron Hurricane from Egypt across India, arriving in Burma in January 1942. The Japanese had every advantage over the Allies as there was no radar or early warning of an attack; 17 Squadron's base at Rangoon's Mingledon airfield was attacked daily. The day after arrival, Batchelar went after a Japanese Army 95 biplane, thinking it would be an easy target, but it proved much more agile than the Hurricane, and faced the approaching aircraft by twisting and turning; Batchelar lost him in the haze. On return to the airfield, Batchelar found quite a few holes in his aircraft.

A Hurricane Tac R Mk IIB of 28 Squadron flying a low-level reconnaissance sortie off Mandalay in support of the 14th Army, passing the Ava Bridge over the Irrawaddy River. (*IWM*)

No. 3 PRU operated unarmed Hurricane Mk IICs on reconnaissance duties over Burma from 6 June 1942. (*IWM*)

There was a constant shortage of aircraft most of the time, and at night the aircraft were dispersed to remote sites to avoid their destruction by enemy bombing. To the pilots, it appeared that they were fighting a losing battle, the squadrons withdrawing to rear bases in the middle and top of Burma.

On one strafe attack, Batchelar was hit in the canopy with the bullet clipping the back of his helmet—the line of the bullet being right where his head would have been if he had not leant forward to look through the gun sight. Near the end of 1942, Batchelar was posted from 135 Squadron to become a flight commander of 17 Squadron, operating in the defence of Calcutta from a long straight road called Red Road, which had been the approach road to the Governor's Palace in the big central park in the heart of Calcutta. Eric Batchelar operated from 'The Mall', leading to 'Buckingham Palace', where 17 Squadron operated for a couple of months. The approach on finals to land was between blocks of flats, which the camber of the road made demanding.

Flying over the featureless jungle was challenging as there was no radar, the HF radios were unreliable, the country was not mapped, and there were few landmarks. The only way to maintain an idea of position was to begin to recognise the shape of the ranges of hills. The Hurricane was excellent for ground strafing, with two 500-lb (227-kg) bombs and four 20-mm cannons. When Hurricanes were operating on interdiction sorties in the Chin Hills, the Japanese put up trip wires across the valleys over the rivers to try to catch the aircraft at low level. Some of the sorties lasted three hours or more, with many returning to base with very low fuel. Over a period of six months no pilots were lost, but they were withdrawn for a rest because of the high levels of strain.

The first two Hurricane PR IIBs arrived at Dum Dum in April, with two more in May, and four in June, allowing photo reconnaissance sorties to commence on 6 June 1942 over northern Burma, but without long-range fuel tanks, the sortie radius was limited to 300 miles. With the arrival of suitable 44-gallon fuel drop tanks in November, the Hurricane PR IIs could just reach Mandalay and Rangoon from Calcutta. In January 1943, 3 PRU was renumbered 681 Squadron and continued to fly short range reconnaissance with up to six Hurricanes until replaced by Spitfire PR XIs and Mosquito PR XVIs in September 1944.

From February to June 1943, Hurricanes were used for escort duties covering the dropping of supplies by RAF Dakotas into the jungle to resupply the Chindit commando-style operations behind enemy lines in northern Burma led by Brigadier Orde Wingate. However, there was little Japanese opposition as the enemy were moving their aircraft to the Pacific islands where US forces were causing a serious threat, and Hurricane escorts were scaled back.

By mid-1943, Blenheim bombers were being retired from front-line duties, and during the monsoon season Hurricane Mk IIBs and IICs were issued to 11, 34, 42, 60, and 113 Squadrons. In addition, Hurricane Mk IID anti-armour ground-attack fighters had been delivered to India from the Middle East. Although the aircraft were issued to 5 and 20 Squadrons, the 40-mm ammunition did not arrive until the end of the year. By December, there were up to 970 Hurricanes in India, including forty-six Mk Is in use with 151 OTU on the North-West Frontier, where pilots from all over the Commonwealth were trained for the new Hurricane units. The Indian Air Force had been supplied with ex-RAF Hurricane Mk IIAs and IIBs—

Hurricane Mk IIDs armed with a pair of underwing 40-mm cannons were used against enemy ground troops. (*P. H. T. Green collection*)

Equipped with Hurricane Mk IIDs from Middle East stocks in mid-1943, 20 Squadron did not take delivery of the 40-mm ammunition until the end of the year. (*P. H. T. Green collection*)

1 Squadron was declared operational at the end of the year. Hurricanes in the air-defence role were starting to be replaced by new Spitfire squadrons, which were able to inflict heavy enemy casualties when raids resumed against Calcutta in December.

By the end of the year, Admiral Mountbatten headed South-East Asia Command, with Peirse in overall command of the Allied Air Forces, and the time was judged right for a new Allied offensive operation to be launched. With the monsoon season over at the end of 1943, Allied forces were much better equipped and prepared to forestall a Japanese threat on Chittagong by once again planning to recapture Akyah and Arakan. The main Allied thrust was led by the 7th Indian Division, setting out from Cox's Bazaar in November and capturing Sinzweya by 6 February. Japanese forces then cut the vital supply route, isolating and encircling the Allies, so that the only method of supply was by air using RAF Dakotas and USAAF C-47s making air drops, escorted by five squadrons of Hurricanes and two of Spitfires. This battle raged for a month until reinforcements arrived in the shape of the 5th Indian Division, which was landed on the coast. This allowed an Allied break out to encircle the enemy, who fought to the death rather than surrender.

Meanwhile, other Japanese forces attacked on a central front in Burma, with three divisions intending to cut the main overland route supplying the air bridge to China, which had been established after the loss of the Burma Road. The villages of Imphal and Kohima were surrounded by the enemy, and most of Kohima was occupied, resulting in the only method of supply again being by air. Reinforcements from the 33rd Indian Corps were flown into Dinapur with an escort of Hurricane Mk IIC fighter bombers, which included 1 Squadron

A Hurricane Mk II, being armed with ammunition for the 20-mm cannons and loaded with 250-lb bombs for ground-attack duties on the Arakan front in Burma. (*Author's collection*)

No. 1. (IAF) Squadron received some ex-RAF Hurricane Mk IIs and was declared operational in Assam at the end of 1943. (*RAF Museum*)

Indian Air Force (IAF). Hurricanes provided close air support for the advance to relieve Kohima, and with total air superiority, Hurricanes flew 2,200 sorties in sixteen days, dropping 2,500 bombs on the Japanese 31st Division. At Imphal, the Allies were able to maintain a fairly large perimeter with room to prepare six airstrips within the horseshoe-shaped valley, and as combat troops of the 5th Indian Division were flown in aboard USAAF C-46 Commandos and C-47 Skytrains; many injured and non-combat personnel were evacuated. Three Hurricane squadrons from Kohima joined 28 Squadron and two Spitfire units at Imphal. During the first two weeks of April, Hurricanes flew around 6,000 sorties out of a total of 10,000.

A brand-new batch of Hurricane Tac R Mk IICs had been supplied to 28 Squadron, with one flight's fitted with a single vertical camera in the rear fuselage, and the other flight's equipped with an oblique camera. At least one Hurricane was kept airborne during the hours of daylight to maintain continuous reconnaissance for the ground forces in the rugged terrain. The squadron was also responsible for locating targets for air attack, an example being a Japanese motorised battalion that was spotted at dusk moving towards Imphal. The resulting attack by thirty-three Hurricane fighter bombers, with the aid of landing lights, dropping bombs and firing cannons stopped the advance and killed some 220 enemy troops. Soon after, a local tribesman brought details of an enemy headquarters concealed in the jungle. On returning to the tribe, members surrounded the target and at the appropriate time laid out red blankets on the ground to guide the dozen 250-lb bomb-carrying Hurricanes into the attack, causing some 100 enemy casualties.

Servicing conditions of Hurricanes could be a bit basic, like this example at Palembang. (*Author's collection*)

Two Hurricane squadrons had been supporting the second Chindit operation since December, the aim of the combined Ghurka, American, and Chinese forces was to cut the Indaw to Myitkyina railway and capture Myitkyina and Mogaung. With the approaching monsoon season, Japanese resistance strengthened, and it was not until early June that Imphal and Kohima were finally captured by the Allies, followed by Mogaung on 20 June, just as the monsoon started. The rains in Assam restricted Allied operations and brought the Japanese to a standstill, resulting in Myitkyina not being taken until 3 August.

By 1 July, Peirse had a total of thirty-eight squadrons under his command, of which twenty-one were operating Hurricanes. Those units with Hurricane Mk IIC fighter bombers based in India and operating over the Burma front were 30, 34, 42, 60, 113, 134, 146, 261, and 9 (IAF) Squadrons. Hurricane Mk IIDs were flown by 20 Squadron on anti-armour duties in Burma until the end of hostilities in September 1945. Hurricane Tac R Mk IICs were operated over the Burma front by 4 and 6 (IAF) Squadrons gathering reconnaissance information, and 17 and 135 Squadrons were tasked with the air defence of Ceylon, although 17 Squadron was in the process of converting to Spitfires. The remaining 5, 11, 28, 79, 123, 258, and 1(IAF) Squadrons were mainly operating from India on ground-attack, reconnaissance, and bomber-escort duties.

The Indian Air Force operated Hurricanes, ending the war with eight squadrons, and fought alongside the RAF in February 1944 to relieve the siege of Imphal. Bob Doe was sent to India to help form the Indian Air Force, taking command of 10 Squadron based at Risslepore in the North-West Frontier. They were then posted to Bihar, where they changed

With the retirement of Blenheims in mid-1943, 34 Squadron re-equipped with Hurricane Mk IIs, seen here sharing an airfield with a USAAF P-47 Thunderbolt. (*IWM*)

Another Blenheim unit to re-equip with Hurricanes was 42 Squadron, an example being Mk IV LB858:AW-Y at dispersal. (*Author's collection*)

When the Blenheims were withdrawn from operational service in mid-1943, among the bomber squadrons converted to fighters was 60 Squadron, a flight from which here is being prepared for the next combat. (*Author's collection*)

Field maintenance on a 60 Squadron Hurricane, which worked well out of the monsoon season. (*Author's collection*)

A line-up of 146 Squadron Hurricane Mk IIBs at Dum Dum, with three more flying over in times of reduced tension. (*IWM*)

Hurricane Mk IIC HV845 of 79 Squadron ready for take-off was one of the aircraft allocated to the defence of Calcutta as well as offensive operations over Burma from December 1942. (*IWM*)

from being a fighter unit to a bomber squadron flying Hurribombers, eventually moving to Burma just inland from Cox's Bazaar, the first operation being just before Christmas 1944.

The role of the Hurribombers became army co-operation, with the aircraft called up for treetop-level attacks at targets hidden in the jungle, providing close support for the soldiers at the front, with anti-aircraft defences practically non-existent, unlike the war in Europe. Flying in the monsoon was very demanding, with heavy rain and cloud going up from ground level to 30,000 feet (9,144 metres), and because the Hurricanes did not have oxygen, the pilots rarely went above 6,000 feet (1,828 metres). Two types of bomb were used: the type that went off on impact, which were dropped from higher up; and ones with an eleven-second delay. Care had to be taken when firing the cannons, as if attempting to fire a long burst there could be a stoppage causing the wing without a stoppage to swing right around.

Although there was little hazard from enemy anti-aircraft fire in Burma, there could be dangers due to accidents or mechanical failure. Taking to the parachute over the impenetrable jungle was particularly hazardous. Records published after the war showed that of 176 pilots who baled out over the Burmese jungle or Japanese-occupied territory, 166 were never located or seen alive again, with only ten surviving. Colin Ellis was one of the lucky ten.

It was customary for Hurricanes to attacks to be in line astern, each behind and below the aircraft in front. During the change of formation, Ellis collided with his number two and lost his tail. With a complete loss of control, he abandoned his Hurricane at around 6,000 feet over Japanese territory. Before leaving his base, Ellis had picked up a parachute for someone obviously much taller and the shoulder straps were very loose. When he fell out of the Hurricane the shoulder straps fell off, and the harness went down to his feet, sending Ellis down headfirst. When he was at 1,000 feet, the aircraft crashed in the jungle nearby, burning fiercely. Luckily, Ellis went through the trees head first and avoided being hung up on the branches where he would be stuck with no way to get down, or otherwise fall from a great height to the ground. He wanted to get away from his burning aircraft in case it attracted enemy soldiers. Knowing roughly where he was and using a compass in his survival kit, he headed west up and over the north-south ridges, avoiding any movements along the valleys. It took five days to return to the Allied lines, surviving on his emergency rations, and sterilising tablets for the local water. Late afternoon on the fourth day, Colin bumped into two Burmese, who gave him shelter for the night and provided guides the next day, later making contact with some West Africans who were fighting the Japanese. Colin's number two was not so lucky and was never found.

Even in the final campaign for the liberation of Burma, Hurricanes were the most numerous Allied aircraft. They mainly provided close air support as their ease of maintenance made them readily available, and by this time there was little sign of Japanese aircraft in the skies. The conquest was led by General Slim with IV, XV, and XXXIII Corps representing the Fourteenth Army, and American and Chinese forces occupied the northern Shan States. The aim was to first retake Mandalay, but the terrain was very rugged and made ground fighting difficult. Using the 'cab-rank' tactic, Hurricanes and Thunderbolts waited aloft ready to be called down to assist the ground forces when required, attacking any resistance including tanks. Mandalay was taken according to plan on 21 March, and the liberating forces also

No. 20 Squadron operated against Japanese ground forces with Hurricane RP-firing Mk IVs until the end of the War in Asia. (*P. H. T. Green collection*)

captured the strategic road, rail, and river junction at Meiktila, 80 miles to the south. General Slim's forces consolidated for about two weeks to allow the resupply of ammunition, fuel, and other logistical necessaries; with the monsoon due to start within six weeks, it was essential to capture Rangoon before then. Eight Hurricane squadrons were moved forward from Mandalay to within 20 miles behind the advancing Allied troops, operating a total of 118 Mk IIC bombers and Tac R Mk IICs.

Equipped with anti-armour Hurricane Mk IVs, 20 Squadron, together with 28 Squadron on tactical reconnaissance, commenced operations from Thedaw airstrip on 13 April 1945 while the runways were still being repaired. The targets were enemy road and river transport. The Allied advance was so rapid that the front line was soon beyond the range of Hurricanes, and a move was made to Tennant airstrip, which brought the main Japanese escape route at Pegu and Sittaung Ferry within range. Both squadrons became operational on arrival at the rudimentary landing ground on 28 April—the Hurricane Mk IVs harrying river transport and the Mk IIDs attacking bottlenecks of fleeing motor transport. After four months of Hurricane air support and with the fall of Rangoon imminent on 30 April, it was clear that despite difficult conditions, the Hurricane pilots and ground crews had made a major contribution to the final defeat of Japan in the jungles of Burma.

14

Foreign Air Forces

HURRICANE MANUFACTURE AND service with the RCAF, both in Canada and Britain, has already been covered, but Hurricanes were licence-built and operated in a number of countries both during and after the Second World War—Belgium, Russia, Yugoslavia, and India have already been mentioned as having operated Hurricanes.

In the 1930s, many of the smaller European countries believed that any aggression against them would be of little benefit, and without the modern equivalent of NATO, there would be no justification for spending large sums of money on defence, even though Hitler had made quite clear his ambitions of European domination. However, some of the close neighbouring countries recognised the growing danger and allocated funds for the updating of their armed forces. When Albania and Italy came to a number of political agreements that strengthened their co-operation Yugoslavia felt threatened, despite the signing of an Italo-Yugoslav settlement in March 1937. The Yugoslav government therefore made a request to Britain for the supply of Hurricanes as a move to modernise from the existing Hawker Furies and Hind bombers, which was approved as part of Britain's support for Allied nations. The initial order was for twelve Hurricane Mk Is from RAF early production batches with fabric-covered wings. The first two were delivered by air from Brooklands via France and Italy on 15 December 1938. This initial batch was soon followed by a second order for twelve Hurricanes with metal-covered wings and powered by Merlin III engines driving de Havilland propellers, with deliveries commencing in February 1940.

In addition, a licence agreement was also negotiated with the British Government for Hurricanes to be built in Yugoslavia by the PSFAZ Rogozarski factory in Belgrade, and the Fabrika Aeroplana I Hidroplana plant in Zemun, to build forty and sixty Hurricanes respectively at the rate of twelve a month. When the German forces attacked Yugoslavia in April 1941, the Royal Yugoslav Air Force had a total of thirty-eight Hurricane Mk Is on charge; eighteen with the 51 Fighter Squadron at Sarajevo, fourteen with 33 Fighter Squadron

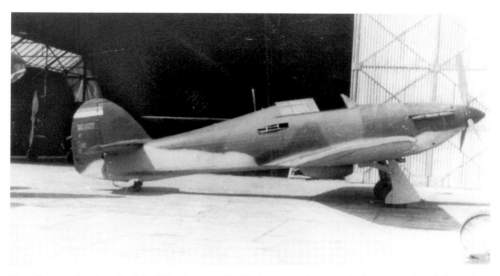

Yugoslavia ordered twelve Mk I Hurricanes with fabric-covered wings, the first two being delivered on 15 December 1938, followed by a second order with metal-covered wings delivered from February 1940. These were followed by licence production, which ceased when the German forces invaded Yugoslavia. The Yugoslav Air Force Hurricane Mk I BR2347 was from the Yugoslav production but was captured by the Germans and at Zemun in April 1941. (*P. H. T. Green collection*)

at Zagreb, and six with 34 Fighter Squadron. The eventual fate of the Yugoslav Air Force Hurricanes is covered in Chapter 11 under the Mediterranean Campaign.

Interest was expressed by the South African defence minister, Oswald Pirow, who had initiated an expansion programme for the SAAF in 1934 with a licence agreement to build Hawker Hartebeeste in Pretoria. A follow-up with the British Government in mid-1938 resulted in the Air Ministry agreeing to supply seven Hurricanes from storage, which were dismantled and shipped to Cape Town in November, where they were reassembled and flown to Pretoria for 1 Squadron SAAF. As these Hurricanes were not fitted with tropical filters, they were unsuitable for combat duties. However, a number of SAAF squadrons were formed as part of the Commonwealth air forces, supporting the RAF in the North African Campaign and in East Africa, as covered in Chapter 12. Some Hurricane Mk IIBs and IICs were taken out of storage in the Middle East after war service, with 1, 3, 40, and 41 Squadrons (SAAF) despatched to South Africa at the end of the war, a few seeing service with the fighter OTU for a short time before being withdrawn from use.

During an official visit to Britain by King Carol of Romania, he was invited to watch a display of RAF squadrons at Odiham in November 1938, and interest was shown in Hurricanes. As a result, an order was placed for twelve Hurricanes taken from existing RAF batches, which were replaced by new aircraft added on to the current production. The Romanian aircraft were delivered from August 1939 and the remainder within a year.

In return, the British Government hoped to support the Balkan opposition to German access to the vital Romanian oilfields, but this was not successful due to delays in the final

Romania ordered twelve Hurricane Mk Is in November 1938, and although they did not see much combat, this aircraft was allocated to *Escadrilla 53* around June 1941. (*P. H. T. Green collection*)

Hurricane deliveries. Romania's signing of The Axis Tripartite Treaty gave Germany access to the oil supplies in return for non-aggression, making it unlikely that any of the Romanian Hurricanes saw any action, but were used in the operational training role.

A military mission from a number of Middle Eastern countries in March 1939 resulted in an order from Iran for eighteen Hurricanes, but due to the lengthy development of tropical air filters, deliveries were delayed and only one aircraft was delivered by September, followed by another in 1940—neither of which were fitted with the tropical filter. Due to a shortage of shipping space and the uncertainties following the start of the Second World War, the remainder of the order was delayed until after the war, although ten Hurricanes were transferred from RAF stocks during hostilities. The order was updated in 1946–1947 when sixteen Hurricane Mk IICs and two two-seaters were purchased for use as fighter trainers by the Advanced Fighter Training Group of the Iranian Air Force's Flying Training School. In the two-seater Hurricane, a second cockpit was located behind the existing cockpit fitted with dual controls and a basic instrument panel, but without radio.

To provide some safety should the aircraft become inverted on the ground, a strengthened bulkhead and pylon was fitted between the two cockpits, albeit without canopies. However, it was found during flight testing that at speeds in excess of 280 mph, the occupant of the rear cockpit was subjected to considerable turbulence, and an adaptation of the Hawker Tempest sliding canopy was fitted over the rear cockpit. The first of the two aircraft was flown on 27 September 1946, and both were delivered to Iran in 1947.

Iran ordered eighteen Hurricanes, but only two were delivered before the start of the war. The order was updated in 1946 with sixteen Mk IICs and a pair of two-seaters. Iranian Hurricane Mk IIC was used for advanced flight training with the cannon ports blanked off. (*RAF Museum*)

Initially, the two-seat Iranian Air Force Hurricanes had both cockpits open, but the rear crew member was subjected to unacceptable turbulence. Hurricane Mk IIC 2-31 was ex RAF KZ232. (*BAe photo*)

Two-seat Iranian Hurricane Mk IIC 2-31 was fitted with a Tempest canopy over the rear cockpit to overcome the violent turbulence. (*P. H. T. Green collection*)

The initial order from Turkey was for fifteen Hurricane Mk Is, which were delivered by sea in September 1939. Further aircraft were taken from RAF Middle Eastern stocks for the Turkish Air Force, including Mk IIC HV608, here having an engine run. (IWM)

The Belgian Government ordered twenty Hurricane Mk Is with Watts wooden propellers in March 1939, and followed this with an order for eighty under licence production in Belgium. The aircraft were lined up on parade, instead of being dispersed around the airfield. This was what greeted the Luftwaffe when they approached over the woods in the background on 10 May 1940, destroying the entire complement of Belgian Air Force Hurricanes of *2-eme Escadrille* at Schaffen-Diest. (*AELR Air Museum, Brussels*)

At about the same time as the original Iranian sale, the Turkish Government also placed an order for fifteen Hurricanes as part of a plan to modernise the air force, with Britain keen to create allies in the eastern Mediterranean. The outbreak of war made deliveries more urgent and the entire batch was shipped by sea in September 1939, all without tropical filters.

Nearer home, the Belgian Government, with memories of the German hostility in 1914 and their location beyond the northern limits of the French Maginot fortifications, were acutely aware of their vulnerability. Among their defensive preparations was an order for twenty Hurricanes from the Kingston production line in March 1939, the first three of which were delivered the following month.

To help spread the production process and avoid delays from Britain, a licence agreement was signed for Hurricanes to be built by Avions Fairey with an order for eighty aircraft. By the time war broke out, the Kingston-built aircraft had been delivered to the early production standard with Merlin IIs driving two-blade Watts propellers, and the first licence-produced example was completed by the end of the year at Gosselies. The intention was to replace the wing armament of eight .303-inch Browning machine guns with four 12.7-mm heavy machine guns, but because of development delays only two aircraft were completed to this standard when the Germans invaded on 10 May. In the event, some twenty aircraft were delivered from the Belgian factory, all armed with the standard eight machine guns, and from

One of the wrecked Hurricane Mk Is of the Belgian Air Force after the Luftwaffe attack on 10 May 1940. (*Author's collection*)

January 1940, all engines delivered by Rolls-Royce were Merlin IIIs. Before the Belgian Air Force was overrun and destroyed (as covered in Chapter 5), the last two aircraft were fitted with Rotol constant-speed propellers.

The final pre-war order for Hurricanes came from Poland, who were probably more in need of fighters than most other countries, but had a misplaced confidence in their own preparedness. They may well have been relying in the protection of Britain and France following their guarantees of support for their sovereign rights against German aggression. The Hurricane order was for one aircraft for evaluation purposes, with an option for nine more. The evaluation aircraft was shipped in July 1939 and confirmed as unloaded at Stettin on 8 August. The fate of this aircraft is unknown—the other nine aircraft were shipped to the Middle East for RAF use. The Polish pilots who were able to escape to Britain certainly made a significant contribution to the Battle of Britain, as outlined in Chapter 6, as well as in offensive operations from 1941.

In March 1940, the Air Ministry authorised twelve Hurricane Mk Is, from stocks held by 19 and 20 MUs at St Athan and Aston Down, to help Finland in the closing stages of the Winter War with the Soviet Union. The Hurricanes were delivered by air via northern Scotland and Norway, one of which crashed in bad weather at Stavenger. By the time the aircraft were delivered, an armistice had been agreed between Finland and Russia, and the Hurricanes equipped HLeLv 30. In June 1941, hostilities between Russia and Finland resumed in what was to become the Continuation War. HLeLv 30 was allocated to the defence of Helsinki, with the Hurricanes being in action on the northern front against Russian bomber and reconnaissance aircraft.

Hurricanes were operated by the Finnish Air Force in local air defence during the Second World War, HU460 being an example. (*P. H. T. Green collection*)

Maintaining and flying the Hurricanes in Russia was a challenge during the war, with many accidents. Even if the damage was not too serious, there were insufficient spares and skills to make repairs. This is ex-RAF Mk IIB Z3577 with the Soviet Air Force after a forced landing in Finland in 1942. (*P. H. T. Green collection*)

Hurricane Mk IIB BM959 '60' Soviet Air Force crash-landed in Finland during 1942. (*P. H. T. Green collection*)

Ex-RAF Hurricane Mk IIs were operated by the Royal Norwegian Air Force after the Second World War. (*P. H. T. Green collection*)

Ex-RAF Hurricane Mk I Z5252 was one of 2,952 Hurricanes supplied to Russia during the Second World War. (*IWM*)

Hurricanes were not particularly popular with Finish pilots; the surviving aircraft were used as operational trainers until 1944 when the Russian onslaught brought about the collapse of Finland. The Fins were then forced to co-operate with the Russian forces in driving out the Germans from their homeland.

Many of the Allies acquired Hurricanes during the Second World War including Russia, who took delivery of some 2,952 as mentioned in Chapter 8, and India, covered to some extent in Chapter 13, while some of the ones supplied to Egypt, Yugoslavia, and Turkey surprisingly survived the war. The Royal Egyptian Air Force operated some Mk Is with 1 (Fighter Reconnaissance) Squadron while Mk IICs were with 2 (Fighter) Squadron at Almaza—all ex-RAF aircraft released from Middle East stocks. The Free French Air Force operated some fifteen Sea Hurricane Mk IICs and Mk XIIs in 1944 and 1945 in North Africa, some of which were still flying into early 1946.

The Irish Air Corps during the war was able to obtain, by various means, up to nineteen Hurricane Mk Is and Mk IICs, which were sufficient to equip 1 Squadron IAC at Baldonnel. The first to arrive was a Mk I, which forced landed during the Battle of Britain, and was soon followed by two more. After lengthy negotiations with the British Government, two were returned in exchange for three early Hurricane Mk Is. A fourth Hurricane was delivered from Northern Ireland in 1943, followed by seven Mk Is and six Mk IICs in 1943 and 1944; some remained in service until 1947.

Egypt acquired surplus Hurricanes from RAF Middle Eastern stocks, an example being Mk IIC KZ886 on the strength of 2 Squadron Egyptian Air Force in early 1945. (*P. H. T. Green collection*)

The Free French Air Force operated some ex-RAF Hurricane Mk IIBs in Algeria and Tunisia, an example being BG707. (*Author's collection*)

A line-up of Irish Air Corps Hurricane Mk IIs at Baldonnel in 1945. Some remained in service until 1947. (*P. H. T. Green collection*)

Portuguese Hurricane Mk IIC 646 at Sintra in 1946. (*P. H. T. Green collection*)

The ultimate Hurricane export order was from Portugal in 1945, where the aircraft served until 1951. (*IWM*)

Hurricane Mk IIC of XV Squadron Portuguese Air Force in 1948. (RAF Museum)

The Portuguese Hurricane Mk IIC that appeared in the film 'Angels One Five' as US-P at Kenley. (*P. H. T. Green collection*)

With the end of the war, Hawker were keen to re-establish their place in the export market. Their first customer came as a result of a government-to-government agreement between Britain and Portugal, wherein Portugal allowed Britain to use the Azores as a military and naval base. In 1943, Britain had already supplied fifteen Mk IICs to Base Aérea No.2 at Ota and from stocks held at maintenance units. Fifty of late-series Mk IICs were released to Hawker at Langley for the preparation of forty for delivery to Portugal, together with a large stock of spares. These aircraft were shipped to Lisbon to serve with Aerial Base 3 at Tancos and with the Lisbon Fighter Defence Flight until January 1952, when they were replaced by F-47D Thunderbolts. A few returned to Britain to star in the film Angels One Five made at Kenley in 1952.

15

Rebuilding Hurricanes

Tony Ditheridge and his staff at Hawker Engineering gained considerable experience manufacturing from scratch twenty-one First World War aircraft. When New Zealand-based Sir Tim Wallace contracted him to restore Hurricane Mk I P3351 from wreckage recovered from Russia, Ditheridge formed Hawker Restorations in 1993. Due to the scale of manufacturing required, Ditheridge decided to build an initial batch of three Hurricanes, the first of which was completed and flown in New Zealand on 12 January 2000. The next two were soon allocated to keen customers: Paul Allen acquired G-KAMM/BW881, a Canadian-built Mk XII that was finished as 5429 Z:135 Squadron RCAF for the Everett-based Flying Heritage Collection; and Sea Hurricane Mk II AE977 for Chino Warbirds as N33TF, now back in Britain. This latter Hurricane had been abandoned by its pilot when based at Yeovilton and crashed into a peat bog near the airfield from which it was later recovered in mid-1980 and stored in a garage. In 2013, this Hurricane was marked as P3886 UF-K:601 Squadron to commemorate the American volunteers who formed the Eagle Squadrons before the USA had formally entered the Second World War. Hurricane Mk I P3886 was flown by Billy Fiske and Carl R. Davis, both Cambridge graduates who joined 601 Squadron (RAuxAF). Billy Fiske joined the RAF when war was declared claiming he was a Canadian, but died from his injuries after a forced landing at Tangmere on 16 August 1940. Carl Davis was born in South Africa to American parents and took British citizenship in 1932, joining the RAF in 1936. He had a total of 9.5 victories, but in a final combat on 6 September 1940 before moving to Exeter for a rest tour, he was shot down and was killed at Matfield, Kent.

When a Hurricane arrives at Hawker Restorations it is often a collection of wreckage with the steel and aluminium components corroded beyond recovery. However, the Hurricane structure was held together by stainless steel plates, which are generally in good condition, allowing on average some 85 per cent to be used again.

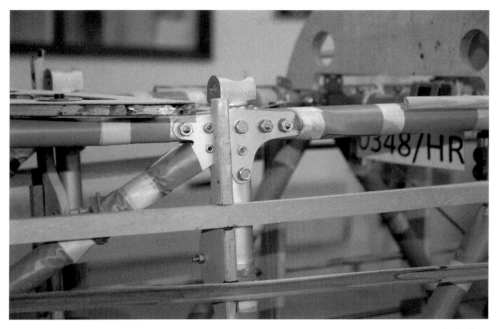

A salvaged stainless steel fish-plate joint for the fuselage structure, the tubular structure of which is new build. (*Author's photo*)

In some cases, the heavy castings, such as the undercarriage legs and axles, can be reused after non-destructive testing. While Hawker Engineering can manufacture any parts, it is preferable to use the original wherever possible. The Merlin engines recovered with the projects are generally unusable, but Eyetech Engineering provide engines overhauled to a very high standard.

When Sydney Camm designed the robust Hurricane, his previous experience had been with mainly wooden structures, particularly the classic Hawker biplane combat aircraft. However, he realised that with the power of a Rolls-Royce Merlin engine he would have to introduce a primary metal structure in the fuselage, although he did not believe in welded construction. To replace the square section wood members, he specified a tubular structure, which was a circular section with square ends at each bay in the fuselage for the fasteners, requiring the development of specialised steels and extensive jigs and tools. The structure was produced to a very high tolerance, in the order of 0.0005 inches, with the fastener holes drilled and then reamed for a tight fit, which avoided the need for large assembly jigs. Where bolts were used as fasteners, the holes were also bushed to avoid over-tightening, while other holes were fastened by hollow rivets. The many joints in the fuselage can consist of anywhere between twenty to 150 parts.

Hawker Restorations can undertake the full restoration task of the complex Hurricane airframe, from detail manufacture, metal and wood fabrication, aircraft assembly, fabric covering and painting, with each aircraft requiring a total of some 25,000 man hours to

The end joint of the wing centre-section main spar with the twelve-sided rolled high-tensile spring steel spar booms. (*Author's photo*)

complete, although from time to time some work is sub-contracted out. Because of the high precision required in the manufacture of parts for the Hurricanes, Hawker Restorations employ four tool-makers for the metal work, and one pattern-maker for the woodwork.

The most challenging task for Hawker Restorations, once the vital information had been acquired, is to manufacture the wing centre-section and similarly structured fin and tailplane. The front and rear spars' top and bottom sections consist of twelve-sided HT180 72-ton spring steel, which is progressively roll-formed and assembled one tube inside the other with an interference fit to a very tight tolerance. Following the rolling of the section, the spar booms are heat treated before assembly. To achieve the correctly finished spar sections, over 120 pairs of specialised rolls have to be designed and manufactured to be fitted to the sole remaining roll-forming machine in Britain. Once complete, the rolled sections are attached to a shear spar web, which are reinforced by a series of squared end tubes. At each end of the centre-section spar booms are forged fittings, which pick up with the outer wings. The Hurricane was the first monoplane fighter with a very complicated snap locking gear to house the inward retracting undercarriage into the stub wings, and the fuselage centre-section also housed one of the three fuel tanks.

Ditheridge has produced a stock of twenty spar sets of material, and since the special steel and the rolling machine no longer exist, he has enough spars for another ten rebuilds before no more Hurricanes can be rebuilt to fly. Any damage on existing aircraft relating to the spars usually entails replacing them, so some of this valuable stock could be used to keep current

The wing centre-section of P2902, showing the main undercarriage and its retraction mechanism—much of the latter was refurbished from original wreckage. (*Author's photo*)

aircraft in the air—spars were recently replaced, for example, by Hawker Restorations for the Battle of Britain Memorial Flight Hurricane PZ865.

Building the wings requires four unique wing spar shapes consisting of double 'T' extrusions, which correspond to the aerofoil sections on the front and rear spars. These consist of hundreds of small hand-made components, all of which are assembled as a basic structure in a sophisticated jig, following which the wings are skinned with aluminium, and the leading edge and wing tips are attached. Some customers request fitting the original Browning machine guns—deactivated, of course—together with the ammunition boxes, feeds, pneumatics, and associated equipment before the wing is attached to the fuselage.

The fin and tailplane are smaller versions of the centre section in terms of overall structure, with the tailplane consisting of front and rear spars made from eight-sided rolled high tensile steel booms with overlapping spars, which are separated by diagonal roll-formed booms. The shape is then achieved by attaching ribs, ready for an aluminium skin covering. The fin has a similar spar construction, but in addition has a slight bend close to the base. The elevators and rudder use steel torque tubes with soldered and riveted cleats attaching a series of ribs manufactured from round tube, which is formed to give an aerofoil 'P' section. As with the wing spars, the special steel and rolling mill are no longer available.

The shape of the Hurricane fuselage is achieved by attaching a series of wooden formers to the primary metal structure on which individual wooden stringers are mounted around the fuselage.

The complex fuselage structure and closely packed systems are shown in this external view of the port side of P3717/G-HITT at Milden in May 2013. This aircraft was at Turweston being prepared for flight at the time of writing in June 2016. (*Author's photo*)

The cockpit—which houses the pilot, instrumentation, controls, canopy, and windscreen—is faired in by a moulded plywood 'dog kennel', together with three removable under fairings beneath the aircraft, giving the ventral fin area around the tailwheel and the radiator intake under the nose.

All the wooden structure is covered in traditional hand-stitched, doped Irish linen. The Merlin engine is faired in by sixteen hand-made aluminium cowlings, which are created by compound curve wheeling. All the metal work is primed and the complete aircraft finished by being painted in authentic camouflage, often with the markings carried in RAF service. The grass field adjacent to Hawker Engineering is not large enough to test fly Hurricanes, so they have been dismantled and taken by road to their eventual home base, or somewhere suitable close by.

During my initial visit to Hawker Engineering, there were three Hurricanes under restoration. Probably the most interesting was Mk I P2902, which is registered G-ROBT. This aircraft was built by Gloster Aircraft and made its maiden flight on, or around, 20 October 1939. By May 1940, the aircraft was on the strength of 245 Squadron based at Drem on the East Coast of Scotland and allocated to coastal shipping patrols. The squadron moved south to Hawkinge on 28 May 1940 for the Battle of France, and while over the beach at Dunkirk was flown by Pilot Officer Kenneth McGlashan. The aircraft was shot down by a Bf 109 on 31 May. In the battle, he received slight wounds and was temporarily blinded by leaking oil

The fully equipped pilot's cockpit of P2902/G-ROBT. (*Author's photo*)

Hurricane Mk I P2902/G-ROBT under restoration at Milden in May 2013. This aircraft first flew on 20 October 1939 and was delivered to 245 Squadron. It was damaged during the Battle of France and force-landed on the beach at Dunkirk on 31 May 1940, from where it was later recovered. (*Author's photo*)

and glycol coolant from the engine. He put the aircraft into a dive and, by the time his sight cleared, was close to the ground. Pulling out of the dive, he made a successful forced landing and was rescued by some British troops, who initially thought he was German. McGlashan walked along the beach and managed to get aboard a Thames paddle steamer, landing at Margate, and return to his squadron at Hawkinge, although he had been initially posted as missing, failed to return. Hurricane P2902 was recovered by French enthusiasts in 1988 in the presence of Kenneth McGlashan, and the remains were stored pending its restoration to flying condition carrying the markings DX-R for R. A. Roberts. By mid-2016, the work on the rebuild was some 80 per cent complete and is expected to fly during 2017; it will be based at the former Battle of Britain airfield of North Weald.

McGlashan continued to serve with 245 Squadron during the Battle of Britain and was promoted to Flying Officer on 6 November. On 17 December 1940, he was posted to 96 Squadron, which was forming up for night-fighter operations at Cranage. He was promoted to Flight Lieutenant on 6 November and left 96 Squadron on 17 November 1941 when he was posted to 60 OTU at East Fortune as an instructor, joining 87 Squadron at Charmy Down on 20 July 1942. He participated in the Dieppe raid on 19 August making strafing attacks, and was posted to 536 Squadron at Predannack on 12 September 1942, which operated Turbinlite Havocs on night-fighting duties. With the disbandment of 536 Squadron on 25 January 1943 due to the concept being ineffective, McGlashan joined 264 Squadron at Warmwell where he served until 15 June 1944, following which he was posted to Cairo to assist BOAC in the opening of the air routes in the Middle East. He returned to Britain in January 1946 and, after further RAF service with 54 OTU and commanding 25 Squadron at West Malling, was promoted to Squadron Leader. He left the RAF on 29 August 1958 and immigrated to Australia with his family in 1964. Before he died, Kenneth McGlashan was reunited with his Dunkirk Hurricane during the early stages of its rebuild at Hawker Restorations.

Next to P2902 was Hurricane G-HITT/P3717, which was originally built as a Mk I but later converted to a Mk II. It entered service with 253 Squadron at Kirton-in-Lindsey on 13 July 1940, where the squadron was rebuilding after sustaining heavy losses in the Battle of France, and was flown by Fg Off. W. M. C. Samolinski, taking part in the Battle of Britain while based at Kenley, when he claimed a Bf 110 over Redhill on 30 August 1940. The aircraft was later one of many delivered to Russia, and its remains were returned to Britain for restoration as SW-P, the markings it carried with 253 Squadron. The aircraft was moved by road to Turweston, Northamptonshire, on 10 February 2015 for Hugh Taylor, where it awaits CAA clearance to fly at the time of writing.

A third Hurricane in the early stages of its restoration was V7497/G-HRLI, which is 50 per cent owned by Hawker Restorations, with the other 50 per cent owned by Peter Kirkpatrick based in Cambridge. It was initially intended to be configured as a two-seater to allow the carriage of passengers, but it is now being rebuilt as a stock single-seat Hurricane, with completion anticipated by April 2017. This Mk I was flown in the Battle of Britain, serving with 501 Squadron RAF, and was shot down on 30 September 1940 when being flown by Fg Off. Rogers, who successfully abandoned his aircraft.

The Hurricane Mk I P2902 DX-R rebuild has progressed over three years, and it is hoped to be able to fly in late 2016. (*Author's photo*)

Hurricane Mk I V7497/G-HRLI at Milden in May 2013, served with 501 Squadron and crashed on 28 September 1940. Subsequently salvaged, the plan was to complete the restoration with a second seat under the existing canopy. (*Author's photo*)

Hurricane V7497/G-HRLI, which has progressed over a period of three years, with the fuselage being equipped. (*Author's photo*)

For many years, Hawker Restorations have been based at Milden, where Hawker Engineering rebuilds classic cars, but there is not sufficient room to fly Hurricanes from the adjacent fields. The aircraft projects are to be moved to Elmscott near Wattisham, where there is a 900-metre grass strip. A new bespoke hangar was erected by the end of 2016, employing 35 per cent more skilled staff and equipped with a full 'C' and 'C' machine shop. Hawker Restorations now have full Battle of Britain contractor approval, and David Wenham has invested in the Company to allow this major development to take place.

Hurricanes Rebuilt by Hawker Restorations

P3351/ZK-TPK Mk I RAF and Russia-converted to Mk IIA 'DR393' for Tim Wallace, Wanaka, New Zealand. Its first flight was on 12 January 2000 at Christchurch.
BW881/G-KAMM Mk XII '5429' Z:135 Sq RCAF for Flying Heritage Collection, Everett.
AE977/N33TF Mk X Sea Hurricane for Chino Warbirds/Tim Friedkin, LE-D:242 Sq, to Biggin Hill in early 2012.
5487/G-CBOE CCF Canadian Mk IIB, in which Hawker Restorations supplied the complete airframe, plus systems and a wing kit ready for equipping.
R4118/G-HUPW MK I. Its first flight was on 23 December 2004. 'UP-W:605 Sq' Peter Vacher, ex-India.

BE505/G-HHII Mk IIB XP-L:174 Sq f/f North Weald 22.1.09 ex-RCAF Mk XII 5403 Hangar 11.
KZ321/G-HURY/CF-TPM Mk IV ex-6 Sq RAF for Vintage Wings of Canada, 2006.
P2902/G-ROBT Mk I crashed at Dunkirk on 31 May 1940. Designated DX-R:245 Sq, after rebuild.
P3717/G-HITT Mk I SW-P:253 Sq B of B, to Mk II in Russia, under rebuild.
V7497/G-HRLI Mk I ex-501 Sq, crashed 28 September 1940, under rebuild to a two-seater.

Phoenix Aero Services, Thruxton Airport

Based at Thruxton Airport, Hampshire, Phoenix Aero Services Ltd had CAA A8-20 approval for restoration of a wide range of vintage aircraft including two Hurricanes under restoration, with a third in storage.

G-CBOE Mk XII (RCAF 5487)

Built by the Canadian Car & Foundry Company, 5487 was allocated to 127 Squadron RCAF based at Gander for coastal patrol duties in mid-1941. At 22.30 on 22 November 1942, while apparently performing aerobatics at night, the pilot, Flight Sergeant Taylor, lost control and crashed into heavy snow near Indian Bay Pond, Newfoundland, suffering minor injuries.

Hurricane XII 5487/G-CBOE flew with 127 Squadron RCAF from Gander and crashed on 22 November 1942. It was acquired by Classic Aero in 2002 and the basic airframe was rebuilt by Hawker Restorations, after which it was returned to Thruxton. The project was taken over by Phoenix Aero in 2011, and with completion planned in 2013, it was advertised for sale at £2.395 million. (*Author's photo*)

The aircraft was recovered and stored until declared a write-off in March 1943. Its history, following a subsequent sale, was unknown until it was recovered from a farm by Hawker Restorations Ltd in the 1990s. It was purchased by Classic Aero Engineering Ltd in 2002, who dismantled the wreck and recovered all the usable original parts, which were incorporated into a rebuilt fuselage, centre section, and engine bearers by Hawker Restorations and returned to Classic Aero for completion.

In 2011, Classic Aero ceased trading and the project was purchased by Phoenix Aero Services Ltd, which continued with the restoration. A return to flight was scheduled for autumn 2013.

G-BYDL Mk IIB (RAF Z5207)

This airframe was a tropicalised version built by Gloster Aircraft in mid-1941 and shipped on HMS Argus to Russia in August 1941 for service with 151 Wing, consisting of 81 and 134 Squadrons, tasked with the air defence of the naval base at Murmansk.

On 7 September, eight Hurricanes were flown off HMS Argus to Vaenga Airfield on the Kola Peninsula, Z5207 becoming the mount of Sgt 'Avro' Anson of 81 Squadron. Between

Hurricane Mk IIB Z5207/G-BYDL was delivered to 20 MU at Aston Down on 22 July 1941 and shipped to Russia in August 1941. The aircraft was issued to 81 Squadron, part of 151 Wing at Vaenga, for the air defence of Murmansk, and passed to the Soviet Air Force on 11 October when 151 Wing ceased operations. It crashed on 16 November 1941 and the wreckage was recovered in the 1980s. The aircraft is about 50 per cent restored, with work stopped pending the completion of G-CBOE. (*Author's photo*)

early September and the last operational patrol on 8 October, Z5207 completed fifteen sorties, and the pilots claimed one and one-third Bf 109Es destroyed. When the RAF left Russia on 11 October 1941, the Hurricanes were passed to the Soviet Air Force. Z5207 was part of a formation of three aircraft that hit rising ground together in bad weather near Lake Pjalve on 16 November 1941, killing all the pilots. The wreckage was left where it was as there were no facilities for the reconstruction of the aircraft.

Recovered in the 1980s by Jim Pearce, Z5207 was acquired by Retro Track and Air and subsequently sold to Mr Phillip Lawton. Restoration was contracted to Classic Aero Engineering Ltd, who had completed approximately half the work using a large quantity of original components at the time they ceased trading.

Following the formation of Phoenix Aero Services Ltd in 2011 by Mr Lawton, work stopped on Z5207 to allow for the completion and sale of G-CBOE, leaving Z5207 as a fuselage and centre-section standing on its undercarriage. When completed, this will be one of the most original Hurricanes in airworthy condition.

It was planned to paint this aircraft in Finnish Continuation War colours to represent HC465, a captured Soviet Air Force Hurricane Mk IIA Z2582, which crash-landed on Lake Tuoppajärvi, Finland, in mid-1942, and was restored to flying condition for the Finnish Air Force.

G-RLEF Mk XII (RCAF 5385)

Purchased as an unregistered, partly completed project by Mr Lawton in 2008, this airframe was originally intended for restoration but found to be in poor condition due to the use of incorrect grade materials. It has been dismantled to salvage the useable original components, which have been put in storage and could form the basis of a rebuild sometime in the future.

When Phillip Lawton found a customer for his flying Hurricane G-CBOE, who turned out to be Munich based Karl-Friedmann Grimminger, he made an offer for the entire package, which was accepted. The assets of Phoenix Aero were transferred in December 2014 to Kaelin Aero Technologies near Stuttgart where the restoration of Z5207 continues.

Cambridge Bomber and Fighter Society (CBFS), Little Gransden

Tucked away in the back of a hangar at Little Gransden is the restoration to non-flying condition of Hurricane Mk I L1639, which was flown by Peter Townsend as VY-Q:85 Squadron, initially at Debden, and then with the BEF during the Battle of France. Built at Brooklands by Hawker Aircraft in 1938, it is one of only two Hurricanes to survive with fabric-covered wings, the other being L1592 in the Science Museum, and this will be the only survivor fitted with the wooden fixed-pitch Watts two-blade propeller. With the gradual withdrawal of the RAF from France, L1639 passed to 504 Squadron and was shot down over the Franco-Belgian border on 14 May 1940, killing Sqn Ldr Parnell and staying where it crashed until the site was excavated in 1999.

Hurricane Mk I L1639 under non-flying restoration as S/Ldr Peter Townsend's VY-Q:85 Squadron, which crashed during the final stages of the Battle of France on 14 May 1940. (*Author's photo*)

The CBFS was formed in 1996 by Paul Rogers, who was inspired by his father, Joe, who served as a member of 85 Squadron ground crew and initially helped to maintain the earliest Hurricanes during the Battle of France. He was then put in charge of looking after L1639 for Sqn Ldr Peter Townsend.

It was the enthusiasm of his father that determined Paul Rogers to recover the wreck and restore it to a very high standard for static display in one of Britain's national museums. The restoration is being carried out by a group of enthusiastic volunteers led by Rogers, with a timescale of rolling the aircraft out of the hangar in 2020.

In the excavation, about 20 per cent of the original aircraft was recovered, and with the addition of parts from two wrecks in Russia, the excavation of nine other wreck sites, and the discarded remains of BBMF Hurricane Mk II LF363 following its crash landing at Wittering, Rogers claims the restoration will contain some 70 per cent restored original parts. All the other parts are being made to the original drawings by Rogers using the facilities at Cambridge University, where he used to work.

The restoration commenced in a workshop at a farm near Fenton, where a Fury Fighter is now being rebuilt. The Fury Fighter is based on K1928, which served with 43 Squadron, where Peter Townsend was a member before joining 85 Squadron.

The Hurricane project moved to Little Gransden in 2009, where there is just enough room to assemble the aircraft with its wings. Seven Merlin engines were excavated from various sites, the usable parts being combined into one engine, which after a seven-year restoration was run for the first time on 9 August 2009. Once the fuselage structure had been completed and the systems and equipment fitted, work then started on the starboard wing structure, including the fitting of four dummy .303-inch machine guns. During the first seven years of work on the Hurricane, the project used about 800,000 hours of volunteer time, and Paul Rogers is always on the lookout for sponsorship that may help complete the project sooner. However, even if none is forthcoming, he will continue to work on the aircraft.

Appendix I

Preserved Hurricanes

UK-built Hurricanes

Identity	Mk	Location	Status
L1592	I	London Science Museum	Public viewing
L1639	I	Little Gransden, UK	Restoration to static condition
L1866/ RCAF323	II	Hawker Restorations, Milden, UK	Restoration to air-worthy condition
L1988	I	Norwegian Aviation Museum, Bodo	Stored wreck
N2394/HC-452	I	Aviation Museum of Central Finland, Luonetjarvi AB	Public viewing
P2617	I	RAF Museum, Hendon	Public viewing
P2902	I	Hawker Restorations, Milden	Restoration to fly
P3173	I	W Sussex, UK	Stored wreck static restoration.
P3175	I	RAF Museum, Hendon	Conserved wreck, public viewing
P3179	I	Tangmere Military Aviation Museum, W Sussex, UK	Conserved cockpit and engine, public viewing
P3311	I	Denver, Colorado USA	Wreck, being rebuilt to fly
P3351/ DR393	I	Cannes-Mandelieu, France	Restored to fly
P3554	I	Air Defence Collection, Andover	Static rebuild from many parts
P3708	I	Norfolk & Suffolk Museum, Flixton	Static rebuild from excavated wreck
P3717/ DR348	I/IIA	Turweston, Northants	Restored to flying condition by Hawker Restorations, Milden
R4118	I	Old Warden	Recovered from India by Peter Vacher and restored to fly

V7350	I	Romney Marsh Wartime Collection	Forward fuselage from excavation of wreck
V7497	I	Hawker Restorations, Milden	Rebuilt from wreck to fly
Z2330	IIA	Hamilton, Ontario, Canada	Long term restoration to fly
Z2389	IIA	Brooklands Museum, Weybridge	Restoration to taxiable condition
Z2461	IIC	Murmansk, Russia	Restored for static display
Z2768	IIA	MAM, Virginia Beach, USA	Stored partly restored
Z3055	IIA	Malta Aviation Museum	Restored to static display
Z5207	IIB	Munich, Germany	Under restoration to fly
Z5227	IIB	San Martin, Ca, USA	Wreck stored
Z5252	IIB	Moscow (unconfirmed)	Stored wreck
Z5663	IIB	Bewdley, Works, UK	Composite static restoration
AP740	IIB	Technical Museum, Moscow	Public static display
BD731	IIB	Wings Museum, Balcombe, UK	Wreck on public display
BE146	IIB	IWM Duxford, UK	Public display as 'Z2315'
BH238	IIB	Sandown, IOW, UK	Stored wreck
KX829	IV	Birmingham	Public display
KZ191	IV	East Garston, Berks, UK	Stored wreck
KZ321	IV	Vintage Wings of Canada, Ottawa	Airworthy in Canada
LD619	IIC	Saxonwold, S Africa	Public static display
LD975	IV	Belgrade, Serbia	Public static display
LF363	IIC	BBMF, Coningsby, UK	Airworthy
LF658	IIC	Brussels, Belgium	Public display
LF686	IIC	Dulles Airport USA	Public display
LF738	IIC	RAF Museum, Cosford	Public display
LF751	IIC	Manston, Kent, UK	Public display
PZ865	IIC	BBMF, Coningsby, UK	Airworthy

Canadian-built Hurricanes

Identity	Mk	Location	Status
Z7015	IB	Shuttleworth Collection, UK	Airworthy
Z7059	I/X	Indian AF Museum, New Delhi	Public static display
AE977	I/X	Biggin Hill, UK	Airworthy
AM274	IIB	Brasschaat, Belgium	Restoration to fly

BW853	IB/XIIA	Cotswold Airport, Kemble, UK	Stored
BW862	IB/XIIA	Hamilton, Ontario, Canada	Stored
BW881	IB/XIIA	Paine Field, Everett, Wa, USA	Airworthy
RCAF 1374	I/XIIA	North Weald, UK	Airworthy
RCAF 5389	XII	Wetaskiwin, Alberta, Canada	Public static display
RCAF 5400	XII	Polk City, Fl, USA	Stored
RCAF 5418	XII	Reynolds Museum, Wetaskiwin	Public static display
RCAF 5447	XII	Vintage Wings of Canada, Quebec	Restoration
RCAF 5461	XII	Brandon, Manitoba, Canada	Static restoration
RCAF 5481	XII	Scone, NSW, Australia	Restoration to fly
RCAF 5487	XIIA	Munich, Germany	Airworthy as BW874
RCAF 5584	XII	Rockcliffe, Ottawa, Canada	Public static display
RCAF 5662	XII	Pima Air Museum, Tucson, USA	Public static display
RCAF 5666	XII	White Rock, BC, Canada	Wreck stored
RCAF 5667	XII	MAM Virginia Beach, USA	Airworthy
RCAF 5708	XII	Lone Star Flight Museum, USA	Stored
RCAF 5711	XII	Historic Aircraft, Duxford, UK	Airworthy

Appendix II Specifications

Mk	Type	Span	Length	Height	Wing Area	Engine	Power	Loaded Weight	Max. Speed	Climb to 20,000 feet	Ceiling	Range	Armament
Prot.	Fighter	40 feet/12.2 m	31.5 feet/9.6 m	13.5 feet/4.11 m	257.5 ft²/23.92 m²	Merlin 'C'	1,025 hp	5,672 lb/2,578 kg	312 mph/501 kph	12 minutes	33,000 feet	500 miles	8 × .303-inch MGs
I	Fighter	40 feet/12.2 m	31.33 feet/9.6 m	13 feet/3.95 m	257.5 ft²/23.92 m²	Merlin II/III	1,030 hp	6,666/3,030	335 mph/536 kph	9 minutes	36,000 feet	525 miles	8 × .303-inch MGs
I Trop	Fighter	40 feet/12.2m	31.33 feet/9.6m	13 feet/3.95m	257.5 ft²/23.92 m²	Merlin II/III	1,030 hp	6,850lb/3,113kg	317 mph/509 kph	9.5 minutes	33,000 feet	460 miles	8 × .303-inch MGs
Sea IA	Naval Fighter	40 feet/12.2m	31.33 feet/9.6m	13 feet/3.95m	257.5 ft²/23.92 m²	Merlin III	1,030 hp	6,780lb/3,082kg	302 mph/485 kph	11.6 minutes	31,000 feet	505 miles	8 × .303-inch MGs
Sea IB	Naval Fighter	40 feet/12.2m	31.33 feet/9.6m	13 feet/3.95m	257.5 ft²/23.92 m²	Merlin III	1,030 hp	6,800lb/3,091kg	296 mph/475 kph	12 minutes	30,000 feet	505 miles	8 × .303-inch MGs
IIA	Fighter	40 feet/12.2m	32.19 feet/9.83m	13.08 feet/3.99m	257.5 ft²/23.92 m²	Merlin XX	1,185 hp	7,014lb/3,188kg	340 mph/546 kph	7 minutes	41,000 feet	468 miles	8 × .303-inch MGs
IIB/XI	Fighter	40 feet/12.2m	32.19 feet/9.83m	13.08 feet/3.99m	257.5 ft²/23.92 m²	Merlin XX	1,185 hp	7,440lb/3,382kg	340 mph/546 kph	7.5 minutes	40,000 feet	465 miles	6, 8, or 12 × .303-inch MGs
IIB	Fighter Bomber	40 feet/12.2m	32.19 feet/9.83m	13.08 feet/3.99m	257.5 ft²/23.92 m²	Merlin XX	1,185 hp	8,470lb/3,850kg	320 mph/514 kph	9.3/10.5 minutes	30,000 feet or 33,000 feet	460 miles	6, 8, or 12 × .303-inchMG + 2 × 250-/500-lb bombs
IIC	Fighter Bomber	40 feet/12.2m	32.19 feet/9.83m	13.08 feet/3.99m	257.5 ft²/23.92 m²	Merlin XX	1,185 hp	7,670lb/3,486kg	334 mph/536 kph	7.6 minutes	36,000 feet	460 miles	4 × 20-mm cannons + 2 × 250-/500-lb bombs
IID	Anti-Armour	40 feet/12.2m	32.19 feet/9.83m	13.08 feet/3.99m	257.5 ft²/23.92 m²	Merlin XX	1,185 hp	7,850lb/3,568kg	322 mph/517 kph	12.4 minutes	32,100 feet	420 miles	2 × 40-mm cannons + 2 × .303-inch MGs
Sea IIC	Naval Fighter	40 feet/12.2m	32.19 feet/9.83m	13.08 feet/3.99m	257.5 ft²/23.92 m²	Merlin XX	1,185 hp	7,618lb/3,462kg	301 mph/484 kph	12 minutes	35,600 feet	452 miles	4 × 20-mm cannons + 2 × 250-/500-lb bombs
IV	Ground attack	40 feet/12.2m	32.19 feet/9.83m	13.08 feet/3.99m	257.5 ft²/23.92 m²	Merlin 27	1,185 hp	8,462lb/3,846kg	280 mph/450 kph	12 minutes	29,100 feet	450 miles	4 × 20-mm or 2 × 40-mm cannons + 8 × RP or 2 × 250-lb bombs
X	Fighter	40 feet/12.2m	31.33 feet/9.6m	13ft/3.95m	275.5 ft²/23.92 m²	Packard Merlin 28	1,300 hp	7,160lb/3,251kg	330 mph/531 kph	9.9 minutes	35,000 feet	N/a	8 × .303-inch MGs
XII	Fighter Bomber	40 feet/12.2m	31.33 feet/9.6m	13ft/3.95m	275 ft²/23.92 m²	Packard Merlin 29	1,300 hp	7,360lb/3,341kg	330 mph/531 kph	9.9 minutes	36,500 feet	N/a	12 × .303-inch MGs+ 2 × 250-/500-lb bombs

Appendix III

Production

Prototype

K5083 ordered under contract 357483/34 to Air Ministry Specification F.36/34 and first flown 6 November 1935.

600 Hawker-built Mk Is Ordered 3 June 1936 to Specification 15/36

L1547–L2146 Contract No. 527112/36, powered by Rolls-Royce Merlin II with Watts two-blade wooden fixed-pitch propeller and fabric-covered wings, delivered between 15 December 1937 and 6 October 1939.

L1708, L1710, and L1711 to SAAF.

L1751(1–205), L1752(2–206), L1837(3–291), L1838(4–292), L1839(5–293), L1840(6–294), L1858(7–312), L1859(8–313), L1860(9–314), L1861(10–315), L1862(11–316), and L1863(12–317) to Yugoslav Air Force (serials in brackets).

L2077, L2078, L2085, L2093 to L2097, L2104, and L2112 to L2114 to Romanian Air Force August to September 1939.

L1759(310), L1760(311), L1761(312), L1762(313), L1763(314), L1878(315), L1879(316), L1880(317), L1881(318), L1882(319), L1883(320), L1884(321), L1885(322), L1886(323), L1887(324), L1888(325), L1890(326), L2021(327), L2022(328), L2023(329) to RCAF.

L1918(1), L1919(2), L1920(3), L1993(4), L1994(5), L1995(6), L1996(7), L1997(8), L2040(9), L2041(10), L2042(11), L2043(12), L2044(13), L2105(14), L2106(15), L2107(16), L2108(17), L2109(18), L2110(19), and L2111(20) to Belgian Air Force.

L2048 to Poland 24 July 1939.

L2079(252) to Iran.

L2024, L2025, L2027–L2033, and L2125–L2139 to Turkey, delivered 14 September to 6 October 1939.

300 Hawker-built Mk Is

N2318–N2367, N2380–N2409, N2422–N2441, N2453–N2502, N2520–N2559, N2582–N2631, and N2645–N2729 Contract No. 751458/38, powered by R-R Merlin III with de Havilland three-blade variable-pitch propeller. The first eighty aircraft had fabric-covered wings and the remainder metal-covered. Delivered 29 September 1939 to 1 May 1940.

N2718–N2729 to Yugoslav Air Force March 1940.

500 Gloster-built Mk Is

P2535–P2584, P2614–P2653, P2672–P2701, P2713–P2732, P2751–P2770, P2792–P2836, P2854–P2888, P2900–P2924, P2946–P2995, P3030–P3069, P3080–P3124, P3140–P3179, P3200–P3234, and P3250–P3264. Contract No. 962371/38/C.23a, powered by Rolls-Royce Merlin IIIs, with de Havilland or Rotol three-blade variable-pitch propeller, delivered November 1939 to April 1940.

P2968(107) to Ireland.

500 Hawker-built Mk Is, Plus Forty-Four Attrition Replacement

P3265–P3279, P3300–P3324, P3345–P3364, P3380–P3429, P3348–P3492, P3515–P3554, P3574–P3623, P3640–P3684, P3700–P3739, P3755–P3789, P3802–P3836, P3854–P3903, P3920–P3944, P3960–P3984, plus replacements P8809–P8818, R2680–R2689, T9519–T9538, and W6667–W6670. Contract No. 962371/38 powered by Rolls-Royce Merlin II with de Havilland or Rotol three-blade variable-pitch propeller, delivered 21 February 1940 to 20 July 1940.

P3269 prototype Mk II.

P3416(108) to Ireland, November 1943.

P3620 to Sea Hurricane Mk IA.

P3720 to Iran as 252, November 1940.

100 Gloster-built Mk Is

R4074–R4123, R4171–R4200, and R4213–R4132. Contract 19773/39/23 powered by Rolls-Royce Merlin III with de Havilland or Rotol three-blade variable-pitch propeller, delivered May 1940 to July 1940.

R4103 and R4104 to SAAF, July 1940.

500 Gloster-built Mk Is

V6533–V6582, V6600–V6649, V6665–V6704, V6722–V6761, V6776–V6825, V6840–V6889, V6913–V6962, V6979–V7028, V7042–V7081, V7099–V7138, and V7156–V7195. Contract No. 85730/40/C.23a powered by Rolls-Royce Merlin III with de Havilland or Rotol three-blade variable-pitch propeller, delivered July to November 1940.

V6576(111), V7158(110), and V7173(109) to Ireland.

500 Hawker-built Mk Is

V7200–V7209, V7221–V7260, V7276–V7318, V7337–V7386, V7400–V7446, V7461–V7510, V7533–V7572, V7588–V7627, V7644–V7690, V7705–V7737, V7741–V7780, V7795–V7838, V7851–V7862, and AS987–AS990. Contract No. 62305/39 powered by Rolls-Royce Merlin III with de Havilland or Rotol three-blade variable-pitch propeller, delivered 2 July 1940 to 5 February 1941.

V7411(104), V7435(112), V7463(114), and V7540(105) to Ireland.

200 Gloster-built Mk Is

W9110–W9159, W9170–W9209, W9215–W9244, W9260–W9279, W9290–W9329, and W9340–W9359. Contract No. 85730/40/C.23a powered by Rolls-Royce Merlin III with de Havilland or Rotol three-blade variable-pitch propeller, delivered November 1940.

W9206, W9215–W9224 to Sea Hurricane Mk I November 1940.

W9314 to Mk IIC prototype.

1,000 Hawker-built Mk IIs

Z2308–Z2357, Z2382–Z2426, Z2446–Z2465, Z2479–Z2528, Z2560–Z2594, Z2624–Z2643, Z2661–Z2705, Z2741–Z2775, Z2791–Z2840, Z2882–Z2931, Z2959–Z2999, Z3017–Z3036, Z3050–Z3099, Z3143–Z3187, Z3221–Z3276, Z3310–Z3359, Z3385–Z3404, Z3421–Z3470, Z3489–Z3523, Z3554–Z3598, Z3642–Z3691, Z3740–Z3784, Z3826–Z3845, Z3885–Z3919, and Z3969–Z4018. Contract No. 62305/39 powered by Rolls-Royce Merlin XX with de Havilland or Rotol three-blade variable-pitch propeller, delivered 14 January 1941 to 28 July 1941.

Z4015 to Sea Hurricane Mk IC.

-400 Gloster-built Mk Is

Z4022–Z4071, Z4085–Z4119, Z4161–Z4205, Z4223–Z4272, Z4308–Z4327, Z4347–Z4391,

Z4415–Z4434, Z4482–Z4516, Z4532–Z4851, and Z4603–Z4652. Contract No. 85730/40/C.23a powered by Rolls-Royce Merlin III with de Havilland or Rotol three-blade variable-pitch propeller, delivered December 1940 to March 1941.

Z4037(106) to Ireland.

600 Gloster-built Mk IIAs/IIBs

Z4686–Z4720, Z4760–Z4809, Z4832–Z4876, Z4920–Z4939, IIA Z4940–Z4969, Z4987–Z4989, LLB Z4990–Z5006, Z5038–Z5087, Z5117–Z5161, Z5202–Z5236, Z5252–Z5271, Z5302–Z5351, Z5376–Z5395, Z5434–Z5483, Z5529–Z5563, Z5580–Z5629, and Z5649–Z5693. Contract No. 85730/40/C.23a powered by Rolls-Royce Merlin XX with de Havilland or Rotol three-blade variable-pitch propeller. Gloster built 140 as Mk IIAs and the remaining 341 as Mk IIBs were delivered by 3 September 1941.

Z5159, Z5210–Z5213, Z5227, Z5236, Z5259, Z5262, Z5263, Z5480 to Russia 1941–1942
Z4846, Z4847, Z4849, Z4851–Z4854, Z4867, Z4873, Z4874, Z4876, Z4920–Z4926, Z4929, Z4931, Z4933, Z4935–Z4939, and Z5440 converted to Sea Hurricane Mk IA/IB.

300 Austin Motors-built Mk IIs

AP516–AP550, AP564–AP613, AP629–AP648, AP670–AP714, AP732–AP781, AP801–AP825, AP849–AP898, and AP912–AP936. Powered by Rolls-Royce Merlin XX with de Havilland or Rotol three-blade variable-pitch propeller.

Some 250 aircraft allocated to Russia October 1941, but some delivered to the RAF.

450 Gloster-built Mk IIAs/IIBs/IICs

BG674–BG723, BG737–BG771, BG783–BG832, BG844–BG888, BG901–BG920, BG933–BG977, BG990–BG999, BH115–BH154, BH167–BH201, BH215–BH264, BH277–BH296, and BH312–BH361. Powered by Rolls-Royce Merlin XX with de Havilland or Rotol three-blade variable-pitch propeller, delivered September 1941 to December 1941.

Russia received 400 and the remainder were sent to the Middle East.

1,350 Hawker-built Mk IIs

BD696–BD745, BD759–BD793, BD818–BD837, BD855–BD899, BD914–BD963, BD980–BD986, BE105–BE117, BE130–BE174, BE193–BE242, BE274–BE308, BE323–BE372, BE394–BE428, BE468–BE517, BE546–BE590, BE632–BE651, BE667–BE716, BM898–BM936, BM947–BM996, BN103–BN142, BN155–BN189, BN203–BN242, BN265–BN298,

BN311–BN337, BN346–BN389, BN399–BN435, BN449–BN497, BN512–BN547, BN559–BN603, BN624–BN654, BN667–BN705, BN719–BN759, BN773–BN802, BN818–BN846, BN859–BN882, BN896–BN940, and BN953–BN987. Powered by Rolls-Royce Merlin XX with de Havilland or Rotol three-blade variable-pitch propeller, delivered 24 July 1941 to 18 March 1942.

BD709, BD731, BD956, BE162, BE470, BN416, BN471, BN481, and BN428 to Russia, 1942. BD787 to Sea Hurricane Mk IA.

1,888 Hawker-built Mk IIs

BN988–BN992, BP109–BP141, BP154–BP200, BP217–BP245, BP259–BP302, BP316–BP362, BP378–BP416, BP430–BP479, BP493–BP526, BP538–BP566, BP579–BP614, BP628–BP675, BP692–BP711, BP734–BP772, HL544–HL591, HL603–HL634, HL654–HL683, HL698–HL747, HL767–HL809, HL828–HL867, HL879–HL913, HL925–HL941, HL953–HL997, HM110–HM157, HV275–HV317, HV333–NV370, HV396–HV445, HV468–HV516, HV534–HV560, HV577–HV612, HV634–HV674, HV696–HV745, HV768–HV799, HV815–HV858, HV873–HV921, HV943–HV989, HWE115–HW146, HW167–HW207, HW229–HW278, HW291–HW323, HW345–HW373, HW399–HW444, HW467–HW501, HW533–HW572, HW596–HW624, HW651–HW686, HW713–HW757, HW779–HW808, and HW834–HW881. Contract No. 62305/39/B, powered by Rolls-Royce Merlin XX with de Havilland or Rotol three-blade variable-pitch propeller, delivered 17 March 1942 to 23 November 1942.

BP657, HL629, HL992, HL994, HV362, HV364, HV840, HV844, HV880, HW117, HW143, HW233, HW347, HW364, HW471, HW551, HW552, HW557, and HW571 Mk IICs shipped to Russia in 1943

HL549 and HL665 shipped to Russia and converted to two–seaters.

HV279, HV287, HV293, HV556, HV593, HW168, HW205, HW300, HW357, HW371, HW406, HW686, HW715, HW868, HW872, and HW879 Mk IIDs shipped to Russia in 1943.

HV513 an HV551 tropical Mk IICs to Turkey in October and November 1942.

HL673 to Sea Hurricane Mk IC.

1,200 Hawker-built Mk IIs and Mk IVs

KW745–KW777, KW791–KW832, KW846–KW881, KW893–KW936, KW949–KW 982, KX101–KX146, KX162–KX202, KX220–KX261, KX280–KX307, KX321–KX369, KX382–KX425, KX452–KX491, KX521–KX567, KX579–KX621, KX691–KX736, KX749–KX784, KX796–KX838, KX851–KX892, KX922–KX967, KZ111–KZ156, KZ169–KZ201, KZ216–KZ250, KZ266–KZ301, KZ319–KZ356, KZ370–KZ412, KZ424–KZ470, KZ483–KZ526, KZ540–KZ582, KZ597–KZ612, plus NF668–NF703 Sea Hurricane Mk IIC conversions. Contract No. 62305/39/C, powered by Rolls-Royce Merlin XX with de Havilland or Rotol three-blade variable-pitch propeller, delivered 20 November 1942 to 19 April 1943.

KW770(NF668), KW774(NF671), KW791(NF669), KW792(NF670), KW799(NF672), KW800(NF673), KW804(NF674), KW807(NF677), KW808(NF675), KW809(NF678), KW810(NF676), KW816(NF679), KW817(NF680), KW827(NF681), KW828(NF682), KW849(NF683), KW850(NF684), KW860(NF685), KW862(NF686), KW868(NF687), KW870(NF688), KW878(NF689), KW880(NF690), KW897(NF691), KW899(NF692), KW908(NF693), KW909(NF694), KW910(NF695), KW911(NF696), KW918(NF697), KW919(NF698), KW920(NF699), KW921(NF700), KW928(NF701), KW929(NF702), and KLW930(NF703) conversions to Sea Hurricane Mk IICs with new serial numbers in brackets.

KW706, KW723, KX113, KX125, KX137, KX538, KX545, KZ234 Mk IICs; KW777, KX177, KX181, KZ301 Mk IIDsKX813, KX865, and KX888 Mk IVs; KZ509 Sea Hurricane Mk IICs all shipped to Russia in 1943.

KX405 and KZ193 converted to Mk Vs.

1,205 Hawker-built Mk IIs and Mk IVs

KZ613–KZ632, KZ646–KZ689, KZ702–KZ750, KZ766–KZ801, KZ817–KZ862, KZ877–KZ920, KZ933–KZ949, LA101–LA144, LB542–LB575, LB588–LB624, LB639–LB687, LB707–LB744, LB769–LB801, LB827–LB862, LB873–LB913, LB927–LB973, LB986–LB999, LD100–LD131, LD157–LD185, LD199–LD219, LD232–LD266, LD287–LD315, LD334–LD351, LD369–LD416, LD435–LD470, LD487–LD508, LD524–LD539, LD557–LD580, LD594–LD632, LD651–LD695, LD723–LD749, LD772–LD809, LD827–LD866, LD885–LD905, LD931–LD979, and LD993–LD999. Contract No. 62305/39/C, powered by Rolls-Royce Merlin XX with de Havilland or Rotol three-blade variable-pitch propeller, delivered 18 April 1943 to 29 September 1943.

KZ858, LB991, and LD205 to Russia, 1943–1944.

LB602, LB664, and LB732, plus others, to Indian Air Force.

1,357 Hawker-built Mk IIs and Mk IVs

LE121–LE146, LE163–LE183, LE201–LE214, LE247–LE273, LE291–LE309, LE334–LE368, LE387–LE405, LE432–LE449, LE456–LE484, LE499–LE535, LE552–LE593, LE617–LE665, LE679–LE713, LE737–LE769, LE784–LE816, LR829–LE867, LE885–LR925, LE938–LE966, LE979–LE999, LF101–LF135, LF153–LF184, LF197–LF237, LF256–LF298, LF313–LF346, LF359–LF405, LF418–LF435, LF451–LF482, LF494–LF516, LF529–LF542, LF559–LF601, LF620–LF660, LF674–LF721, LF737–LF774, MW335–MW373, PG425–PG456, PG469–PG499, PG512–PG554, PG567–PG610, PZ730–PZ778, PZ791–PZ835, and PZ848–PZ865. Contract No. 62305/39/C, powered by Rolls-Royce Merlin XX with de Havilland or Rotol three-blade variable-pitch propeller, delivered 29 September 1943 to 24 May 1944.

LE529, LF463, LF470, LF473, LF481, LF509, LF510, LF592, LF595, LF596 to Russia 1944
LF342, LF133, LF360, LF383, LF422, LF425, LF514, LF564, LF565, LF568, LF570, LF586,

LF620, LF699, LF706, LF717, LF757, LF772, MW373, PG521, PG535, PG538, PG543, PG599, PG610, PZ735, PZ738, PZ745, and PZ759 to Portugal 1945–1946.

LF541(116), LF624(118), and PZ796(120) to Ireland.

PZ865 to Hawker as G–AMAU.

One Hawker-built Mk V NL255 prototype.

Total UK Production: 12,952.

CANADIAN PRODUCTION

160 Canadian Car and Foundry-built Mk Is

P5170–P5209, T9519–T9538, Z6983–Z7017, Z7049–Z7093, and Z7143–Z7162. Powered by Rolls-Royce Merlin II with de Havilland three-blade variable-pitch propeller, the majority shipped to UK March–November 1940.

P5176(93) to Ireland 1942.

340 Canadian Car and Foundry-built Mk Xs

AE958–AE977, AF945–AF999, AG100–AG286, AG287–AG344, and AG665–AG684. Powered by Packard Merlin 28 with three-blade Hamilton Hydromatic variable-pitch propeller. Some 100 completed with eight .303-inch gun wing and the remainder with twelve .303-inch gun wing.

AG287(1374), AG293–AG296 (1377, 1368, 1375, 1376), AG299(1378), AG300(1380), AG302(1379), AG304–319 (1372, 1363, 1366, 1367, 1371, 1362, 1365, 1361, 1356, 1358, 1354, 1357, 1353, 1355, 1352), AG323(1351), AG325–AG327(1359, 1373, 1369), AG330(1370), and AG332 (1360) all to RCAF.

AE958–AE962, AE964–AE969, AE975, AE977, AF945–AF947, AF949–AF955, AF962, AF963, AF965, AF967, AF969, AF971, AF973, AF974, AF976, AF981, and AF982 to Sea Hurricane Mk IIBs
AG672–AG984 to Russia.

100 Canadian Car and Foundry-built Mk Xs

AM270 AM369, and AP138. Powered by Packard Merlin 28 with Hamilton Hydromatic three-blade variable-pitch propeller. Originally built with eight .303-inch gun wings, but many converted to twelve gun or four cannon armament.

AM367 to Russia.

50 Canadian Car and Foundry-built Mk XIIA

BW835–BW884. Powered by Packard Merlin 28 with Hamilton Hydromatic three-blade variable-pitch propeller. To RCAF as Sea Hurricanes on lend-lease contract.

150 Canadian Car and Foundry-built Mk XIs

BW885–BW999, and BX100–BX134. Powered by Packard Merlin 28 with Hamilton Hydromatic three-blade variable-pitch propeller. Originally built with eight .303-inch gun wings, but many converted to twelve gun or four cannon armament.

BW920, BW922, BW926, BW984, BX102, BX108–BX111, and BX119–BX124 to Russia, with remainder to RAF.

248 Canadian Car and Foundry-built Mk XIs and Mk XIIs

JS219–JS371, JS374–JS420(twelve–gun wings), and JS421–JS468 (most converted in UK to four 20-mm cannon armament, powered by Packard Merlin 28 or 29 with Hamilton Hydromatic three-blade variable-pitch propeller.

JS219–JS221, JS225, JS227–JS229, JS232, JS233, JS235, JS237, JS240, JS241, JS256, JS257, JS300, JS309, JS317, JS391, JS396–JS399, JS405–JS412, JS415, and JS419 shipped to Russia.

Remainder to RCAF, RCN, RAF & FAA.

150 Canadian Car and Foundry-built Mk XIIAs

PJ660–PJ695, PJ711–PJ758, PJ779–PJ813, PJ842–PJ872. Powered by Packard Merlin 29 with Hamilton Hydromatic three-blade variable-pitch propeller, built with eight .303-inch gun wings and many converted to twelve gun or four cannon armament. Most of this batch were shipped to Russia or the Asian Campaign, with a few retained in Canada for conversion to Sea Hurricane Mk XIIAs.

200 Canadian Car and Foundry-built Mk XIIs

5376–5775. Powered by Packard Merlin 28 or 29 with Hamilton Hydromatic three-blade variable-pitch propellers, built with eight .303-inch gun wings and all allocated to RCAF.

Total Canadian Production: 1,398

Total Combined Production: 14,350 Hurricanes

Appendix IV

Hurricane Units

Role Abbreviations

AAC	Anti-aircraft Co-operation
Army Co-op	Army Co-operation
ASR	Air Sea Rescue
Calib	Calibration
Comms	Communications
COpsT	Combined Operations Training
F	Day Fighter
FB	Fighter Bomber
FR	Fighter Reconnaissance
NF	Night Fighter
PR	Photo Reconnaissance
Recce	Reconnaissance
Tac Recce	Tactical Reconnaissance
Tblt	Turbinlite

NB: The list covers the main locations of the units, which are in the overall order, but to reduce space no mention is made of any return to an airfield. In addition, Hurricanes were in service with a number of FAA, training and miscellaneous units.

Royal Air Force

Unit	Role	Code	Mk	Dates	Bases
1 Sqn	F	N/A	I	10/1938–04/1941	Tangmere, France, Northolt, Wittering, Kenley and Croydon
	F	JX	I	04/1942–07/1942	Tangmere
	F	JX	IIA	02/1941–06/1941	Kenley, Croydon and Redhill
	F	JX	IIB	04/1941–01/1942	Croydon, Redhill, Kenley and Tangmere
	F	JX	IIB	06/1942–09/1942	Tangmere
	F	JX	IIC	07/1941–09/1942	Tangmere, Acklington
3 Sqn	F	OP	I	03/1938–07/1938	Kenley
	F	OP	I	05/1939–04/1941	Biggin Hill, Hawkinge, Kenley, France, Wick, Castletown, Turnhouse, Skaebrae
	NF	QO	IIB	04/1941–10/1941	Martlesham Heath, Debden, Stapleford Tawney, Hunsdon
	NF	QO	IIC	04/1941–02/1943	Martlesham, Stapleford, Hunsdon
5 Sqn	FB		IIC/D	06/1943–10/1944	Khangpur, Yelahanka, India/Burma
6 Sqn	F	JV	I	03/1941–07/1941	Tobruk
	F		I	09/1941–02/1942	Egypt, Libya
	FB	JV	IIC	12/1942–02/1943	Egypt, Libya
	FB	JV	IID	05/1942–09/1943	Egypt, Libya, Tunisia
	FB	JV	IV	07/1943–01/1947	Egypt, Italy, Palestine, Cyprus
11 Sqn	F		IIC	08/1943–06/1945	India, Burma
17 Sqn	F	UV	I	06/1939–02/1941	North Weald, Croydon, Debden, Hawkinge, Kenley, France, Tangmere, Martlesham
	F	YB	IIA	02/1941–04/1941	Croydon, Martlesham
	F	YB	IIB	07/1941–11/1941	Elgin, Dyce, Tain, Catterick
	F	YB	IIA	01/1942–06/1942	Asia
	F	YB	IIB	06/1942–08/42	Jessore Asia
	F	YB	IIC	08/1942–06/1944	Alipore, Agartala, China Bay, Minneriya
20 Sqn	F		IID	03/1943–09/1945	Charra India/Burma
	FB		IIC	08/1944–10/1944	Sapan India/Burma
	FB		IV	11/1944–09/1945	Sapan India/Burma
28 Sqn	Army Co-op		IIB	12/1942–12/1944	India/Burma
			IIC/IV	03/1944–07/1945	India, Burma, Malaya
29 Sqn	F		I	08/1940–12/1940	Wellingore
30 Sqn	F	RS	I	06/1941–08/1942	Alexandria, Ratmalana Ceylon
	F		IIB	08/1941–08/1942	Ceylon, Burma
	F	RS	IIC	08/1942–09/1944	Ceylon, Burma

Unit	Role	Code	Mk	Dates	Bases
32 Sqn	F	KT	I	10/1938–1942	Biggin Hill, Gravesend, Manston, Wittering, Acklington, Middle Wallop, Ibsley, Pembrey, Angle, West Malling
	F	GZ	IIB	07/1941–11/1942	Angle, Manston, West Malling, Friston, Honiley, Baginton
	F	GZ	IIC	11/1941–08/1943	Manston, West Malling, Friston, Baginton, Algeria, Tunisia
33 Sqn	F	NW	I	09/1940–02/1942	Egypt, Greece, Libya
	FB		IIB	03/1942–06/1942	Egypt, Libya
	FB		IIC	06/1942–12/1943	Egypt, Libya
34 Sqn	FB	8Q	IIC	08/1943–04/1945	Burma, India
	FB		IIB	12/1943–12/1944	Burma, India
	AAC		IIC		Horsham St Faith
42 Sqn	FB	AW	IV	10/1943–06/1945	Burma, India
	FB	AW	IIC	09/1944–12/1944, 04/1945–06/1945	Burma, India
43 Sqn	F	NQ	I	11/1938–07/1941	Tangmere, Acklington, Wick, Northolt, Usworth, Drem, Crail
	F	FT	I	09/1942–11/1942	Kirton-in-Lindsey
	F	FT	IIB	04/1941–09/1942	Drem, Acklington, Tangmere
	F	FT	IIC	11/1942–03/1943	Algiers (Maison Blanche)
46 Sqn	F	RJ/ PO	I	03/1939–05/1941,	Digby, Acklington, Norway, Stapleford, North Weald, Church Fenton, Sherburn-in-Elmet
	F		IIC	06/1941–07/1941	Malta
56 Sqn	F	LR/ US	I	04/1938–02/1941	North Weald, Martlesham, France, Digby, Wittering, Boscombe Down, Middle Wallop
	F	US	IIB	02/1941–03/1942	North Weald, Martlesham, Duxford
60 Sqn	FB	MU	IIC	07/1943–06/1945	Burma, India
63 Sqn	Tac R	UB	IIC/IV	03/1944–05/1944	Turnhouse, Woodvale
	Tac R		IIC	09/1944–12/1944	North Weald, Manston
67 Sqn	FB	RD	IIB	02/1942–06/1942	Burma, India
	FB		IIC	06/1942–02/1944	Burma, India
69 Sqn	Recce		I/II	04/1941–02/1942	Malta
71 Sqn	F	XR	I	11/1940–05/1941	Church Fenton, Kirton-in-Lindsey, Martlesham
	F	XR	IIA	05/1941–08/1941	Martlesham, North Weald
73 Sqn	F/NF	HV/ TP	I	07/1938–01/1942	Digby, France, Church Fenton, Castle Camps, Egypt, Libya
	NF		IIB	1942–02/1942	Egypt, Libya
74 Sqn	F		IIB	12/1942–08/1943	Persia, Iraq, Palestine, Egypt

Unit	Role	Code	Mk	Dates	Bases
79 Sqn	F	AL	I	11/1938–1941	Biggin Hill, Manston, Digby, France, Hawkinge, Sealand, Acklington, Pembrey, Fairwood Common
	F	NV	IIB	1941–12/1941	Pembrey, Fairwood Common
	FB	NV	IIC	06/1942–09/1944	Burma, India
80 Sqn	F	AP	I	06/1940–01/1942	Egypt, Greece, Palestine, Syria
	F	AP	II	01/1942–04/1943	Egypt, Libya, Palestine
81 Sqn	F		IIB	07/1941–11/1941	Leconfield, Russia
85 Sqn	NF	NO/VY	I	09/1938–04/1941	Aldergrove, Debden, France, Martlesham, Croydon, Castle Camps, Church Fenton, Kirton-in-Lindsey, Gravesend, Hunsdon, West Malling, Swannington
87 Sqn	NF	PD/LK	I	07/1938–09/1942	Debden, France, Church Fenton, Colerne, Charmy Down
	NF	LK	IIC	06/1941–03/1944	Charmy Down, Algeria, Gibraltar, Morocco, Sicily
94 Sqn	NF/FB	GO	I	05/1941–12/1941	Egypt, Iraq
	F		I	06/1942–08/1942	Egypt, Libya
	FB		IIB	12/1941–01/1942	Egypt, Libya
	FB	GO	IIC	06/1942–05/1944	Egypt, Libya
95 Sqn	F		I	07/1941–10/1941	Sierra Leone
96 Sqn	NF	ZJ	I/IIC	10/1940–03/1942	Cranage
98 Sqn	F		I	06/1941–07/1941	Kaldarnes, Iceland
111 Sqn	F	TM/JU	I	12/1937–04/1941	Northolt, Acklington, Drem, Wick, Digby, North Weald, Croydon, Debden, Dyce
113 Sqn	FB		IIC	09/1943–04/1945	India, Burma
116 Sqn	Calib		I/IIA	11/1941–05/1945	Hendon, Heston, Croydon, North Weald, Gatwick, Redhill, Hornchurch
121 Sqn	F	AV	I	05/1941–07/1941	Kirton-in-Lindsey, Digby
	F	AV	IIB	07/1941–11/1941	Kirton-in-Lindsey, North Weald
123 Sqn	FB		IIC	11/1942–09/1944	Persia, Egypt, Asia
126 Sqn	F		IIA/b	06/1941–04/1942	Malta
127 Sqn	F	BZ	I	06/1941–07/1941	Syria, Iraq
	F		I	02/1942–06/1942	Palestine
	F		IIB	06/1942–10/1943	Egypt
	F		IIB	08/1943–04/1944	Egypt, Palestine
128 Sqn	F	WG	I/IIB	10/1941–03/1943	Sierra Leone

Unit	Role	Code	Mk	Dates	Bases
133 Sqn	F	MD	IIB	08/1941–12/1941	Coltishall, Duxford, Colly Weston, Fowlmere, Eglington
134 Sqn	F	GQ/ GA	IIB	31/07/1941– 10/1941	Leconfield, Russia
	F	GV	IIB	01/1943–10/1943	Egypt, Libya
135 Sqn	F		IIA	15/08/1941–1942	Baginton, Honiley, Burma, India
	F		IIB	02/1942–10/1943	Burma, India
	F		IIC	11/1941–1941	Burma, India
	FB		IIC	10/1943–09/1944	Ceylon
136 Sqn	FB	HM	IIA	08/1941–11/1941	Kirton-in-Lindsey
	FB		IIB/C	03/1942–10/1943	India, Burma
137 Sqn	FB	SF	IV	06/1943–01/1944	Rochford, Manston, Lympne
145 Sqn	F	SO	I	03/1940–02/1941	Croydon, France, Filton, Tangmere, Westhampnett, Drem, Dyce
146 Sqn	F		IIB	05/1942–01/1944	India, Burma
151 Sqn	NF	GG/ DZ	I	12/1938–06/1941	North Weald, Martlesham, France, Stapleford, Digby, Bramcote, Wittering
	NF		IIC	04/1941–01/1942	Wittering
153 Sqn	FB		IIC	08/1944–09/1944	Algeria
164 Sqn	FB	FJ	IID/ IV	02/1943–02/1944	Middle Wallop, Warmwell, Manston, Fairlop, Twinwood Farm
173 Sqn	Com		I	07/1942–1943	Heliopolis
174 Sqn	FB	XP	IIB	03/1942–04/1943	Manston, Fowlmere, Warmwell, Odiham, Chilbolton, Grove, Zeals
175 Sqn	FB	HH	IIB	03/1942–04/1943	Warmwell, Harrowbeer, Gatwick, Odiham, Stony Cross, Lasham
176 Sqn	AAC		IIC	05/1943–01/1944	India
181 Sqn	FB	EL	I	09/1942–1943	Duxford, Snailwell
182 Sqn	FB	XM	I	09/1942–1943	Martlesham, Sawbridgeworth
183 Sqn	FB	HF	I	11/1942–1943	Church Fenton
184 Sqn	Anti-tank	BR	IID	12/1942–/1943	Colerne, Chilbolton, Eastchurch, Merston, Manston
	FB	BR	IV	1943–1944	Merston, Manston, Detling, Odiham
185 Sqn	F		I	05/1941–06/1942	Malta
	F		IIA	05/1941–06/1942	Malta
186 Sqn	Army Co-op	AP	IV	08/1943–11/1943	Ayr
193 Sqn	FB	DP	I/IIC	01/1943–02/1943	Harrowbeer
195 Sqn	F		I	11/1942–03/1943	Duxford, Hutton Cranswick

Unit	Role	Code	Mk	Dates	Bases
208 Sqn	Army Co-op		I	11/1940–1942	Egypt, Libya, Greece, Palestine
			IIA/B/C	05/1942–12/1943	Egypt, Libya, Iraq, Syria, Palestine
213 Sqn	F	AK	I	01/1939–1942	Wittering, France, Biggin Hill, Exeter, Tangmere, Leconfield, Driffield, Nicosia, Egypt
	FB	AK	IIC	01/1942–05/1944	Egypt, Libya
225 Sqn	FR	WU	I	01/1942–06/1942	Thruxton
	FR		IIB/C	02/1942–04/1943	Thruxton, Algeria, Tunisia
229 Sqn	F	RE	I	30/1940–05/1941	Digby, Wittering, Northolt, Speke
	FB	HB	IIC	09/1941–04/1942	Egypt, Libya, Malta
232 Sqn	F	EF	I	07/1940–11/1941	Sumburgh, Castletown, Skitten, Drem, Montrose, Abbotsinch, Ouston
	F		IIB	08/1941–02/1942	Ouston, Singapore
237 Sqn	F		I	01/1942–12/1942	Egypt, Libya, Iraq, Persia
	F		IIC	02/1943–12/1943	Egypt, Libya
238 Sqn	F	VK	I	06/1940–03/1941	Middle Wallop, St Eval, Chilbolton
	F	VK	I	02/1942–05/1942	Egypt, Libya
	F	VK	IIA	03/1941–05/1941	Chilbolton, Pembrey
	F		IIC	09/1941–02/1942	Egypt, Libya
	FB		IIC	10/1942–09/1943	Egypt, Libya
	Anti-tank		IIB	05/1942–10/1942	Egypt, Libya
239 Sqn	Army Co-op	HB	I/IIC	01/1942–05/1942	Hatfield, Gatwick
241 Sqn	Army Co-op	RZ	IIC	10./1942–01/1944	Ayr, Algeria, Tunisia
242 Sqn	F	LE	I	02/1940–04/1941	Church Fenton, Biggin Hill, France, Coltishall, Duxford, Martlesham
	F	LE	IIB	02/1941–03/1942	Martlesham, Stapleford, North Weald, Manston, Valley, Singapore, Sumatra/Java
	FB		IIC	1941–09/1941	Stapleford, North Weald, Manston
245 Sqn	F	DX	I	03/1940–1941	Leconfield, Drem, Turnhouse, Aldergrove, Ballyhalbert
	FB	MR	IIB	08/1941–1942	Chilbolton, Warmwell, Middle Wallop
	NF		IIC	1942–01/1943	Charmy Down
247 Sqn	F	HP	I	12/1940–06/1941	Roborough, St Eval, Portreath
	F	HP	IIA	06/1941–12/1941	Predannack, Exeter
	F		IIB	08/1941–12/1941	Predannack, Exeter
	NF		IIB	08/1942–03/1943	High Ercall, Middle Wallop
	NF	ZY	IIC	08/1941–03/1943	Predannack, High Ercall, Middle Wallop
249 Sqn	F	GN	I	05/1940–1941	Church Fenton, Leconfield, Boscombe Down, North Weald

Unit	Role	Code	Mk	Dates	Bases
	FB		I	05/1941–1942	Malta
	FB		IIA	02/1941–1942	North Weald, Malta
	FB		IIB	1942–03/1942	Malta
250 Sqn	NF		I/IIC	02/1942–04/1942	Egypt
253 Sqn	F	SW	I	01/1940–09/1941	Manston, Northolt, Kenley, Kirton-in-Lindsey, Turnhouse, Prestwick, Leconfield, Skeabrae
	NF		IIB	07/1941–09/1942	Skeabrae, Hibaldstow, Shoreham, Friston
	NF		IIC	01/1942–09/1942	Hibaldstow, Shoreham, Friston
	F		IIC	11/1942–09/1943	Algeria, Tunisia
255 Sqn	NF		I	03/1941–07/1941	Kirton-in-Lindsey, Hibaldstow
256 Sqn	NF	JT	I	03/1941–05/1942	Sqnuires Gate
257 Sqn	F	DT	I	06/1940–06/1941	Hendon, Northolt, Debden, Martlesham, North Weald, Coltishall
	Army Co-op	DT	I	04/1942–07/1942	Honiley, High Ercall
	F		IIC	04/1941–08/1941	Coltishall
	Army Co-op	FM	IIB	06/1941–09/1942	Coltishall, Honiley, High Ercall
258 Sqn	F	ZT	I	12/1940–04/1941	Leconfield, Duxford, Drem, Acklington, Jurby
	F		I	03/1942–1943	Java, Ceylon
	F		IIA	04/1941–02/1942	Kenley, Redhill, Martlesham, Singapore
	F		IIB	03/1942–12/1943	Java, India
	FB		IIC	11/1943–08/1944	India, Burma
260 Sqn	F		I	12/1940–02/1942	Castletown, Drem, Palestine, Egypt, Libya
261 Sqn	F		I	08/1940–05/1941	Malta
	F		I	07/1941–03/1942	Iraq, Palestine, India
	F		IIB	03/1942–11/1943	Ceylon, India, Burma
	FB		IIC	10/1943–06/1944	India, Burma
263 Sqn	F	HE	I	06/1940–11/1940	Drem, Grangemouth
273 Sqn	F		I	08/1942–1942	Ceylon
	F		IIA/B	08/1942–1942	Ceylon
	F		IIC	12/1943–05/1944	Ceylon
274 Sqn	F	YK	I	08/1940–1941	Egypt, Malta
	FB	NH	IIB	10/1941–05/1942	Greece, Egypt, Libya
	FB	NH	IIC	1942–11/1943	Egypt, Libya, Cyprus
276 Sqn	ASR		II	12/1941–1942	Harrowbeer
279 Sqn	ASR		IIC/IV	04/1945–06/1945	Thornaby
283 Sqn	ASR		II	1944–1945	N Africa

Unit	Role	Code	Mk	Dates	Bases
284 Sqn	ASR		II	09/1944–03/1945	Tunisia
285 Sqn	AAC		IIC	01/1944–06/1945	Woodvale, Andover, North Weald
286 Sqn	AAC		IIC/IV	11/1942–05/1945	Filton, Lulsgate, Colerne, Zeals, Locking, Weston Zoyland, Culmhead
287 Sqn	AAC	KZ	IIB/IV	11/1941–02/1944	Croydon
288 Sqn	AAC	RP	IIC/IV	11/1941–1944	Digby, Wellingore, Coleby Grange, Collyweston
289 Sqn	AAC	YE	IIC/IV	12/1941–06/1945	Kirknewton, Turnhouse, Acklington, Eshott, Andover
290 Sqn	AAC		IIC	12/1943–01/1945	Newtownards, Long Kesh, Turnhouse
291 Sqn	ASR	8Q	IIC	03/1944–06/1945	Hutton Cranswick
302 Sqn Polish	F	WX	I	07/1940–03/1941	Leconfield, Northolt, Westhampnett
	F		I	05/1941–07/1941	Jurby
	F		IIA	03/1941–05/1941	Westhampnett
	F		IIB	07/1941–10/1941	Jurby, Church Stanton, Warmwell
303 Sqn Polish	F	RF	I	08/1940–01/1941	Northolt, Leconfield
	F		I	08/1941–10/1941	Speke
306 Sqn Polish	F	UZ	I	08/1940–07/1941	Church Fenton, Tern Hill
	F	UZ	IIA	04/1941–07/1941	Northolt
308 Sqn Polish	F	ZF	I	11/1940–04/1941	Baginton
309 Sqn Polish	Army Co-op	WC	IIC/IV	04/1944–10/1944	Drem, Hutton Cranswick, Acklington, Peterhead
310 Sqn Czech	F	NN	I	07/1940–03/1941	Duxford
	F		IIA	03/1941–12/1941	Martlesham, Dyce
	F		IIB	06/1941–11/1941	Dyce
312 Sqn Czech	F	DU	I	08/1940–05/1941	Duxford, Speke, Valley, Jurby
	F		IIB	05/1941–12/1941	Kenley, Martlesham, Ayr
315 Sqn Polish	F	PK	I	02/1941–07/1941	Acklington, Speke
316 Sqn Polish	F	SZ	I	02/1941–06/1941	Pembrey, Colerne
	F		IIA/B	06/1941–11/1941	Colerne, Church Stanton
317 Sqn Polish	F	JH	I	02/1941–07/1941	Acklington, Ouston, Colerne, Fairwood Common
	F		IIA/b	07/1941–10/1941	Exeter

Unit	Role	Code	Mk	Dates	Bases
318 Sqn Polish	Tac Recce		I	03/1943–08/1943	Detling
			IIB	90./1943–02/1944	Palestine, Egypt
331 Sqn Norway	F	FN	I	07/1941–08/1941	Catterick
	F	FN	IIB	08/1941–11/1941	Castletown, Skeabrae
335 Sqn Greece	F	FG	I	10/1941–09/1942	Palestine
	FB		IIB	08/1942–10/1943	Egypt, Libya
	FB		IIC	10/1943–01/1944	Egypt, Libya
336 Sqn Greece	F		IIC	02/1943–08/1944	Egypt, Libya
351 Sqn Yugo	FB		IIC	07/1944–09/1944	Libya
	FB		IV	09/1944–06/1945	Italy, Yugoslavia
352 Sqn Yugo	FB		IIC	04/1944–06/1944	Libya
401 Sqn RCAF	F	YO	I	06/1940–02/1941	Middle Wallop, Croydon, Northolt, Prestwick, Castletown
	F		IIB	02/1941–09/1941	Driffield, Digby
402 Sqn RCAF	F	AE	I	12/1940–05/1941	Digby
	F		IIA	05/1941–08/1941	Wellingore, Martlesham, Ayr
	FB	AE	IIB	08/1941–03/1942	Rochford, Warmwell
417 Sqn	F	AN	IIB	09/1942–10/1942	Egypt
	F		IIC	09/1942–01/1943	Cyprus
438 Sqn RCAF	FB	F3	IV	11/1943–04/1944	Digby, Wittering, Ayr, Hurn, Funtington
439 Sqn RCAF	FB	5V	IV	01/1944–04/1944	Wellingore, Ayr, Hurn, Funtington
440 Sqn RCAF	FB	18	IV	02/1944–03/1944	Ayr, Hurn
450 Sqn RAAF	FB	OK	I	05/1941–12/1941	Egypt, Palestine, Syria
451 Sqn RAAF	F		I	07/1941–01/1943	Egypt, Libya, Syria, Cyprus, Palestine
	Army Co-op		IIC	02/1943–10/1943	Egypt
486 Sqn RNZAF	NF	SA	I/IIB	03/1942–07/1942	Kirton-in-Lindsey, Wittering, Hibaldstow
488 Sqn RNZAF	F		I	01/1942–02/1942	Singapore

Unit	Role	Code	Mk	Dates	Bases
501 Sqn RAuxAF	F	ZH/ SD	I	03/1939–05/1941	Filton, Tangmere, France, Croydon, Middle Wallop, Gravesend, Kenley, Colerne
504 RAuxAF	F	TM	I	08/1939–07/1941	Hucknall, Digby, Debden, France, Wick, Castletown, Catterick, Hendon, Filton, Exeter
	F		IIB	07/1941–11/1941	Fairwood Common, Chilbolton, Ballyhalbert
516 Sqn	COps T		II	12/1943–12/1944	Dundonald
518 Sqn	Met	Y3	IIC	09/1945–10/1946	Aldergrove
520 Sqn	Met		IIC	06/1944–04/1946	Gibraltar
521 Sqn	Met		IIC	08/1944–02/1946	Docking, Langham, Chivenor
527 Sqn	Calib	WN	I/IIB	06/1943–04/1945	Castle Camps, ll, Digby
530 Sqn	Tblt		I	09/1942–01/1943	Hunsdon
531 Sqn 1452 Flt	Tblt		IIC	05/1942–01/1943	West Malling, Debden
532 Sqn 1453 Flt	Tblt		IIC/ XII	07/1941–02/1943	Wittering, Hibaldstow
533 Sqn 1454 Flt	Tblt		IIC/ XIB	07/1941–01/1943	Colerne, Charmy Down
534 Sqn 1455 Flt	Tblt		IIC/X	07/1941–01/1943	Tangmere
535 Sqn 1456 Flt	Tblt		IIC	11/1941–09/1942	Honiley, High Ercall
536 Sqn 1457 Flt	Tblt		IIC	08/1941–09/1942	Colerne, Predannack, Fairwood Common
537 Sqn 1458 Flt	Tblt		IIC/ XII	12/1941–01/1943	Middle Wallop
538 Sqn 1459 Flt	Tblt		IIC	09/1941–01/1943	Hunsdon, Hibaldstow
539 Sqn 1460 Flt	Tblt		IIC/X	12/1941–01/1943	Acklington
567 Sqn	AAC	14	IIC/IV	12/1943–06/1945	Detling, Hornchurch, Hawkinge
577 Sqn	AAC		IIC/IV	12/1943–07/1945	Castle Bromwich
587 Sqn	AAC	M4	IIC/IV	12/1943–06/1945	Weston Zoyland, Culmhead
595 Sqn	AAC		IIC/IV	12/1943–12/1944	Aberporth
598 Sqn	AAC		IIC	02/1944–04/1945	Peterhead, Bircham Newton
601 Sqn RAuxAF	F	UF	I	02/1940–09/1940	Tangmere, France, Middle Wallop, Debden, Exeter, Northolt
	F	UF	IIB	09/1940–1941	Northolt, Manston, Matlaske, Duxford
605 Sqn RAuxAF	F	UP	I	08/1939–12/1940	Tangmere, Leuchars, Wick, Hawkinge, Drem, Croydon
	F		IIA	11/1940–08/1941	Croydon, Martlesham, Tern Hill, Baginton
	F		IIB	08/1941–03/1942	Baginton, Kenley, Sealand, Sumatra

Unit	Role	Code	Mk	Dates	Bases
	F		IIB	01/1942–02/1942	Malta
607 Sqn RAuxAF	F	AF	I	03/1940–06/1941	France, Croydon, Usworth, Tangmere, Turnhouse, Drem, MacMerry, Skitten
	FB		IIA	06/1941–08/1941	Skitten, Castletown
	FB		IIB	07/1941–03/1942	Castletown, Martlesham, Manston
	FB		IIB	02/1943–12/1943	India, Burma
	FB		IIC	06/1942–02/1943	India, Burma
	FB		IIC	07/1943–09/1943	India, Burma
610 Sqn RAuxAF	F		I	09/1939	Hooton Park
615 Sqn RAuxAF	F	KW	I	04/1940–02/1941	France, Kenley, Prestwick, Northolt
	F		I	04/1941–07/1941	Valley
	F		IIA	02/1941–04/1941	Kenley
	F		IIB	07/1941–1942	Valley, Manston, Angle, Fairwood Common
	F		IIC	07/1941–03/1942	Valley, Manston, Angle, Fairwood Common
	F		IIC	06/1942–09/1943	India, Burma
631 Sqn	AAC	6D	IIC	03/1944–07/1945	Towyn, Llanbedr
639 Sqn	AAC		IV	08/1944–04/1945	Cleave
650 Sqn	AAC		IV	04/1944–06/1945	Cark, Bordogan
667 Sqn	AAC		I/IIC	06/1944–12/1945	Gosport
679 Sqn	AAC		IIC/IV	12/1943–06/1945	Ipswich
680 Sqn	PR		I/II	02/1943–12/1944	North Africa
681 Sqn	PR		II	01/1943–11/1943	India
691 Sqn	AAC	5S	I/IIC	12/1943–08/1945	Roborough, Harrowbeer
695 Sqn	AAC		IIC	12/1943–09/1945	Bircham Newton

Commonwealth and Allied

Unit	Role	Code	Mk	Dates	Bases
3 Sqn RAAF	F		I	02/1941–07/1941	Egypt, Libya, Palestine
2 Sqn Egypt AF	FB		IIC	01/1944–01/1945	Egypt
1 Sqn RCAF	F	NA/YO	I	02/1939–06/1940	Calgary Alberta
	F		I	06/1940–02/1941	Middle Wallop, Croydon, Northolt, Prestwick, Castletown, Driffield
123 Sqn RCAF	Army Co-op	VD	I/XII	11/1942–10/1943	Rockcliffe Ontario

125 Sqn ECAF	F	BA	I/XII	04/1942–05/1943	Sydney Nova Scotia
126 Sqn RCAF	F	BV	XII	04/1942–05/1945	Dartmouth Nova Scotia
127 Sqn RCAF	F	TF	XII	07/1942–12/1943	Dartmouth Nova Scotia
128 Sqn RCAF	F	RA	I/XII	06/1942–03/1944	Sydney Nova Scotia
129 Sqn RCAF	F	HA	XII	08/1942–09/1944	Dartmouth Nova Scotia
130 Sqn RCAF	F	AE	XII	09/1942–03/1944	Mont Joli Quebec
133 Sqn RCAF	F	FN	XII	07/1942–03/1944	Lethbridge Alberta
135 Sqn RCAF	F	XP	XII	07/1942–05/1944	Mossbank Saskatchewan/Patricia Bay BC
1 Sqn India AF	FB		IIB/IIC	09/1942–03/1946	India, Burma
2 Sqn India AF	FB		IIB	09/1942–02/1946	India, Burma
3 Sqn India AF	FB		IIC	11/1943–11/1945	India, Burma
4 Sqn India AF	FB		IIC	08/1943–08/1946	India, Burma, Japan
6 Sqn India AF	FB		IIB/IIC	02/1943–01/1945	India, Burma
7 Sqn India AF	FB		IIC	11/1944–03/1946	India, Burma
9 Sqn India AF	FB		IIC	01/1944–05/1945	India, Burma
10 Sqn India AF	FB		IIC	04/1944–04/1945	India, Burma
1 Sqn SAAF	F		I	12/1940–04/1941	East Africa, Egypt, Libya
	FB		IIB/IIC	04/1941–11/1942	Egypt, Libya
3 Sqn SAAF	F		I	12/1940–04/1943	East Africa, Aden
	FB		IIB/IIC	04/1943–03/1944	Egypt, Libya
7 Sqn SAAF	FB		IIB/IIC	05/1942–08/1943	Egypt, Libya
40 Sqn SAAF	F		I	01/1942–11/1942	Egypt, Libya
	FB		IIB	11/1942–05/1943	Egypt, Libya, Tunisia
41 Sqn SAAF	FB		IIB/IIC	05/1943–05/1944	Egypt, Libya

Further Reading

Barclay, G., *Battle of Britain Pilot*, (Somerset: Haynes, 2012)

Birtles, P., *Battle of Britain Airfields* (Hersham: Midland, 2010)

Birtles, P., *Hurricane: The Illustrated History* (Somerset: Patrick Stephens, 2001)

David, D., *Hurricane* (London: Grub Street, 2000)

Fozard, J., *Sydney Camm and the Hurricane* (Shrewsbury: Airlife, 1991)

Jackson, R., *Hawker Hurricane* (London: Blandford, 1987)

Jefford, C. G., *RAF Squadrons* (Shrewsbury: Airlife, 1988)

Mason, F. K., *Hawker Hurricane* (Shrewsbury: Aston, 1987)

Molson, K. M., Taylor H. A, *Canadian Aircraft since 1909* (Sittsville, ON: Canada's Wings, 1982)

Milton, B., *Hurricane: The Last Witnesses* (London: Andre Deutsch, 2015)

Rawlings, J. D. R., *Fighter Squadrons of the RAF* (London: Macdonald, 1969)

Riley, G., *Hawker Hurricane Survivors* (London: Grub Street, 2015)

Robertson, B., *Sopwith: The Man and his Aircraft* (Letchworth: Harleyford, 1970)

Shores, C., *Royal Canadian Air Force* (Toronto: Royce Publications, 2008)

Sturtivant R., *British Naval Aviation*, published by (London: Arms and Armour, 1990)

Sturtivant, R., *The Squadrons of the Fleet Air Arm* (Tonbridge: Air Britain, 1984)

Thomas, N., *RAF Top Gun: The Story of Battle of Britain Ace and World Air Speed Holder 'Teddy' Donaldson CB, CBE, DSO, AFC* (Pen & Sword, Barnsely, 2008)